Is the Holocaust Unique?

SECOND EDITION

Is the Holocaust Unique?

PERSPECTIVES ON COMPARATIVE GENOCIDE

edited and with an Introduction by

Alan S. Rosenbaum

with a Foreword by

Israel W. Charny

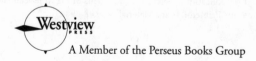

A Member of the Perseus Books Group

Copyright © 2001 by Westview Press, A Member of the Perseus Books Group

Published in 2001 in the United States of America by Westview Press, 5500 Central Avenue, Boulder, Colorado 80301-2877, and in the United Kingdom by Westview Press, 12 Hid's Copse Road, Cumnor Hill, Oxford OX2 9JJ

Find us on the World Wide Web at www.westviewpress.com

Library of Congress Cataloging-in-Publication Data

Is the Holocaust unique? : perspectives on comparative genocide / edited by Alan S. Rosenbaum. — 2nd ed.
    p. cm.
Includes bibliographical references and index.
ISBN 0-8133-3686-4
1. Holocaust, Jewish 1939–1945)—Historiography.   2. Genocide.   I. Rosenbaum, Alan S.

D804.348 .I8 2000
940.53'18'072—dc21   00-047712

The paper used in this publication meets the requirements of the American National Standard for Permanence of Paper for Printed Library Materials Z39.48-1984.

10   9   8   7   6   5   4   3   2   1

I dedicate this volume to my wife Pamela Sue;
to my children Emily, Jascha, Libby, and Alexandra;
and to my grandchildren Rebecca and Sophie,
and
to the younger generations who are inheriting
a world not of their design but one
summoning their most courageous impulses against
the rising tides of intolerance, hatred,
and attempts at genocide.

The only thing necessary for the triumph of evil is for good men to do nothing.

Attributed to Edmund Burke (1729–1797)

Contents

Foreword

ISRAEL W. CHARNY

I am stunned and upset by this book and very grateful to its editor, Alan S. Rosenbaum, for creating it.

It is, as I will attempt to explain, a daring compilation of contemporary academic thinking about the Holocaust in a comparative perspective, so that in the process it also concerns, and in some cases also presents, important new information about other cases of genocide, including the following:

- the genocide of the Romani, or Gypsies, in the very same process of the Holocaust (which Ian Hancock correctly argues "deserves acknowledgment far beyond that which it now receives," especially by the Jewish establishment);
- the Armenian genocide, both in its own monumental right and then also as a prototype of genocide that many scholars see as the precursor, and in a sense also as a facilitator, of the Holocaust;
- too-little-known information about the genocides of so many indigenous peoples—the native Americans;
- genocide in Nigeria-Biafra;
- the ethnic cleansing and genocide that occurred in the former Yugoslavia throughout the first half of the 1990s;
- a stunning historical analysis of the Atlantic slave trade that argues—for the first time that I, as a genocide scholar, have seen—for it to constitute genocide;
- the Ukrainian famine genocide;
- and more, making it clear to all people that genocide has been, is, and will continue to be the fate of many different peoples—and one must be careful that even legitimate considerations of the uniqueness of a given genocide (such as the archetypal event of the Holocaust) not blind us to the enormity of the problem of mass murders of many different peoples, especially toward our collective future on this planet.

This book is so daring, I now add, that in my opinion it includes several chapters and substantial sections of chapters that should never have been accepted for publication by a responsible editor *save for his intention to show the difficult truth of the jingoistic/ideological wars (above and beyond a healthy diversity of ideas and emphases) that are going on in Holocaust and genocide studies.* For, along with the devotion and scholarly skills of an increasing number of researchers unearthing more knowledge of the Holocaust and other genocides, there is a disquieting pattern of claims of the "incomparable uniqueness" of the Holocaust and a good deal of political power used in many places in academia, museums, and communities to back up these claims by pushing down and out nonadherents.

No less disturbing, many of the counterclaims—however justified in epistemological and moral intent to place the genocides of *all* peoples on the same level of tragedy and evil—go on to minimize the horror of the Holocaust and display a nasty lack of reverence for the victims of the Holocaust. And though such counterclaims correctly try to pull the Holocaust back into a comparative perspective and prove that the Holocaust was not uniquely more punishing, cruel, and betraying of human civilization than all other cases of genocide, they introduce serious factual distortions regarding the history of the Holocaust (e.g., the preposterous claim that Jews had it *easier* than victims in other genocides because the Nazi death machinery was so efficient). Yet at times the treatment of the subject of the Holocaust takes on the semblance of a competitive or prestige issue for academicians, progressing to a point that deeply violates reverence for the Holocaust, both as an enormous specific tragedy and as a watershed event in our century that has finally brought before our human civilization the denied subject of genocide as an all-too-frequent and, indeed, universal phenomenon.

The central question in this book is whether it is possible to say, as one contributor says explicitly and several others say more guardedly, "Not all mass murders are genocide."

Can there be any case of mass murder which is not genocide? I do not believe so. *Can there be any case of mass murder that is not with or without intention? with or without a plan to kill all the victim people? with or without a murder-enabling and camouflaging context of war against the victim nationality or against another people with whom the victims are or are not allied? with or without territorial, economic, or political motives? with or without religious, ethnic, or other historic enmity, memory, or cause for revenge for a previous genocide? that is even for "no reason"—other than the atavistic rotten cannibalism and sadistic cruelty that is, tragically, a serious part of human nature and potential?*

In a presentation to the Raphael Lemkin Symposium on Genocide at Yale University Law School (see annotated references following this foreword), I proposed recognizing all cases of mass murder as genocide *and*, at the same time, subclassifying various cases of genocide into subgroups of similar events, so that we have a series of categories of types of genocide, with study and analysis of the differences and similarities in contexts, dynamics, methods, outcomes, possibilities for intervention, and so on. It is no different than a book about cancer diseases that kill; the various killer cancers are similar *and* different. We do not suffer competitions between different types of cancer as to which is to be celebrated as unique or worst.

I believe that all cases of genocide are similar and different, special and unique, and appropriately subject to comparative analysis. /

For each person whose loved ones were killed in any genocide, for each people whose co-nationals were variously persecuted, tortured, driven into exile, and/or murdered, each genocide is inherently unique.

Moreover, each configuration of historical, political, military, societal, and psychological processes that define a given genocidal process is inherently unique.

I object to any statement that in any way minimizes the significance or sacredness of any people's losses, even when the understandable and legitimate purpose is to honor one's own people's tragedy, or even the specific tragedy of any other given people that one is respectfully researching or is committed to remembering.

I also object to scholars who transform the material of genocide scholarship predominantly into definitional arguments about what is or is not "genocide." I call this "definitionalism," or such an intense concern with establishing the boundaries of a definition that the reality of the phenomenon—in this case, human tragedy and infamy—is banished to a secondary position and no longer genuinely experienced.

Even more regrettable are those scholars who, patently, are more concerned with *their* ideas and with *their* political standing in academia or the community than with a commitment to all human lives.

※ ※ ※

I recommend to the readers, and certainly to students who will be using this book in a university setting, that as one reads each chapter, ask the following questions about each scholar's work:

- *Does the author convey a genuine and unstinting concern with the tragedy and immorality of each and every genocide to which he refers in his comparative analysis?*
- *Does the author appear more concerned with perpetuating his own people's memory of their genocide than with a concern for all human lives?*
- *Does the author appear more involved with his own ideas and scholarship than with battling the evil of genocide?*
- *Does the author use all-or-none thinking and black-and-white argumentation to create diametrically opposed differences between different cases of*

genocide to the point where deaths in the one instance are claimed to be more terrible than in the other?

- *Does the author utilize* post hoc *fallacious reasoning?* The following are examples of such fallacies that will be found in contributions to this book:
  - *Most of the Armenians in Istanbul survived the Armenian genocide at the hands of the Turks; therefore, one cannot say the Turks intended or committed genocide, because genocide means the murder of an entire people.*
  - *There is no evidence the Nazis planned to kill all the Jews outside of Europe; therefore, one cannot say they intended total annihilation of the Jewish people.*
  - *When the Nazis faced defeat, many of them were willing to stop killing the Jews; hence, one cannot say they had been adherents to a pseudoreligious commitment to murder all the Jews.*

This book is outstanding because it brings together in one volume the contentious and often unsavory Tower of Babel of scholars' voices in the field of Holocaust and genocide studies. In effect, editor Alan S. Rosenbaum has pitted the assembled scholars against one another in a grand gladiatorial coliseum, where he also lets us see many of the scholars in their naked reactions when they are consumed with proving something or other about their chosen genocide versus other genocides.

Rosenbaum himself is very clear in the Introduction that "the Holocaust is in many crucial aspects an unparalleled or singular event" but that this does not mean it is "unique" and, indeed, that the Holocaust is of great significance because it leads us to universal lessons about other "unqualified evil." It, therefore, can appear paradoxical that he has accepted for publication in his volume the following:

- A chapter that argues for the undisputed uniqueness of the Holocaust and utilizes the appearances of comparative analysis of other genocides to minimize every single one of them. One should note that in the penultimate version of this chapter, which served as the *final* version until just days before this volume went to press, statistical data about the Armenian genocide were presented that do not correspond to the press reports in *The New York Times* at the time of the genocide, to the published archives of U.S. diplomats, or to major historians such as Toynbee and Sachar, the purpose of the data being to minimize the fatalities in the genocide, and these data were also accompanied by a reference to a full-blown revisionist source, that is a known denier of that genocide. While the numerical details of this data will not, after all, be included in these pages, the skewed conclusion they support remains.

- A chapter that insists that state murder of 6 million Ukrainian people by starvation was never *intended* as murder but rather as a coercive political strategy with a necessary policy that overrode any concern for the dying; therefore, the whole process and the mass deaths by starvation did not constitute genocide.
- A chapter that—although correctly battling for recognition of all mass-murdered peoples as victims of an ugly universal process of genocide and courageously analyzing the relationship between denials of genocide and claims of uniqueness—insults and polarizes scholarship in the field no less than it criticizes and corrects errors and contains some of the worst insults to the enormity of the Holocaust, including the illustration given earlier of reasoning that *since Nazis did not kill all the Jews, they did not intend to kill them all in the first place.*
- Chapters that contain many absolute assertions and interpretations of truth without humility or struggle and without references to alternative ideas.

The editor has clearly decided to allow all sides of the debate to speak in a wholly uncensored or even uncorrected way. One might disagree with this decision, but one can understand why he made it. Although the reader needs to be alerted to the fact that there are gross distortions courtesy of full-blown and irresponsible revisionists (there are others in addition to the case referred to earlier), there may not be any other way for the editor to give us a serious opportunity to see ourselves as we really are in the field of holocaust and genocide studies. I value what Rosenbaum has dared achieve for us, even as I, personally, don't like much of what I see. It seems to me that there are too many parts spun from the same cloth of all-or-nothing, ideologically driven thinking, prejudice, arrogance, or degradation, and posturing for power—all elements that our true common enemy, the genocidal process, also builds on. For my soul and academic self, I believe holocaust and genocide studies should be dedicated to be a beacon of reverence and caring for *all* human life.

Jerusalem
August 1995

ANNOTATED REFERENCES TO SELECTED PUBLICATIONS
WRITTEN BY ISRAEL W. CHARNY ON A "GENERIC"
AND "HUMANISTIC" DEFINITION OF GENOCIDE

"Genocide: The Ultimate Human Rights Problem," *Social Issues Resource Series: Human Rights*, vol. 2, article 57 (1986), reprinted in *Social Education* 49(6) (1985): 448–452.

"The issue is the *wanton* murder of a group of human beings on the basis of any identity whatsoever that they share: national, ethnic, racial, religious, political, geographical, ideological. I reject out of hand that there can ever be any identity process that in itself will justify the murder of men, women and children 'because' they are anti some 'ism' or because their physical characteristics are high or low cheekboned, short or long eared, or green or orange colored" (*Social Education,* p. 448).

"Genocide and Mass Destruction: Doing Harm to Others as a Missing Dimension in Psychopathology," *Psychiatry* 49(2) (1986): 144–157.

A proposal to expand traditional mental health diagnosis from its usual emphasis on the harm people do to *themselves* and their own capacity to function, to include diagnosis of the harm people do to *other* human beings and their capacity to function.

"How to Avoid (Legally) Convictions for Crimes of Genocide (a One-Act Reading)," *Social Science Record* 24(2) (1987): 89–93.

A satire on a legal consultation pursued by the unholy alliance of Hitler, Stalin, Pol Pot, Talaal, and Idi Amin at the law offices of a top firm of international lawyers: Satan, Conformist, and Whore. The clients want to know how to protect themselves against possible international penalties for genocide. Their legal counsel propose that they be careful not to terminate a single victim people at one time but that they had best get their victim group when it is embedded within a larger population, for example, many Jews within the total population of New York City, and thus perhaps escape some of the pedantic stipulations in current genocide law.

Unpublished Typescript, Fiction. April 2018. Intergalactic Council for Protection of Ethnic and Planetary Human Rights and the Prevention of Genocide. *Internet on the Holocaust and Genocide, Special Double Issue 25/26 on the Seventy-Fifth Anniversary of the Armenian Genocide,* April 1990, pp. 13–14.

A satire about an interplanetary body in the future that rules the Holocaust qualifies only as *attempted genocide* and *humancide,* because in the final analysis it constituted only partial destruction of the Jewish people, many of whom survived, in contrast with *genocide,* which refers only to instances of actual total extinction of a people, and *planetcide,* which is the full extermination of an entire planet. The tiny country of Israel on Planet Earth votes against the proposal but loses, but the Armenians on Earth take revenge on Israel for past denials and minimization of their genocide by voting for the proposal.

"The Psychology of Denial of Known Genocides," in Israel W. Charny, ed., *Genocide: A Critical Bibliographic Review,* vol. 2 (London: Mansell Publishing, and New York: Facts on File, 1991), pp. 3–37.

A classification of different types of denial of known genocides and an analysis of the psychological dynamics of such denials, including to further incite violence, against the same and other victim peoples, in the future; humiliation of the victims and their survivors; "stealing" the record of history and rationality from human civilization—all further acts of aggression against humanity.

"Which Genocide Matters More? Learning to Care About Humanity," in *Genocide in the Twentieth Century: Critical Essays and Eyewitness Accounts,* ed. Samuel Totten, William S. Parsons, and Israel W. Charny (New York: Garland, 1995), pp. 535–542.

The concluding chapter of a book that, along with chapters that focus on a succession of genocides in the twentieth century, presents first-person accounts of genocides, creating an anthem of the voices of victims from a series of peoples in their common humanity. Usually, oral histories and first-person accounts appear in publications devoted to a single, specific people, and the voices of different peoples are rarely heard together.

"Toward a Generic Definition of Genocide," in *Genocide: Conceptual and Historical Dimensions,* ed. George Andreopoulos (Philadelphia: University of Pennsylvania Press, 1994), pp. 64–94 (presented at the Raphael Lemkin Symposium on Genocide, Yale University Law School, February 1991).

A proposal of a comprehensive classification of different forms of genocide, each category as a separate conceptual entity for legal and social science purposes, but all within a unifying generic concept of genocide as all cases of mass murder; so that no situation can arise where any form of mass murder can be denied recognition as *genocide.*

Preface

The reader should expect that the viewpoints expressed by some of the contributors to this collection are controversial and, despite their scholarly frame of reference, may occasion some challenging exchanges in response well beyond what has already occurred elsewhere. I, as editor, reaffirm that the purpose of this volume is to disclose to the reading public some cardinal aspects of the character and dimensions of this ongoing and sometimes impassioned debate. Each contributor is a recognized expert in his or her chosen area of scholarship and is understood to stand behind his or her claims as expressed herein.

Alan S. Rosenbaum

Acknowledgments

I wish to thank the following individuals, whose expertise and assistance in a variety of areas helped to guide me in the preparation of the manuscript: Spencer Carr and Rob Williams (Editors, Westview Press); Dr. Michael Berenbaum (Project Director of the United States Holocaust Memorial, Washington, D.C.); Dr. Joseph P. DeMarch (Chairman, Department of Philosophy, Cleveland State University, Cleveland, Ohio); Barry Epstein (President, Eppco Enterprises, Cleveland, Ohio); Ricardo Teamor, Esq. (Teamor, Thomson, and Associates); Bonnie Orgovan (Philosophy Department Secretary).

The things I saw beggar description. . . . The visual evidence and the verbal testimony of starvation, cruelty and bestiality were . . . overpowering. . . . I made the visit deliberately in order to be in a position to give first-hand evidence of these things if ever, in the future, there develops a tendency to charge these allegations merely to "propaganda."

General Dwight D. Eisenhower, April 15, 1945

There Were No Nazi 'Gas Chambers'; the Holocaust was "propaganda."

Marco Polo, *a Japanese magazine,* **February 1995**

The best medicine for the vulgar exercise of comparative victimization is not the copious assertion of Jewish uniqueness, but an end to the fruitless debate between the uniqueness and universality of suffering in the first place.

David Biale, TIKKUN, January/February 1995

The uniqueness of the Jewish experience can best be documented by comparing it with the Nazi treatment of other persecuted populations. The study of the Holocaust can provide insights that have universal import for the destiny of all humanity.

Michael Berenbaum, A Mosaic of Victims, *1990*

Events happen because they are possible. If they were possible once, they are possible again. In that sense the Holocaust is not unique, but a warning for the future.

Yehuda Bauer, The Holocaust in Historical Perspective, *1978*

Introduction to the First Edition

ALAN S. ROSENBAUM

The time has come to fix the place of the Nazi-engineered Holocaust against the Jews, Gypsies, and millions of others so that it may be accurately integrated into the mainstream of recorded history. For it remains disturbingly obvious, even to those with merely a passing exposure to this area of scholarship, that the variety of radically different opinions on this matter may contribute unwittingly to the nihilistic impression that any one view is as valid or invalid as any other view. This outcome would be most unfortunate and would be rejected unequivocally by this editor and the contributors to this book.

Normalizing the Holocaust in this manner recognizes both its continuities and discontinuities with the past. It is not an attempt to marginalize or dilute its horror but rather to point out that a social phenomenon that is treated as external to history and literally beyond the reach of human understanding (which it may be to those who endured and survived its ravages) will undoubtedly be seen quite differently from the perspectives of future generations. Indeed, some theorists in the scholarly world are in the throes of a struggle to articulate the abiding significance of the Holocaust. The purpose of the process of normalization is to influence responsible opinion about this matter in the future, now that the fiftieth anniversary of the liberation of Auschwitz—the "largest Jewish cemetery in the world" and the worst of the Nazi's death camps—and the defeat of the Third Reich have passed. Unfortunately, this historiographic process has become burdened with serious impediments. The most critical problem concerns how best to characterize the Holocaust: Should it be regarded as a unique historical phenomenon?

If indeed it is true that the Holocaust is genuinely and significantly unique and unprecedented, as a number of prominent scholars argue, then questions arise as to whether that perspective assures that future generations will better understand this historical phenomenon than would otherwise be so. Accordingly, we may ask: Is this claim about uniqueness historically inconsequential because it is an understandable expression, perhaps based in a mixture of motives and circumstances, of a generation of people who were in some way personally touched by the effects of World War II? Is it inevitable, as many people today fear, that the attenuating hold it has on our generation will gradually yield to a more generalized notion that the Holocaust was merely only one of many significant horrors that occurred in this century's most horrific conflict? Are the authentic victims of the Holocaust and the proponents of the claim of its uniqueness ultimately asserting in this unusual mode of expression a fearful plea for remembrance? Will the current exercise in the "politics" of uniqueness be displaced by the sheer quantity and magnitude of atrocities that have occurred as they become better known (as in Mao's China) and, unfortunately, happen in the future? And will the received concept of the Jewish-centeredness of the Holocaust be overwhelmed by the persistent cries of other aggrieved groups and by new evidence attesting to their own serious losses in the Holocaust? Of course, none of these questions can definitely be answered now. Nevertheless, some considered reflections about these matters can be offered based on the idea that the chapters in this volume are written by scholars who regard the overall issue of uniqueness very worthy of response.

Granted, history is replete with instances of mass death in a "widening circle of genocide." In order to avoid the unseemly appearance of a competitive martyrdom in attributing a certain specialness sui generis to the Holocaust, a sound defense of this ascription must be marshaled by its proponents at the very least in the context of the relevant empirical demographics of this history. The chapters in this volume are intended to promote clarity and understanding of the various claims about the comparability of other egregious instances of mass killing and death to the Holocaust. In this context, the term *Holocaust* usually refers to what the Nazis called the "Final Solution to the Jewish question," namely, the deliberate, systematic extermination of all Jewish people (nota bene: They succeeded in murdering at least 6 million people, including over 1.5 million children; this means that Jewish losses amounted to two-thirds of European Jewry). It also encompasses the relentless persecution, enslavement, and murder of many millions more: Gypsies (or Roma, or Romani), Poles, Slavs, gays, the mentally ill, the handicapped, and political dissidents. Of these non-Jewish victims of the Holocaust, numbering some 5.5 million people, it is clear that the fate of the Gypsies is generally accepted as being nearest to that of the Jews in the Nazi vision of a future "world without Jews" and Judaism.[1] As a more complete record becomes known, it may well be that the Gypsies can no longer be assumed to share a relatively separate experience from the Jews under the Nazi regime. Therefore, some scholars assert that "uniqueness" must also be held to encompass the Gypsy genocide. This is the cardinal point of Chapter 3, by Ian Hancock. In any case, the arguments marshaled in defense of the uniqueness of the Holocaust are almost never drawn on the basis of numbers of people killed alone, because Russia under Stalin and China under Mao had considerably larger numbers of people slain than did Germany under Hitler. Thus, the focus is usually placed on the Nazis' ideologically motivated intent to exterminate wholly the seed of the Jewish people—all men, women, and children everywhere.

In general, this book is premised upon the life-affirming proposition that no determinate group's suffering ought to be consigned to perpetual misconception, insignificance, invisibility, or silence. For, if it could, the collective voice of every group would seek to have its anguished cries of suffering and pain both heard and accurately enshrined in history's Book of Life as a legacy of instruction about warning signs of a possible recurrence for future generations to heed. Inasmuch as this is the only way to rescue a historical reality such as the Holocaust from oblivion—in that history does not speak for itself because it is dead and silent and, in and of itself, teaches us nothing—great care and attention must be dedicated to documentable specifics. Also, our focus must include contextual and interpretive considerations in the scholarly enterprise of framing and conveying information and establishing perspective from which future generations may learn, particularly so that those who are able to recall the genocidal past will move to thwart its recurrence (as the sanguine philosopher George Santayana once implicitly counseled).

Therefore, as I note at the outset and reaffirm here, any presumption about the uniqueness of the Holocaust may be entirely warranted provided that, upon proper scrutiny, it does not in any manner diminish or still the certain moral authority that must be accorded to other groups whose members have also been forced to endure unspeakable atrocities during their history. And yet any acknowledgment of the persecutions and mass deaths endured by members of other groups should not be construed as vitiating or denying, in the absence of honest and rational debate, claims as to the uniqueness of the Holocaust.

Too often, however, philosophical reflections and theoretical discussions about historically significant realities such as the Holocaust are sterile because they trade in some unnecessarily vacuous abstractions. These abstractions only serve to confuse, undermine, and prevent a full and accurate grasp of the realities in question. Typical of such dialogues, which are pointless because they arrest further constructive thought, is the tendency to attribute the occurrence of the Holocaust, or, for that matter, *any* act of violence, to "Man's inhumanity to Man" or to a presumed "evil or bestial human instinct."[2] Two other well-known approaches that yield a similar sterile outcome concern: first, a mystification that ensues from treating the Holocaust as essentially unthinkable owing to its extrahistorical and profoundly idiosyncratic, evil nature; and, second, a trivialization of its unprecedented character that accrues to the notion that the Holocaust, like *all* other sociohistorical events, is unique. Recourse to such abstract universalisms fails to account for real event-specifics like context, scope, and dimension; intention; methods; opportunity; blame; and responsibility. These chapters seek to avoid such usage because it obscures the genocidal realities that the contributors propose to compare and evaluate. In any case, there is a rational and honest disagreement among them about a precise, adequate definition of uniqueness itself.

It is in this spirit that the distinguished contributors to this book intend to assess the claims about whether the Holocaust is unique as viewed from the standpoint of other well-known and apparently analogous instances of genocide or mass deaths. Each chapter has been written specifically for this book, prompted by the firestorm of controversy surrounding, among other things, how best to remember the Holocaust and integrate our understanding into the historical mainstream of the scholarly literature. Hence, it is to be expected that prominent scholars in the interrelated areas of history, political science, religion, and philosophy have important contributions to make toward advancing a fair and reasonable resolution to this dispute.

One particularly insidious and nasty undercurrent of all this is a newfound cottage industry dedicated to voicing distortions and contrived falsifications of history in the form of "Holocaust denials."[3] It is reasonable to conjecture that this industry will be transitory, despite the fear, indignation, and outrage it currently provokes, because the testamentary evidence to the contrary is so overwhelming that it has become institutionalized (e.g., the United States Holocaust Memorial Museum) and readily accessible to the general public. In addition, responsible scholars[4] have made timely and persuasive refutations of specific fraudulent claims, laying bare the Holocaust deniers' incredulity and antisemitic motivation.

Nevertheless, when Holocaust denials are considered in tandem with another set of recent tendencies to "normalize," historicize, relativize, marginalize, and trivialize the reality of the Holocaust, the debate seriously intensifies. In this sense, efforts to deny its uniqueness converge with attempts to deny its existence altogether. Again, the core issue in this debate is whether the Holocaust has a special or unique place on history's continuum of persecution, genocide, and mass death. It appears that it does on its face, if we consider such factors as the magnitude of murders, ideology, and prior government planning and executions, the wholesale involvement of the legal and medical professions, the major business and industrial enterprises, academic institutions, the military forces, and the civil service, as well as the widespread bureaucratization and technoindustrialization of genocide.

However, if such normative inferences about "uniqueness"—much like its paradigmatic character of genocide and of evil—are to be warranted and enduring given the factors noted above, the Holocaust requires a rigorous, empirical comparison to other historical instances of mass death with sufficiently relevant similarities. For this reason, I have chosen to include such tragedies as the Atlantic slave trade, which is examined by Seymour Drescher in Chapter 6; the Soviet-engineered Ukrainian famine and mass kulak killings and population transfers, as discussed by Barbara B. Green in Chapter 9; the decimation and population transfers of Native American peoples, addressed by both Steven T. Katz (Chapter 4) and David E. Stannard (Chapter 13); and the Gypsy holocaust and the Armenian genocide at the hands of the Turks, analyzed by Vahakn N. Dadrian (Chapter 8) and also by Katz. References to the recent civil strife in the Balkans, Rwanda, and Cambodia will also be presented for the reader's analysis, particularly in Chapter 7, by Robert F. Melson. Again, the idea is not to invite a cynical politics of competitive suffering but rather to offer an assessment of the uniqueness claim regarding the Holocaust in light of other commonly cited and seemingly comparable instances of mass death.

There exists some question as to why some people think it important to attribute a "uniqueness" to the Holocaust[5] or to mount a rebuttal to the attribution,[6] given that there are a number of other historical events that are patently "unique" in a nontrivial sense. For instance, no such necessity seems to prompt those scholars who readily acknowledge a definite uniqueness to the nuclear devastation of the Japanese cities of Hiroshima and Nagasaki at the end of World War II to engage in a debate about its specialness, to challenge the ascription or uniqueness, or, for that matter, to deny its existence. Of course, some dispute has surrounded the matter of the rationale behind the putative military necessity to drop the bombs (for example, in a revanchist spirit some Japanese politicians, not unlike some disingenuous Germans who point to the Allied saturation bombing of Dresden as a moral equalizer, seek to cast Japan either as a co-sufferer or victim with equal moral standing alongside the true victims of Japanese militarism such as the people of Nanking in the 1930s or as would-be liberators of Asia from Western colonial domination as justification for its attack on Pearl Harbor on December 7, 1941). But no thinking person would seriously contest the uniqueness of the use of atomic weaponry on Japan. So why are Holocaust studies burdened with this curious challenge? I think the answer is conveyed in the words of Oxford professor Isaiah Berlin: "There must be a good deal more to the question of uniqueness—the 'placing in context' of this event than a mere historical assessment of an objective kind. It has a conspicuously political motive."[7] Nowhere else is this impression better confirmed than in the German historians' debate (the *Historikerstreit*) about reshaping a positive German national identity post-Auschwitz[8] and in the recent cultural politics of Jewish history and identity.

The debate among (mostly) German historians involves the question of interpreting Germany's Nazi past and the evil criminality of the Holocaust in view of certain current political purposes. One such purpose is to provide a special conceptual historicist framework for understanding and evaluating the Holocaust by reference to Hitler's antibolshevism (equally if not more important than his antisemitism) and a general violent and unavoidable response to rapid industrialization. Ernst Nolte, the German theorist, articulated this stratagem for minimizing Nazi genocide by attempting to rationalize and justify it.[9] The problem with this approach concerns, among other things, an attempted justification for Nazi wrongdoing by casting aside moral and legal principles to serve preferred political ends, for example, burying the past without really confronting it or downplaying the responsibility of the German nation today in view of its antisemitic and Nazi past. It is a transparent form of rationalizing evil by relativizing (or worse) its occurrence.

Another approach that politicizes history is found in claims that the Third Reich's actions as regards the Holocaust basically were no different than what others have done in furthering national interests in war or peace: destroy enemies by whatever means are at their disposal. This view also seeks to normalize the Holocaust. Still others argue that the future cannot be faced squarely unless and until former adversaries reconcile and agree to leave behind past wartime antagonisms. In this vein, we have a 1985 event that triggered a bitter worldwide dispute—the wreath-laying ceremony by U.S. President Ronald Reagan and German Chancellor Helmut Kohl at Germany's Bitburg cemetery, the burial ground for some German soldiers and Nazi SS criminals. A wave of indignation swept over those who felt this ill-conceived political effort at reconciliation came at the expense of a fair and honest appraisal of Germany's responsibility for its Nazi past. At the same time, however, many others were able to embrace the notion that the demands of future international relations and affairs required leaving the past behind by unfettering Germany from the stultifying grip of its shameful and blameworthy past, that is, from its moral and historical responsibility for the Holocaust. The political nature of continuing attempts to rehabilitate Germany by short-circuiting well-founded charges of culpability and responsibility, in a strategy designed to blunt criticism against Germany, is mentioned earlier (i.e., the deliberate recasting of the Dresden firestorm as a victimization of Germany that assigns it—or so the expositors of this notion hold—a standing worthy of equal moral consideration with the victims of German aggression).

Among some scholars, both Jewish and non-Jewish, there continues to be a certain current of thought that strives to retrieve the pain and suffering of the Jewish people in the Holocaust, arguably the worst fate to have befallen the Jews from time immemorial, and to give it a permanent and uniquely significant place in the annals both of Jewish and world history.[10] As may be expected, variations on this theme range from a plea for universal and perpetual recognition of the Holocaust as the worst case of genocide ever (as Katz proposes), certainly as the ineradicable nadir in all Jewish history as crucial to Jewish identity[11] and to the right to have its identity publicly validated; to the quasireligious concept of evil as best exemplified and embodied in the Holocaust;[12] to the theological query concerning God's whereabouts during the exterminative process of His Chosen People at the hands of the Nazis and their co-persecutors.[13]

As the chapters in this book demonstrate, the Holocaust is in many crucial respects an unparalleled or singular event. The historical singularity of the Holocaust does not imply by that fact alone that it is "unique" in some significant sense. And though an assertion of its uniqueness appears unavoidably to invite invidious comparisons with others' pain and suffering, this consequence alone should not render the inquiry fruitless.

In my opinion, research, argument, and clarity of comprehension belie any charge of fruitlessness because accurate empirical differentiation between instances of mass death and killing demonstrate how the Holocaust will probably be remembered, not only as "the epitome of evil, of cruelty," in the words of Elie

Wiesel, but also as an event unlike any other and thus with special significance for all humanity.[14]

In this editor's opinion, one of the universal lessons that Holocaust study aspires to teach involves, above all else, the honest consideration about how we ought to respond in the future when confronted with unqualified evil. If "evil" means the use of a maleficent power to deliberately destroy the physical, cultural, or spiritual being of an individual human being or a people,[15] then, in the wake of the Holocaust, we must forthrightly acknowledge its presence and resist a modern cultural bias to blur the distinction between good and evil. Second, our deepest sense of moral redemption demands unequivocal resistance to the workings of evil in any feasible manner; or at the very least to make the doers of evil accountable for their actions. Finally, the enduring significance implicit in sustained teaching or preaching of contempt and hatred for others who differ from ourselves or, in a word, to satanize others simply because they are and not for what they may have done, will lead, we now know, under a conducive mix of circumstances, to a policy of relentless persecution and even extermination.[16] For there is certainly an abiding wisdom in the recognition that the Holocaust has seared into the collective historical consciousness of humanity a new, indefeasible standard of evil. In other words, it may be that George Santayana's trite admonition about remembering the past as a way of not condemning ourselves to repeating it might also occasion among future genocidists a recollection of barbaric Nazi methods for more efficiently destroying their enemies. So we must be ever vigilant about the warning signs of a possible turn toward genocide. In light of these many lessons, only thus may we salvage our humanity and reaffirm the fundamental values at the heart of our civilization: respect for individual human life, dignity, and freedom; for human rights; and for a just rule of law.[17]

NOTES

1. In support of this view, we may cite the following authoritative works: Michael Berenbaum, "The Uniqueness and Universality of the Holocaust," in *A Mosaic of Victims*, ed. M. Berenbaum (New York: New York University Press, 1990), p. 33 (where Berenbaum argues that the Roma "shared much but not all the horrors assigned to the Jews"); Steven T. Katz, *The Holocaust in Historical Context*, vol. 1 (New York: Oxford University Press, 1994), pp. 27–63; and George L. Mosse, *Toward the Final Solution: A History of European Racism* (Madison: University of Wisconsin Press, 1978), pp. 220–221 (Mosse cited the Nazi expert, Eva Justin, on the Gypsy question). For contrary views, see Angus Fraser, *Gypsies* (Oxford: Blackwell Publishers, 1992); and Gerhard L. Weinberg, *Germany, Hitler, and World War Two* (New York: Cambridge University Press, 1995), pp. 218–219.

2. For instance, see "Freeing the Survivors," *U.S. News and World Report*, April 3, 1995, p. 65; also, for a variation on the same theme, see Alan S. Rosenbaum, *Prosecuting Nazi War Criminals* (Boulder: Westview Press, 1993), pp. 5, 9 at n. 4.

3. Deborah L. Lipstadt, *Denying the Holocaust: The Growing Assault on Truth and Memory* (New York: Free Press and Plume, 1994).

4. In this regard, such prominent scholars as Deborah Lipstadt and Harold Brackman have exposed the distortions and falsifications of some pseudohistorical but dangerous antisemitic tracts published by such organizations as the Institute of Historical Review and the Nation of Islam.

5. The substance of this multifaceted dispute is recorded in Gina Thomas, ed., *The Unresolved Past: A Debate in German History* (New York: St. Martin's Press, 1990); and *Forever in the Shadow of Hitler?*, trans. James Knowlton and Truett Cates (Atlantic Highlands, N.J.: Humanities Press, 1993).

6. See Pierre Papazian, "A 'Unique Uniqueness'?" in *Midstream*, April 1984, pp. 14–18.

7. See Isaiah Berlin's remarks in Thomas, *The Unresolved Past*, p. 19.

8. For a Holocaust-related philosophical discussion of "history as identity," notably Jürgen Habermas's idea of "historical consciousness as the 'medium' for national self-consciousness," see Charles S. Maier, *The Unmasterable Past* (Cambridge: Harvard University Press, 1988), pp. 121–159, esp. pp. 151–154. See also Anne-Marie Le Gloanec, "On German Identity," in *Daedalus*, Winter 1994, pp. 129–148.

9. Nolte is quoted in Saul Friedlander, *Memory, History, and the Extermination of the Jews of Europe* (Bloomington: Indiana University Press, 1993), p. 34. An informative critique of Nolte's view is offered by Wolfgang J. Mommsen, "Neither Denial nor Forgetfulness Will Free Us from the Past," in Knowlton and Cates, *Forever in the Shadow of Hitler?*, pp. 202–215.

10. For example, see Alice L. Eckardt and A. Roy Eckardt, *Long Night's Journey into Day: A Revised Retrospective on the Holocaust* (Detroit: Wayne State University Press, 1988), pp. 52–59.

11. It is quite evident that some theorists resist any attempt to build the idea of victimization in the Holocaust into Jewish identity. However, it is my opinion that the Jewish people are probably the smallest numerically and the only group to have survived almost 2,000 years of intermittent and often devastating persecution at the hands of one dominant group after another, the Holocaust being the worst case. Arguably, the history of the Jewish people will continue to have a crucial impact on that group's identity. Accordingly, one scholar observes that Jews have generally become most concerned in our post-Holocaust world about physical and cultural survival as a group. In view of this experience, there is today a palpable undercurrent of nervous insecurity textured into the collective consciousness and memory of the Jewish community. Consequently, any discernible antisemitic threat or attack on the state of Israel or intermarriage between Jews and non-Jews quickens the fear of many Jews that Hitler may, after all, be handed a posthumous victory. See Jack Wertheimer, *A People Divided* (New York: Basic Books, 1993), esp. pp. 28–34. On the related post-Holocaust identity issue regarding Jews who wish to retain their European heritage while remaking their homes in Europe, see Mark Kurlansky, *A Chosen Few* (Reading, Mass.: Addison-Wesley, 1995), pp. ix–xiv; Emil L. Fackenheim, *To Mend the World: Foundations of Post-Holocaust Jewish Thought*, Midland ed. (Bloomington: Indiana University Press, 1994), pp. 294–313; on Jews in America and the impact of the Holocaust on their identity, see Seymour Martin Lipset and Earl Raab, *Jews and the New American Scene* (Cambridge: Harvard University Press, 1995), pp. 108–109; 118–119; 126.

12. See Fackenheim, *To Mend the World*, pp. 233–240.

13. Aaron Hass, *The Aftermath: Living with the Holocaust* (New York: Cambridge University Press, 1995), pp. 143–160. Hass surveys some responses by survivors and theologians to the question, "Was God Watching This?" For a succinct summary of some Jewish and non-Jewish theologians' views on this matter, see David Ariel, *What Do Jews Believe?* (New York: Schocken Books, 1995), pp. 105–107.

14. See Cargas's interview with Emil Fackenheim, in Harry James Cargas, *Voices from the Holocaust* (Lexington: University Press of Kentucky, 1993), p. 134.

15. A similar definition of evil is found in Fred E. Katz, *Ordinary People and Extraordinary Evil* (Albany: State University of New York Press, 1993), p. 5.

16. Lawrence L. Langer, *Admitting the Holocaust* (New York: Oxford University Press, 1995), pp. 179 and 184.

17. In philosopher Richard Rorty's words, which generally express a similar sentiment: "It does not diminish the memory of the Holocaust to say that our response to it should not be a claim to have gained a new understanding of human nature or of human history, but rather a willingness to pick ourselves up and try again." Richard Rorty, "Human Rights, Rationality, and Sentimentality," in *On Human Rights: The Oxford Amnesty Lectures 1993*, ed. Stephen Shute and Susan Hurley (New York: Basic Books, 1993), p. 246 at n. 7.

Introduction to
the Second Edition

ALAN S. ROSENBAUM

$\mathcal{T}$he essential but unfortunate academic, cultural and institutional battles being waged over securing the controlling or authoritative interpretation of the Holocaust and its fitting place in history, politics, ethics, religion and in the popular imagination, continues to arouse interest, frustration and anger. As memory yields to history, the debates center upon such questions as: How ought the Holocaust be remembered, represented, commemorated, and also understood, e.g., as in the context of other instances of mass suffering—from persecution to genocide? What were the principal causes of the Holocaust?[1] And, is it possible to prevent or stem the severity of future genocidal tendencies, if lessons may be drawn from careful studies of the Holocaust? This volume will focus upon the more limited question about how the Holocaust ought to be understood in the framework of selected other similar instances of mass death and genocide.

An increasingly common millennial pronouncement among some observers is that the twentieth century has been the bloodiest in history. We have only to cite the creation of concentration camps, large-scale genocides, especially the Holocaust, two world wars and countless other wars to drive this point home. Certainly, Hitler's Germany deserves its reputation as the century's paradigmatic dictatorship.[2] If this observation is defensible, then, as 'the past bleeds into the present,' it is in my opinion a mistake to merely accept this sweeping but probably justifiable observation without further consideration of real event-specifics construed in terms of factors like context, scope and dimensions, intentions, nature of participants, methods, opportunity, blame and responsibility. Otherwise, any discussion or reflection upon the correctness of the predication will remain emotional, sterile, or vacuous, and with a tinge of resignation, regret and hope that the centuries to come will not be similarly characterized. In other words, comparative genocide studies are neither unreasonable nor invidious exercises in comparative suffering nor a betrayal of deeply held memories and sentiments about the cases of persecution, suffering, and victimization at the hands of genocidists who have targeted one's own people or group. (Analogously, although death is a common denominator of manslaughter and murder, legal systems like ours recognize for various purposes a distinction between various types of homicide). In summary, there are substantial differences among instances of genocide; hence, these must be noted and properly classified, despite that they all have murder in common.

Furthermore, conceptual clarity, historical accuracy, official accountability for criminal wrongdoing, coupled with a special *caveat* about unnecessarily politicizing genocide studies, are likely crucial future outcomes of reasonable scholarly attempts to establish legal and ethical standards for understanding genocide in its various forms to date, and for appreciating the kinds of suffering and victimization some peoples may be made to endure. Such studies generally are premised on the notion that claims about the alleged incomprehensibility of the Holocaust (or any historical phenomenon) are rooted in an ahistorical and abstract theorizing. Yet silence as the only credible response to the abyss of the Holocaust seems to be germane mainly to those who witnessed and suffered first-hand. Whether or not the Holocaust is profoundly unique (but not inexplicable), and whether current conscientious reflections and writings about its full significance as standard-setting or perspective-giving may be established for the contemplation and guidance of future generations, is plausibly at the heart of the debate about its singularly enduring value.

This editor believes that a major contribution to this debate, and to fixing for most informed reasonable people the significant uniqueness of the Holocaust in the future, lies mainly—but not exclusively—in studies of comparative genocide (of course, historians in the future are always free to write as they wish.) In this vein, some prominent scholars assert that the Holocaust is significantly and unalterably unique,[3] hoping thereby to enshrine it as the current universal standard for the classification and measurement of the various instances of mass death, cruelty, human rights abuse, evil and, particularly, genocide. Other scholars reject this claim on various grounds, as some important media attention in response to the first edition has shown. Still others find such exchanges both odious and necessary.[4] In any case, comparative genocide studies appear to be emerging as an important disciplined way for reasonable and educated people to speak and write intelligently about this matter and to avoid the passions of demogogues, of extreme nationalists and antisemites who trivialize or deny the existence of the Holocaust. Indeed, I hope the original edition advanced this trend as some in the mainstream media and academies have affirmed.[5] For this reason, the new contributors, as with those in the first edition, were selected carefully for their expertise in important areas of comparative genocide studies which require attention but were either implicit or undeveloped in the earlier edition.

Accordingly, in addition to those previously included, the new chapters will address the question of the ethics involved in attributing a special uniqueness to the

Holocaust (by Distinguished Professor John K. Roth); an analysis of Bosnian war crimes and the prosecution of their perpetrators by the United Nations *ad hoc* tribunal in the Hague as they impact the issue concerning the uniqueness of the Holocaust (by Justice Richard J. Goldstone, former United Nations Chief Prosecutor); the matter of inquiries into stolen assets from Jewish Holocaust victims by Switzerland, Sweden, Germany, and other nations (by Dr. Shimon Samuels, Director of the Paris office of the Wiesenthal Documentation Center). In his chapter, Samuels will discuss whether matters of restitution and reparations constitute an important and precedent-setting arrangement with impact upon the 'uniqueness' debate.[6] Another new section will examine the core of some crucial similarities and dissimilarities between the Holocaust and Japanese atrocities (in particular the medical experiments "conducted by Unit 731 and the Rape of Nanking") during Japan's occupation of China in the 1930s (authored by Kinue Tokudome, a leading journalist in the struggle to convince the Japanese government to fully and honestly confront its past). Finally, the issue of the impact of contemporary German historians and their writings upon the assertion of the uniqueness of the Holocaust will be addressed[7] (by Professor Wulf Kansteiner, an historian whose expertise lies in German historiography).

Some significant changes have occurred in history and in scholarship, which justify the publication of this newly expanded collection of essays written specifically for this volume. However, it should be noted at the outset that the sum of these changes does not signal a final resolution of the issues and debates concerning the uniqueness of the Holocaust,[8] despite some firm words of assurance from some distinguished Holocaust scholars.[9]

Indeed, substantial differences of opinion remain at the heart of the matter, not the least of which still concerns the overall value of a well-reasoned, well-documented analysis, classification and assessment of instances of similar forms of genocide; the nontrivial meaning of the term 'uniqueness' itself; and whether "the Holocaust" ought to refer exclusively to the Jewish victims of the Nazi German state (and not, also, for example, to the Roma or Gypsy people of whom it has been claimed suffered a fate much like that of the Jews). This new edition will aspire to contribute only to a further clarification of the first two aforementioned items; the third item will require additional research by well-informed scholars, and will likely find its home in a future volume.[10]

In a superficial sense, the fact that the term "Holocaust" has recently been applied to so many different types of calamities appears to reinforce its dramatic affect as a well-known paradigmatic or defining case of genocide and of evil.[11] In brief, instances of inflationary usage may be found in such book (sub-) titles as *American Holocaust*[12] or "The Forgotten Holocaust of World War II",[13] and in labels about disparate tragedies, misfortunes or ideological or self-promoting declamations like certain Eco-disasters, Y2K "cyber-Holocaust", diseases (AIDS, Cancer clusters), the Atlantic Slave Trade and abortion. Hence, some Holocaust scholars have opted for the Hebrew term "Shoah" in reference to the Nazi

Holocaust (whose prime target for extermination was the Jewish people, every man, woman and child) as a kind of insurance against inappropriate 'word-napping'. In any event, it is a commonplace, but still worth noting that no one person or group has a perpetual monopoly on any particular word's usage.[14]

On the other hand, the turbid waters of inflated usage of "the Holocaust" are better clarified or avoided as comparable genocides are analyzed and grounded upon conceptual clarity, defensible methods of inquiry with supportable evidence, and upon reasonable interpretations by competent scholars. If the Holocaust can then be shown, which I believe it can, to be the unparalleled case of genocide to date, then as some other instances of atrocities are demonstrated to share a greater number of core similarities than dissimilarities to the Holocaust, they become more convincing or justifiable as instances of genocide,[15] and as well its perpetrators prosecutable based on the justiciable evidence gathered. However, this editor would disclaim and repudiate again any conclusion that one aggrieved group's suffering is in some way inherently or universally more valuable than any other group's suffering. There is no intention or consequence in genocide studies that implies a moral hierarchy or algorithm of pain and suffering among peoples or groups.

It is undoubtedly true that, barring any new genocidal catastrophe in the near future, the Holocaust will probably always be accepted by most Jews as the worst calamity to have befallen the Jewish people. But whether or not it will be accepted as the paradigm instance of genocide from the collective perspective of expert scholarly opinion and the popular mind in the broader context of genocide and world history has to be persistently argued, and not merely assumed or denied.[16]

A number of major news and professional media reviewed or mentioned the original volume in a favorable light, if not each and every chapter.[17] It is clear from these responses that the issue about the significant uniqueness of the Holocaust is well worthy of continued scholarly attention because it is likely to help determine its abiding value in future historical, philosophical, and theological reflections on the phenomenon of genocide; to legitimize and promote comparative genocide studies (as repugnant as these are); and finally to defend against ever present efforts to trivialize, distort, or deny the Holocaust. In addition, the proliferation and overall acceptance of academic programs, conferences, organizations, memorials, and museums, and the sheer volume of books and articles dedicated to the Holocaust and its primarily Jewish victims in relation to other genocidal or similar catastrophic events tend to institutionalize remembrance as they encourage comparative genocide studies.

Finally, the creation by the United Nations Organization of the two *ad hoc* tribunals for Bosnian and Rwandan war crimes, coupled with the ratification in July 1998 of the International Criminal Court for bringing some former and future genocidists to justice, will also invariably serve to enhance comparative studies of genocide. They do so because the Nuremberg precedent,[18] given its influence upon the recent Genocide and Geneva Conventions, Human Rights Protocols and Covenants, and treaties (including anti-terrorism and anti-rape provisions), in the development of international law involving war crimes, crimes against humanity and against the peace, necessarily appropriates the core elements of criminal wrongdoing with respect to the Holocaust and German (and collaborationist) atrocities, and applies them to other forms of mass death, especially in cases where the atrocities are government-sponsored or -driven.

For instance, the United Nations has initiated an official investigation of atrocities in Cambodia under the Pol Pot (Khmer Rouge) regime (1975–1979) to determine if sufficient justiciable evidence is available to prosecute specific individuals for these barbarous crimes, despite obvious political threats, liabilities, and other conflicts (i.e., realistic warnings of serious civil unrest by some former Khmer Rouge if war crimes trials are held). In consequence, if trials do take place, documentable evidence for patterns of crimes will be expected to be well established, and hence less impeachable as future generations try to comprehend the past for contemporary purposes.

Although some different methods exist for dealing with past genocidal occurrences, it is clearly unacceptable for reasons of morality and legal accountability to bury these malevolent episodes in history.[19] Well-founded and widely supported institutional prosecutions of war criminals not only may result in official accountability, including punishment upon conviction of individuals found guilty, but also a permanent record of the nature and scope of the crimes committed will be publicly accessible to future generations. In addition, some measure of justice will have been achieved.

Without offering a detailed argument here for or against the relative merits of truth (or historical clarification) commissions as an alternative to trials or to blanket amnesty without accountability, some general observations may be helpful; at least they represent another type of method ancillary to getting at specific truths and individual cases of complicity in serious and widespread rights abuses and mass deaths. (Perhaps the international community and the Cambodians respectively may benefit from just such a commission instead of leaving grievances from all sides unaddressed or bringing to justice the alleged perpetrators of genocide or prosecuting only the surviving leadership of the Khmer Rouge: regardless of which option is finally selected, the ideal of a just national reconciliation is at stake). Of course, the price to be paid by the victims for truth about politically motivated abuses is official amnesty for the criminal victimizers. Otherwise, unless some credible action is taken to confront the past, the genocide will remain–in the absence of trials or truth commissions—substantially less well documented and national healing will remain evermore remote,[20]

South Africa, El Salvador and Argentina may be cited as examples of nations whose successor governments had instituted a truth commission. The ultimate purpose of a truth commission is to seek a national reconciliation, no matter how imperfect the findings may be for all parties to the conflict. Those who are alleged criminals, if their criminality had a political motive, will be granted amnesty for truthfully admitting the specifics of their abuses and culpability. Those who are prime suspects and who refuse to testify, or who testify untruthfully, are subject to prosecution. However, "amnesties are invalid when they conflict with international treaties that obligate states to prosecute and punish."[21]

A close scrutiny of the political process and results of truth commissions tells us that at best their impact upon all parties to the conflict in the countries mentioned above is decidedly mixed.[22]

In any case, I underscore the main point that historical (and judicial) records from a successful official proceeding, namely, putting suspected criminals in the dock or requiring them to testify truthfully and fully before a national or aptly empowered reconciliation commission, become more complete and permanent, and better enable historians and other scholars to draw well-documented comparisons with other instances of mass death.

One final reflection on the matter of (international) justice is warranted now. The arrest, detention, and, (possibly) extradition of former Chilean dictator Augusto Pinochet for prosecution by countries other than his own exemplifies the global trend toward accountability and justice. The grounds for his liability for crimes committed during his military junta's rule in Chile (1974–1990), is another facet about the positive developments in international law with regard to criminal responsibility and legal accountability (no matter how much time has elapsed or no matter where the crimes were committed). More to the point, the growing body of international law, coupled with the political will to use it, makes a sea-change in accountability for even domestic crimes (e.g., the "auto-genocide" in Cambodia and the genocidal atrocities committed by government agents against groups of Mayan people during the 1981–83 critical period in the Guatemalan civil war) and probably spells the beginnings of an authoritative record keeping which will possibly make the politics of genocide less "politicized" and distorting of particular cases in relation to other similar ones. It also means no perpetrator of serious crimes (including leaders) will likely enjoy lifelong immunity from prosecution.

Although public trials and national—or international—commissions of reconciliation attempt to get at "the truth," it always remains the case that writers with their own motives and personal agendas may reflect upon past crimes and, if not given to outright denials about their occurrence, place them in a preferred context which may distort or inaccurately portray or interpret reality. Curiously, some writers use a postmodernist approach to events like the Holocaust, with a consequent loss of proper perspective. Its influence is most noticeable in philosophical literature, law, history and the social sciences.[23]

Postmodernist criticism seems to aspire, through a strategy of deconstructing relevant contexts, texts and narratives, to dismantle and eradicate faith in a basic belief in universally valid standards of truth, fact, reason, objectivity, and valuation.[24] Given these standards, it is difficult enough to bring reasonable people to agreement about the character or nature of certain events. However, in the absence of universal standards, what remains regarding inquiry is an absurd epistemological nihilism, which results in either a vacuous or a chaotic democracy of perspectives where no one claim or viewpoint (e.g., or 'truth' or 'story') is better or worse than any other claim. Accordingly, some postmodernists seem dedicated to a sophistical relegation of the Holocaust to a "constellation of events" too complex for a simple 'yes' or 'no' as to its genocidal nature and meaning; hence, instead of viewing the Holocaust as radical or as unspeakable evil, and the nadir point on a continuum of genocide they prefer "meaning choices" as an attempt at interpretation or explanation about what had happened. And the language of "meaning choices" is, for them, reducible to 'power' and 'interest' relationships and the inequitable or uneven distribution of power. He who holds the power controls the definition of whose interests are to be served. Since the present task does not permit a full-blown critique of the rampant subjectivism and arbitrariness involved in postmodernist analysis and also how it feeds the currents of irrationalism, suffice it to say that whatever redeeming value it may have, it may do an egregious disservice to those who seek or grasp the rock bottom certainties about the good life and the forces which destroy and dehumanize it. In other words, everything is not simply relative to the situation, or to the "truths," stories, and language used to interpret it. We may expect realistically that, over time and with sufficient debate, commonsense, a good will, competence, and honesty, it is possible to formulate defensible truth-claims and perspectives. What is ultimately at stake, in my view, is a fuller understanding and assessment of the Holocaust, Hitler's Germany and genocide in the broader context of world history, using explicit and sufficiently supportable concepts and standards.

As I noted in the Introduction to the first edition, this perspective is not furthered by unnecessarily politicizing and/or relativizing the selected realities. Moreover, caution should also be exercised where, like with oppressors, persecutors, and genocidists, some criminal wrongdoers and their apologists try to seize for themselves a mantle of victimhood, and thereby seek to inhabit the same sanctified moral space reserved for innocent, real victims.

The reason many victimizers masquerade as victims is to create the perception of a certain moral equality between 'harm done' and 'harm suffered,' so that they may eschew blame and accountability for their wrongful actions. In other words, victimhood confers a special moral authority, which lies beyond criticism. In any case, the *true* victims of suffering, persecution and/or genocide are often made to endure, unacceptably, not only a rewrite and falsification of history, but also an outrageous convolution of moral status (where victimizers cloak themselves as victims). An example of this situation may be found in the aftermath of World War II. The Displaced Persons camps often contained Holocaust survivors and their persecutors standing side-by-side, as if both, equally, are casualties of the war, the latter giving the appearance of being truly innocent victims.[25] Another illustration is found in the Japanese governments current unwillingness to admit (and not merely "regret") wrongdoing beyond the comfort women issue and offer reparations to the victims of its brutal occupation of China in the mid-1930s.[26] Perhaps its rationale may reside in a popular sentiment among the Japanese people that they, too, were made to suffer the thermonuclear devastation of Nagasaki and Hiroshima, and indiscriminate bombing of Tokyo. Thus, the implication from their perspective is a collapse of the distinction between victim and victimizer and an ephemeral strategy to escape accountability for Japan's atrocities, one that I believe will eventually fail.

In conclusion, the basic interests of truth and justice on a global scale are best served when there are in place credible institutional mechanisms, such as courts, treaties, investigation, and truth commissions, and as well the popular will to use them. We seem to have entered a new era of official accountability for serious and widespread wrongs done. An inevitable concomitant and substratum of organized efforts at global accountability is a determined mission to find and disclose the historic facts relevant to each instance of deliberate atrocities and mass deaths. On an optimistic note, comparative studies of such atrocities, especially genocide, should bring perspective and balance to the responsible voices of organized groups who seek to have their cries of sorrow publicly validated. They also provide a substantial informational weapon in campaigns against exaggeration, distortion, falsification, or denial of any given calamity.

NOTES

1. For example, the Goldhagen thesis (that Hitler gave deadly vent to the Germans' pent-up and ages-old, pathological antisemitism) and its detractors (R. Hilberg, C. Browning, et al.) are of notable significance here. See: Daniel Goldhagen's *Hitler's Willing Executioners* (New York: Alfred A. Knoff, 1996); Christopher Browning's *Ordinary Men* (New York, 1992); Norman Finkelstein and Ruth Bettina's *A Nation on Trial* (New York: Henry Holt and Company, 1998); and Richard Breitman's *Official Secrets* (New York: Hill & Wang, 1998). Breitman's book suggests that evidence is available showing that, contrary to Goldhagen's view, many ordinary Germans were not up to "racial" murders (pp. 225–7 and throughout). For a similarly nuanced view, see Marion Kaplan, *Between Dignity and Despair* (New York: Oxford University Press, 1998), pp 234–5.

2. See: Ian Kershaw, *Hitler* (New York: W.W. Norton, 1999), p. xix.

3. For example, see: Lawrence Langer, "Moralizing the Holocaust," in *Dimensions: A Journal of Holocaust Studies*, Vol. 12, No. 1 (New York: Braun Holocaust Institute, 1998), p. 5.

4. See: Aryeh Neier, *War Crimes* (New York: Times Books, 1998), pp. xii, 22.

5. Notable are a number of professional conferences on Holocaust-related themes that include comparative genocide issues, e.g., in Seattle, 1998 ("The Holocaust and the Churches") and again in Nassau, 1999; in Boston, 1998 ("20th World Congress of Philosophy"); and prospectively, in Oxford, England, 2000 ("Remembering For the Future III").

6. Cf. Christian Pross, *Paying for the Past* (Baltimore: Johns Hopkins University Press, 1998), p. viii.

7. An excellent but too brief outline of some recent developments in how some historians in Germany deal with its Nazi past, is: Georg G. Iggers, "The German Historians and the Burden of the Nazi Past," in *Dimensions*, pp. 21–8.

8. E.g., see: Lawrence Langer, *Preempting the Past* (New Haven: Yale University Press, 1998), p. xvii.

9. For example, see: *The Holocaust and History*. Eds. M. Berenbaum and A. Peck (Bloomington: Indiana University Press; and Washington, D.C.: United States Holocaust Memorial Museum, 1998), pp. 16, 22 (Y. Bauer); 84–5 (O. Bartov); and, 230–2 (F. Littell).

10. It may well be true that the Nazis' motivation for murdering Jews systematically differed from that in the Roma case, but is the difference in motivation sufficient to exclude the latter from "the Holocaust"? (See Note #15 below.)

11. For example, L. Langer observes that the dominent moral and spiritual metaphor of hierarchy, viz., the bottom-most as Hell, has been dubiously linked to Auschwitz. He suggests that perhaps a more creative metaphor might be found as a challenge to "the modern intelligence," *Preempting the Past*, pp. xvii–xix.

12. David Stannard, *American Holocaust* (New York: Oxford University Press, 1992).

13. Iris Chang, *The Rape of Nanking* (New York: Basic Books, 1997).

14. See: Samuel G. Freedman, "Laying Claim to Sorrow Beyond Words," *The New York Times* (December 13, 1997), pp. A11, A13.

15. See my entry about 'uniqueness' and genocide in the *Encyclopedia of Genocide*, Vol. 2 (London: A; B; C Clio, 1999), pp. 567, 569–571. Also, see: Gavriel D. Rosenfeld, "The Politics of Uniqueness: Reflections on the Recent Polemical Turn in Holocaust and Genocide Scholarship," in *Holocaust and Genocide Studies*, Vol. 13 N1 (Spring, 1999), pp. 28–61. In this article, Rosenfeld presents a compelling overview of the more recent arguments about the uniqueness of the Holocaust and their political significance.

16. The case for persistence in writing and teaching is starkly exemplified in a recent poll among Germans; almost 20% of 14–17 year olds know nothing about "Auschwitz," and another 18% believe reports of Auschwitz are inflated. See *Response*, Vol. 20, No. 1 (Winter/Spring, 1999), p.5.

17. For instance, see: Christopher Shea, "How Unique Was the Holocaust? A New Book Ignites a Debate," *The Chronicle of Higher Education* Vol. XLII, No. 38 (May 31, 1996), pp. A6–7, 12; *London Times Higher Education Supplement* (July 15, 1996), p. 17; *The New York Review of Books* (June 26, 1997); *Der Tages Spiegal: Politische Literatur (Germany)*.

18. Christian Tomuschat, "International Criminal Prosecution: The Precedent of Nuremberg Confirmed," in *The Prosecution of International Crimes*, eds. R. S. Clark & M. Sann (New Brunswick: Transaction Publishers, 1996), pp. 17–27.

19. Accordingly, one measure of how well Germany confronts its past is how effectively its government deals with neo-Nazi racist and xenophobic hate crimes today.

20. It is unlikely at the present time that Cambodia could conduct its own trials fairly since its legal infrastructure by almost all accounts is virtually nonexistent or highly corrupt. Thus, the United Nations would need to sponsor either trials or a truth commission or any other mechanism for securing accountability and the prospect of national reconciliation. For an excellent overview of various responses to national healing, see: Martha Minow, *Between Vengeance and Forgiveness* (Boston: Beacon Press, 1998).

21. Aryeh Neier, p. 98.

22. In February, 1999, the President of the Union of South Africa, Nelson Mandela, criticized his country's Truth Commission for giving the appearance of balance in its findings whereas it failed to distinguish between the different motives for violence, namely, those violent actions to oppress people and those done to liberate them. Also, see: Aryeh Neier, Ch. 7.

23. See: Daniel Farber and Suzanna Sherry, *Beyond All Reason* (New York: Oxford University Press, 1997).

24. See my succinct review of *Postmodernism and the Holocaust,* eds. A. Milchman and A. Rosenberg in *Choice,* Vol. 36, No. 6 (February, 1999).

25. Alan S. Rosenbaum, *Prosecuting Nazi War Criminals* (Boulder: Westview Press, 1993), pp. 67–8.

26. Iris Chang, *The Rape of Nanking* (New York: Basic Books, 1997), pp. 224–5. Also, see: Ralph Blumenthal, "Comparing the Unspeakable to the Unthinkable," *The New York Times* (March 7, 1999); and Ralph Blumenthal and Judith Miller, "Japanese Germ-War Atrocities: A Half-Century of Stonewalling the World," *The New York Times* (March 4, 1999), p. A10.

❀ 1 ❀

The Ethics of Uniqueness

JOHN K. ROTH

The debate is blurred by the vagueness of the idea of an episode being unique.
Every event is in some ways unique and in other ways not.

Jonathan Glover,
Humanity: A Moral History of the Twentieth Century

*I*s the Holocaust unique? As this revised edition of Alan S. Rosenbaum's book indicates, debate about that vexing question has been going on for some time. Nor will it go away any time soon. The reasons for the persistence of this issue include the point that Jonathan Glover underscores in this essay's epigraph.[1] There is unlikely to be universal agreement about how events are or are not "unique," and thus closure on the question of the Holocaust's uniqueness—no matter how extensive the scholarship, to say nothing of what future events might produce—should not be expected. For that reason, it is important to consider Gavriel D. Rosenfeld's observation that the Holocaust uniqueness debate raises "important questions concerning the utility of the uniqueness concept."[2] Rosenfeld's observation appears at the end of his primarily historiographical analysis of the uniqueness debate. He approaches but does not enlarge what I shall call the ethics of uniqueness, the topic on which my reflections here will dwell.

As I understand the Holocaust, it was the systematic, state-organized persecution and murder of nearly six million Jews by Nazi Germany and its collaborators.[3] They slaughtered two-thirds of the Europe's Jews and one-third of the world's Jewish population. In addition, Nazi Germany's genocidal policies destroyed millions of other defenseless people, including Roma and Sinti (Gypsies), Polish citizens, and Soviet prisoners of war, as well as homosexuals, the handicapped, Jehovah's Witnesses, and other political and religious dissidents within Germany itself.

At least four terms name this immense tragedy, which continues to raise questions concerning why and how it happened. Masters of euphemistic language, the

Nazis spoke of *die Endlösung*, "the Final Solution" of their so-called Jewish question. In the early 1940s, eastern European Jews turned to Jewish scripture and used a Yiddish word, *Churb'n*, which means "destruction," or the Hebrew term, *Shoah*, which means "catastrophe," to name the disaster confronting their people.

Although *Shoah* is widely used in Israel and the official remembrance day for the Holocaust is called *Yom Hashoah*, "Holocaust," a term that began to achieve prominence in the 1950s, still remains the most common name. It derives from the Septuagint, an ancient Greek translation of the Hebrew Bible, which employs *holokaustos* for the Hebrew *olah*. Those biblical words refer to a completely consumed burnt offering. While the destruction perpetrated by Nazi Germany must be named lest it be forgotten, the problematic religious connotations surrounding the term "Holocaust" suggest that no name can do it justice.

Genocide swirls through the Holocaust uniqueness debate. As I understand genocide, it involves state-organized destruction of a people because of what the political scientist R. J. Rummel calls "their indelible group membership (race, ethnicity, religion, language)."[4] Nazi Germany's destruction of European Jewry was genocide or nothing could be. But what of the Holocaust's uniqueness?

Arguments for the Holocaust's uniqueness do not depend primarily on the number of Jewish victims or the way in which they were killed. Rather, as Steven T. Katz maintains, the uniqueness claim rests on "the fact that never before has a state set out, as a matter of intentional principle and actualized policy, to annihilate physically every man, woman, and child belonging to a specific people. . . . Only in the case of Jewry under the Third Reich was such all-inclusive, noncompromising, unmitigated murder intended."[5]

The Nazis intended to destroy all Jews. That aim was neither restricted to specific territory nor based primarily on what Jews had done. Instead, the Nazis' apocalyptic ideology defined Jews to be so inferior racially, so threatening, that their existence had to be eliminated root and branch. While I find this analysis persuasive, and thus I am a defender of what Glover calls the "distinctive darkness" of the Holocaust, I do not devote my life to study of the Holocaust primarily because of its purported uniqueness. One of a kind or not, the Holocaust remains immensely important, so much so that the reasons for studying it ought not to hinge on something as ambiguous as its uniqueness. Moreover, there is no doubt about it: the uniqueness debate does leave us in ambiguous territory.

Some scholars contend, for example, that Nazi Germany's targeting of the Sinti and Roma did not differ substantially from the fate intended for the Jews. Others fear that the uniqueness claim banishes other genocides to undeserved second-class status. How those disagreements will continue to unfold remains to be seen, but I believe that the debate ought to be contextualized by ethical considerations more than it has been to date. We need to ask: What is the most important issue at stake in our consideration of the Holocaust and genocide? Surely it cannot simply be uniqueness issues or even exact historical accuracy, crucial though such accuracy is, for historical understanding is scarcely an end in itself. Historical study presupposes values that are not contained in historical study alone. Intentionally or unintentionally, it functions in ways that affect the present the and the future. As the Holocaust survivor Elie Wiesel so often suggests, we remember not only for the dead but perhaps even more for the living. To remember *for* implies "on behalf of" and "for the sake of." Such remembering serves goals and perceived goods that go beyond the remembering itself.

Any debate about the Holocaust's uniqueness or about the relation of the Holocaust to other genocides is worthwhile just to the extent that it never loses sight of the fact that *ethical reasons* are the most important ones for studying these dark chapters in human history. The historian Yehuda Bauer, a defender of the Holocaust's uniqueness, offers a proper qualifying reminder along these lines when he writes: "Events happen because they are possible. If they were possible once, they are possible again. In that sense, the Holocaust is not unique, but a warning for the future."[6]

To elaborate this essay's key thesis—the most important reasons for studying the Holocaust and genocide are ethical—I want to step back from encountering the uniqueness debate directly and consider instead what education about the Holocaust and genocide involves. Doing so will then help to focus further the ethics of uniqueness.

Charlotte Delbo was not Jewish, but her arrest for resisting the Nazi occupation of her native France made her experience the Holocaust when she was deported to Auschwitz in January 1943. Delbo survived the Nazi onslaught. In 1946, she began to write the trilogy that came to be called *Auschwitz and After*. Her work's anguished visual descriptions, profound reflections on memory, and diverse writing styles make it an unrivaled Holocaust testimony. As the trilogy draws to a close, Delbo writes, "I do not know / if you can still / make something of me / If you have the courage to try . . . "[7] She contextualizes those words in two ways that have special significance as we think about the direction of Holocaust and genocide studies—and issues about the ethics of uniqueness—in the 21st Century. First, Delbo stressed that her experience in Auschwitz and then in the Nazi concentration camp at Ravensbrück gave her what she called "useless knowledge," a concept to which I shall return later in this chapter. Second, just before the lines I have quoted from *Auschwitz and After*, Delbo remembers Françoise, one of the French women who survived Auschwitz with her. Memory made Françoise mourn. When she thought of the waste and devastation she had experienced and could not forget, the permanently scarring "useless knowledge" it involved, Françoise insisted that the advice one often hears (start over, begin again, put the past behind you) rings hollow as it mocks what cannot be forgotten. "Make one's life over," Françoise protested, "what an expression . . . "[8]

Françoise was not the only survivor on Delbo's mind in *Auschwitz and After*. She had not forgotten Poupette, Marie-Louis, Ida, and many others who were with her in the camps. Nor could Delbo forget how Auschwitz forever divided, besieged, and diminished her own life. Thus, as though she were speaking for her survivor friends, as well as for herself, Delbo wondered "if you can still / make something of me."

To the best of my knowledge, Delbo did not participate in debates about the Holocaust's uniqueness. I expect she would have found them quite beside the point. Yet issues about the ethics of uniqueness are not far removed from her reflection, because the uniqueness debate needs to confront a challenge that Delbo poses: What can and cannot be done with the Holocaust? What must and must not be made of that catastrophe? If we have the courage to study, research, and teach about the Holocaust and other genocides, even to try to learn from them, what awareness should that courage embody, what questions must it raise, what pitfalls does it have to avoid?

Toward the end of the annual Claremont course on the Holocaust course that I concluded in January 2000, my students and I studied Delbo's trilogy. They also wrote papers about that book. The one submitted by an art major named Sarah Yates was distinctive. Inspired by Delbo's reflection that she has two faces (one ruined, another full of light), Sarah's "paper" consisted of a handsome oak box, dark-stained and lacquered. The accompanying written text noted that the box could be "something one might set on a coffee table next to a plate of cookies or a vase of tulips." Like the appearance of Delbo's post-Holocaust life, it could seem to be normal and even decorative. However, Sarah went on to say, "when opened, the box reveals its other 'face,'" an interior of memory fragments, which are not "normal," let alone decorative.

Sure enough, inside Sarah's "Box of Memories," as she called her project, there were carefully crafted wooden puzzle pieces. Some fitted together; others did not. Each piece was delicately inscribed on both sides. The inscriptions were words not only from Charlotte Delbo but also from Primo Levi, Gerda Weissmann Klein, Dr. Elchanan Elkes, Raul Hilberg, and other Holocaust-related writers we had read. Their words did not fit together easily, any more than the puzzle pieces themselves, but Sarah's advice was to "dump the pieces out onto your floor or your desk, and then to try making and 'reading' different arrangements." Each time the configuration, the narratives and meanings, would change, and yet they would not be entirely different. The fragments were real. Many things could be done with them, but not anything or everything, at least not if one respected the memories the box contained.

Doing as Sarah instructed, I observed—but not closely enough—that the "Box of Memories" was layered. Deep down, covering what turned out to be a face painted at the bottom of the box, there were levels where the puzzle pieces did fit together in a recognizable way that just matched the box's interior. Before I knew it, the fragments were out of the box, and I was arranging them to see what the combinations could be. But when the time came to put the pieces back in the box, I discovered that I could not make them fit.

Without replacing the bottom layers as Sarah had originally arranged them, the pieces would not go back into the box in a way that permitted its lid to be closed.

Sarah had color-coded the edges of the bottom layers so she could remember how they went together, but even then, she confessed, closing the "Box of Memories" was hard to do. Later, when Sarah shared her "Box of Memories" with her classmates during a period at the end of the semester when the students reported about work they had been doing, a few of the carefully carved memory fragments disappeared. Regretting their loss, Sarah made others—not to replace the irreplaceable but to fill the "Box of Memories" again so that it could not easily be closed.

Experience with Charlotte Delbo's writing and with Sarah Yates's artistic reflection on it, I believe, makes two clusters of suggestions about the overall direction of Holocaust and genocide studies in the 21st Century and, in particular, the ethics of uniqueness. First, just as is true of the magnitude of these events themselves, study and research about the Holocaust and genocide are increasingly overwhelming tasks. They will be no less so in the future, because the aspects we have to study are not "color-coded," and they do not and will not all fit neatly into boxes of memory, let alone into the departments and compartments of scholarship—including definitions and debates about uniqueness.

It is not just that whole fields of scholarly inquiry scarcely imagined twenty, ten, or even five years ago have emerged and loom large. Where the Holocaust alone is involved one thinks of restitution issues, new archival materials, concerns about women, and renewed controversy about the Vatican and Pope Pius XII, to name just a few. Each genocide will entail its own expanded fields of inquiry as study proceeds. In addition, the issue also involves different ways in which scholarly investigation is carried on. It takes place not just in archives and libraries, not just in the conventional forms of lecturing, writing, and publishing, but also electronically through E-mail networks and the Internet as well as through oral history and the breaking of daily news. Given the magnitude of the events under study, the fact that no one can keep up with all that is going on in Holocaust and genocide studies is fitting, but the realization is disorienting nonetheless and especially as we think of Delbo's challenge: "I do not know / if you can still / make something of me / If you have the courage to try . . . "

Second, because Holocaust and genocide studies will overwhelm us all, it will take some courage to try to direct these studies well in the 21st Century. With that fact in mind, it is worth asking: How important is it to continue the debate about the Holocaust's uniqueness? Certainly it is important to defend the Holocaust's particularity—the same is true of every genocide—so that these disasters are not universalized to the point of abstraction and banality. The ethics of uniqueness requires us never to forget that it is always particular people who are targeted and that they are targeted by specific people and powers. The ethics of uniqueness also requires us to remember that particularity is no guarantee against becoming a victim or a perpetrator, a point that has led Yehuda Bauer to make three additions to the biblical Ten Commandments: Thou shalt not be a perpetrator. Thou shalt not be a victim. Thou shalt not be a bystander.

With these concerns in mind, I spent some time in my recent Holocaust course asking Sarah Yates and her classmates what they thought about six topics: (1) Why should the Holocaust be studied? (2) How should the Holocaust be investigated or taught? (3) What goals should be emphasized in teaching and learning about the Holocaust? (4) What criteria should be used to judge whether study and teaching about the Holocaust are successful? (5) What question(s) about the Holocaust remain most on your mind as our study draws to a close? (6) How do you think study about and research on the Holocaust might change, or should change, in the future? What do we need to know about the Holocaust that we seem not to know?

I want to share some of the things that my students said. I do so not because they are "experts" in the field, but because they are "thoughtful amateurs" whose intuitions, fallible though they are, contain valuable reminders. The students' intuitions can do so, I believe, because of the ways in which they avoid the uniqueness debate while still keeping attention focused on the particularity of the Holocaust and genocide.

The question "Why should the Holocaust be studied?" elicited responses that overlapped with "What goals should be emphasized in teaching and learning about the Holocaust?" With respect to the former, the responses included: We should study to understand, to learn, to prevent, for the sake of the future, to remember and honor those who were victimized. Other responses said, we should study the Holocaust because this event is a defining moment, because of the extreme evil it involved, and "because it happened." The students were clearly concerned about the Holocaust's particularity. They also understood something about the uniqueness debate, but this debate rarely, if ever, became their central concern because they were overwhelmingly preoccupied with the implications of the Holocaust for their own lives.

As for the goals that should be emphasized, there were two that came out repeatedly: one goal in teaching and learning about the Holocaust should be *understanding* how and why it happened. The other goal should be *prevention*. When it came to the question about how the Holocaust should be studied, the following themes were most pronounced: there should be historical objectivity, but facts alone are not enough; "all sides" should be explored, and multiple approaches are required; the importance of first hand reports (especially from survivors) is crucial. When the students emphasized that "all sides" should be studied, they were neither relativizing nor universalizing the Holocaust. At least after a few weeks of study, they were gripped by the particularity and specificity of the Holocaust's history. That focus was what underwrote their insistence that the actions of perpetrators, victims, bystanders, neighbors, rescuers, and people active in resistance all had to be taken into account. The reasons for taking all of them into account was partly because the history could only be adequately encountered by doing so, but also because such an accounting was essential for the students' reflection about how their own lives ought to be lived.

The responses to the question about criteria for successful teaching about the Holocaust were the most tentative. Several said they were not sure there could be criteria. Others stressed greater understanding of the history. Still others said that measures of success might include: never forgetting the Holocaust, the elimination of Holocaust denial, greater tolerance, and prevention of related disasters. One of the most focused and succinct responses said success would depend on answers to three questions: Has one learned about what happened? Has one been affected (emotionally, spiritually) by the teaching? Has one wrestled deeply and been disturbed by the content of the study?

There were variations on the theme concerning lingering questions, but one student spoke for several others by saying that the key question was "how to place the Holocaust in history."

That comment suggested not only the importance of continued searching for detail and the relation of one event to another, including how to place the Holocaust in relation to other genocides, but also larger issues that are not matters of history alone, a factor that one student underscored by asking, "What now? What about outside the classroom? What should I do with what I learned?" The question was not a naive request for "lessons of the Holocaust," for these students were acquainted with what Charlotte Delbo meant when she spoke of "useless knowledge." And so the student's questions remain, and they are questions that ask why, at the end of the day, one should care so much that the history of the Holocaust and genocide is studied, researched, and taught. Why, in particular, should non-Jews—for most of my Holocaust students are not Jewish—as well as Jews care that memory of the Holocaust is institutionalized and preserved?

Even when, indeed especially when, differences of opinion exist about such issues, clarity about them seems important, because, without such clarity, it is not likely that very many people will continue serious study of the Holocaust. Some clarity about those issues may be found by noting what some of these "informed amateurs" had to say when the question was "How do you think study about and research on the Holocaust might change, or should change, in the future? What do we need to know about the Holocaust that we seem not to know?"

First, there was widespread concern that study and research will change because, as one student put it, "all the survivors will soon be dead and so will most others who have a vivid memory of that time." In a similar vein, another student was not entirely off the mark when she said, "soon all we will have left are books about the Holocaust." And, she might have added, quite a few of those books will contain lots of arguments about the Holocaust's uniqueness. If I read accurately between the lines, these student concerns imply worry that, as the Holocaust and perhaps other 20th Century instances of genocide recede further into the past, they will become more and more a matter of purely historical interest and investigation. Continued debate about the Holocaust's uniqueness, ironically, could contribute to that result. It could become a largely scholastic argument that keeps swirling around itself. Such an outcome could make Holocaust and genocide studies less and less significant for the present and the future unless the historical investigation is carried on in tandem with an ongoing emphasis and evaluation of the political, ethical, and religious implications of the Holocaust and genocide.

Sarah Yates had something like this in mind, I believe, when she wrote, "I think as the last living survivors pass away, it will become important to 'let the Holocaust in.' If it is taught and [researched] with more detachment, as is the tendency with receding history, a crucial element will be lost. People must honestly, carefully, and humbly pick up the fragile pieces. They must never be scattered." Too much debate by proponents and opponents of the thesis that the Holocaust is unique fails to pick up the fragile pieces humbly. Instead, the desire is to win an argument. True, the arguments are important because they involve historical accuracy and the integrity of the particularity of events. But what can be lost—the scattering of the pieces that Sarah deplored—is an emphasis on why the historical accuracy and the integrity of the particularity are so crucial: namely, that they help us to discern what we ought to do in the present and the future, which means that the "winning" of arguments about uniqueness takes a distant second place to the task of trying to forestall further genocidal wasting of human life in years to come.

After one of the class sessions in which we had discussed some of these questions, I played a brief videocassette vignette in which Elie Wiesel can be heard to say that, from his point of view, there is one fundamental reason to study the Holocaust: namely, to make people more sensitive. What Wiesel means by *sensitive* is that we should be more concerned about people, especially defenseless people who are potential or actual victims of persons and powers that lay waste to human life. Sensitivity means prevention and protest against such harm-doing; it means help and intervention on behalf of those in need.

I played the Wiesel video clip for my students because his emphasis on sensitivity is rightly placed. My own study and teaching about the Holocaust are governed largely by ethical concerns, and for that reason debate about the Holocaust's uniqueness plays a relatively small part in them, for other issues seem to be of much greater importance. As Sarah Yates once suggested, the uniqueness debate may frame the way some people *think* about the Holocaust, but sensitivity and concern for others should frame the way all people *live* after the Holocaust. Therein, she, added, lies all the difference in the world.

The study of any instance of genocide, I believe, is fundamentally a moral enterprise to check the repetition of the worst that people—always particular people in concrete and specific situations—have done and may do again. In *Reading the Holocaust*, Inga Clendinnen makes this point in a related way when she "reads" the Holocaust to dispel what she calls "the 'Gorgon effect'—the sickening of imagination and curiosity and the draining of the will which afflicts so many of us when we try to look squarely at the persons and processes implicated in the Holocaust. . . . Such perplexity," she goes on to say, "is dangerous . . . an indulgence we cannot afford."[9]

The rationale for Holocaust education makes ethical considerations—especially one such as Wiesel's emphasis on sensitivity—of primary concern. We seek not only to learn *about* the Holocaust but to learn *from* it. The ethics of uniqueness urges that the debates about the Holocaust's uniqueness are worth pursuing just to the extent that they enable us to learn *from* them, which means learning increased sensitivity of Wiesel's ethical kind.

Neither learning about nor learning from the Holocaust is easily done. There are those who question how or whether the latter happens *even if* we have learned *about* the Holocaust. Indeed, *because of* what we learn about the Holocaust, there are those who question how or whether learning *from* the Holocaust takes place. In the first case, one might point out that the slogan "Never again" is mocked by another ("Again and again") where the history of genocide in the 20th Century and beyond is concerned. Let me concentrate, however, on a more subtle but especially crucial issue for Holocaust pedagogy and its intersection with uniqueness debates. This issue has to do with the idea that learning about the Holocaust will not let us take very much from the Holocaust when it comes to lessons, moral insights, and determination to check genocidal tendencies.

To get at those challenges, I want to return to Charlotte Delbo and her "useless knowledge" before turning to two Holocaust scholars, Lawrence L. Langer and Peter Novick, who also make important contributions to my reflections. When Delbo speaks about "useless knowledge," she refers to Auschwitz experiences that are so dark as to be unforgettable but also so overpowering that the more one encounters their stark realities—even in reading about them, let alone in the flesh or in personal memory—the more we are likely to be disoriented and overwhelmed by them. If we are to learn from the Holocaust, that prospect looms large. Delbo makes us wonder how we should try to cope with the likelihood that what we try to learn from the Holocaust will be overcome by the "useless knowledge" we obtain as we learn about it.

One of the first American interpreters of Charlotte Delbo, and she taught him a great deal, is the literary critic Lawrence Langer. Echoing Delbo, Langer suggests that we can learn nothing—at least nothing edifying—from Holocaust testimonies that describe a baby torn in two or a woman buried alive. The Holocaust, he thinks, is a watershed event. It is so partly because knowledge about it leaves us largely estranged from a moral universe that we might nostalgically yearn to inhabit but that has been ruined by Auschwitz and Treblinka.

If I read Langer correctly, the perplexity that Inga Clendinnen wants to mitigate is less the problem than what he identifies as an understandable but problematic inclination to "pre-empt" the Holocaust, which involves using—even abusing—the Holocaust to shore up ethical or religious beliefs. Langer makes us wonder how we can learn from the Holocaust without pre-empting it. The best response to Langer's challenge is not an argument or a theory, including arguments and theories about uniqueness, but instead deeds and lives that actually move from study of the Holocaust and genocide to greater caring for those in our world who are most in need and defenseless against power that oppresses them.

In a *New York Times* article on June 27, 1999, Langer gave credit to the author of the book he was reviewing for drawing the "sensible if unpopular conclusion that we should study a historical event like the Holocaust not to extract lessons but to appreciate its complexities and contradictions."[10] He went on to say that such a conclusion "will please a few readers but probably upset many more." Langer made those comments about Peter Novick's *The Holocaust in American Life*, which also raises complicating questions related to the ethics of uniqueness.

In addition to asking "Why now? and "Why here?" when it comes to discerning the American concern about the Holocaust, Novick is skeptical about the value of such concern. In particular, he is dubious about "the idea of 'lessons of the Holocaust,'" and early on in his book he emphasizes two reasons for his skepticism.[11] The first is pedagogic. The Holocaust's very extremity, he argues, makes it an unlikely source of "lessons for dealing with the sorts of issues that confront us in ordinary life."[12] He doubts that there is anything that is necessarily "morally therapeutic" in "the mere act of walking through a Holocaust museum, or viewing a Holocaust movie," or, we might add, studying the Holocaust and genocide.[13]

Novick is more skeptical than he needs to be at this point. Some thirty years of Holocaust-related teaching convinces me that the right kind of study about the Holocaust and genocide can have a profound moral effect on students. Novick resists such evidence as anecdotal, but the changed lives and their testimony exist nonetheless. In the context of this essay, however, Novick helps us to ask whether debates about uniqueness have, even anecdotally, such a salutary impact. My judgment may be wrong, but here I would share some of Novick's Holocaust-related skepticism. I doubt that uniqueness debates do very much to improve the ethical quality of our lives, which is not in any way to accept Novick's conclusion that study of the Holocaust and genocide does not have a key role to play in developing moral sensitivity of the kind I am defending here.

My comments anticipate the second reason for Novick's skepticism, which is pragmatic. That is to say he is dubious that there will be much to show when one asks "what is the payoff" of learning from the Holocaust that is supposed to be ethical. Novick does not deny that Holocaust study might sometimes sensitize people to resist "oppression and atrocity," but he contends that emphasis on the Holocaust (especially emphasis that insists on the Holocaust's "uniqueness") "works in precisely the opposite direction, trivializing crimes of lesser magnitude."[14] At least for most Americans, Novick contends, "contemplating the Holocaust is virtually cost-free: a few cheap tears." Yet in another sense he reckons that such contemplation is not cost-free at all, because "it promotes *evasion* of moral and historical responsibility" as far as the American's own history is concerned.[15]

Here Novick's challenge runs as follows: How do Americans—or any people—study and teach about the Holocaust and genocide without evading moral and historical responsibilities that belong to them as they confront their past, present, and future? If people do not evade those responsibilities, will efforts to learn about and from the Holocaust and genocide deserve the attention now being devoted to them? Novick's questions are as good as they are tough, and they are better than some of his responses to them. For instance, his implication that study of the Holocaust and genocide is at odds with a broadening intensification of moral concern fails to obtain the empirical validation needed to validate it. At least anecdotally, the evidence seems to be overwhelmingly on the other side. Nevertheless, whatever the virtues that study of the Holocaust and genocide involve and produce, such study is not an end in itself. Even more so that principle applies to uniqueness debates. Those debates may not be incompatible with an intensification of moral concern, but their content and impact do not seem to move primarily in that direction. Thus, they bear watching and need evaluating from a moral perspective that asks: How do these debates contribute to practically visible moral sensitivity. To the extent that these debates do not make such a contribution, it would be well to call them off.

"I do not know," wrote Charlotte Delbo, "if you can still make something of me / If you have the courage to try . . ." As the 21st Century develops, the challenge we face in thinking about uniqueness debates in particular and the direction of Holocaust and genocide studies in general is the following: *We should avoid the ultimate irony that would result if Holocaust and genocide studies—including debates about uniqueness—become a kind of useless knowledge.* That fate is likely to be avoided only if the direction of Holocaust and genocide studies in the 21st Century is oriented by increasingly articulated ethical responses to the question: Why do research, study, and teach about the Holocaust and genocide? Or, in words that Charlotte Delbo wrote in *Auschwitz and After*, words that epitomize the ethics of uniqueness, words that every Holocaust and genocide scholar would do well to inscribe where they can be seen each day one works: "I beg you / do something / learn a dance step / something to justify your existence / something that gives you the right / to be dressed in your skin in your body hair / learn to walk and to laugh / because it would be too senseless / after all / for so many to have died / while you live / doing nothing with your life."[16]

NOTES

1. Jonathan Glover, *Humanity: A Moral History of the Twentieth Century* (London: Jonathan Cape, 1999), 396. Glover's impressive book devotes several chapters to Nazi Germany and the Holocaust. His discussion of what he calls "the distinctive Nazi darkness" is brief but pointed. He defends the view that the Holocaust has "a terrible darkness all its own," which he defines by citing Eberhard's Jäckel's statement that "the National-Socialist murder of the Jews was unique because never before had a nation with the authority of its leader decided and announced that it would kill off as completely as possible a particular group of humans, including old people, women, and children, and infants, and actually

put this decision into practice, using all the means of governmental power at its disposal." (See Glover, 396). Significantly, Glover points out this "terrible darkness" not simply to defend its distinctiveness but for the ethical lessons that he believes the darkness suggests. See Glover, 396.

2. Gavriel D. Rosenfeld, "The Politics of Uniqueness: Reflections on the Recent Polemical Turns in Holocaust and Genocide Scholarship," *Holocaust and Genocide Studies* 13 (Spring 1999): 47. Rosenfeld's article provides an excellent overview and critique of the positions held by major proponents and opponents of the Holocaust's uniqueness.

3. In the following preliminary statements, which define my understanding of the Holocaust and briefly outline the underpinning argument concerning the Holocaust's distinctiveness, I draw on material I prepared for John K. Roth et al., *The Holocaust Chronicle: A History in Words and Pictures* (Lincolnwood, IL: Publications International, 2000).

4. R. J. Rummel, *Death by Government* (New Brunswick, NJ: Transaction Publishers, 1997), 31.

5. Steven T. Katz, "The Uniqueness of the Holocaust: The Historical Dimension," in Alan S. Rosenbaum, ed., *Is the Holocaust Unique?: Perspectives on Comparative Genocide* (Boulder, CO: Westview Press, 1996), 19–20.

6. Yehuda Bauer, *The Holocaust in Historical Perspective* (Seattle: University of Washington Press, 1978), 37.

7. Charlotte Delbo, *Auschwitz and After*, trans Rosette C. Lamont (New Haven: Yale University Press, 1995), 352.

8. Ibid., 351.

9. Inga Clendinnen, *Reading the Holocaust* (Cambridge: Cambridge University Press, 1999), 4.

10. When Langer stresses the sensible thing is to appreciate the Holocaust's complexities and contradictions, as opposed to extracting lessons from the Holocaust, I am both sympathetic and puzzled. I agree that the complexities and contradictions are crucial. The devil is found in their details. Without those details, encounters with the Holocaust remain inaccurate, abstract, and trite. My puzzlement, however, involves what it could mean to *appreciate* the complexities and contradictions if that appreciation has little, if anything, to do with understanding that is in basic ways ethical or moral. If we do not experience the Holocaust's complexities and contradictions as ethical dilemmas that point, at least in part, toward the need for greater ethical sensitivity, then I remain quizzical about what it could mean to appreciate them. If Langer resists the idea that study of the Holocaust is fundamentally an ethical task, I believe that his many years of distinguished scholarship in the field are nevertheless contributions to ethical reflection of the highest importance, and I further believe that his own passion for the scholarship he does so well can only by understood as springing from ethical motivations and suppositions.

11. Peter Novick, *The Holocaust in American Life* (Boston: Houghton Mifflin, 1999), 13.

12. Ibid.

13. Ibid.

14. Ibid., 14.

15. Ibid., 15.

16. Delbo, *Auschwitz and After*, 230.

❀ 2 ❀

Religion and the Uniqueness of the Holocaust

RICHARD L. RUBENSTEIN

$\mathcal{F}$ew events of the twentieth century have been the object of as much persistent popular interest as the Holocaust. When the United States Holocaust Memorial Museum opened its doors in April 1993, museum officials estimated that 1 million people would visit the museum during its first year. They vastly underestimated the actual number that first year, hosting approximately 2 million visitors, two-thirds of whom were non-Jews. It is difficult to account for this interest simply in terms of the number of Holocaust victims or the fact that the Shoah was perpetrated by the government of one of the best-educated and technically competent nations in the world, although that fact cannot be discounted. There have been many other large-scale, demographic catastrophes perpetrated by human beings in the twentieth century. Nevertheless, it is unlikely that a museum devoted to Stalin's murders or the Armenian genocide of 1915 would consistently draw so large a number of visitors as has the Holocaust Museum.

What, then, accounts for the persistence of interest in the Holocaust half a century after the end of World War II? It is, I believe, the fact that the Holocaust, more than any other twentieth-century disaster, resonates with the religio-mythic traditions of biblical religion, the dominant religious tradition of Western civilization. Put differently, the response to the Holocaust reflects the pervasiveness in Western civilization of what Stephen R. Haynes has called the "witness-people myth"—the belief that whatever happens to the Jews, for good or ill, is an expression of God's providential justice and, as such, is a sign "for God's church."[1] According to Haynes, the witness-people myth is "a deep structure in the Christian imagination . . . a complex of ideas and symbols that, often precritically and unconsciously, informs ideas about Jews among persons who share a cultural heritage." The myth has its roots in the biblical doctrine that God has chosen Israelis as His people by bestowing upon them a covenant stipulating that Israel's fidelity would be rewarded by divine protection, as surely as infidelity would be harshly punished. As we know, the rabbis interpreted the Fall of Jerusalem as God's punishment of a sinful Israel for failing to keep the commandments. Christian thinkers agreed that the Fall of Jerusalem was divine punishment, but they argued that the rejection of Jesus as Lord and Messiah was God's motive for laying waste to Jerusalem and the Holy Temple. According to the Christian interpretation, the Jews could only regain God's favor by truly accepting baptism. As long as they refused, God would condemn them to the suffering, humiliation, and indignity of exile. The suffering of the witness people was thus understood as a confirmation of Christian faith, and Jews were seen as justly paying a bitter price for their refusal to accept the truth as taught by Christianity.

Given the enormous weight Judaism and Christianity place on the interpretation of Jewish disaster as an expression of God's justice and providence, it was inevitable that both Jews and Christians would respond to the Holocaust in accordance with their respective traditions. It is, for example, possible for believing Christians to view the Armenian genocide or the Pol Pot massacres in Kampuchea as purely secular events without raising the question of whether transcendent religious meaning is involved in such events. Not so the Holocaust. The Holocaust almost inevitably elicits some form of religious interpretation at every level of intellectual sophistication, as is evident in the popular response to the Holocaust museum. The same phenomenon can be seen in the rise of Holocaust theology as a distinctive discipline among a large number of post–World War II Jewish theologians and a smaller but influential group of Christian thinkers. The latter include John Pawlikowski, Paul van Buren, Franklin Littell, Alice and Roy Eckhardt, and John K. Roth. Never before in Jewish history had there been a catastrophe of such magnitude, and if one believes, as do most Jews and Christians, in a God who is the ultimate author of the drama of history, then the question of divine involvement in the Holocaust is bound to arise.

No matter how the question of God's involvement is resolved, neither academically trained theologians nor ordinary laypersons can entirely ignore it. For some, the Holocaust is ipso facto proof that a sinful Israel had been justly punished by a righteous God. Many others—both Jewish and Christian—are unable either to abandon some semblance of faith in the biblical God-who-acts-in-history or to assert that the Holocaust was in any sense God's righteous judgment. Unable to abandon either position, they are impaled on the horns of a dilemma, made more painful by their respective liturgical traditions that stress the righteous and saving acts of the Lord.

Most academically trained historians argue that events like the Holocaust can be adequately explained in terms of the conflicting material interests of the perpetrators and their victims. Undoubtedly, much can be learned from a socioeconomic reading of history. Nevertheless, such a reading underestimates the power of religion and myth to define reality. The overwhelming majority of human beings understand the world in terms of the way their religions and cultures define reality for them. A given society's religio-mythic inheritance is normally opaque to critical scrutiny by its members, because that same inheritance is a crucially important part of the interpretive matrix by which individuals comprehend reality.

Even in a relatively secular age, the power of religion to define reality largely determines the experiences available to Jews and Christians alike, at least in relation to each other. In the case of the witness-people myth, most Christians can be said to *dwell within the myth* and to comprehend Jewish history and experience in and through it.[2] That is why the deicide accusation has been so potent a force throughout the ages. That is also why the image of Judas has played so important a role in determining the way Jews have been perceived by Christians, especially in times of stress.[3]

The fate of the Jews as a distinctive people is too closely connected with the religio-mythic inheritance of both Judaism and Christianity for the Holocaust to have lacked profound religious significance for either believing Jews or Christians, especially at the level of unreflective, pretheoretical consciousness. The Holocaust is linked to the Fall of Jerusalem in 586 B.C.E. (to the Babylonians) and in 70 C.E. (to the Romans). It is also linked to the responses to those events of the prophets, the rabbis, the authors of the New Testament, and the Church Fathers as is no other event in modern history.

No other instance of genocide or attempted genocide in modern times elicits associations so directly to the Bible and its worldview as does the Holocaust. Other peoples have depicted themselves as "Christ among the nations" and have interpreted their suffering as an assault on God's people, but in no other instance did the event occur to those who were directly linked to the biblical drama of God's involvement in history as the Jews. More people died under Stalin than in the Holocaust, albeit a lesser proportion of the peoples of the Soviet Union perished than was the case with Europe's Jewish population. Ethnic cleansing in former Yugoslavia and the recent massacres in Rwanda are horrendous examples of mass slaughter and inhumanity. Nevertheless, these events do not have the same religio-mythic overtones for Jews and Christians as does the Holocaust.

My conviction that the religious dimension is responsible for the uniqueness of the Holocaust has been strengthened by frequent visits to Asia. Starting in the late 1970s, I have made more than fifteen trips to Japan and Korea. As I came to know Japanese, Chinese, and Korean scholars, it became apparent that, except for the Christians among them, the Holocaust had very little meaning for them. It did not happen on their continent, and, terrible as it was, it was perceived as simply one of the many bloody chapters in human history, of no distinctive importance in and of itself. The scholars were by no means indifferent to human suffering. Nevertheless, except for Asian Christians, the Holocaust was seen as a purely Western secular event.

Most Asians do not respond to Jews, either positively or negatively, in as emotionally complex a manner as do Westerners. During World War II, for example, even Japanese antisemites were largely incapable of the kind of visceral anti-

Jewish hatred that pervaded much of Europe.[4] Japanese antisemitism first became a significant force in the aftermath of the Bolshevik Revolution when the 75,000-man Japanese Expeditionary Force and its White Russian allies were defeated by the Bolsheviks and forced to retreat from eastern Siberia. According to the defeated White Russian officers who fought alongside the Japanese, the Bolshevik Revolution was the result of a secret Jewish conspiracy for world domination. The Japanese found this explanation credible. As "proof," White Russians had offered an infamous forgery, *The Protocols of the Elders of Zion*, which was speedily translated into Japanese. In addition to finding the Bolshevik system repugnant given their profound reverence of the emperor, the Japanese were horrified at the murder of Tsar Nicholas II and his family. Convinced that the Jews were deeply implicated in the revolution, a group of Japanese officers and ultranationalists began to study Jews and Judaism in the 1920s. They concluded that many of the disorders brought about by modernity were deliberate elements in a grandiose Jewish plot. Although they saw the Jews as a potential danger to Japan, in the 1930s they decided on a radically different strategy than that of the National Socialists in dealing with them. If the Jews were as powerful and as potentially dangerous as the *Protocols* alleged, they were to be handled with great care in order to turn their alleged abilities and influence into an advantage for Japan.

In the 1920s and 1930s, Captain Norihigo Yasue and naval Lieutenant Koteshige Inuzuka were regarded as leading "experts" on Jews and Judaism. Both had been attached to the White Russian military command during the unsuccessful campaign against the Bolsheviks. Captain Yasue translated the *Protocols* into Japanese. He was also the author of several tracts warning of a Jewish conspiracy to take over the world. In 1927, the Foreign Ministry borrowed Yasue from the army and sent him to Europe and the Middle East, where he met with Zionist leaders such as David Ben Gurion, Chaim Weizman, and Menahem Ussishkins, as well as rabbis and ordinary Jews. He was impressed by the *kibbutzim*, which he believed the Jews would use to colonize the countries they would eventually conquer. Nevertheless, he reported honestly to his superiors that he heard no hint of any conspiracy for world domination while among the Jews of Palestine.[5]

Like Yasue, Lieutenant Inuzuka was as convinced of a Jewish world conspiracy as any hard-core Nazi, but he and his fellow "experts" reacted very differently than did the Nazis. In a January 18, 1939, report to the navy's general staff, Inuzuka spelled out the difference: "[The Jews are] just like a *fugu* [blowfish] dish. It is very delicious but unless one knows well how to cook it, it may prove fatal to his life."[6] The *fugu* fish is regarded by the Japanese as a great delicacy *when properly prepared*. There is, however, no margin for error. An improperly prepared *fugu* can result in almost instantaneous death. However, the "experts" were convinced that they knew how to prepare this particular *fugu*.

Yasue was also a key figure in protecting the 17,000 Jews residing in Shanghai during the war. In July 1942, Colonel Joseph Meisinger—the Gestapo chief for Japan, China, and Manchukuo—and two other German officials met with local authorities in Shanghai to demand that the Japanese exterminate their Jewish charges "like garbage" on Rosh Hashanah.[7] Meisinger had previously served in Warsaw in 1939. Shanghai's Japanese authorities were initially inclined to accede to Meisinger's demands, but Vice Consul Mitsugi Shibata found both Meisinger and his proposals revolting. He took the highly unusual step of warning the leaders of Shanghai's Jewish community. He urged them to use their contacts in the Japanese government to thwart Meisinger. Shibata was imprisoned and dismissed from the Consular Service when his activities became known to local Japanese authorities.[8] Nevertheless, the Shanghai Jews got word to Dr. Abraham Kaufman, a leading Jew in Harbin, Manchuria, who enjoyed the favor of some of Japan's most important leaders, including members of the ultranationalist Black Dragon Society. When Kaufman used his contacts to apprise Foreign Minister Y[amo]suke Matsuoka and Colonel Norihigo Yasue of the impending danger, the Japanese government rejected Meisinger's proposals.[9] To appease its German ally, the government decreed on February 18, 1943, that "stateless refugees" would be confined to a ghetto in the Hongkew section of Shanghai, one of the poorest sections of the metropolis. Nevertheless, within Hongkew, the Jews were not harmed.

In spite of persistent German efforts to bring Japan's policy into line with national socialism on the "Jewish question," more than 20,000 Jews found a safe haven during the war in Japanese-occupied Shanghai, several other Chinese cities controlled by Japan, and the puppet-state of Manchukuo (Manchuria). Moreover, with a few exceptions, some of Japan's leading antisemites were among the most effective protectors of the Jewish refugees. Protecting Jews under their own names, they followed a consistent pattern of writing and translating antisemitic tracts under pseudonyms.

There have been periods, such as the present, when Japan has been flooded with antisemitic literature.[10] World War II was such a period, but Japanese anti-Jewish feeling has never had the emotionally overladen content that has characterized European antisemitism. The reason is fairly obvious: The vast majority of Japanese are not Christians influenced by the witness-people myth. The emotions engendered by the Judeo-Christian rivalry are largely absent among the Japanese.

As noted, many Japanese have seen Jews as responsible for the Bolshevik Revolution. Today, some Japanese blame the Jews for the strengthening of the yen and the newly activist U.S. trade policies toward Japan. Nevertheless, the Jews have not been perceived as deicides, and Jewish history is not seen as a continuing record of divine chastisement for failure to accept Christ as Lord, something the overwhelming majority of Japanese have yet to do.

Thus, the Holocaust is not a unique event for the Japanese or for most other Asians. The same cannot be said of the Western world, where it is difficult to extricate the Holocaust from the matrix of meanings concerning Jews and Judaism to be found in the biblical religions. To repeat, as a catastrophic event in Jewish history, the Holocaust can only be compared to the Fall of Jerusalem in ancient times. Inevitably, it elicits a religious response as did the earlier catastrophe. This is especially true in the United States, with its pervasive biblical tradition. For a very large number of Americans, by no means all of them Fundamentalists or Dispensationalists, the Bible is a living document, and contemporary events tend to be comprehended in its terms. Moreover, far more Christians than care to say so in public regard the Holocaust, as did the early Christians at the time of the Fall of Jerusalem to the Romans, as God's punishment for Israel's continuing refusal to accept faith in Christ.

Elsewhere, I have written that the Holocaust was a holy war in which post-Enlightenment European Christendom's goal of eliminating Jews and Judaism from its midst was fulfilled by Hitler, albeit by means other than most religious authorities would have preferred. Put differently, far more Europeans objected to the methods Hitler employed to eliminate the Jews than to his objectives.

In spite of national socialism's unremittingly racist antisemitism, Europe's motives for seeking the elimination of the Jews were largely religious. To understand the Holocaust as a modern holy war, we must keep in mind the fact that in Europe's formative centuries all those who rejected baptism, apart from the Jews, were either expelled or exterminated.[11] For example, in 1995, Norway celebrated a millennium of adherence to Christian religion. It is instructive, however, to remember how Christianity won the day in that country: According to the Norse sagas, in 995 King Olaf I Tryggvason returned from Dublin to give Norwegians a stark choice—death or baptism.[12]

Put differently, the king was offering his subjects the choice of death or becoming Europeans. For the king, as well as for Europe's princes and prelates in the centuries that followed, the price of admission to full participation in European civilization was membership in the Christian church. Moreover, today, no less than yesterday, few aspects of European civilization—art, literature, music, philosophy, religion, politics, universities, status hierarchies—can be entirely divorced from their Christian roots. Even European secularism is an unintended consequence of Europe's Christian culture, as Max Weber and others have recognized.[13]

My characterization of the Holocaust as a modern version of a Christian holy war carried out by a neopagan National Socialist state hostile to Christianity is based in part on the answer to the following question: *Which groups and institutions in the 1930s regarded the total elimination of the Jews and Judaism from Europe as a long-term benefit?* The answer is clear: *All those for whom the integrity of the Christian symbolic universe was indispensable to a genuinely civilized existence.* In 1939, the overwhelming majority of European Christian leaders were convinced that the greatest threats to the integrity of their symbolic universe came from two sources: bolshevism and unconverted Jews, whether religious, socialist, Zionist, secular, or assimilationist. Moreover, these same leaders thought of bolshevism as largely Jewish in origin and spirit. In their minds, the two often merged into one.

Europe has never valued genuine religious diversity. Whenever a group or a movement arose to challenge the primacy of Christianity anywhere in Europe—

whether it was the external challenge of Islam or the internal challenge of the Cathari in thirteenth-century southern France—the response of European Christendom was to eliminate the nonbeliever. Before the Enlightenment, Jews were tolerated in parts of Europe as long as they were perceived as useful. When that perception no longer held, they were expelled.

As a result of the Enlightenment, the Jews came to participate in European life under conditions of more or less civic equality. This resulted in the rise of a class of Jewish writers, thinkers, intellectuals, and academics who for a time were able to influence European Christendom from within. Neither the Catholic Church nor the Protestant churches found that development acceptable. After the Bolshevik Revolution, perceived by both the churches and the European right as a Jewish assault on Christendom, the Jewish presence within European Christendom became intolerable to important political and religious elites throughout the continent. All that remained was for someone to find a feasible method of population elimination. As was the case with the Cathari in the thirteenth century, it was only a question of time before the highly popular objective of eliminating the Jews from the European continent was achieved. Although never proclaimed as such, the Holocaust bore much resemblance to a holy war in which the Nazis did the dirty work for institutions that were destined to outlast them.

It is the religious element that makes the Holocaust unique. The Holocaust can be likened to a one-sided holy war or a latter-day crusade, most closely resembling the Albigensian Crusade. Never before in history was one religion eliminated so brutally or so efficiently by adherents of another religion with almost no protest. Like the Fall of Jerusalem, the Holocaust arouses speculation concerning God's absence or presence in history for Jews and Christians alike. Although the motives for initiating the Holocaust were by no means solely religious, the event did achieve an extraordinarily important goal for most Europeans—the elimination for all practical purposes of the Jewish demographic presence and Jewish religio-cultural influence within European Christendom. In vast areas of central and eastern Europe, today's surviving Jews constitute little more than a living museum to be exhibited or suppressed as suits the momentary political objectives of the governing elite.

NOTES

1. See the introduction to Stephen R. Haynes, *Jews and the Christian Imagination: Reluctant Witness* (Louisville, Ky.: Westminster/John Knox Press, 1995), pp. 8ff.

2. Ibid., p. 9.

3. On the influence of Judas on Christian perceptions of Jews, see Richard L. Rubenstein, *After Auschwitz: History, Theology, and Contemporary Judaism*, 2d ed. (Baltimore: Johns Hopkins University Press, 1992), pp. 21–22, 45, 50–51.

4. For an examination of Japanese attitudes toward Jews during World War II, see David Kranzler, *Japanese, Nazis, and Jews: The Jewish Refugee Community of Shanghai, 1935–1945* (Hoboken, N.J.: KTAV, 1988).

5. Marvin Tokayer and Mary Swartz, *The Fugu Plan: The Untold Story of the Japanese and the Jews During World War II* (New York: Paddington Press, 1979), p. 49.

6. Cited by Kranzler, *Japanese, Nazis, and Jews*, p. 169.

7. Tokayer and Swartz, *The Fugu Plan*, pp. 222–226.

8. Kranzler, *Japanese, Nazis, and Jews*, pp. 478–479.

9. The sources disagree concerning Colonel Yasue's first name. Kranzler, *in Japanese, Nazis, and Jews*, lists the name as "Senko." Tetsu Kohno lists the name as "Norihigo." I have accepted the latter. See Tetsu Kohno, "The Jewish Question in Japan," in *Jewish Journal of Sociology* 29(1) (June 1987).

10. See David G. Goodman, "Japanese Anti-Semitism," *World and I* (November 1987).

11. On this point, see Robert Bartlett, *The Making of Europe: Conquest, Colonization, and Cultural Change, 950–1350* (Princeton: Princeton University Press, 1993).

12. "Norway Celebrates a Millennium of Christianity Despite Fires," *New York Times*, June 4, 1995.

13. For a brief discussion of the Christian roots of secularization, see Peter Berger, *The Sacred Canopy: Elements of a Sociological Theory of Religion* (Garden City, N.Y.: Anchor Books, 1969), pp. 105–126.

❀ 3 ❀

From the Holocaust: Some Legal and Moral Implications

RICHARD J. GOLDSTONE

*I*t was with some misgivings that I agreed to contribute a chapter to the second edition of this book. My hesitation arose primarily for reasons that are well articulated in the editor's introduction. In particular, Rosenbaum says that ". . . an assertion of [the Holocaust's] uniqueness appears unavoidably to invite invidious comparisons with others' pain and suffering . . ." The contents of some of the chapters in this book amply demonstrate the truth of this assertion. I do not propose to take issue with the many statements, views and theories which appear in those chapters, with which I disagree and thereby compound the hurt to victims.

My decision to accept the editor's invitation was based upon the recognition that there are some comparisons that are not invidious and that are helpful to an understanding of genocides which have been perpetrated since the Holocaust. I hope in this chapter to refer to some unique features which fall into this benign category. I would refer first to the very substantial political and material acknowledgement which victims of the Holocaust have received, particularly from Germany. Substantial reparations have been paid over a period of many years to individual victims or their families. Claims continue to be recognized and now the German legislature has decided to build a memorial to the victims of the Holocaust in Berlin. Notoriously stringent Swiss bank secrecy laws have been forced to bend before the claims of Holocaust survivors. The victims of no other genocide have received this kind of acknowledgement. Neither have the Roma or the other non-Jewish victims of the Holocaust.

Secondly, there were the criminal law consequences of the Holocaust. The Nuremberg trials brought to justice many of the leaders and executioners responsible for the massacre of the victims, both Jewish and non-Jewish. And, the trial of Adolph Eichmann resulted in the execution of one of the people most re-

sponsible for the "Final Solution". There have been trials of Nazi officials and collaborators in a number of European countries. This feature of the Holocaust was
probably unique until the establishment of the United Nations ad hoc tribunals
for the former Yugoslavia and Rwanda. (As I shall attempt to demonstrate, however, neither of these tribunals would have been established but for the consequences of the Holocaust.)

The former leader of Republika Srpska, Radovan Karadzic, has been indicted
as a war criminal on charges which include genocide and crimes against humanity and Slobodan Milosevic, the President of the Federal Republic of Yugoslavia,
has been indicted for crimes against humanity allegedly perpetrated against the
Albanian population of Kosovo. Other lesser officials have been tried and sentenced to long terms of imprisonment. In Arusha, the Rwanda Tribunal has sentenced senior former Hutu leaders, among them Jean Kambanda, former Prime
Minister of the Rwandan Interim Government, to long periods of imprisonment.
Others are on trial.

Thirdly there has been a remarkable scholarship which has emerged in consequence of the Holocaust. No other genocide has evoked this response from the
international academic community. Holocaust writings have come from political
scientists, philosophers and sociologists, to mention the most obvious. Hardly a
week passes without a new volume on some or other aspect of the Holocaust.

However in my opinion, the most permanent, important and unique feature of
the Holocaust is that it gave birth to the international human rights movement
and the recognition of an international jurisdiction for the prosecution of war
criminals. Prior to World War II states rather than individuals were considered
the subjects of international law. The shock to the conscience of humankind triggered by the Holocaust gave rise to the realisation that it was necessary for the law
of nations to protect individual members of the human race. The effect of that
realisation was manifested in 1945 in the provisions of the Charter of the United
Nations.[1] In the Preamble one finds a reaffirmation of "faith in human rights, in
the dignity and worth of the human person, in the equal rights of men and
women". One of the purposes of the United Nations, referred to in Article 1(3),
is "promoting and encouraging respect for human rights and for fundamental
freedoms for all without distinction to race, sex, language, or religion". Promotion
of human rights and fundamental freedoms is to be found throughout the
Charter.[2] This was effectively the birth of the international human rights movement. It was followed in 1948 by the Universal Declaration of Human Rights.[3] In
a silent but obvious reference to the Holocaust one reads in its preamble of the
"disregard and contempt for human rights" which resulted in "barbarous acts
which have outraged the conscience of mankind".

It took almost two decades for the effect of the Universal Declaration of
Human Rights to spawn the human rights conventions of the 1960s, and in par-
ticular the International Covenant on Civil and Political Rights[4] and the
International Covenant on Economic, Social and Cultural Rights.[5] Both were ap-

proved by the General Assembly in 1966 although it was to take another decade before each received the number of ratifications necessary to bring it into operation. Today human rights instruments are more than declarations of intent. They have led states to undertake tangible initiatives in enforcing human rights. In the Americas, the Inter-American Court, in Europe, the European Court of Human Rights and in Africa, the proposed African Court of Peoples' and Human Rights are all vehicles by which individuals may challenge the conduct of states.

Prior to the Holocaust it was widely accepted, whether explicitly or implicitly, that historical and cultural differences between continents and nations precluded the development of common international values and norms. A consequence of that acceptance was the universal recognition of state sovereignty. The manner in which a government behaved towards its own people was not the business of other states or of the international community. It was indeed a corollary of national sovereignty that individual human beings were not recognised as subjects of international law. Only nations and their governments were granted standing before international tribunals. It was in such a world order that colonialism could exist and flourish. The patchwork boundaries which still bedevil parts of Africa and Asia are a constant reminder of that era.

It was the Holocaust and the manner in which the Nazi war machine targeted innocent civilians in Germany and the countries it occupied that dealt a mortal blow to the inviolability of national sovereignty. This fundamental change manifested itself in a number of ways. The first was the reworking of the idea that certain huge war crimes could constitute "crimes against humanity." Although the concept of a crime against humanity was not new, the manner in which the term was used in the Nuremberg Charter was innovative.

> The seeds of the [Nuremberg] Charter's 'crimes against humanity' provision were planted in the First Hague Convention of 1899 on the Laws and Customs of War and Fourth Hague Convention of 1907, and in their annexed Regulations Respecting the Laws and Customs of War on Land. The Preamble of the two conventions used the term 'laws of humanity' and they based their normative prescriptions on these unarticulated values. Prior to the Charter, the words used in the Preamble of the Two Hague Conventions are the only references in conventional international law which approach the term 'crimes against humanity'. Though the Hague Conventions concerned 'war crimes' in the narrow and specific sense, they derived from the larger meaning of violations of 'laws of humanity'. Thus these words were intended to provide an overarching concept to protect against unspecified violations whose identification in positive law was left to future normative development.[6]

In the Charter the expression was used to cover the massive and systematic war crimes committed by the Nazis. The idea gained currency that those crimes were so egregious and shocking that they constituted crimes not only against the immediate victims or their families and not only against the people in the country in which they were perpetrated. They were truly crimes committed against all humankind. As such any nation, no matter how far removed from the site of the crimes, had jurisdiction to put the perpetrators on trial and, if found guilty, to punish them. The recognition of this new and broad concept of crimes against humanity was confirmed by the General Assembly of the United Nations when it unanimously affirmed the substantive principles of the Nuremberg Charter and Judgement in 1950.[7] Albeit unintended, the recognition in international law of crimes against humanity became the Achilles heel of national sovereignty. It spawned a new universal jurisdiction for egregious crimes.

Although the Convention on the Prevention and Suppression of the Crime of Genocide,[8] adopted by the General Assembly in 1948, does not explicitly provide for the principle of universal jurisdiction, the Convention's confirmation of the crime of genocide as a crime under international law compels an appreciation of the attendant universal jurisdiction. Every state that has ratified the Convention, is obliged to bring to justice any individual reasonably suspected of committing genocide, no matter where the acts were committed and irrespective of a connection with armed conflict.

In 1949, the definition of war crimes contained in the Nuremberg Charter was incorporated in the four Geneva Conventions of that year.[9] These conventions recognized a new species of war crimes known as "grave breaches". Incumbent on every State bound by these Conventions is the obligation to bring to justice any person suspected of having perpetrated a grave breach. If the authorities of such a nation refuse or are unable to bring such persons before its courts, the suspect is required to be handed over to the authorities of a nation that is prepared to do so. These provisions, unlike those of the Genocide Convention, apply only where there is a state of international armed conflict at the time of the commission of the alleged violations.

Any doubts which may have persisted as to the application of universal jurisdiction to the crimes of genocide, grave breaches and crimes against humanity have vanished in contemporary times. In his report pursuant to the Statute of the International Tribunal for the Former Yugoslavia,[10] the Secretary-General of the United Nations declared that only those crimes to which, incontrovertibly, universal jurisdiction attached would be included within the Tribunal's Statute— those crimes being genocide, crimes against humanity and war crimes. It was a measure designed to ensure that all states, everywhere, would be able to surrender those individuals within their territory, accused of committing the crimes set out in the Tribunal's Statute.

We see then that the horrors of the Holocaust gave rise to a new international value—respect for the right of all people to be protected from such horrors regardless of international borders. That value, in turn, spawned a new norm compelling the international community to accept the principle of universal jurisdiction in respect of certain grave war crimes. That principle of international law soon found a place in the domestic law of many countries. Thus, suspected Nazi war criminals have been brought to trial in the domestic courts of a number of nations whether or not such crimes were committed within the borders of those nations. In terms of this principle citizens of one state have been tried by the courts of other nations without the consent of the government of the nation of which the accused is a citizen. Before the Holocaust that could not have happened.

Universal jurisdiction provided the judges of Adolph Eichmann with an answer to one of his defenses, asserting that the State of Israel, which had indicted him, was not in existence at the time his crimes were alleged to have been committed and was thus devoid of jurisdiction to hear the matter.[11] The judges in Jerusalem relied on the universal principle and the passive personality and protective principles (more traditional principles of jurisdiction) to try the offences which constituted crimes against humanity. Some twenty years later, Israel wished to try John Demjanjuk, allegedly a former SS member who had served at Treblinka, under the same laws used to prosecute Eichmann—the Nazis and Nazi Collaborators (Punishment) Law of 1950. Demjanjuk, then residing in the United States of America, sought to challenge his surrender to Israel by raising a defense similar to Eichmann's—that the State of Israel had not been in existence at the time of the alleged crimes. The court, this time citing only the principle of universality held that Demjanjuk could indeed be prosecuted in Israel for the alleged crimes.[12] The employment of the universal principle, without more, signalled the increasingly robust nature with which it was perceived. A more recent dramatic illustration of this principle was the arrest in 1998, in London, of General Pinochet, the former head of the state of Chile, on a request from a Spanish prosecutor, for war crimes allegedly committed in Chile some two decades earlier. A citizen of one country may now be prosecuted by the courts of second country for crimes committed in a third country. That would have been quite unthinkable before 1945.

There has been resistance to these changes. China, in particular, has consistently resisted the interference by other nations or the international community in what it regards as being its internal affairs. How it treats its own citizens, its leaders assert, is their business alone. It was a surprise to most international lawyers and political analysts when, in May 1993, the Security Council unanimously established the International Criminal Tribunal for the former Yugoslavia and some 18 months later the International Criminal Tribunal for Rwanda.[13] The statute setting up the Yugoslavia Tribunal was adopted unanimously by the Security Council and the General Assembly participated fully in the election of the judges and the voting of funds for its operations. China abstained in the vote on the Rwanda Tribunal but only in sympathy for the Government of Rwanda which had changed its mind on the establishment after initially having requested it.

The United States has for decades jealously guarded its sovereignty and claimed the right to object to its citizens being tried by foreign courts or international tribunals. It was this sensitivity that caused the United States to be one of the last nations to ratify the Genocide Convention—a delay of some forty years after its approval in the General Assembly. This, presumably, is also the reason for it being one of only two nations not to have ratified the Convention on the Rights of the Child. The other nation is Somalia. It is this same sensitivity which has led the United States to vote alongside only six other nations against the terms of the 1998 Rome Statute establishing a permanent International Criminal Court.[14] Its principle objection was that its citizens might be prosecuted before such a court without the consent of its government.

There can be little doubt that a permanent International Criminal Court will begin work during the first decade of the new century. There can be no doubt, too, that the United States will eventually take the lead in ensuring that such a court works efficiently. It was after all, the government of President Clinton that ensured the viability of the Yugoslavia and Rwanda tribunals and secured support for the processes culminating in the Rome Statute. The people and governments of the great majority of nations have come to recognize that without international criminal jurisdiction war criminals will continue, as in the past, to enjoy effective impunity.

There have thus been impressive and substantial developments in the internationalization of war crimes and the jurisdiction of domestic and international courts to try war criminals. As the world continues to shrink, it will become more and more difficult for indicted war criminals to find sanctuary. It may well be in the self interest of a successor government in Belgrade to deliver Slobodan Milosevic for trial in the Hague. So, too, Radovan Karadzic from Bosnia. The people of those lands will not for too long wish to remain outside the community of nations, and they will not be allowed in for as long as they harbour their war criminals.

If future perpetrators of genocide, crimes against humanity and serious war crimes are brought to justice and appropriately punished then the millions of innocent victims who perished in the Holocaust will not have died in vain. Their memory will remain alive and they will be remembered when future war criminals are brought to justice. And, it is certainly not too much to hope that efficient justice will also serve to deter war crimes in the future and so protect the untold numbers of potential victims.

NOTES

1. U.N.C.I.O. XV 335.

2. See Articles 13(1)(b), 55, 62(2) and 68.

3. G.A. Res. 217 A (III) UN Doc. A 1810 (1948).

4. 999 U.N.T.S.171.

5. G.A. Res. 2200 A (XXI) UN Doc. A/6316 (1966) 993 U.N.T.S. 3.

6. M Cherif Bassiouni, *Crimes Against Humanity in International Criminal Law*, 1992, Nijhoff Publishers, at 165–6.

7. Nuremberg Principles: Principles of International Law Recognized in the Charter of the Nuremberg Tribunal and in the Judgement of the Tribunal. U.N.G.A.O.R. 5th Session, Supp. No.12, UN Doc. A/1316 (1950).

8. 78 U.N.T.S 277.

9. 75 U.N.T.S. 31, 75 U.N.T.S. 85, 75 U.N.T.S. 135, 75 U.N.T.S. 287.

10. United Nations: Secretary-General's Report on Aspects of Establishing an International Tribunal for the Prosecution of Persons Responsible for Serious Violations of International Humanitarian Law Committed in the Territory of the Former Yugoslavia (May 3, 1993), 32 *International Legal Materials* 1159 (1993) at 1174.

11. *Attorney General v Eichmann* 36 *International Law Reports* 5.

12. *Demjanjuk v Petrovsky* 79 *International Law Reports* 535.

13. Statute of the International Tribunal for the Former Yugoslavia (1993), Security Council Resolution 827, *International Legal Materials*, 1993, 1192. Statute for the International Tribunal for Rwanda (1994) Security Council Resolution 955, *International Legal Materials*, 1994, 1598.

14. United Nations Diplomatic Conference on Plenipotentiaries on the Establishment of an International Criminal Court, Rome, Italy, 15 July–17 July 1998, A/CONF. 183/9, 17 July 1998.

❊ 4 ❊

The Uniqueness of the Holocaust: The Historical Dimension

STEVEN T. KATZ

I

Introduction

Given the focus of this book on the issue of the uniqueness of the Holocaust, I wish to state clearly at the outset my position on this matter: The Holocaust, that is, the intentional murder of European Jewry during World War II, is historically and phenomenologically unique. No other case discussed in this book parallels it. My burden in the remainder of this chapter is to document and defend this statement.

In arguing for the uniqueness of the Holocaust, I am *not* making a *moral* claim, in other words, that the Holocaust was more evil than the other events discussed in this collection, for example, the murder of Armenians in World War I, the devastation of the Native American communities over the centuries, the decimation of Ukraine by Stalin, the treatment of the Gypsies during World War II, and the enslavement and mass death of black Africans during the enterprise of New World slavery. I know of no method or technique that would allow one to weigh up, to quantify and compare, such massive evil and suffering, and I therefore avoid altogether this sort of counterproductive argument about what one might describe as comparative suffering.

In addition, I am not suggesting that the Holocaust involved the greatest number of victims of any mass crime. It did not. Numbers of victims will not establish the uniqueness of the Holocaust—quite the contrary.

When I argue for the uniqueness of the Holocaust I intend only to claim that the Holocaust is phenomenologically unique by virtue of the fact that never before has a state set out, as a matter of intentional principle and actualized policy, to annihilate physically every man, woman, and child belonging to a specific people. A close study of the relevant comparative historical data will show that only

49

in the case of Jewry under the Third Reich was such all-inclusive, noncompromising, unmitigated murder intended.

Given the limits of this short chapter, my presentation must be selective and schematic. I will, therefore, consider only three of the cases discussed by others in this volume in order to show how they differ from the Holocaust. If space allowed, a similar decipherment in support of *difference* could be made in every case said to be comparable to the Holocaust in this collection.[1]

II

The Case of the Native Americans:
Colonial America and the United States

The Native American people(s) have been the subject of exploitation, despoliation, rape, violence, and murder since the arrival of Columbus. This centuries-long record of subjugation and abuse is incontrovertible and tragic. However, I would argue that the structure, the character, of the assault against the Native American peoples differs radically from that represented by the Holocaust for several fundamental reasons, the most basic of which is the role that disease has played in this history. That is to say: All serious contemporary students of the demographic collapse of the Indian peoples of America (that is, populations north of Mexico) are now agreed that its primary cause, whatever other factors contributed to this phenomenon, was newly imported pathogens against which the native community, estimated at anywhere between 1 million (plus or minus 10 percent) and 18 million, had no immunity. Henry Dobyns lists ninety-three pandemics and epidemics, most of which occurred in the territory that now comprises the United States, caused by European pathogens that struck the Native American peoples between 1500 and 1900. And for the sixteenth century alone—the period of the greatest decimation—Alfred W. Crosby Jr. cites fourteen major epidemics between 1524 and 1600.

As occurred also in the unparalleled demographic collapse of the South American Indian population in the sixteenth century, not only did the American aborigines lack the biological ability, the immunological prerequisites, to resist the unfamiliar and unfriendly microbes that now assaulted them, the European invaders and settlers who were directly responsible for their (often unknowing) importation lacked the scientific knowledge required to halt their deadly work once it had begun. Thus, infectious killers were unintentionally let loose within the Americas, and literally nothing was able to intervene to limit the massive damage they would do.

This phenomenon defined the history of the Native American peoples right through the nineteenth century. In the most complete analysis of nineteenth-century Indian demography undertaken to date, Henry Dobyns enumerates no less than twenty-seven epidemic outbreaks during that century, the most deadly of which were thirteen smallpox epidemics, the two worst occurring in 1801–1802 and 1836–1840. During the first of these, James Mooney estimates that, for example, "the prairie tribes . . . lost more than half of their population at this time, while the Wichita, Caddo, and others in the South suffered almost as severely."[2] Nearly everywhere in the United States, Indians continued to die, and disease was the primary cause of their death.

For example, Sherburne Cook attributes only 8.64 percent of the decline in California's Indian population to military casualties, most of the remainder, that is, the rate of loss, being due to disease. This ratio of loss due to disease versus other factors evidenced in California also obtained more generally, with modification from location to location, throughout the country in Indian-white relations. Thus, Cook concluded that only approximately 6,750 Indians had been killed by white settlers in New England between 1634 and 1676, even though this half-century included the Pequot War of 1637 (and saw the native population of New England decline by many times that number). Even Russell Thornton, who has vigorously attempted to highlight the roles of warfare and genocide in the decline of the Indian population, is forced by the unassailable demographic evidence to conclude that, at most, "45,000 American Indians [were] killed in wars with Europeans and Americans between 1775–1890. To this might be added . . . 8,500 American Indians killed in individual conflicts during the period, to arrive at a total of 53,000 killed."[3]

That is to say, in a period of 115 years, during which the indigenous population declined by over 1.5 million, only 53,000 casualties, or 3.7 percent of the total lost, can be counted as having been intentionally murdered. For the pre-1775 period, the percentage of loss due to warfare (and individual murder) is even lower. Thornton, for example, in attempting to configure losses in the prerevolutionary era, suggests doubling the post-1775 figure of 53,000 to arrive at the pre-1775 aggregate. Accordingly, if we follow this suggestion, if only for purposes of argument, we have a projection, however crudely arrived at, of 106,000 casualties due to war and conflict situations in this earlier epoch. However, given the much higher total native population in this initial contact period—anywhere up to 10 or more times as great as what it was after 1775—the percentage of loss represented by this hypothesized 106,000 casualties shrinks to some fraction of 1 percent.

When mass death occurred among the Indians of America, and it did occur, it was almost without exception caused by microbes, not militia—although militias were much in evidence and did their damage—that is, this depopulation happened unwittingly rather than by design, even transpiring in direct opposition to the expressed and self-interested will of the white empire-builder or settler. This is true for the colonial era as well as for the period of American domination. It should be specifically remarked, contra the genocidal reading of these historical events, that after the discovery of the smallpox vaccination in 1797, all Indians were encouraged to be vaccinated, and following the epidemic of 1831–1832, U.S. government policy required the vaccination of Indians. The resistance of the western tribes to this statute contributed directly to their decimation by epidemics in the late 1830s and early 1840s.

Certainly the fatigue, the unaccustomed and punishing hunger, and a host of related psychological dilemmas that attended white conquest, in conjunction with direct military conflicts and acts of violence, reduced the inherent ability of the native population to withstand the heretofore unencountered pathogens. Yet these important factors do not alter the *unintentional* character of the spread of these infectious visitations—the primary killer—nor our appreciation of the notorious inability to control these pandemics once they began. Moreover, in contradistinction to those who would overemphasize the nonpathogenic causes of Indian decline, it needs to be understood that the most widespread and demographically significant epidemics—claiming an estimated one-third or more of the still very large native population—were the very earliest ones, in other words, those connected with the initial contact, that occurred *prior* to any full-scale program of enforced labor or removals north of Mexico.

Disease unaided, disease per se, along with the internal social and communal dislocations it created, was the primary, unavoidable, and ubiquitous agency of death among North American Indians between 1492 and 1900.

In addition, further mediating factors are to be considered in drawing the disjunction between the Native American case and the Holocaust. Foremost among these is the vast enterprise of mission that was first established and supported by all the colonial powers and then continued under American auspices.

After American independence, between 1787 and 1820, eleven denominational and interchurch groups created missionary agencies, the most active being the American Board of Commissioners for Foreign Missions, an interdenominational group with a predominance of Presbyterian and Congregational missionaries founded in 1810. By 1824, twenty-one missionary schools were being supported by federal and private funds—six by the American Board of Commissioners, five by the Baptists, four by the United Foreign Missionary Society, four by the Methodists, and one each by the Moravians, Presbyterians, Cumberland Missionary Society, and the Catholics. The Indian Department reported in 1824–1825 that in 1824 a total of $192,064.48 had been spent on Indian education from all sources (government, Indian annuities, and private donations) and that this amount had increased to $202,070.85 by 1825. By 1826, the total of Indian missionary schools had grown to thirty-eight, and a number of new missionary societies had come into being. These thirty-eight schools had 281 teachers and 1,159 students and received $13,550 from the federal government. The most notable conversionary successes were in the South among those nations later known as the Five Civilized Tribes, the Cherokee, Choctaw, Chickasaw, Creek, and Seminole, with the Cherokee providing the single most remarkable case in point.

By the 1830s, despite significant setbacks connected with the Jacksonian removals, which had seriously divided the diverse missionary groups (and differing denominations), both Protestant and Catholic missionaries were working intensively among the Native Americans from Florida to California and from New York to the Great Northwest. In the 1840s, Jesuits were active in Idaho, Washington, and the Dakota Territory, and Presbyterians, Methodists, and Congregationalists were to be found in the Dakota Territory and in the Northwest. The 1850s witnessed the spread of missions to the Santee and the Ojibway in Minnesota. Now, too, the Mormons established missions to the Shoshoni and Delaware in Utah, Wyoming, Kansas, and Idaho. All this at the cost of many millions of dollars. For example, between 1818 and 1830 the Choctaw Mission in Mississippi, which converted a total of 360 individuals and established four small churches, spent $140,000 on its relatively limited activities, and the Baptists spent on its missionary work in the West $131,888 ($72,184 provided by the federal government) between 1826 and 1842 and an additional $139,750 ($69,475 from the federal government) between 1843 and 1864. By 1865, the American Board of Commissioners of Foreign Missions had spent no less than $1.25 million on its Indian missionary activity.

After the Civil War, President Ulysses Grant's "peace policy," begun in 1869, encouraged still more intensive missionary activity under the leadership of the Quakers. At Grant's request, the Board of Indian Commissioners, composed of wealthy and influential Protestant laymen (no Catholics were nominated), was established by an act of Congress on April 10, 1869. Along with the creation of this new board, the selection of Indian agents, with obvious disregard for the First Amendment, was, at least in part, given over to church groups in the hope that they would be able to reform and improve the Indian service. In all, thirteen denominations came to control seventy-three agencies dealing with approximately 235,000 Indians. However, their inexperience and lack of a coherent design in such matters proved fatal, and, in the end, this reformist system, for all its considerable ambition and undoubted goodwill, did not work. By 1882, this Christian reform program was abandoned—even the Quakers having lost faith in it; in its place the country moved to adopt a radically alternative strategy for solving the "Indian problem"—the allotment of Indian lands.

What is of particular and compelling interest vis-à-vis the post-1880 reformist effort to resolve the fate of the Indian peoples is the naive, quasi-Utopian, exceedingly insensitive, ultimately destructive, though kindly meant, ideology that governed this short-lived experiment. At the core of this initiative, undertaken by well-intended, thoroughly ethnocentric men, was the orthodox white opinion that Indian culture was inferior and that in order to "advance," the Indians had to shed their traditions as they "progressed" up the ladder of "civilization." The Indian modes of existence (personal and corporate), in all their distinctive particulars, were, by definition, doomed. Like the liberals of Europe who a priori demanded the complete eradication of Jewish identity as the fair, obligatory price for Jewish emancipation and civic equality before and after the French Revolution, the "friends" of the Indian, with clear consciences, demanded a comparable extinguishing of Native American identity. The liberals in both Europe and America—and this is what made them liberals—were for the rapid acculturation and (eventual) equality of the Jew and the Indian respectively, but only after all vestiges of their traditional *tribal* consciousness and classical forms of life had been eliminated. As such, the most revolutionary constructions of ethnocide were seen not only as thoroughly compatible with authentic friendship for the Native American (and the European Jew) but, actually, as an entailment of that friendship. "Poor Indian, Poor Jew, savages and primitive obscurantists respectively, we know better." Native American*ism* (like Juda*ism*) would be, had to be, exterminated—but through an ethnocidally generous process that preserved the fundamental Native American stock now to be refashioned and recycled in a more acceptable majoritarian image.

Put simply, the reality of mission, the implication of all the conversionary activity here described, is contragenocidal in its intent.

The creation of Indian reservations also bears directly on this issue of putative Indian genocide. In fact, after 1850, the policy of reservations became the primary national response to the "Indian question," because, unless the indigenous peoples could be protected against the tidal flow of white settlement that was in the process of creating a vast settler nation stretching from the Atlantic to the Pacific, all hope of preventing the extinction of the Indian would prove a cruel illusion. That is, *as an alternative to extinction*, and as a new, if in many ways equivocal, manifestation of America's historic paternalistic and imperialistic colonial attitudes toward the nation's aboriginal peoples, a second round of Indian removals, now to newly established reservations, began. This policy, first articulated in a programmatic way by William Medill, commissioner of Indian affairs in the James Polk administration, allowed the majority of western Indian territory to be opened up to white settlement while establishing a "controlled" and protected environment—all too often actually uncontrolled and unprotected—wherein intercourse, laws, white-directed educational reform (there were forty-two Indian schools by 1842 with some 2,000 pupils of both sexes), and missionary activity could, working together, begin to transform the indigene into a peasant-style Christian farmer. Indian culture would give way to "civilization," but the Indians themselves, that is, as a biological entity, would survive, if in a starkly different sociocultural guise.

Beginning in the early 1850s, under the administration of President Millard Fillmore, the implementation of this policy on a broad scale was accelerated. For example, the Fort Berthold Indian Reservation was created in 1851 for the Hedatsa, Mandan, and Arikara; the Otoe were moved to the Blue River Reservation in Nebraska and Kansas in 1854; and the Cheyenne and Arapaho were "settled," temporarily as it turned out—for they had another decade of overt resistance left in their system—in areas south of the Arkansas. Various California Indian nations were enclosed on the Fresno Farm Reservation in 1852, the El Tejon Reservation in 1853, and the Nome Lackee Reservation in 1854, with six additional loci created between 1856 and 1870 (though only three of these reservations remained open by 1871). The Chippewa of Michigan and Wisconsin began their entry onto reservations in 1854. In fact, in 1854 alone, the various Indian nations ceded, in twelve treaties, 18 million acres in return for reservations of 1.5 million acres. In 1865, the Kiowa, Comanche, and Kiowa-Apache were established in northern Texas and western Oklahoma. In 1866, the Santee Reservation was created in Nebraska, and, in 1867, the White Earth Reservation was created for the Chippewa. In 1868, the Navajo were moved to a reservation in northern New Mexico and Arizona; the Utes were relocated to western Colorado and parts of Utah; and a number of other Utah tribes were installed in the Uintah Valley. The Sioux, under the Treaty of Fort Laramie, settled in Montana and the Dakotas after 1868, and the Oglala Sioux settled at the Red Cloud Reservation in 1870. In 1873, the Mescaleros were lodged on a reservation in their traditional lands in south-central New Mexico; in 1869, a final settlement with the Southern Cheyenne and Southern Arapaho was reached that created a nearly 4.3-million-acre reservation in western Oklahoma; in 1874, the Kickapoo, who had previously been moved west of the Mississippi, were moved once more to a newly created reservation; the Pawnee were installed on a reservation in Indian Territory in 1875; and then in 1876–1877, following further wars and General George Custer's massacre, the Northern Cheyenne were likewise moved to this territory. In the Northwest beginning in 1855, the Nez Percé were given a 3-million-acre territory in the Grande Ronde, Clearwater, and Snake and Salmon Valleys of Idaho; the Cayuse, Umatilla, and Wallawalla were provided with a grant of 800 square miles in the Blue Mountains beginning in 1855; and the Klikitat, Yakima, and Paloo (Palouse) were settled on the Yakima River in the Washington Territory. The Flathead, Upper Pend d'Oreille, and Kutenai were ceded a 1.25-million-acre reserve in northern Montana. In Oregon, the indigenous peoples were contained in the Warm Springs Reservation, and the Numa (Northern Paiute) who spread across parts of Oregon, California, Idaho, and Nevada were removed to the Walker Lake and Pyramid Lake (and other) reservations after the Pyramid Lake War of 1860. By 1876, even some Apache had accepted their fate and joined reservations. Indeed, by the mid-1870s Secretary of the Interior Columbus Delano estimated that Indian reservations outside of the Indian Territory occupied 96,155,785 acres (containing 172,000 people). Accordingly, as late as 1887, Indian lands totaled 156 million acres.

This enterprise of protected resettlement was, ultimately but not surprisingly, unable to transcend the broader crosscurrents and deeply partisan politics of the period. Pressure to reduce Indian landholdings continued, justified by various reformist ideologies as well as outright avarice, often offering only a "fig leaf." However, even a cursory study of the inventory of the reservations already listed indicates that the U.S. government, despite the inhumanity and injustice incarnate in this grossly unfair resolution of the territorial question, never came, relative to the American Indian, to the Hitlerian conclusion: "You cannot live at all." During this era physical abuse and moral indifference were present in abundance in Indian affairs, but the substantial criminality and severe neglect that reigned supreme were not the consequence of, and were not accompanied by, a consciously enacted program of extermination.

In the years following the Civil War, especially during President Grant's terms in office, the U.S. government carried through its decision that the Indian people qua a people could not live *among* the white population but could continue their separate communal life in their degraded and reduced circumstances, with official America's consent in the special Indian territories created for this purpose. It did so because, as the commissioner of Indian affairs wrote in 1867, the policy of "preservation by gradual concentration on territorial reserves [was the only alternative to] swift extermination by the sword and famine."[4] This was not a noble choice. White society, even as it "saved" the aboriginal inhabitants of the land, was guilty of colossal wrongdoing. Yet, despite the monumentality and endurance of the crime, this was not a crime without limits and self-imposed constraints. The maintenance of 141 reservations (by 1880), controlling well over 100 million acres (including the Indian territory), inhabited by hundreds of thousands of Indians—housing 11,328 students in school, 177 church buildings, and 27,215 Indian church members—is indisputable evidence of this. The reservation, for all the ethical and existential transgressions that it represents, is a concession to survival, a commitment to continued individual and tribal existence. (As proof of its success in at least providing for native survival, I note that in the mid-1980s, the Native American population of the United States was put at 1.532 million by the U.S. Census Bureau, with 631,574 persons still living on 278 reservations; the 1990 census put the native Indian population at over 1.8 million.)

In this often misrepresented historical context, it is important to recognize explicitly that the Indian Wars, begun in the 1850s and 1860s against the great western tribes (Navajo, Comanche, Sioux, and Apache), were fought not to exterminate the Indians outright but rather to break their serious and continued resistance to removal to reservations. The federal government and the U.S. Army sought to crush Indian autonomy, eradicate Indian territorial attachments, put an end to the extremely expensive Indian Wars, and reduce the Indians to a subservient and acquiescent mode of behavior that would allow the national authorities to dictate the sociopolitical, economic, and existential conditions of Indian life. This description applies even to such humanly costly encounters as occurred, for example, in the Washington Territory in the mid-1850s during the Rogue River War and the Yakima War. For these military conflicts, too, were fought so that the federal authorities could successfully relocate Indian tribes drawn from Oregon and Washington onto eight reservations established for them. This nonexterminatory reading of the great Indian Wars is reinforced, moreover, by the treatment of (to take just one example) the Nez Percé, who chose not to join their Northwest Indian neighbors in the military conflicts of the 1850s and were, at least for a time, spared their depredations as a consequence. That is to say, reflective of a larger, conscious American design, there was no national homicidal scheme directed at the Washington and Oregon Indians.

Likewise, the great climactic Indian Wars on the plains in the 1870s and 1880s against the Kiowa, Cheyenne, Arapaho, Comanche, and Sioux, among others, were, for all their lethal ferocity, a continuation of the dominant-submissive pattern that the federal authorities now sought to impose on white-Indian relations. Contra the misconceived genocidal school of historical interpreters, it is here relevant to recognize the salient fact—not forgetting particular massacres perpetrated by American military forces, indeed, precisely in light of them—that once the U.S. Army had subdued the great western tribes on the field of battle, it could have slaughtered all the remaining tribal members had genocide been its determinate purpose. It was not and it did not.

III
The Famine in Ukraine

The widespread and consequential famine in Ukraine between 1930 and 1933 also has to be accounted for in light of the current argument contra genocide. There are two main lines of scholarly interpretation as to what happened in Ukraine and why. The first of these emphasizes the nationalist dimensions of the event. Under this interpretation, both the indigenous Ukrainian population and the alien Soviet ruling class knew that Ukraine, as recently as 1918, had been independent—with its own separate historical and cultural traditions—and that it wished to be politically independent again. Accordingly, the confrontation of the late 1910s and of the 1920s and 1930s in this region is seen as having been defined by the collision of two competing claims to sovereignty: one nationalist and the other putatively internationalist, though, increasingly, the latter was merely a cover for an ever more visible Russian national chauvinism. For Stalin, the ultimate objective is seen to have been the full integration without national remainder of Ukraine into the larger, ideally homogenized, Soviet state. Anything less was dangerous, both practically—because it would interfere with Bolshevik control of the agricultural market and the essential issue of grain collection and distribution, a circumstance that often divided the local leadership—and potentially—because of the geopolitically divisive character of nationalist aspirations. In consequence, Stalin, under this nationalist reading, consciously decided on a deadly campaign—most accurately described through the political category of internal colonialism—to eradicate this recurring threat to Soviet hegemony. Beginning with the purge of Ukrainian academics and political and cultural leaders that began in April 1929 and continued into 1930, Stalin is believed to have set in motion a movement that would eventually consume literally millions of Ukrainians.

The object of the entire terror campaign was, under this exegesis, the complete annihilation of Ukrainian nationalism (a goal that was also consistent with the larger Stalinist policy of the socialization of agriculture). Much like Hitler's later strategy in, for example, Poland (and elsewhere in eastern Europe), Stalin sought to expunge local autonomy and all manifestations of cultural and political independence in order to facilitate continued domination from Moscow. Here, as in many other cases that easily come to mind (Cambodia, Nigeria, Sudan, and, most recently, Rwanda), the purpose of state-organized violence is the maintenance of political control.

Given the importance of the independent, economically autonomous peasantry in Ukraine's socioeconomic structures, Stalin's plan for the extermination of national identity required—in addition to the removal of the national intelligentsia—a crusade against this "protocapitalist" strata. As Semen O. Pidhainy has described it, Stalin had to move against Ukrainian nationalism's "social base"—the individual landholdings.[5] "Only a mass terror throughout the body of the nation—that is, the peasantry—could reduce the nation to submission."[6] As long as the *selianym* (a euphemism now for all free Ukrainian peasants) existed, nationalist (and capitalist) sentiment would remain: Both needed to be crushed.

The dominant method used to achieve this collective submission to socialism, this elimination of the base of Ukrainian national sentiment, was the forced collectivization of the agricultural sector. At the same time, and not unimportant, such a centralized agrarian policy gave the Communist Party—in the form of the All-Union Commissariat of Agriculture—control over the region's grain supply. It was the task and responsibility of this commissariat, in conjunction with the Soviet planners, to calculate, coordinate, and organize the yearly grain harvest, in other words, to set and oversee the state exactions to be levied and collected. In the event, when this direct control was expressed in an overly demanding target for grain exports from the region—ostensibly justified by the increased program of industrialization that was to be financed by the agricultural surplus—it effectively translated into a man-made famine in Ukraine in 1931 that grew worse in 1932 and 1933. For example, in 1931, the procurement quota for the region was set at 7 million tons out of a total of 18.3 million tons (much of which had been lost to inefficient collective harvesting). Such a level of national procurement almost certainly spelled trouble for the local community. Matters of food supply only got worse in 1932 when the procurement total was again set at 7 million tons while that year's harvest, due to drought, inefficiency, and a decline in the number of acres sown—the last partly in protest to Stalinist policy—came in at the very reduced level of 14.7 million tons. Although the local leadership, in the face of the total decline in tonnage, managed to persuade Moscow, at great cost to itself in the suspicions of disloyalty (and suspect nationalism) that such appeals raised, to reduce the quota to 6.6 million tons—itself a target never fulfilled—even this reduced sum was still far too high to make it possible to avoid massive starvation. Stalin, despite the mounting death toll, did not believe, or did not *want* to believe, the claim that the harvest was too small both to feed the Ukrainian people and to provide sufficient grain for export. Instead, already intensely suspicious of Ukrainian separatism and fearful of local disloyalty, he chose to interpret the failure to meet the inordinate quotas sent down from the center as deliberate acts of "sabotage," the peasants as no better than "wreckers" of the socialist dream. Therefore, in a deliberate act intended to punish the population of Ukraine—though justified as an act of socialist self-defense—he continued to export grain from the region, if at a lower rate: 1.73 million tons in 1932 and 1.68 million tons in 1933, compared to 5.2 million tons in 1931. This export of grain, given the greatly reduced supplies, turned an already grave situation into an occasion of mass death.

Increased pressure was now also applied against the *selianym*-class enemy, local party officials (37.3 percent of the new Ukrainian Communist Party members and candidate members were purged and 75 percent of local Soviets and members of local committees were replaced, with many of those who were replaced being arrested for failing to produce the required quota), those involved in local agricultural middle management (many of these officials were arrested in the second half of 1932 for sabotaging Bolshevik policy), and all channels of Ukrainian economic, cultural, and nutritional self-sufficiency. On December 14, 1932, the Central Committee of the All-Union Communist Party accused the leadership of the Ukrainian Communist Party "of tolerating a Ukrainian nationalist deviation in its ranks"[7] and then proceeded, on January 24, 1933, to replace it with a new ruling clique headed by Pavel Postyshev. At the same time, all available food aid to the stricken population, it is argued, was consciously denied, existing grain reserves in the region and elsewhere were not made available, and the importation of food was stopped at the border of Ukraine—all while Stalin, in an act of depravity, continued, as already noted, to export more than 3 million tons of grain in 1932 and 1933. As a result, there was massive—under this decoding, *intentional*—starvation throughout Ukraine climaxing in 1933 and 1934. Of a peasant population of upwards of 25 million, I estimate that up to 5 million persons, or 20 percent of the rural population, plus from 500,000 to 750,000 persons in the urban areas of Ukraine, died from lack of food and related medical problems in this period. In some areas, the death rate was as low as 10 percent, in others nearly 100 percent, depending largely upon local agricultural and ecological conditions, for example, and most importantly, the ability to find other sources of nutrition, such as fish or wildlife—in many places this also led to cannibalism and infanticide—to replace the lost grain harvests.

So goes the nationalist account of the Ukrainian famine interpreted as an intentional, man-made "genocide." Stalin purposely killed 5 million or more Ukrainians, plus hundreds of thousands of additional individuals belonging to other ethnic groups, such as the Volga Germans and Kuban Cossacks, in order both to decapitate opposition to agricultural collectivization and to eradicate Ukrainian, and other, nationalist aspirations.

Now, accepting this nationalist interpretation of Ukrainian history, at least for the sake of argument, what are we to conclude about these events constituting an instance of genocide? This is neither an irrelevant nor a trivial question given the size of the human losses involved and the evil will that is asserted to have directly caused, to have been knowingly responsible for, these losses. Moreover, I do not want to support any diminution or denial of this vast collective tragedy, the existence of which is not in doubt. However—and here I recognize that given the loss of millions of persons this conclusion will seem at first counterintuitive—even if the nationalist intentionalist thesis is correct, the results—at least 5 million deaths—do *not* constitute the technical crime of genocide, and the event, in its phenomenological specificity and totality, is not, for all of its murderous ferocity and demographic enormity, comparable to the Shoah. I would argue—assuming the correctness of this account—that the ruthless campaign against Ukrainian nationalism that destroyed a majority of the indigenous Ukrainian cultural and political elite, in addition to a significant segment of the peasant population of the region, is most correctly categorized as an instance of nationalist conflict and internal colonialism rather than as an example of genocide. Stalin did not intend to exterminate the entire population of Ukraine.

This conclusion finds immediate support from the apposite statistical indicators: Though the human carnage was enormous—approaching the number of Jewish victims during the Second World War—the portion of the Ukrainian peasant population lost was somewhere near 20 percent (plus or minus 5 percent), and the losses for the Ukrainian population as a whole were in the area of 15 percent. These demographic results resemble (if being slightly higher than) the figures for population decline in those eastern European countries overrun by the Nazis, and in both cases the numbers do not indicate that a policy of total population eradication was pursued. Had Stalin in Ukraine—and Hitler in eastern Europe—sought to pursue a genocidal war, given the destructive possibilities that lay open to him, more than 15 percent of the population would have been done away with. More people were not killed because, amid the murder that did occur, there was, odd as this may seem, restraint. There was restraint because Stalin did not want to eradicate the people of Ukraine; he wanted to exploit them. Eliminating the whole of a vanquished helot population makes no more sense than slaughtering one's slaves. However, in contrast, eliminating a conquered people's controlling elite, leaving it leaderless, anxious, and vertiginous, is a rational and functional strategy, long pursued by conquerors and adopted by Stalin, in order to achieve both enduring subordination of the subjugated and political stability in one's empire. This is not a humane imperial strategy—a regular course of action to be recommended as a form of empire maintenance—but neither is it genocide.

Ironically, this judgment is confirmed by the heartrending condition of the children, especially infants and the newborn. Throughout Ukraine, youthful cadavers lay strewn across the landscape; the entire territory had become a crude necropolis for children under the age of twelve who were unable to obtain enough nourishment to stay alive. Yet even here, in the midst of the most intense human suffering, the relevant population statistics require careful decipherment. The latest demographic data indicate that fewer than 760,000 children died,[8] largely from starvation, between 1932 and 1934. This represents, depending on one's estimation of other relevant demographic variables, between 6 percent and 33.5 percent of the age cohort and a significant percentage of the total population decline. However, recognizing the great tragedy that occurred here, even the maximum loss rate of 33.5 percent does not support a genocidal reading of this event. For, on these numbers, that is, a loss rate of between 6 and 33.5 percent, 66.5 percent of Ukrainian children, at a minimum, survived. Once the famine was past its peak in May 1933, the surviving two out of three children were not singled out for further harassment or worse. Most of those who survived the crisis of 1932–1933 survived.

This historical outcome regarding the children is not trivial. What makes the Ukrainian case non-genocidal, and what makes it different from the Holocaust, is the fact that the majority of Ukrainian children survived and, still more, that they were *permitted* to survive. Even the mountain of evidence pertaining to Stalin's evil actions produced by the proponents of the nationalist-genocide thesis—for example, James Mace and Robert Conquest—does not indicate an intent to eliminate, or any motive that would plausibly justify the extermination of, the Ukrainian biological stock. Though the number of Ukrainian children who died and, under the intentionalist reading, were murdered, was almost as high as (or higher than) the number of Jewish children who were exterminated, their deaths were the consequence of, represented, and intended something wholly different from what the murder of Jewish children at Auschwitz and Treblinka represented and intended. In the Ukrainian case, the focused object of the violence and death was national enfeeblement and political dismemberment. In the Shoah, the focused object, given its racial determinants, was physical genocide. Stalin intended that after the famine there should still be Ukrainians, though not Ukrainianism; Hitler intended that after Auschwitz there would be neither Jews nor Judaism. The loss of every child in both contexts, employing the calculus of the talmudic sages, was the loss of a world. The death of each child was an act of equal immorality. Nonetheless, there is an important, nonreductive, phenomenological difference to be drawn between mass murder (including children) and complete group extinction (including children), between a war for political and territorial domination (including children) and a war of unlimited biological annihilation (including children).

The issue, the interpretive inquiry, the dialectic of evidence and meaning regarding the Ukrainian tragedy, is still more complex. For, as noted (nonpolemically) at the outset of this analysis, there are two possible explanations of the Ukrainian tragedy. The second possible, plausible, non-nationalist deconstruction of the Ukrainian tragedy argues that the famine was neither intended nor man-made—though, ultimately, it was the result of human errors connected with the program of forced collectivization. That is to say, under this alternative reading, the famine, the reality and extent of which no one denies, was not the consequence of a premeditated plan to murder large numbers of Ukrainians in support of an antinationalist political outcome in the region. Therefore, by definition, what transpired, though baleful and full of bile, was not genocide.

The case for this very different interpretation has been made by a number of scholars including, most recently, J. Arch Getty, Walter Laqueur, Mark B. Tauger, and R. W. Davies, and is supported by both Robert C. Tucker's narrative in his *Stalin in Power* and Adam Ulam's conclusion in his *Stalin: The Man and His Era:* "Stalin and his closest collaborators had not willed the famine."[9]

Now, under either interpretation of the Ukrainian tragedy, the fact is that, though something very terrible occurred in Ukraine, what happened was a very different sort of thing—structurally and as regards intention—than what transpired in the Holocaust.

IV
The Armenian Tragedy

The Armenian tragedy was an enormous historical outrage. As I understand this event, the controlling ambition, the collective civic agenda, behind Turkish inhumanity was primarily nationalist in character and, in practice, limited in scope and purpose. The Armenian massacres were an indecent, radicalized manifestation of a most primitive jingoism activated by the exigencies of war from without and the revolutionary collapse of the Ottoman empire from within. Turkish nationalism—the extreme nationalist elites in control of the Turkish state—now under the violent cover of war, envisioned and pursued the elimination of (*not* the murder of) *all* non-Turkish elements—and most especially and specifically the eradication of the Armenian community—from the national context. The anti-Armenian crusade was, therefore, for all its lethal extravagance, a delimited political crusade. Of course, mixed into the noxious brew that represented itself as national destiny were other obsessions: a loathing of Christians if not all non-Muslims, xenophobia, greed, jealousy, fear, desire, and the like. But, above all else, the "war against the Armenians" was a vulgar and desperate manifestation of raw nationalist politics.

As a direct and immediate consequence, anti-Armenianism is not expressed in the baroque language of metaphysical evil, nor does it require (paraphrasing Heinrich Himmler's assertion that "all Jews without exception must die") the complete annihilation of *every* Armenian man, woman, and child. It does not represent a racial collision as that term came to be understood in the ornate ontological schema of Nazism. There is no assertion of primordial reciprocity between power and being, between intrahuman aggression and metahistoric causations, between biological contingencies and noumenological principles. Rather, the elemental rationale almost universally cited by the Turks in defense of their actions is political: The Armenians were secessionists, Russian spies, fifth-columnists, and divisive nationalists who would subvert the Turkish people's revolution and destroy Turkish national and political integrity. This explanatory tack, this nationalist warrant, is already determinative in the prewar Turkish interpretation of, for example, the Armenian massacres at Adana in April 1909, and it reappears in full force in the explication of the events of 1915–1916. Repeated Turkish reference to the Armenian revolution at Van in 1915 is perhaps the outstanding example of this "legitimating" mode of moral-political reasoning.

This is to argue that contrary to, for example, Helen Fein's contention that the Armenians were "enemies by definition,"[10] that is, on a priori ideological or racial grounds—thereby allowing her erroneously to equate the action against Jews and Gypsies in World War II with that against the Armenians in World War I—the Armenians were "enemies" to the degree that they were enemies in this context, on practical and political grounds centering around long-standing policies of internal colonialism, the implications—and machinations—of national self-determination, and the provocative issue of loyalty in time of war. Accordingly, the objective of Turkish action, when it came in 1915–1916, was the destruction, once and for all, of Armenian national identity. The criminality of the Armenians did not require (as I shall show in detail in a moment) the biological extinction of every Armenian man, woman, and child—especially if such individual and collective survival took place outside Turkish national boundaries and, therefore, made no claims upon Turkish sovereignty or national territory.

This is not to ignore the magnitude of the crime perpetrated against the Armenian people, the misery and death entailed by the mass deportations, the continual abuse of Armenian women, the mix of ideology, sadism, and self-interest in the massacre of Armenian men, and the theft and murder of infants and children. It is, however, to insist that these deliberate acts of despoliation and near-unlimited cruelty be deciphered aright. To decipher them aright means recognizing their particular strategic causation that (odd as this may sound, given the vast inhuman carnage that occurred) entailed limits. Being a political-national assault against a political enemy, the Young Turks could achieve their preeminent goal—the protection of the nation as they defined it—without requiring the complete physical extirpation of every person of Armenian heritage. To this degree (and here I make only this limited and very precise claim), the intentionality behind, as well as the actualized structure of, the Turkish program for the eradication of Armenian national existence was *unlike* the biocentric war that Nazism carried on against the Jews—because the "Armenian question" differed in its quintessential character from the "Jewish question." The former had been a conflicted political issue for nearly a century, had created manifold pressures and functional compromises for the Ottoman state, and now could be, once and for all, resolved by the annihilation of the organized Armenian *community* within Turkey. In contrast, the Jewish question, which had likewise been a central, exceedingly controversial, political concern in Europe since the beginning of Jewish emancipation in the eighteenth century, was categorically transformed by Hitler into an inescapable metaphysical challenge ("blood" in the Nazi universe of discourse being understood as the elementary vehicle by which ontological values become incarnate in history) that could *only* be resolved by an uncompromisingly genocidal assault. The Third Reich, therefore, insisted not only on the elimination of Jewish collective identity and communal existence, but also on the murder of *every* Jewish person of whatever age and gender.

At this juncture of our argument, three seminal factors that strengthen the morphological *dis*analogy between the Armenian tragedy and the Holocaust need to be introduced. They are: (1) the possibility of Armenian Christian conversion to Islam as a way of avoiding deportation and worse; (2) the specific character of the forced deportations; and (3) the *nontotalistic* nature of the anti-Armenian crusade.

As regards the mediating role of conversion to Islam, the eyewitness accounts of the tragedy repeatedly mention this lifesaving, though communally destructive, possibility. Both "willingly" and unwillingly, large numbers of Armenians became Muslims. In particular, there appears to have been extensive, forced proselytization of Armenian women and children. It is difficult to ascertain just what role official Ittihadist ideology played in these coerced prophylactic rituals, though it is clear that the Committee of Union and Progress (CUP), devoid as it was of a racist ideology, did not oppose such re-creative, death-deflecting actions. Indeed, to the degree that Islamicization constructively reinforced the Young Turks' normative political agenda—Islam being a fundamental buttress of Turkification (whereas Christianity was the key element in Armenian self-identity)—this survivalist (flagrantly inhumane) program was consistent with CUP ambitions; and it found wide instantiation. So wide, in fact, that Johannes Lepsius again and again excoriates the Turkish government for allowing, even encouraging, this tyrannical policy, and Arnold Toynbee accusingly refers to "survival being purchased by apostatizing to Islam."[11] Likewise, the German, U.S., British, and other governments are on record as protesting this unwelcome practice.

In that neither Islam nor Turkism is predicated on inelastic, biologistic concepts, both possess absorptive capacities that create existential as well as sociopolitical possibilities unavailable in Nazism. Accordingly, the "other" is not only defined differently by the Ittihad elites than in Hitler's Reich—not genetically and without reference to metaphysical canons of ontic pollution and decadence—but the required response to the "other" allows for the remaking of the "other," primarily through the mysterious rite of conversion, so as to obviate still more complete—that is, exterminatory—forms of overcoming. We have evidence that the children in Christian orphanages were converted en masse. It was not only women and children who were forcibly converted. Lepsius, for example, records that the entire male medical staff of the German Mission Hospital in Urfa were coerced into becoming Muslim, as were Armenian army physicians at Sivas.[12] In Aleppo, the entire Armenian labor battalion was converted in February 1916, and further large-scale conversions of Armenian males occurred in March and April 1916. Lepsius also reports that "all Armenian villages in the Samsun area and in

Unich has been Islamicized. No favors were granted to anyone, apart from renegades."[13] In fact, Lepsius conservatively estimates that 200,000 men, women, and children, approximately 12 to 13.5 percent of the entire Armenian community, were forcibly converted and thereby saved,[14] however objectionable the instrument of their salvation. In this respect, Turkish policy reproduces medieval procedures of cultural homogenization, not modern procedures of physical genocide. As such, it kept Armenians, if not Armenianism, alive.

Secondly, the Armenian deportations were not uniform events of total annihilation. Though these Armenian removals, carried out under the most brutal conditions, were regularly occasions of mass death that sealed the fate of hundreds of thousands, several hundred thousand Armenians did survive these horrific journeys. Lepsius, for example, (under)estimates the remnant at 200,000 individuals. Toynbee cites a total of 600,000 Armenian survivors up to 1916—the combined total of those who lived through the deportations and those who fled into Russian territory. He summarizes:

> In general wastage [death during the deportations] seems to fluctuate, with a wide oscillation, on either side of 50 percent; 600 out of 2,500 (24 percent) reached Aleppo from a village in the Harpout district; 60 percent arrived there out of the first convoy from the village of E. (near H.), and 46 percent out of the second; 25 percent arrived out of a convoy from the village of D. in the same neighborhood. We shall certainly be well within the mark if we estimate that at least half those condemned to massacre or deportation have actually perished.[15]

Supporting these large estimates of the number of those who were *not* killed during these forced evacuations are the figures for Armenians who found refuge in Arab countries and then, later, in western Europe and the United States. Richard Hovannisian, writing of their acceptance in the Arab world, indicates that "many of the deportees suffered a cruel fate at the hands of certain Bedouin tribes in the Syrian desert, but most were accorded sympathetic asylum by the Arab peoples, who had themselves endured four centuries of Ottoman domination. In all, the number of Armenian deportees who found refuge in Arab lands, by 1925, is estimated at well over 200,000."[16] This figure excludes the 50,000 persons who found refuge in Iran. More specifically, Hovannisian breaks these refugee figures down as follows: Syria accepted 100,000 Armenian refugees; Lebanon, 50,000; Palestine and Jordan, 10,000; Egypt, 40,000; Iraq, 25,000; and Iran, 50,000, making a total of 275,000 survivors. These numbers are supported by later governmental statistics issued by the respective Arab countries. Census data released between 1931 and 1945 by the individual Middle East states indicate that Syria had an Armenian population of 125,550 (1945); Lebanon, 72,797 (1944); Palestine, 3,802 (1931); and Egypt, 19,596 (1937). Moreover, in addition to these aggregates, we also have evidence in various national census counts of the inter-war period of sizable new Armenian communities, in France, Greece,

Cyprus, Bulgaria, and the United States, with additional small populations in Czechoslovakia, Switzerland, Greece, Hungary, Austria, Yugoslavia, Italy, and Canada. (The population figures for these communities overlap with Hovannesian's figures for the Arab World—though to what exact degree is uncertain.) Therefore, if we put the number of survivors of these inhumane transfers at between 300,000 and 400,000, we shall be on secure grounds—or at least grounds that are as secure as possible given all the statistical uncertainties—remembering that Hovannisian's total of 275,000 does not include any survivors in Russia, Europe, or the United States. This translates into a survival rate somewhere between 17.7 percent (300,000 out of 1.7 million, the maximum Armenian population) and 26.6 percent (400,000 out of 1.5 million, the minimum Armenian population). Then, too, beyond the mathematics alone, these substantial statistics indicate that the Turkish oppressor did not require nor demand the death of all Armenians. The Turks had all of these individuals, this entire defenseless population, within their control and could have murdered them all, despite the practical difficulties involved in murdering an entire people in a country as large as Turkey, had they so desired. Evidently, this was not necessary.

Thirdly, the enacted policy of deporting Armenians was not universally applied even within the borders of Turkey. The Armenians of Constantinople, numbering up to 200,000, and the Armenians of other large cities—for example, Smyrna, where between 6,000 and 20,000 Armenians lived, Kutahia, and, to some degree, Aleppo—were not uprooted en masse during the entire war period. Lepsius estimated (and, in his own words, perhaps "overestimated") that the number of Armenians so protected represented one-seventh to one-ninth of the total Armenian population, or some 204,700 persons (out of what he projected as an original Armenian population of 1,845,450).[17] Although recent studies[18] require that we temper Lepsius's figures and indicate that up to 30,000 Armenians were, in fact, deported from Constantinople, the need to modify all generalizations as to Turkish intentions, given the very real limitations placed upon evictions from Constantinople and elsewhere, stands.

To gain a full picture of all the relevant statistics bearing upon the question of Armenian survival, we must also add in the 300,000 or so Armenians who retreated with the Russian army back into Russian territory after the final defeat at Van in the summer of 1915 and the 4,200 who survived the famous battle at Musa Dagh and were rescued by the French in mid-September 1915. Accordingly, the comprehensive demographic picture regarding casualties and survival looks like this:

1914 Armenian Population	1,500,000–1,700,000
Converts to Islam	200,000–300,000
Survive Deportations (outside Turkey)	300,000–400,000
Survive in large Turkish Cities	170,000–220,000
Survive in Russia	250,000–300,000
Survivors of Musa Dagh	4,200–4,200

TOTAL SURVIVORS   924,200–1,224,200
TOTAL DEATHS (1915–1918, based on 1,700,000 total)   475,800–775,800

This is not the Holocaust.

V
Conclusion

The spatial limits imposed on this chapter prevent further comparative review and analysis. However, I believe that in all the other cases that are said to parallel the Holocaust, close study would show that they also are dissimilar insofar as they, too, would not be examples of an unlimited war that required complete annihilation—the death of every man, woman, and child—of the victim population. The Holocaust is a unique historical reality.

NOTES

1. I discuss all of these historical events at great length in volume 2 of my study entitled *The Holocaust in Historical Context* (New York: Oxford University Press), forthcoming. Volume 1, published in 1994, deals with premodern cases, for example, medieval antisemitism, the witch craze, the medieval crusades against heretics, and the French wars of religion, that bear on this subject.

2. James Mooney, "Calendar History of the Kiowa Indians," in the *Seventeenth Annual Report of the Bureau of American Ethnology, 1895–1896* (Washington, D.C.: Bureau of Ethnology, 1898), part 1.

3. Russell Thornton, *American Indian Holocaust and Survival* (Norman: University of Oklahoma Press, 1987), p. 49.

4. Cited from Brian Dippie, *The Vanishing American: White Attitudes and U.S. Indian Policy* (Middletown, Conn.: Wesleyan University Press, 1982), p. 151.

5. Semen O. Pidhainy et al., eds., *The Black Deeds of the Kremlin: A White Book*, vol. 1 (Detroit, 1955), p. 205.

6. Robert Conquest, *The Harvest of Sorrow: Soviet Collectivization and the Terror-Famine* (New York: Oxford University Press, 1986), p. 219. Repeated in the *U.S. Commission on the Ukraine Famine* (Washington, D.C., 1990), p. xiii: "Crushing the Ukrainian peasantry made it possible for Stalin to curtail Ukrainian national self-assertion."

7. Cited from George O. Liber, *Soviet Nationality Policy* (Cambridge: Cambridge University Press, 1992), p. 166. On these political activities, interpreted from a radical Ukrainian perspective, see Hryhory Kostiuk, *Stalinist Rule in the Ukraine* (New York: Praeger, 1960), pp. 18–37; and from a less ideological perspective, see Robert S. Sullivant, *Soviet Politics in the Ukraine* (New York: Columbia University Press, 1962), pp. 195–208.

8. Robert Conquest's maximum total of child deaths of 4 million—3 million as a result of the famine and 1 million due to the program of dekulakization—appears, based on currently available evidence, too high. See *Harvest of Sorrow*, p. 297. Moreover, this total in-

cludes non-Ukrainian children, for example, those of Kazakhstan, thus reducing the number and percentage of child losses in Ukraine (even on Conquest's numbers) significantly.

9. Adam Ulam, *Stalin: The Man and His Era* (New York: Viking, 1973), p. 349.

10. Helen Fein, *Accounting for Genocide* (New York: Free Press, 1979), p. 30.

11. Arnold Toynbee, "The Murderous Tyranny of the Turks" (pamphlet: New York, 1917).

12. Johannes Lepsius, *Deutschland und Armenien, 1914–1918* (Potsdam: Tempelverlag, 1919), p. 283.

13. Ibid., p. 160.

14. Ibid., p. lxv.

15. Arnold Toynbee in Viscount Bryce, *The Treatment of the Armenians in the Ottoman Empire, 1915–1916* (London: The Knickerbocker Press [for His Majesty's Stationery Office], 1916), p. 650.

16. Richard Hovannisian, "Ebb and Flow of the Armenian Minority in the Arab Middle East," *Middle East Journal* 1(28) (Winter 1974):20.

17. I will provide a fuller accounting of these statistics in my analysis of the Armenian Tragedy in Vol. 2 of my *Holocaust in Historical Context*.

18. See Vahakn N. Dadrian's important qualification regarding the Armenians of Constantinople, "Genocide as a Problem of National and International Law: The World War I Armenian Case and Its Contemporary Legal Ramifications," *Yale Journal of International Law* 14(2) (Summer 1989):262, n. 131; and again, "The Documentation of the World War I Armenian Massacres in the Proceedings of the Turkish Military Tribunal," *International Journal of Middle East Studies* 23(4) (November 1991):570, n. 26. According to Dadrian's reconstruction, based on the testimony of German Ambassador Wolff-Metternich on December 7, 1915, who gave as his source the Turkish chief of policy, 30,000 Armenians were deported from Constantinople and more deportations were feared.

❀ 5 ❀

Responses to the Porrajmos: The Romani Holocaust[1]

IAN HANCOCK

Ignorance and arrogance are in full flower ... [including] the notion that not only Jews ... but Gypsies were chosen by the Nazis for annihilation.
Edward Alexander, "Review of Lopate," 1990[2]

√

"Holocaust" has been used to encompass more than the murder of the Jews. From the casualties in our Civil War to the wholesale murder of gypsies in World War II.
William Safire, "On Language: Long Time No See," 1983[3]

*J*ust four years after the fall of the Third Reich, Dora Yates, the Jewish secretary of the Gypsy Lore Society, noted in the pages of *Commentary* that:

It is more than time that civilized men and women were aware of the Nazi crime against the Gypsies as well as the Jews. Both bear witness to the fantastic dynamic of the 20th century racial fanaticism, for these two people shared the horror of martyrdom at the hands of the Nazis for no other reason than that they were—they existed. The Gypsies, like the Jews, stand alone.[4]

And, the following year, the *Wiener Library Bulletin*, organ of what is now the Jewish Institute of Contemporary History in London, published the statement that "Germany had in 1938 a gipsy population of 16,275. Of these, 85 percent were thrown into concentration camps, and no more than 12 percent survived."[5]

Despite these very early observations[6] and the overwhelming amount of documentation relating to the fate of the Gypsies in Nazi Germany, which has been examined during the fourteen years the U.S. Holocaust Memorial Council has been in existence, that body, more than any other, rigorously persists in underestimating and underrepresenting that truth, made plain forty-five years ago, a position reflected in the permanent exhibit in the United States Holocaust Memorial Museum—whose staff, it should be said, has generally been much more favorably disposed to the Gypsy case. In their 1989 book *Holocaust: Religious and Philosophical Implications*, editors John Roth and Michael Berenbaum ask, "Why should the fate of the Jews be treated differently than the fate of the Gypsies or the Poles. . . . The answer will be found in these essays."[7] But the answer to that question, at least for the Gypsy case, appears nowhere in any of the twenty-three essays that appear in the book. More recently still, Martin Gilbert, in his foreword to Carrie Supple's *From Prejudice to Genocide: Learning About the Holocaust*, published for use in British schools, refers to the Holocaust as "the attempt by the Nazis to destroy all the Jews of Europe between 1941 and 1945," then mentions the fate of the Romani victims as being among "other attempts at genocide, such as the slaughter of the Armenians,"[8] thereby placing Gypsies with a group outside of the Holocaust altogether and echoing the statement in his *The Holocaust* that "it was the Jews alone who were marked out to be destroyed in their entirety."[9] And though Michael Burleigh and Wolfgang Wippermann discuss in detail a "final solution" of the "Gypsy problem" in their book *The Racial State*, Antony Polonsky is still moved in his introduction to that book to maintain that "as emerges clearly from the arguments of Burleigh and Wippermann, the mass murder of the Jews *was* unique in that every Jew, man, woman and child, assimilated or deeply orthodox, was singled out for destruction."[10] It is abundantly clear that some historians see only what they want to see, that a very blind eye is being turned in the direction of Gypsy history, and that where the Romani genocide in Nazi Germany is acknowledged, it is kept, with the fewest of exceptions,[11] carefully separated from the Jewish experience. Some authors, such as Emil Fackenheim and Charles S. Maier, seem not yet to have made up their minds about whether to include Gypsies or not: "With the possible exception of the Gypsies, Jews were the only people killed for the 'crime'" of existing."[12] And in Maier's words:

> Why . . . does it seem important to insist on the uniqueness of the Nazi crimes? Because nowhere else but in Nazi-occupied Europe from 1941 to 1945 was there an apparatus so single-mindedly established to carry out mass murder as a process in its own right. And not just mass murder, but ethnic extermination—killing, without even a pretext of individual wrongdoing, an entire people (if gypsies are counted, two peoples).[13]

Similarly, Richard Breitman admits that Gypsies might eventually also get higher billing once more details become available: "The Nazis did try to wipe out virtually all Jews, whereas their murderous policies for other groups were more selective. In some cases, for example with the gypsies, further research is needed to show what distinctions were made, why some were killed and others spared."[14]

This is a profoundly emotionally charged issue, one fraught with subjective interpretation and response. Assumptions are made, and repeated with confidence, by individuals who have no special expertise in (Romani) holocaust history, and unqualified statements are reiterated that automatically assume a lesser status for Gypsies in the ranking of human abuse. These take the form of entire articles, such as that by Steven Katz.[15] He systematically compares the fate of Jews in the Holocaust with the medieval witch craze, North American Indians, black slavery, Gypsies under the Nazis, homosexuals during World War II, and Polish and Ukrainian losses during World War II, concluding that "all . . . are to be fundamentally distinguished from the Holocaust, even when they reveal horrifyingly large casualty figures."[16] The same is found in the writings of Yehuda Bauer, who states with assurance in his entry on "Gypsies" in *Encyclopedia of the Holocaust* that "the fate of the Gypsies was in line with Nazi thought as a whole: Gypsies were not Jews, and therefore there was no need to kill all of them."[17] Then, like Katz, he substantiates this claim by selectively citing sources (none more recent than 1979) and makes no comparisons with Jewish populations that were also exempted from death and for whom there was likewise "no need to kill all." The three-and-a-half-page "Gypsies" entry in the two-volume, 2,000-page *Encyclopedia of the Holocaust*, incidentally, amounts to less than one-quarter of 1 percent of the whole book, despite the enormity of Gypsy losses by 1945, which proportionately at least matched, and possibly exceeded, losses of Jewish victims. In his more recent book, Katz elaborates upon these comparisons and expands upon the criterion of "intentionality," which, he says, characterized the fate of Jews in the Holocaust but not that of any other victims of mass-scale murder. Indeed, he claims that "the Nazi attack on the Jews was the only true genocide in history."[18]

Typically accompanying these statements and assumptions is the acknowledgment that yes, there were other victims of Nazism, but they belong under a separate heading of non-Jews, and their fate was different. Berenbaum places the Gypsy victims in a category we might easily call "unnamed afterthought" in his own definition of the Holocaust—"the systematic state-sponsored murder of six million Jews by the Nazis and their collaborators during World War II; as night descended, millions of others were killed in their wake."[19] Berenbaum presumed what the effect of the United States Holocaust Memorial Museum upon the public consciousness would be fully five years before its opening, in *Newsday*, when he said, "People had to grow. Jews had to learn to be sensitive to non-Jewish victims, and they, in turn, had to learn to be sensitive to the uniqueness of the Jewish experience."[20] The central issue rests squarely upon this notion of "uniqueness"; it was the basis of my presentation at the first "Remembering for the Future" conference in Oxford, which was published in an expanded version in my *Without*

Prejudice.[21] Phillip Lopate seems to be the only writer to have listed the criteria for "uniqueness" in an unequivocal way:

> The position that the Jewish Holocaust was unique tends to rest on the following arguments: (1) scale—the largest number of deaths extracted from one single group; (2) technology—the mechanization of death factories; (3) bureaucracy—the involvement of the state apparatus at previously unheard-of levels; (4) intent—the express purpose being to annihilate every last member of the Jewish people.[22]

I will enumerate these and other principal challenges to the Romani case that have emerged since the Oxford conference and that argue for categorization separately from the Jewish case and thereby support the perceived "uniqueness" of the latter, commenting upon each in turn:

1) Jews were targeted to the last man, woman, and child for complete extermination, a policy that held true for no other population.

There were in fact numbers of categories of Jews who were exempt and who escaped death. Raul Hilberg discusses these in detail in the first chapters of his *The Destruction of the European Jews*.[23] As early as 1938, the Third Reich asked various foreign governments to extend invitations to German Jews as a means of getting them out of the country, but this policy was not extended to include Gypsies. Mention can also be made of the September 1, 1941, law confining Jews and Gypsies to their place of residence, which exempted Jews married to non-Jews but did not similarly spare Gypsies. Ronald Smelser discusses the Brand Mission of 1944 (named for Hungarian Jew Joel Brand, who led this effort to free Jewish countrymen), when Adolf Eichmann himself was prepared to spare the lives of 1 million Jews in return for 10,000 trucks, and the effort of the American Jewish Joint Distribution Committee, which successfully secured the release of 318 Jews from Bergen-Belsen the same year.[24] As the Holocaust intensified, most of these exemptions, for both groups, were progressively rescinded. When making statements of this kind, the year should be specified to incorporate policy changes. Ultimately, *only* Jews and Gypsies were singled out for complete extermination (with the exception of certain exempted groups within each population) on the basis of race and/or ethnicity. No other targeted populations were thus identified, and for this reason Gypsies must not be placed in the residual category of "Others."

2) Gypsies "come closest" to the Jewish situation but, as Messrs. Mais, Bauer, Wiesel, and Berenbaum and others have said, close is still a miss.

In this connection and most recently, Michael Berenbaum has said, in the introduction to *The World Must Know*, "At the center of the tragedy of the Holocaust is the murder of European Jews—men, women and children—killed not for the identity they affirmed or the religion they practiced, but because of the blood of their grandparents. Near that center is the murder of the Gypsies. Historians are still uncertain if there was a single decision for their complete annihilation, an enunciated policy of transcendent meaning to the perpetrators."[25] He further says "Gypsies (Roma and Sinti) had been subject to official discrimination in Germany long before 1933, but even the Nazi regime never promulgated a comprehensive law against them,"[26] a statement that seems to have been paraphrased from David M. Luebke, who wrote that "no comprehensive 'Gypsy Law' was ever promulgated."[27] To this might also be added Richard Breitman's statement that "whatever its weaknesses, 'Final Solution' at least applies to a single, specific group defined by descent. The Nazi are not known to have spoken of the Final Solution of the Polish problem or of the gypsy problem."[28] What makes a decree calling for racial obliteration "comprehensive" or not isn't discussed, but the statement is neither correct nor serves in any way to relegate the fate of the Gypsies to some less stringent category. But, as Penelope Keable asserts in her refutation of those who claim that no so-called Gypsy Law ever existed, "while denial threatens . . . oblivion, facts require repetition if they are to remain facts."[29] There are numerous Nazi policy statements available to us calling for the total elimination of the Romani population, several of which I have included in my chronology, together with references.[30] Thus in the Auschwitz *Memorial Book* we find "the final resolution, as formulated by Himmler, in his 'Decree for Basic Regulations to Resolve the Gypsy Question as Required by the Nature of Race,' of December 8th, 1938, meant that preparations were to begin for the *complete extermination* of the Sinti and Roma."[31] In 1939 Johannes Behrendt of the Office of Racial Hygiene issued a brief stating that "all Gypsies should be treated as hereditarily sick; the only solution is elimination. The aim should therefore be the elimination without hesitation of this defective element in the population." Benno Müller-Hill writes:

> Heydrich, who had been entrusted with the "final solution of the Jewish question" on 31st July 1941, shortly after the German invasion of the USSR, also included the Gypsies in his "final solution." . . . The senior SS officer and Chief of Police for the East, Dr. Landgraf, in Riga, informed Rosenberg's Reich Commissioner for the East, Lohse, of the inclusion of the Gypsies in the "final solution." Thereupon, Lohse gave the order, on 24th December 1941, that the Gypsies "should be given the same treatment as the Jews."[32]

Reinhard Heydrich, who was head of the Reich Main Security Office and the leading organizational architect of the Final Solution, ordered the *Einsatzkommandos* "to kill all Jews, Gypsies and mental patients."[33] Although there is no dispute about the Heydrich directive, in their 1991 work Burleigh and Wippermann draw attention to the fact that not all of the documentation regarding its complete details, relating to both Jews and Gypsies, has been found:

A conference on racial policy organized by Heydrich took place in Berlin on 21 September 1939, which may have decided upon a "Final Solution" of the "Gypsy Question." According to the scant minutes which have survived, four issues were decided: the concentration of Jews in towns; their relocation to Poland; the removal of 30,000 Gypsies to Poland, and the systematic deportation of Jews to German incorporated territories using goods trains. An express letter sent by the Reich Main Security Office on 17th October 1939 to its local agents mentioned that the "Gypsy Question will shortly be regulated throughout the territory of the Reich." . . . At about this time, Adolf Eichmann made the recommendation that the "Gypsy Question" be solved *simultaneously* with the "Jewish Question," . . . Himmler signed the order despatching Germany's Sinti and Roma to Auschwitz on 16th December 1942. The "Final Solution" of the "Gypsy Question" had begun.[34]

The *Memorial Book* for the Roma and Sinti who died at Auschwitz-Birkenau interprets this somewhat differently:

The Himmler decree of December 16th, 1942 (*Auschwitz-Erlaß*), according to which the Gypsies should be deported to Auschwitz-Birkenau, had the same meaning for the Gypsies that the conference at Wannsee on January 20th, 1942, had for the Jews. This decree, and the bulletin that followed on January 29th, 1943, can thus be regarded as a logical consequence of the decision taken at Wannsee. After it had been decided that the fate of the Jews was to end in mass extermination, it was natural for the other group of racially-persecuted people, the Gypsies, to become victims of the same policy, which finally even included soldiers in the *Wehrmacht*.[35]

In a paper delivered at the March 1987 conference on the non-Jewish victims of the Holocaust sponsored by the U.S. Holocaust Memorial Council, Dr. Erika Thurner of the Institut für Neuere Geschichte und Zeitgeschichte at the University of Linz stated:

Heinrich Himmler's infamous Auschwitz decree of December 16th, 1942, can be seen as the final stage of the final solution of the Gypsy Question. The decree served as the basis for complete extermination. According to the implementation instructions of 1943, all Gypsies, irrespective of their racial mix, were to be assigned to concentration camps. The concentration camp for Gypsy families at Auschwitz-Birkenau was foreseen as their final destination . . . opposed to the fact that the decision to seek a final solution for the Gypsy Question came at a later date than that of the Jewish Question, the first steps taken to exterminate the Gypsies were initiated prior to this policy decision; the first gassing operations against Gypsies did indeed take place in Chelmno as early as late 1941/early 1942.[36]

On September 14, 1942, following a meeting in Berlin with Minister of Propaganda Josef Goebbels, *Reichminister* of Justice Otto Thierack wrote that "with respect to the extermination of antisocial forms of life, Dr. Goebbels is of the opinion that the Jews and the Gypsies should simply be exterminated."

Six years earlier, on March 4, 1936, a memorandum was sent to State Secretary of the Interior Hans Pfundtner that addressed the creation of a "Gypsy Law" (the *Reichzigeunergesetz*), the purpose of which was to deal with the complete registration of the Romani population, their sterilization, the restriction of their movement and means of livelihood, and the expulsion of all foreign-born, stateless Gypsies.

3) Another argument, discussed by Emil Fackenheim[37] and most recently given voice by Israeli Rabbi Eliezer Schach, is that "God used the Holocaust to punish Jews for their sins."

This would certainly exclude other groups and is perhaps the most difficult defense of "uniqueness" to address, from a non-Jewish perspective. But no doubt speaking for most of the Jewish religious community, Rabbi Yitzak Kagan of the Lubavitch Foundation of Michigan responded that Schach's statement "borders on heresy";[38] we must wonder how the murder of innocent Jewish babies can possibly be rationalized by this argument. It is of some significance that some Roma and Sinti today have succumbed to survivor's guilt and have also wondered, rhetorically, whether the Holocaust was "punishment" for imagined transgressions.

There is also the argument that the Jewish experience cannot be compared to that of any other people because Jews alone "dwell inside divine history"[39] (or "outside of history," as it has also been stated, for example, by Elie Wiesel). Such an argument is likewise a difficult one to reconcile with prosaic historical detail.

4) Certain Romani groups sedentary for two or more years were to be exempted from death.[40]

This two-year exemption was only a recommendation and was never actually implemented, as it was overridden by Himmler's own directive that all migratory Gypsies be killed and sedentary Gypsies worked to death in labor camps. In any case, this potential situation would only have applied to the Soviet Union and the Baltic lands and nowhere else. A similar situation did, however, operate for Jews in these countries; thus Hilberg writes of the *Gebietskommissar* for northern Lithuania in September 1941 complaining about the killings, explaining that "the Jews were needed as skilled laborers."[41] Hilberg continues, "In October 1941, the Reichskommissar forbade the shooting of Jews ... [and] during the quiet months of the winter and spring of 1942, they began to adjust themselves to their hazardous existence." By the end of 1943, "some tens of thousands of Jews were being kept alive at Lida and Minsk in Byelorussia, and looked forward to evacuation, or death." Nazi extermination of the Baltic Roma was particularly effective, almost the entire population having been destroyed by 1945.

5) Some Gypsies were even allowed to fight in the German army.[42]

Donald Kenrick and Grattan Puxon discuss Gypsies who served in the armed forces, saying that "Gypsies had officially been excluded from the army by law as early as November, 1937 . . . on the grounds of racial policy no more Gypsies should be called up. . . . The release of servicemen took some time and Gypsies could still be found in the army as late as 1943."[43] The sentence following this, however, reads, "*Certain classes of Jews with mixed parentage were retained in the armed forces throughout the war*" (emphasis added).

6) Kenrick and Puxon discuss certain categories of exemptions that applied to Gypsies.[44]

Kenrick and Puxon do deal with these and also include the statement that "these exemptions compare with similar arrangements for Jews."[45] If such an argument is to be used to characterize the treatment of Roma and Sinti, then it must likewise be used to characterize the treatment of Jews. And since it does apply to both populations, it cannot be used to support the "unique" treatment of the latter.

7) It has been claimed, including by the German government itself as a means of avoiding the payment of war crimes reparations, that Roma and Sinti were targeted not for racial reasons but rather for social reasons.

Yehuda Bauer has supported this argument also, stating that "the Gypsies were not murdered for racial reasons, but as so-called asocials . . . nor was their destruction complete."[46] But this argument originates in the deliberate and despicable move on the part of the German government to take advantage of the shattered condition of the surviving Romani population, which was in no condition to contest it and for which the Romani population is still suffering today. The racial identity of the Gypsy people and the genetically based rationale for their extermination are abundantly documented and referenced.[47] "In his report on the matter, the Bonn Correspondent of the *Manchester Guardian* . . . points out that the Supreme Court's decision 'is at direct variance with the known facts of Nazi policies for concentrating and later exterminating the gypsies.'"[48]

It is still the case that Gypsies are widely believed to be a population defined by behavior and social criteria rather than by genetic heritage or ethnicity. Professor Seymour Siegel, former chairman of the U.S. Holocaust Memorial Council, questioned, in the pages of the *Washington Post* and in the context of their right to full inclusion, whether Gypsies did in fact constitute a distinct ethnic people,[49] a particularly insensitive remark since Roma have a far more demonstrable claim to a "racial" identity than do Jews; this latter has been the subject of many studies.[50] A report on the health of the U.S. Romani population by a team of Harvard geneticists, which appeared in the prestigious medical journal *Lancet*, concludes, "Analysis of blood groups, haptoglobin phenotypes, and HLA types establish the Gypsies as a distinct racial group with origins in the Punjab region of India. Also supporting this is the worldwide Gypsy language Romani, which is quite similar to Hindi."[51]

The fact remains, however, that whether Gypsies and Jews are "races" or not does not matter; Hitler believed both populations to constitute a racial threat, and race was his justification for their attempted extermination. Bauer's further observation, that "nor was their destruction complete," is a baseless and peculiar argument, since the same statement applies, mercifully, to Jews, nearly 300 times as many of whom survived the Holocaust than did Gypsies (see Key Point 10, below).

8) Some families of "pure" Gypsies were to be preserved in special camps for future anthropologists to study.[52]

This has also been noted by Bauer, where he includes "pure" Gypsies with yet another category (apparently of his own devising: "racially safe" Gypsies—in direct contradiction of his reference in Key Point 7, above, to Gypsies as a *non*racially targeted population) in his statement that "Gypsies who were of pure blood, or who were not considered dangerous on a racial level, could continue to exist, under strict supervision."[53] In the United States Holocaust Memorial Museum's published Holocaust history we find the same argument made by Mais and Bauer repeated in slightly modified form, that "pure Gypsies were not targeted for extermination until 1942."[54] The wording here gives the impression that there was an existing policy that was then revoked in 1942, rather than its having been (like Key Point 4, above) nothing more than a suggestion, by Himmler, which was mocked by his peers as "one more of Himmler's hare-brained schemes"[55] and rejected outright by Martin Bormann, head of the Nazi Party Chancellery. Thus on December 16 of that same year, in compliance with this rejection of his idea, Himmler issued the order that "all Gypsies are to be deported to the Zigeunerlager at Auschwitz concentration camp, with no regard to their degree of racial impurity." This order may even have been the result of a direct decision from Hitler himself.[56] Nazi SS Officer Percy ("Perry") Broad, who worked in the political division at Auschwitz and participated directly in the murders of several thousand prisoners there, wrote that "it was the will of the all-powerful Reichsführer to have the Gypsies disappear from the face of the earth."[57] Richard Breitman reproduces the statement made by Streckenbach following a policy meeting with Hitler and Heydrich held in Pretsch in June 1940: "The Führer has ordered the liquidation of all Jews, gypsies and communist political functionaries in the entire area of the Soviet Union."[58] Even if Himmler's "Gypsy Zoo" had been a reality, it would only have involved the lives of several dozen individuals, fewer by several hundred percent than the six thousand Karait Jews who were able to argue successfully for their own lives to be spared.

9) Gypsies received kinder treatment because parents and children were allowed to stay together in special family camps, unlike other prisoners.

Lucette M. Lagnado and Sheila Cohn Dekel are among those who have referred to this: "The Gypsies were allowed to stay together, perhaps because they were faithful Christians. Despite their inferior racial stock, it was their one privilege . . . the Gypsies alone among the inmates had the comfort of being with their loved ones."[59] Their unqualified reference to Roma as constituting "inferior racial stock," their guess at their faithful Christianity, and their stunningly unfeeling description of the Gypsy camp in Auschwitz as resembling a "vast playground, an ongoing carnival" can only reflect the authors' stereotypes about Roma and Sinti, and it is abundantly obvious that neither one of them ever spoke to a Romani survivor or was there at the camp at Birkenau. Ulrich König makes it very clear that the "family camps" were not created out of any humanitarian motive or desire to bestow any "privilege" but rather because the Gypsies became completely unmanageable when separated from family members.[60] Michael Zimmermann also discusses this:

> The Nazi institutions involved with the persecution of the Gypsies knew about the particularly close family ties in this ethnic group. If these family ties were not taken into account, as happened in part with the deportation of 2,500 Sinti to Poland in 1940, there were certainly difficulties for the police, which were recorded negatively. To this extent, the RSHA [the *Reichssicherheitshauptamt*, or State Security Office] order of 29 January 1943 to deport the Sinti and Roma to Auschwitz "in families" reflected efforts to keep the friction and resultant bureaucratic problems associated with the deportation and internment as small as possible.[61]

First Lieutenant Walther of Infantry Regiment 734 and head of the execution squad wrote in his *Report on the Executions of the Jews and the Gypsies* that "the execution of the Jews is simpler than that of the Gypsies. One must admit that the Jews go to their deaths very composedly; they remain very calm. The Gypsies, however, wail and scream and move about incessantly as soon as they get to the place of execution." It was simply more expedient and caused the guards less problems to keep families together for processing. König writes of their sometimes having to smash the hands and feet of the Gypsies, who even used loaves of stale bread as weapons, in order to render them docile as they were being herded to the ovens. His book is a monument to Romani heroism and resistance in the camps and should be required reading for any student of the Porrajmos. Romani families were not kept together in every camp, incidentally (compare those shipped to Poland in 1940 referred to above by Zimmermann); this seems to have been a policy enacted at Auschwitz-Birkenau in particular. Jews transported to Auschwitz from Theresienstadt in September 1943, for example, were also allowed to remain together with their families.

> 10) "The denial of the right to live is what singles out the fate of the Jews from all other victims—Gypsies, Poles, Russian prisoners of war, Jehovah's Witnesses ... their fate was different from the fate of the Jews."[62]

Michael Berenbaum, in a better position than most to know the details of the Romani experience during the Holocaust, repeats these arguments in his book, where he says "Gypsies shared much, but not all of the horrors assigned to Jews. Romani were killed in some countries but not others. . . . Even though the Romani were subject to gassing and other forms of extermination, the number of Gypsies was not as vast. . . . In contrast, all Jews lived under an imminent . . . sentence of death."[63] Jews were killed in some countries but not others, too, and the number of Gypsies was "not as vast" because (according to the Nazis' own census conducted by Behrendt in 1939) there were nine times as many Jews as Gypsies to start with at the outbreak of World War II, so obviously the numbers were greater. Selma Steinmetz's argument that "numbers decide" would only be valid if the number of Jews and the number of Gypsies had been equal to begin with.[64] But when we discuss genocide we must do so in the context of the *destruction of entire peoples*, and, in terms of overall percentage, the losses of the Roma and Sinti almost certainly exceeded those of any other group; their *percentage* was "vaster." If there had been 17.4 million Gypsies in 1939 (the government's estimate of the number of Jews in that year), the Nazis would surely have murdered 6 million, too.

The question of the numbers of Roma and Sinti who were killed is a vexed one. Given the nature of their mode of life, no reliable estimate of the prewar European Romani population exists. Similarly, the circumstances of their dispatch at the hands of the Nazis make this a question that can never be fully answered. I dealt with this in some detail but rely on König's statement:

> The count of half a million Sinti and Roma murdered between 1939 and 1945 is too low to be tenable; for example in the Soviet Union many of the Romani dead were listed under non-specific labels such as Liquidierungsübrigen [remainder to be liquidated], "hangers-on" and "partisans." . . . The final number of the dead Sinti and Roma may never be determined. We do not know precisely how many were brought into the concentration camps; not every concentration camp produced statistical material; moreover, Sinti and Roma are often listed under the heading of "remainder to be liquidated," and do not appear in the statistics for Gypsies.[65]

In the eastern territories, Russia especially, Gypsy deaths were sometimes counted into the records under the heading of Jewish deaths. The *Memorial Book* for the Gypsies who perished in Auschwitz-Birkenau also discusses the means of killing Roma:

> Unlike the Jews, the overwhelming majority of whom were murdered in the gas chambers at Birkenau, Belzec, Treblinka and all the other mass extermination camps, the Gypsies outside the Reich were massacred at many places, sometimes only a few at a time, and sometimes by the hundreds. In the *Generalgouvernement* [the eastern territories] alone, 150 sites of Gypsy massacres are known. Research on the Jewish Holocaust can rely on comparison of pre- and post-war census data to help determine the numbers of victims in the countries concerned. However, this is not possible for the Gypsies, as it was only rarely that they were included in national census data. Therefore it is an impossible task to find the actual number of Gypsy victims in Poland, Yugoslavia, White Ruthenia and the Ukraine, *the lands that probably had the greatest numbers of victims.*[66]

This means that statements such as "somewhere between 20 and 50 percent of the entire population of European Gypsies was killed by the Nazis"[67] and the low figure of 250,000 Romani deaths displayed at the United States Holocaust Memorial Museum must be considered underestimations. Several published estimates[68] put the figure in excess of 1 million, and even thirty years ago Louis Pauwels and Jacques Bergier listed it at 750,000.[69] That perhaps an even higher number of Gypsies were murdered in the fields and forests where they lived than were murdered in the camps has been recognized for some time. The most recent reference to this appeared in the *Financial Times* (London) in an article by C. Tyler, who noted that "between 500,000 and 750,000 were killed in the German death camps during the war, and another million may have been shot outside."[70] New information is reaching us all the time that is pushing the death toll upwards. Dr. Paul Polansky of the Iowa-based Czech Historical Research Center recently published a report on his discovery of a hitherto unrecorded concentration camp at Lety in the Czech Republic, which was used for the disposal of Gypsies. Now used as a pig farm, Lety, as well as a chain of other camps, processed mainly Roma, killing them on the spot or sending them on to Auschwitz. Numbers from here, like those from the Gypsy camps in northern Italy, have not yet been figured into the estimate.[71] We should nevertheless rejoice in the numbers of those who lived and not glorify those of the dead in some horrible body count; but if we *are* obliged to argue with numbers and quantity in this peculiarly American way, then let us look at the situation from the other side and count the Romani *survivors* of the Holocaust, only 5,000 of whom are listed in the official register of the Zentralrat Deutscher Sinti und Roma in Heidelberg, only four of whom have been located in the United States, where over 80,000 Jewish survivors live today out of 350,000 still living worldwide. My respected colleague Donald Kenrick, coauthor of *The Destiny of Europe's Gypsies*, the first full-length treatment of the Porrajmos, has claimed with some gladness that his own research points to the *lowest* figures for Romani deaths by 1945; in his new book he estimates that they did not exceed 200,000.[72] Surely this is the kind of dialogue we should be striving for, not a competition over whose losses were greater.

11) The "uniqueness" of the Jewish case should be defended at all costs because it justifies the existence of the Jewish homeland, Israel.

On the main mall of the campus at the University of Texas at Austin, where I teach, there stands a structure some nine feet high, erected by the Jewish Students' Association as a monument to Israel. It is covered with photographs and newspaper articles, and in the very middle of it is a yellow placard bearing the words, "Israel: The Six Million: Never Forget." This is not a new argument; indeed it has been suggested to me by more than one well-disposed U.S. Holocaust Memorial Council member, and Zygmunt Bauman explicitly refers to the way in which "the Jewish state tries to employ the tragic memories as the certificate of its political legitimacy, a safe-conduct pass for its past and future policies, and above all, as the advance payment for the injustices it might itself commit."[73] But it is a specious argument. Israel, a Jewish state, should exist under any circumstances; speaking as a member of a people without a country, I can feel very deeply the emotion associated with the (non)possession of a homeland. To acknowledge that Gypsies received the same treatment as Jews, as Miriam Novitch says, "for the same reasons using the same methods" cannot take anything away from the enormity of the Jewish tragedy or diminish the strength of the right to Israel. I am reminded of Dermot Mulroney's words in *Where the Day Takes You*: "What's mine is mine, and if I share it with you, it becomes less mine!"[74] I cannot imagine that the rest of the world would interpret the Romani claim in this way or see it as a threat to the right to the existence of a Jewish state.

12) No other group was viewed with such disgust and contempt, so relentlessly and methodically persecuted, or selected for total eradication from the face of the earth.

Gypsies don't match this, I have been told, because Gypsies weren't mentioned in *Mein Kampf* or at the Wannsee Conference, because some Gypsies were exempt from the death machine, and because a much higher number of Jews had died by 1945.

Gypsies were not mentioned specifically in the documentation of the Wannsee Conference, because by that time (January 20, 1942) policies against Jews, subsequent to the December 24 directive issued four weeks earlier, automatically applied to the Gypsies. The Wannsee Conference in any case was not a policy or decision-making meeting, although it has acquired that interpretation; its purpose was rather to coordinate existing policies. And no argument was necessary in *Mein Kampf* because it was totally unnecessary on Hitler's part to make any case for anti-Gypsyism. There was simply no need to convince anybody of the subhuman status of Gypsies, against whom laws were already firmly entrenched in Germany, despite the guarantees of the constitution of the Weimar Republic. No public conscience ever provoked a defense of the Romani case, a fact Angus Fraser comments upon in his book *The Gypsies*: "From about 1937 onwards, [Nazi] pressures . . . on Gypsies built up swiftly and remorselessly, with no hostile public reaction, abroad or at home, of the kind which had made the Nazis a little more circumspect in their dealings with the Jews, at least in the early days, because of respect for world opinion."[75]

When the question of this indifference was raised following the war, one French physician commented, rhetorically, that "everyone despises Gypsies, so why exercise restraint? Who will avenge them? Who will bear witness?"[76] Nor can the excuse that the rest of the world was ignorant of what was happening be maintained in the Romani case:

> Whatever the real state of knowledge or ignorance among the German civilian population during the Second World War about the transport and the murder of millions of German and non-German Jews in Europe, the initial internment of the Roma was kept secret from no one. Concentration camps were built on the outskirts of the capital city, and the internment of the Sinti and Roma was not only covered by a number of Berlin newspapers, but was even joked about in their columns. Psychologists engaged in racial research paid official visits to Marzahn to study and take extensive film footage of the Romani children at play there. A major trainline ran right past that camp, and its few survivors recall that train passengers who pitied their situation, and who knew or suspected that the interned Roma were surviving on only minimal rations, occasionally threw packages of food down into the camp enclosure as their train passed by.[77]

German antisemitism, like anti-Gypsyism over the centuries, has bordered upon the pathological,[78] yet there was no one to argue in support of the Gypsies, unlike those who defended the Jewish position. As Burleigh and Wippermann make clear,[79] antisemitism was *not* an undisputed part of the early German racial hygiene movement. Alfred Ploetz and a number of other racial hygienists, such as Wilhelm Schallmayer, fiercely denounced antisemitism; indeed, in his 1895 treatise, Ploetz classified Jews as a part of the superior "white race."[80] On the contrary, in the early 1890s the Swabian Parliament organized a conference on the "Gypsy scum" (*Das Zigeunergeschmeiß*), and in 1899 Alfred Dillmann established the Gypsy Information Agency (*Nachrichtendienst in Bezug auf die Zigeuner*), which began to collect data in the form of genealogical information, fingerprints, and photographs of Gypsies throughout the territory. This led to the publication in 1905 of Dillmann's *Zigeuner-Buch*,[81] which laid the groundwork for what was to come a quarter-century later. It consisted of a lengthy argument for controlling Gypsies, stressing their inherent criminality and calling them "a plague against which society must unflaggingly defend itself." The bulk of the volume consisted of a register of over 5,000 individuals that gave date and place of birth, genealogy, criminal record if any, and so on. The third part of the book consisted of photographs of Gypsies taken from police files throughout the German states. On February 17, 1906, the Prussian minister of the interior issued a directive to "Combat the Gypsy Nuisance" (*Die Bekämpfung des Zigeunerunwesens*) and established bilateral, anti-Gypsy agreements with all neighboring countries. Licenses were required by all Romani people wanting to live and work in Prussia. In 1909 the Swiss Department of Justice began a national register of Gypsies, and in Hungary it was recommended at a "Gypsy Policy Conference" that all Romani people be branded on their bodies for easy identification. In 1912, France introduced the *Carnet Anthropométrique*, a document containing personal data (including photograph and fingerprints) that all Gypsies were henceforth required to carry.

"The first anti-Jewish law was promulgated in 1933,"[82] at a time when scores of anti-Gypsy laws had already been in effect in Germany for centuries. In 1920, the minister of public welfare in Düsseldorf forbade Gypsies from entering any public washing or recreational facilities, such as swimming pools, public baths, spas, or parks; this restriction also came to be applied to Jews after 1933.[83] More ominously, in that same year, Karl Binding and Alfred Hoche published their treatise[84] on "lives undeserving of life" (*Lebensunwertes Leben*), which argued for the killing of those who were seen to be "dead weight" (*Ballastexistenz*) within humanity, including Gypsies. This notion of "unworthy life" was incorporated into Nazi law on July 14, 1933, less than six months after Hitler came to power, in his "Law for the Prevention of Hereditarily Diseased Offspring." In 1934, Roma and Sinti were expelled from the trade unions. In June 1935, the main Nazi institution to deal with Gypsies, the Racial Hygiene and Criminal Biology and Research Unit, was first established, its express purpose being to determine whether Gypsies and blacks were human or subhuman, the groundwork on genetic evaluation that provided the model for the subsequent classification of Jews. Five months later, on November 26, the Ministry of the Interior, which partially funded the Research Unit, circulated an order forbidding marriages between Germans and "Gypsies, Negroes, and their bastard offspring." On September 15, 1935, the *Nürnberger Gesetze* (the "Nuremberg Law for the Protection of Blood and Honor") was passed, making marriage between "Aryan" and "non-Aryan" people illegal. It stated that "of the foreign blood common in Europe, there are only Jews and Gypsies." In 1936, in preparation for the Summer Olympic Games and for fear of negative world opinion, "anti-Semitic posters and placards were temporarily removed" from the streets of Berlin by the Nazis;[85] at the same time, Gypsies were being cleared from those streets as an eyesore, because visitors had to be "spared the sight of the 'Gypsy disgrace,'"[86] just as they were at the 1992 Summer Olympic Games in Barcelona. Just before the Berlin games, 600 Gypsies were forcibly detained in a cemetery and next to a sewage dump at Marzahn, which was "particularly offensive to a people hyper-sensitive about cleanliness";[87] in Spain fifty-six years later, they were placed in the Campo de la Bota outside of the city. More significantly, we have now learned that Nazi propaganda encouraging public support for the incarceration of Gypsies was widely distributed together with the program for those games in 1936. In 1938, more stringent criteria came to be applied to the definition of "Gypsy": If two of an individual's eight great-grandparents were even part Gypsy, that individual later was deemed to have too much "Gypsy blood" to be allowed to live—a criterion twice as strict as that defining who was Jewish. Indeed, if criteria for the latter had applied equally to Gypsies, some 18,000 (nine-tenths of the total Romani population of Germany at that time) would have escaped death.[88] One could argue, therefore, that Gypsies in fact were seen as posing twice the genetic threat to the *Herrenvolk* that Jews did.

According to eyewitness accounts, in January or February 1940, 250 Gypsy children from Brno in the concentration camp at Buchenwald were used as guinea pigs for testing the Zyklon B cyanide gas crystals, a lethal insecticide that from 1941 onward was used for the mass murders at Auschwitz-Birkenau. "At Buchenwald then, for the first time, this gas was used for mass murder, and it was for the murder of innocent Gypsy children."[89]

The night of November 9, 1938, is remembered in the annals of the Jewish Holocaust as *Kristallnacht*, or "The Night of Broken Glass," for it was on this night, in response to the murder of a German embassy official in Paris by a Jewish teenager, that over 1,000 synagogues were desecrated and nearly a hundred Jews were killed, with thousands more arrested. This blatant public display of hatred marked the beginning of the open and official sanctioning of the persecution of an "inferior race." In effect, it sent a message to the general public that such violence had full state approval. From this date onward, anti-Jewish hostility escalated steadily toward the Holocaust. But this was not the first massive anti-Jewish outbreak in twentieth-century Germany; in November 1923, a violent attack took place in Berlin against numbers of eastern European Jews who had come there to live.[90] For the Romani victims, there were also mass roundups and displays of military and police brutality, designed to show them—and the German public—exactly where they stood in the German hierarchy and how they could be treated by ordinary citizens with the approval and encouragement of the government. As early as 1927, between November 23 and November 26, armed raids were carried out in Gypsy communities throughout Prussia to enforce a decree issued on November 3 of that year, which required that all Gypsies be registered through documentation "in the same manner as individuals being sought by means of wanted posters, witnesses, photographs and fingerprints."[91] Even infants were fingerprinted, and those over six years of age were required to carry identity cards bearing fingerprints and photographs. Eight thousand Gypsies were processed as a result of that raid, more than a third of the entire Romani population in Germany. The second such action took place between September 18 and September 25, 1933, when the *Reichsministers* for the interior and for propaganda ordered the apprehension and arrest of Gypsies throughout Germany in accordance with "The Law Against Habitual Criminals." Many were sent to concentration camps as a result, where they were forced to do penal labor and where some underwent sterilization. The most significant military action, however, occurred during the summer of 1938, between June 12 and June 18, when *Zigeunerau-fräumungswoche,* or "Gypsy Clean-Up Week," was ordered. Hundreds of Gypsies throughout Germany and Austria were rounded up, beaten, and imprisoned. In Mannswörth, Austria, 300 were arrested in this way in a single night.

Following the collapse of the Third Reich, nothing was done to assist the Romani survivors, no effort made by the liberators to reorient them; instead, the terms of a 1926 pre-Nazi anti-Gypsy law still in effect ensured that those lacking a trade remained out of sight, hiding in the abandoned camps, for fear of arrest and incarceration. Since that time, all of the programs used by the Nazis to deal with Gypsies have been either suggested or implemented by various European nations—sterilizations in Slovakia, recommendations for incineration in a furnace from an Irish government official, forced incarceration and deportation in Germany.[92] Today, the Romani population faces its severest crisis since the Holocaust; neo-Nazi race crimes against Gypsies have seen rapes, beatings, and murders in Germany, Hungary, and Slovakia; anti-Gypsy pogroms in Romania and Bulgaria, including lynchings and home burnings, are increasing. For my people, the Holocaust is not yet over.

The United States Holocaust Memorial Museum has not yet done enough to educate the world about the Romani experience; there, the "Gypsy" artifacts on display in the "other victims" corner of the museum's third floor consist of a violin, a wagon, and a woman's dress—more Hollywood than Holocaust—and very, very few of the Romani victims and inmates depicted in the photo exhibits (especially those involving Josef Mengele's experiments with twins) are identified as such. Most galling of all was the total absence of the key words "Gypsy," "Rom," "Sinti," "Romani," "Zigeuner," and so on in the computerized question-and-answer bank provided for the public to consult. This led, in June 1993, to an organized protest at the museum by a group represented by Mary Thomas of Adoptive Parents and Friends of Romani Children demanding that more details of the fate of Roma and Sinti be included in the museum. They argued that when their newly acquired children grow older and begin to ask about their background and the history of their people, and about the Holocaust in particular, the United States Holocaust Memorial Museum would not be the place to go for their answers, that the Gypsy story had been downplayed to the extent of differently representing historical fact, of revision by omission. That protest led to the circulation of a petition asking, among other things, that more Romani scholars (rather than non-Gypsy specialists) be directly involved and that more documentation on the Romani holocaust be displayed and made available to visitors to the museum; this has resulted in the inclusion of one or two Gypsy entries in the computerized data bank.

I have been both praised and criticized for bringing attention to these issues. The director of one Holocaust center referred to me as a troublemaker; another writer on the Holocaust called my discussion of the Romani case in the Jewish context "loathsome." A representative of the U.S. Holocaust Memorial Council, whom I have never met, told a researcher who called to find out how to reach me that I was a "wild man." People have walked out when it was my turn to speak at conferences about the Porrajmos, and one former professor at the university where I teach adamantly refused even to *mention* Roma and Sinti in his regular course on the Holocaust. Others have intimated that I should not be pursuing this because I am not a historian and therefore not qualified to engage in this kind of research. If you think these things don't hurt me, they do, deeply. There are those reading this chapter who I'm sure are angered by what is being said in these pages, who are ready to challenge me. Why should this be? I have tried to remain objective and let the facts argue my case. If I can be proven wrong, I am happy to acknowledge that. I am well aware that for some people insistence upon getting all the facts of the Romani experience properly acknowledged has been regarded as confrontational and even threatening; Yehuda Bauer[93] felt that "anti-Gypsy sentiment" in Europe was, in his words, "in competition" with "radical anti-Semitism" there, the "sentiment" in question having led to the murders and pogroms against Gypsies mentioned above, during the same period for which the *1990 Country Report on Human Rights* reported "no incidents of anti-Semitic violence." At the same time, however, an August 1993 report issued by the Nemzetközi Cigány Szöveség quoted a physician from the Romanian town of Teleorman who said "our war against the Gypsies will start in the fall. Until then, preparations will be made to obtain arms; first we are going to acquire chemical sprays. We will not spare minors, either."[94] Events indicating that this persecution began to happen shortly thereafter were described in the December 19, 1993, issue of the *San Francisco Chronicle*, where the following appeared:

> An orgy of mob lynching and house-burning with police collaboration, has turned into something even more sinister for Romania's hated Gypsies: the beginnings of a nationwide campaign of terror launched by groups modeling themselves on the Ku Klux Klan. . . . "We are many, and very determined. We will skin the Gypsies soon. We will take their eyeballs out, smash their teeth, and cut off their noses. The first will be hanged."[95]

Anti-Gypsyism is at an all-time high, and it can only begin to be combated by sensitizing the general public to the details of Romani history and suffering. My purpose in this chapter, a follow-up to a paper given at the 1994 "Remembering for the Future" conference in Oxford, is to get these issues into the open, to air them publicly, in hopes that a more accurate, and more compassionate, attitude will prevail.

Resistance to the Gypsy case must be due at least in part to the lateness of its arrival on the academic scene; scholarship on the Porrajmos is comparatively new, so much so that it has brought charges of "bandwagoning" from some quarters. Our people are traditionally not disposed to keeping alive the terrible memories from our history—nostalgia is a luxury for others, and the Porrajmos was not the first but the second historical attempt to destroy the Roma as a people, following Charles VI's extermination order in 1721. Roma in the United States, for example, have obliterated entirely from their collective memories all recollection of the five and a half centuries of slavery in Romania, which their great-great-grandparents came to America to escape during the last century.[96] Survivors of the Holocaust are today likewise reluctant to speak about their experiences, and so it is that the story is only now beginning to unfold. The task of those collecting testimonies is made all the more difficult because, for some groups, the Sinti in particular, there are cultural restrictions upon speaking about the dead.

It has to be said too that there is an element of racism evident in the Jewish response; after all, Gypsies are a "Third World people of color," as Lopate coins the term in his discussion of the relative value of victimhood; Anton Fojn ("Bubili") wrote of the SS guards' whipping him and his father off the transport and through the gates of Dachau and calling them "Congo niggers" on account of their dark skin.[97] I have been told—off the record—that some U.S. Holocaust Memorial Council members do not want to be judged by the company they fear they might have to keep. In **every** single public opinion poll, including one conducted in the United States (**and** reported in the January 8, 1992, issue of the *New York Times*), Gypsies are listed as the most discriminated-against minority, the most despised ethnic population, and some of the stereotypes have evidently rubbed off on some councilmembers. At one presentation I gave at a Hillel center, I was interrupted by a woman who leapt to her feet and angrily demanded why I was even comparing the Gypsy case to the Jewish case when Jews had given so much to the world and Gypsies were merely parasites and thieves. On another occasion a gentleman in the audience stood up and declared that he would never buy a book on the Holocaust written by a Gypsy. I learned recently from James Michael Holmes of Phoenix Productions International that two Hollywood studios have already declined to consider an updated script of the 1947 film *Golden Earrings*, because it is a screenplay about the Holocaust that does not deal with Jewish victims.

Working to alter attitudes of this kind is a mighty task indeed and was one reason behind my cofounding the Romani-Jewish Alliance some years ago, which works to dispel anti-Jewish and anti-Romani stereotypes and to educate both populations about the other's experience. I should say here, incidentally, in answer to an often-asked question, that there are many Roma and Sinti who are Jewish and many more Romani-Jewish marriages. During the war, such "marriages" characterized one concentration camp in eastern Serbia in particular, where Gypsies and Jews were held before transportation. Even popular attempts to document our story can do more harm than good; an example is the film version of Alexander Ramati's *And the Violins Stopped Playing* (1988), which is so full of misrepresentation and distortions of the truth that it would have been better left undone (among other things it suggests that Gypsies were murdered in Auschwitz, for example, lest they survive as witnesses to the fate of the Jewish prisoners).

It might also be acknowledged that some resistance is grounded simply in disbelief, in the assumption that "if this is true, why haven't we heard about it before?" I must admit that for a very long time, as I searched the "shelves tightly packed," through the innumerable books on the Holocaust looking for references to Gypsies, I would skim right over sections dealing with the non-Romani victims; I am ashamed to say that they just were not as important to me, so consumed was I with my search. It was only later that I began to take the time to learn about what happened to other groups and to be appalled and aggrieved by what I read. When the existence of one's entire people is threatened so barbarously, anything else simply gets in the way. But others have come to do as I did and are examining the cases of those besides their own without prejudgment, and I am encouraged by the responses forthcoming from those who have made the effort, with an open mind, to examine the details of what Roma and Sinti suffered at the hands of the Nazis. I have said many times that only Jews can really come close to understanding the impact the Porrajmos has had on the Romani population, and I venture to think that only Gypsies can come close, on an emotional level, to understanding the Jewish tragedy. The Holocaust, sadly, just doesn't seem to mean as much for anyone else. But neither Jew nor Roma can *fully* understand the other's experience, then or now, nor should either begin to presume to interpret for the other. For this reason I would like to see the individual "uniquenesses," if you like, emphasized by a greater use of the ethnic terminology: *Shoah* or *Khurbn* for the Jewish Holocaust, *Porrajmos* for the Romani. The word "Holocaust," I feel, is used too casually to have the meaning intended for it.

I have been deliberately critical of the U.S. Holocaust Memorial Council and the museum in this chapter and make no apology for that, for our relationship over the past decade has been stormy and has caused me considerable personal frustration. It is, after all, the national memorial to the victims of Nazism and an international educational resource. Many factors, many personalities, have been involved in the misunderstandings and anger generated by the dialogue between Roma and the council. Speaking at the council's conference on non-Jewish victims in Washington, D.C., in 1987, Erika Thurner drew attention to the evident lack of concern for the Holocaust's Romani victims:

> Gypsies have generally been forgotten or been reserved for the footnotes of historical investigation. . . . This very position, as a fringe social group with negligible social status, is responsible for the fact that, after 1945, the Gypsy Holocaust was not acknowledged for so many years, and continues to be neglected to a certain degree to this very day. Ignorance as to the fate of the Sinti and Roma in the Third Reich has made historical reconstruction especially difficult. It has led to further discrimination against Gypsies, and to the *refusal* to recognize their right to restitution of both a material and ideal nature.[98]

In the years since Erika Thurner made those observations, there has been a steadily growing acknowledgment of the Romani tragedy and an acceptance of the fact that the Jews and the Gypsies were equally victim to the techniques and policies of the Nazi death machine. But along with this recognition at the academic and historical levels, so efforts to singularize the Jewish experience have gained, at least for some of its champions, an almost desperate impetus.[99] Perhaps we should be examining not what the challenges are to the procedural and historical details with which scholars attempt to make their case, but rather *why* it is so vitally important to some of them to privatize the Holocaust—why they strive so passionately to do so.

I am confident that open recognition of the Romani position will continue to grow. From having no representation at all on the council we now have one member; from having no Gypsy-related entries in the data bank we now have some. The council has gone so far as to protest formally against anti-Gypsyism at the administrative level.[100] My greatest hope is that we will eventually be moved out of the category of "other victims" and fully recognized as the only population, together with Jews, that was slated for eradication from the face of the earth. I want to be able to thumb through any of the many published treatments of the Holocaust at my local bookstore and find comprehensive information in them about what happened to my people—at present, we're usually not listed in indexes at all. My most recent purchase was Louis Snyder's *Encyclopedia of the Third Reich*; not only does it not contain one single reference to Gypsies, but neither does Robert Ritter nor Eva Justin nor Gerhard Stein nor Sophie Erhardt find a place in its list of entries. This is true also for the *Encyclopedia of the Second World War*,[101] *Who's Who in Nazi Germany*,[102] and *Who Was Who in World War II*,[103] as well as for most other books on the Holocaust. It is an eerie and disheartening feeling to pick up such books and find the attempted genocide of one's people written completely out of the historical record. Perhaps worse, in the English-language translation of at least one book, that by Lucjan Dobroszycki of *The Chronicle of the Lodz Ghetto*, the entire reference to the liquidation of the Gypsy camp there (entry number 22 for April 29 and 30, 1942, in the original work) has been deleted deliberately. I have been told, but have not yet verified, that translations of other works on the Holocaust have also had entries on Roma and Sinti removed. Furthermore, I do not want to read references to the United States Holocaust Memorial Museum in the national press and learn only that it is a monument to "the plight of European Jews," as the *New York Times* told its readers on December 23, 1993. I want to be able to watch epics such as *Schindler's List* and learn that Gypsies were a central part of the Holocaust, too; or other films, such as *Escape from Sobibór*, a Polish camp where, according to Kommandant Franz Stangl in his memoirs, thousands of Roma and Sinti were murdered, and not to hear the word "Gypsy" except once, and then only as the name of somebody's dog. This latter example is not merely offensive, it is cruel and callous. Camp survivor B. Stawska is one who has described the transportation of Sinti and Roma to Sobibor:

In November, 1942, the pogrom against the Jews and Gypsies began, and they were shot on a mass scale in street executions. The Gypsies were driven into the square at the fore of the crowd, and after them the Jews. It was cold, and the Gypsy women were weeping loudly. They had all their possessions on their backs, including eiderdowns; everything that they had, but all of that was taken away from them later. The Jews behaved very calmly, but the Gypsies cried a lot—you could hear one loud sobbing. They were taken to the station and loaded into goods wagons, which were sealed and taken to stations beyond Chełm, to Sobibór, where they were burnt in the ovens.[104]

National Public Radio (NPR) in Washington, D.C., covered extensively the fiftieth anniversary of the liberation of Auschwitz-Birkenau on January 26, 1995, but Gypsies were never once mentioned, despite being well represented at the commemoration. In his closing report on NPR's "Weekend Edition" on January 28, Michael Goldfarb described how "candles were placed along the tracks that delivered Jews and Poles to their death." But it is little wonder that Gypsies weren't mentioned; they were not allowed to participate in the candle ceremony. An article on the Auschwitz commemoration that appeared in the British press (though not in the U.S. press) dated January 28 included a photograph of a group of Roma staring mournfully through a wire fence, with a caption reading "Cold-shouldered: Gipsies, whose ancestors were among Auschwitz victims, are forced to watch the ceremony from outside the compound."[105] In a speech given at that ceremony, Elie Wiesel said that the Jewish people "were singled out for destruction during the Holocaust." The British Broadcasting Corporation's "World at War" segment entitled "Genocide" mentions the 1935 law forbidding Aryans from marrying Jews but fails to say that the very same law also referred to Gypsies; it mentions the Polish victims repeatedly but remains completely silent about Roma, against whom—unlike Poles—the Final Solution *did* operate. The first concentration camp inmates pictured in that documentary are Sinti prisoners at Buchenwald, but the viewer isn't told this. And in Germany, where it all began, Roma and Sinti have even yet to be included in the national Holocaust memorial, an omission that attracted the international media,[106] even though the chairman of the Jewish community in Berlin, Heinz Galinski, speaking at a ceremony commemorating the Romani victims of the Porrajmos fifteen years ago, acknowledged publicly that "Jews and Gypsies were both singled out as 'lives unworthy of life.'"[107] Surely genocide of the magnitude suffered by the Romani people deserves acknowledgment far beyond that which it now receives.

NOTES

1. This chapter is an expanded version of a paper first presented at "Remembering for the Future International Conference on the Holocaust," held at Berlin, Germany, March, 13–17, 1994.

2. *Congress Monthly*, May/June (1990), p. 13.

3. *New York Times Magazine*, September 20, 1983, p. 12.

4. Dora Yates, "Hitler and the Gypsies," *Commentary* 8 (1949):455, reprinted in *On Prejudice: A Global Perspective*, ed. Daniela Gioseffi (New York: Anchor Books 1993), pp. 103–110.

5. *Anon.*, "How the Gipsies Were Persecuted," *Wiener Library Bulletin* 4(3/4) (1950):18.

6. Earlier references to the situation of Roma and Sinti in Nazi Germany are Sultzberger (1939), Max (1946), Kochanowski (1946), and Maximoff (1946).

7. John Roth and Michael Berenbaum, eds., *Holocaust: Religious and Philosophical Implications* (New York: Paragon House, 1989), pp. 6–7.

8. Carrie Supple, *From Prejudice to Genocide: Learning About the Holocaust* (Stoke-on-Trent: Trentham Books, 1993).

9. Martin Gilbert, *The Holocaust: A History of the Jews of Europe During the Second World War* (New York: Henry Holt), 1985.

10. Michael Burleigh and Wolfgang Wippermann, *The Racial State: Germany, 1933–1945* (Cambridge: The University Press, 1991).

11. For example, see Annegret Ehmann, "A Short History of the Discrimination and Persecution of the European Gypsies and Their Fate Under Nazi Rule," Lecture, Institute of Contemporary Jewry, The Hebrew University, January 27, 1981; Sybil Milton, "The Context of the Holocaust," *German Studies Review* 13(2) (1990):269–283, "Gypsies and the Holocaust," *History Teacher* 24(4) (1991):375–417, "The Racial Context of the Holocaust," *Social Education* (February 1991):106–110, "Nazi Policies Towards Roma and Sinti, 1933–1945," *Journal of the Gypsy Lore Society* 2(1), 5th series (1992):1–18; "Antechamber to Birkenau: The *Zigeunerlager* after 1933," in *Die Normalität des Verbrechens*, ed. Helge Grabitz et al. (Berlin: Hentrich, 1994), pp. 241–259, and "Sinti und Roma als 'vergessene Opfergruppe' in der Gedenkstättenarbeit," in *Der Völkermord an den Sinti und Roma in der Gedenkstättenarbeit*, ed. Edgar Bamberger (Heidelberg: Dokumentations-und Kultur-zentrum Deutscher Sinti und Roma, 1994), pp. 53–62; Erika Thurner, "Nazi Policy Against the Gypsies," Paper delivered at the U.S. Holocaust Memorial Council Conference on Other Victims, Washington, D.C., March 1987; and David Young, *A Mulano Place: Paradox and Ambivalence in the Romani Holocaust*, B.A. (Hons.) Thesis, Macquarie University, Sydney, Australia, 1994.

12. Emil Fackenheim, *To Mend the World* (New York: Schocken Books, 1982), p. 12.

13. Charles S. Maier, *The Unmasterable Past: History, Holocaust, and German National Identity* (Cambridge: Harvard University Press, 1988), p. 82.

14. Richard Breitman, *The Architect of Genocide: Himmler and the Final Solution* (Hanover, N.H.: University Press of New England, 1991), p. 19.

15. See Steven Katz, "Quantity and Interpretation: Issues in the Comparative Analysis of the Holocaust," *Remembering for the Future: Jews and Christians During and After the Holocaust*, vol. 3 (Oxford: Pergamon, 1988), pp. 200–216.

16. Ibid., p. 216.

17. Israel Gutman, ed., *Encyclopedia of the Holocaust* (New York: Macmillan, 1990).

18. Steven Katz, *The Holocaust in Historical Context, Volume 1: The Holocaust and Mass Death Before the Modern Age* (Oxford: University Press, 1994); see also David Nemeth, "Contrasting Realities and the Gypsy Holocaust," *Newsletter of the Gypsy Lore Society* 17(3) (August 1994):3–4.

19. Michael Berenbaum, *The World Must Know: The History of the Holocaust as Told in the United States Holocaust Memorial Museum* (Boston: Little, Brown, 1993), p. 1; see also Michael Shermer, "Proving the Holocaust," *Skeptic* 2(4) (1994):32–57.

20. As quoted in Susan Brenna, "Housing the Memories of Genocide," *Newsday*, September 2, 1988, pp. 2–5.

21. Ian Hancock, "'Uniqueness' of the Victims: Gypsies, Jews, and the Holocaust," *Without Prejudice: International Review of Racial Discrimination* 1(2), 1988, pp. 45–67.

22. Phillip Lopate, "Resistance to the Holocaust," in *Testimony: Contemporary Writers Make the Holocaust Personal*, ed. David Rosenberg (New York: Random House, 1989), pp. 285–308.

23. Raul Hilberg, *The Destruction of the European Jews* (Chicago: Quadrangle Books, 1961).

24. Ronald Smelser, "The 'Final Solution' and the War in 1944," unpublished manuscript, University of Utah, Salt Lake City, 1991.

25. Berenbaum, *The World Must Know*, p. 2.

26. Ibid., at p. 51.

27. David M. Luebke, *The Nazi Persecution of Sinti and Ròma*, U.S. Holocaust Memorial Museum Research Brief, April 18, 1990, p. 3.

28. Breitman, *The Architect of Genocide*, p. 20.

29. Penelope Keable, *Creators, Creatures and Victim-Survivors*, doctoral diss., University of Sydney, Australia, 1995, p. 24.

30. See David Crowe and John Kolsti, eds., *The Gypsies of Eastern Europe* (Armonk, N.Y.: E. C. Sharpe, 1991), pp. 11–30.

31. State Museum of Auschwitz-Birkenau (for Documentary and Cultural Centre of German Sintis and Roma), *Memorial Book: The Gypsies at Auschwitz-Birkenau* (Munich: K. G. Saur, 1993), p. xiv (emphasis added).

32. Benno Müller-Hill, *Murderous Science: Elimination by Scientific Selection of Jews, Gypsies, and Others, 1933–1945* (Oxford: University Press, 1988), pp. 58–59.

33. Ibid.

34. Burleigh and Wippermann, *The Racial State*, pp. 121–125.

35. State Museum of Auschwitz-Birkenau, *Memorial Book*, p. 3.

36. Thurner, "Nazi Policy Against the Gypsies."

37. See Emil Fackenheim, *The Jewish Return into History* (Syracuse, N.Y.: University Press, 1978).

38. Kate DeSmet, "Comments Outrage Area Jews," *Detroit News*, December 31, 1990, p. B-3.

39. See, e.g., Vico and Keable.

40. Based on the author's personal correspondence with Yitzchak Mais, dated May 11, 1988.

41. Hilberg, *The Destruction of the European Jews*, pp. 142–144.

42. Based on the author's personal correspondence with Yitzchak Mais, dated May 11, 1988.

43. Donald Kenrick and Grattan Puxon, *The Destiny of Europe's Gypsies* (London: Sussex University Press, Chatto and Heinemann, 1972, new edition in preparation), p. 82.

44. Based on the author's personal correspondence with Yitzchak Mais, dated May 11, 1988.

45. Kenrick and Puxon, *The Destiny of Europe's Gypsies,* p. 78.

46. Yehuda Bauer, "Whose Holocaust?" *Midstream* (November 1980):42–46.

47. See, e.g., Hancock, *Chronology,* in Crowe and Kolsti, *The Gypsies of Eastern Europe.*

48. *Manchester Guardian,* January 9, 1956.

49. Lloyd Grove, "Lament of the Gypsies: 40 Years After Auschwitz, Petitioning for a Place," *Washington Post,* July 21, 1984, p. C4.

50. For example, see C. S. Coon, "Have the Jews a Racial Identity?" in *Jews in a Gentile World,* ed. I. Graeber and S. H. Britt (New York: Greenwood, 1942), pp. 20–37; R. Patai and J. Patai-Wing, *The Myth of the Jewish Race* (Detroit: Wayne State University Press, 1989); and William Petersen, "Jews as a Race," *Midstream* (February-March 1988):35–37.

51. J. D. Thomas et al., "Disease, Lifestyle, and Consanguinity in 58 American Gypsies," *Lancet* 8555 (August 15, 1977):377–379.

52. Based on the author's personal correspondence with Yitzchak Mais, dated May 11, 1988.

53. Bauer, "Whose Holocaust?"

54. Berenbaum, *The World Must Know,* p. 51.

55. Gabrielle Tyrnauer, *The Fate of Gypsies During the Holocaust,* Special Report prepared for the U.S. Holocaust Memorial Council, Washington, D.C., 1985, restricted access document, p. 24.

56. Sybil Milton, "Nazi Policies Towards Roma and Sinti."

57. Percy Broad, "KZ Auschwitz: Erinnerungen eines SS-Mannes," *Hefte von Auschwitz* 9 (1966):7–48.

58. Breitman, *The Architect of Genocide,* p. 164.

59. Lucette M. Lagnado and Sheila Cohn Dekel, *Children of the Flames: The Untold Story of the Twins of Auschwitz* (New York: William Morrow, 1991), p. 82.

60. Ulrich König, *Sinti und Roma unter dem Nationalsozialismus* (Bochum: Brockmeyer Verlag, 1989), pp. 129–133.

61. Michael Zimmermann, "From Discrimination to the 'Family Camp' at Auschwitz: National Socialist Persecution of the Gypsies," *Dachau Review* 2 (1990):87–113, quote at 107–108.

62. Yitzchak Mais, in the brochure published by the Museums at Yad Vashem.

63. Roth and Berenbaum, *Holocaust: Religious and Philosophical Implications,* p. 33.

64. See Selma Steinmetz, *Oesterreichs Zigeuner im NS-Staat,* Monographien zur Zeitgeschichte (Frankfurt: Europa Verlag, 1966).

65. König, *Sinti und Roma unter dem Nationalsozialismus,* pp. 87–89.

66. State Museum of Auschwitz-Birkenau, *Memorial Book,* p. 2 (emphasis added).

67. Berenbaum, *The World Must Know,* p. 129.

68. See references in Hancock, "'Uniqueness' of the Victims."

69. Louis Pauwels and Jacques Bergier, *Le Matin des Magiciens* (Paris: Gallimard, 1960), p. 430.

70. C. Tyler, "Gypsy President," *Financial Times,* March 26, 1994, pp. 3–4.

71. Susan Strandberg, "Researcher Claims Thousands of Gypsies Exterminated by Czechs," *Decorah Journal* (May 5, 1994):1–2.

72. Donald Kenrick, *Gypsies Under the Swastika* (Hatfield: Hertfordshire University Press, 1995).

73. Zygmunt Bauman, *Modernity and the Holocaust* (Cambridge: Polity Press, 1989).

74. Kurt Voss and Mark Rocco, *Where the Day Takes You.* Cinetel Films, Inc., 1992.

75. Angus Fraser, *The Gypsies* (Oxford: Blackwell, 1993), pp. 261–262.

76. Christian Bernadec, *L'Holocaust Oublié* (Paris: Editions France-Empire, 1979), p. 34.

77. Katie Trumpener, "The Time of the Gypsies: A 'People Without History' in the Narratives of the West," *Critical Enquiry* 18(4) (1992):843–884, quote at 844.

78. See especially Stephen Wilson, *Ideology and Experience: Anti-Semitism in France at the Time of the Dreyfuss Affair* (London: Fairleigh Dickinson University Press, 1982), ch. 13, "Racial Anti-Semitism: A Race Apart," pp. 456–495.

79. Burleigh and Wippermann, *The Racial State,* p. 36.

80. Robert Proctor, "From *Anthropologie* to *Rassenkunde* in German Anthropological Tradition." In George W. Stocking, ed., *Romantic Motives: Essays on Anthropological Sensibility* (Madison: University of Wisconsin Press, 1988): 138–179.

81. Alfred Dillmann, *Zigeuner-Buch* (Munich: Wilsche Verlag, 1905).

82. Burleigh and Wippermann, *The Racial State,* p. 4.

83. Ibid., p. 77.

84. Karl Binding and Alfred Hoche, *Die Freigabe der Vernichtung Lebensunwerten Lebens* (Leipzig: Felix Meiner, 1920).

85. Burleigh and Wippermann, *The Racial State,* p. 84.

86. Zimmermann, "From Discrimination to the 'Family Camp' at Auschwitz," p. 91.

87. Burleigh and Wippermann, *The Racial State,* p. 117.

88. Kenrick and Puxon, *The Destiny of Europe's Gypsies,* p. 68; see also Ehmann, "A Short History of the European Gypsies," p. 10.

89. F. Proester, *Nacistická okupace: Vraždeni čs. Cikánů v Buchenwaldu.* Report prepared for Miriam Novitch, Document No. ÚV ČSPB K-135 on deposit in the Archives of the Museum of the Fighters Against Nazism, Prague, 1968.

90. Detlev Peukert, *The Weimar Republic* (New York: Hill and Wang, 1987), p. 160.

91. Eva von Hase-Mihalik and Doris Kreuzkamp, *Du Kriegst Auch einen Schönen Wohnwagen: Zwangslager für Sinti und Roma Während des National-sozialismus in Frankfurt am Main* (Frankfurt: Brandes and Apsel, 1990), p. 140.

92. Stephen Kinzer, "Germany Cracks Down: Gypsies Come First," *New York Times,* September 27, 1992, p. 1.

93. See his "Continuing Ferment in Eastern Europe," *SICSA Report* 4(1/2) (1990):1, 4.

94. Sandor Balogh, "Following in the Footsteps of the Ku Klux Klan: Anti-Gypsy Organization in Romania," Nemzetközi Cigány Szövetség *Bulletin,* No. 5, New York, 1993.

95. Louise Branson, "Romanian Gypsies Being Terrorized," *San Francisco Chronicle,* December 19, 1993, pp. A1, A15.

96. See Ian H. Hancock, *The Pariah Syndrome: An Account of Gypsy Slavery and Persecution,* 2d ed. (Ann Arbor, Mich.: Karoma, 1988).

97. Lopate, "Resistance to the Holocaust," p. 292; Ina R. Friedman, *The Other Victims: First-person Stories of Non-Jews Persecuted by the Nazis* (Boston: Houghton Mifflin Co., 1990): 7–24.

98. Thurner, "Nazi Policy Against the Gypsies," p. 7.

99. For example, see Steven Katz, *The Holocaust in Historical Context, Volume 1.*

100. Harvey Meyerhoff, "Council Decries Germany's Treatment of Gypsies," *U.S. Holocaust Memorial Council Newsletter,* Winter Issue (1992–1993):8.

101. Elizabeth-Anne Wheal, Stephen Pope, and James Taylor, *Encyclopedia of the Second World War* (Secaucus, N.J.: Castle Books, 1989).

102. Robert Wistrich, *Who's Who in Nazi Germany* (New York: Bonanza, 1982).

103. John Keegan, ed., *Who Was Who in World War II* (New York: Thomas Crowell, 1978).

104. In Jerzy Fickowski, *The Gypsies in Poland* (Warsaw: Interpress, 1989), p. 43.

105. Margaret Stapinska, "Faceless, Stateless, Endless Victims," *Yorkshire Post*, January 28, 1995, p. 5.

106. *Anon.*, "Holocaust Memorial Omits Gypsies," *Atlanta Constitution*, July 15, 1992, p. A-5.

107. Heinz Galinski, "Dieses Gedenken sei uns Mahnung zum Handeln," *Sinti und Roma in Ehemaligen KZ Bergen-Belsen am 27 Oktober 1979* (Göttingen: Gesellschaft für Bedröhte Völker, 1980), pp. 76–81, 77.

❀ 6 ❀

The Atlantic Slave Trade and the Holocaust: A Comparative Analysis

SEYMOUR DRESCHER

The Comparative Impulse

*T*he vastness of some historical events and processes attracts scholars into postulates marked by singularity. Like the Holocaust, modern slavery intuitively appeals to the historical imagination as a candidate for uniqueness: "There was nothing quite like black slavery, in scale, importance or consequence," writes one of slavery's recent chroniclers.[1] Beyond slavery's challenge to scholarly understanding, recently, considerable popular pressure has generated a demand that greater attention be paid to the story of slaves and their descendants in the world at large. The enormous increase in scholarly discussion and in the public visibility of the Holocaust in the United States has contributed to corresponding reflections on the place of slavery in American and world history. In April 1995, a *New York Times* front-page story on the commemoration of slavery reported that "some scholars compare this widespread reflection to that of Jews who have vigilantly preserved memories of the Holocaust."[2] Because both phenomena are so intimately tied to stories of mass degradation, dispersion, and death, they elicit not only scholarly analysis but tempt philosophers, theologians, and politicians into competitions over comparative victimization.

In an early comparison, a historian of American slavery attempted to analogize the psychology of Nazi concentration camp inmates with the trauma of enslavement in order to explain what was considered to be the cultural annihilation and long-term infantilization of blacks in America. Subsequent research and discussion of this putative analogy indicated that the original comparison had been premised on deficient knowledge about both systems. Since the 1970s, the research on both subjects has, if anything, widened the distance between the Holocaust and New World slavery. A generation of slavery scholarship has increasingly demonstrated the ability of slaves not only to sustain themselves but to create systems of culture, family, community, enterprise, and consumption from the sixteenth to the nineteenth centuries.[3]

Histories of slavery in the Americas now routinely devote much of their pages to such themes as the development of religion, family life, women and children, leisure and the arts, independent economic activities, consumption patterns, and individual and collective forms of resistance. The whole scholarly enterprise now focuses on a system that endured and expanded for almost four centuries and produced an enormous variety of human interaction. Slaves created patterns of human relationships as complex as any to be found outside the distinctive economy of the Atlantic system. African Americans were part of a durable system in which the enslaved played key roles as actors in "an ever-widening social and economic space."[4]

By contrast, historians of the Holocaust must analyze human behavior, thought, and institutional development within a time-frame of years, not centuries. Analytical questions about intergenerational patterns of production and reproduction, modes of family- and community-building, and the evolution of economic activity over many generations are irrelevant. There were, of course, rapidly changing patterns of work, culture, and even artistic expression, but they unfolded in terms of months and years, not decades, generations, and centuries. Except for isolated individual fugitives hidden by gentiles and pockets of Jewish armed partisans, the Holocaust is a tale of rapidly *narrowing* economic and social space, physical concentration, immiseration, and annihilation.[5] A recognition of the divergence of the two "institutions" was quickly grasped in the wake of the initial comparison. It remains the starting point in any contrast of slavery in the Americas with the Holocaust in Europe.

If there is one aspect of African slavery that might be fruitfully linked to an analysis of the Holocaust, it is probably the process of initial enslavement. Coerced transfers of sub-Saharan Africans fed slave systems of the Mediterranean, Atlantic, and Indian Ocean basins for ten centuries. The largest component of this forced migration after 1500 was the transatlantic slave trade. During three and a half centuries, from the early 1500s to the 1860s, up to 12 million Africans were loaded and transported in dreadful conditions to the tropical and subtropical zones of the Americas. In the process, probably twice as many were seized in the African interior.

One historian has estimated that in the peak century and a half of the intercontinental forced migration from Africa (1700–1850), "twenty-one million persons were captured in Africa, seven million of whom were brought into domestic slavery [within Africa itself]." The human cost of sustaining the combined slave systems to the west, north, and east of sub-Saharan Africa between 1500 and 1900 was an estimated "four million people who lost their lives as a direct result of enslavement," plus others who died prematurely.[6] Of the nearly 12 million in the Atlantic slave trade, around 15 percent, or up to 2 million more, died on the Atlantic voyage—the dreaded "Middle Passage"—and the first year of "seasoning." In the Americas, the death rates dropped gradually to levels approximating those projected in Africa.[7] Averages offer only an inkling of the intensity of suffering in particular regions, communities, barracoons, and slave ships or in the diverse situations to which slaves were delivered in the Americas. In terms of conditions of life as well as of death, the long journey from the African interior was the peak period of pain, discomfort, psychological dislocation, and degradation in the Atlantic system. Within the parameters of the slave trade, comparisons with the Holocaust may, therefore, be more meaningful, even if the differences remain overwhelming.

Market Versus Nonmarket Forces

A fundamental comparison may begin with the terms given by those who organized the two systems. The Holocaust was envisioned as a "final solution" to a problem: Jews were beings whose very existence was a threat and whose physical disappearance was regarded as one of the highest priorities of the Nazi leadership. The success of the enterprise required rapid institutional innovation and was measured in a time frame calculated in months and years. The Atlantic slave trade developed incrementally with millennia of institutional precedents. The initial age of European transoceanic expansion from the fifteenth to the seventeenth centuries slowly added a new dimension to the expansion of African slavery. Europeans discovered by stages that they could best tap the mineral and agricultural potential of the Atlantic basin with massive rearrangements of labor. The rapid depletion of New World populations led to experiments in various forms of imported, coerced labor from both Europe and Africa. In large parts of the New World, as in Africa, slaves proved to be an economically optimal form of labor for slaveholders. The context of the development of the slave trade was, therefore, both long-term and incremental. For hundreds of years, the Americas presented enormous tracts of sparsely populated land and subsoil minerals suitable for profitable production and overseas export. During the same period, Europeans developed capital and communications networks capable of directing the transportation of American production to all parts of the Atlantic world. Simultaneously, Africans expanded and intensified their internal networks of enslavement, and Europeans tapped into those networks of enslavement for long-distance, coerced migration.[8]

Historians of slavery intensely dispute the slave trade's long-term effects on each region of the Atlantic system—whether and how much slavery stimulated or constrained development in Europe, the Americas, and Africa.[9] There is, however, a generally shared consensus about two points. First, there was no single collectivity, whether defined in political, geographical, religious, or racial terms, that dominated the entire trade complex at any point. Indeed, it is the fragmentation of power that assured the system was sustained as a competitive system. Second, whatever groups entered into and departed from this vast complex of human and material transfers, the central mechanism driving its general expansion for well over three centuries was the economic gain accruing to those who remained in it. Economic considerations and the attempt to bend economic outcomes to advantage by additions of political constraints define the terms in which participants entered or exited from the trade.[10]

Almost every scholarly work on the slave trade also acknowledges or infers the primacy of economics or political economy as the nexus of the flow of forced labor within the system.[11] Only the captives, transferred from owner to owner in a network of exchanges that often extended for months from the interior of Africa to the interior of the Americas, had no bargaining power in the stream of transfers. What drove the movement of human beings along the network was the value-added potential at the end of the process and the ability of individuals and states to tap into that delivery system. If the slave trade was what some historians have termed an "uncommon market," *uncommon* is clearly the modifier; *market* is the noun. What ensured that the trade continued was the dream of wealth flowing back into the system as returns on previous investments in human beings. And though the slave trade epitomized the reduction of human beings to the category of things, it was also the slaveholder's conception of the enslaved as potentially *valuable* things that sustained the system of exchange. From the perspective of all those involved in the traffic, the longer that all able-bodied slaves remained alive, the greater was their potential to add to the wealth, status, and power of the traders and slaveholders. The slaves' status as property and as productive instrument, analogous to "laboring cattle," ensured that their disablement or death registered as costs to their owners.[12]

The Holocaust of 1941–1945 developed in a different context and was driven by different motivations. It was confined to a single continent. It reached its greatest intensity in European areas and against populations that had been least directly involved in the Atlantic slave trade. Unlike the latter, it was dominated by one hegemonic political entity: the Nazi regime. It functioned most effectively, according to its own directors, where the Nazis had unimpeded institutional authority to implement their plans. Where Nazi political power was less direct and more limited, the system worked less effectively or thoroughly.[13] Rather than attempting to convert underpopulated or underexploited areas into optimal producers of wealth, the perpetrators conceived of the areas under their influence as already overrun with undesirable populations afflicted with human pollutants. Even before the decision for the Final Solution, the Nazis assigned a very high political priority to methods of quarantine and expulsion of Jews into zones far beyond Europe. Africans, Europeans, and Americans in the Atlantic slave trade measured their success in terms of the numbers of captives landed and sold alive. In the Nazi system, every Jew destroyed was a gain in "racial" security and a once-for-all economic gain in confiscated goods.[14]

The slave trade was an open-ended process. Its voluntary participants (the traders) wished to perpetuate it. As a forced migration, it devastated areas of Africa and changed the balance of population groups within the Americas. Regarding the impact on the population of Africa, a major historical debate revolves around the question of whether the population of western or west-central Africa would have been substantially larger in 1700 or 1850 in the absence of the transatlantic branch of the slave trade. However, it never so depleted western and west-central Africa as to threaten the Atlantic system.[15] By contrast, the Holocaust was directed against specific groups within Europe and had very specific effects on those groups. Millions of Jewish deaths were so concentrated in time and place that the impact of overall and short-term depletion of the target population was dramatic and definitive.

As a "way of death," the slave trade was kept in being by the maintenance of a continuous flow of living human bodies who were a means to the production of labor. The Holocaust was kept in motion by the production of dead human bodies. The two systems, therefore, reveal dramatically different tempos of mortality. Joseph Miller, a historian of the Angolan slave trade, has drawn a profile of "Annualized Mortality Rates Among Slaves from Capture Through Seasoning." He depicts a typical trade cycle extending over four years (fourteen months in transit and almost three years of seasoning in the New World).[16] For African slaves, the highest rate of loss would have occurred in the first fourteen weeks of captivity: on the journey through Africa, within the coastal holding quarters (the barracoons), and during the Atlantic Middle Passage. Ironically, one of Miller's four-year cycles is as long as the whole period of the Holocaust.

The mortality profile of the Holocaust victims is dissimilar from that of Angolan slaves. In some areas, whole communities were massacred on the spot. In the wake of the invasion of Russia in 1941, the *Einsatzgruppen*, or special killing squads, and their auxiliaries rounded up and slaughtered tens of thousands of Jews in open areas near their homes.[17] For one stage of the slave trade, Miller notes that annualizing the death rate in the slave barracoons "would produce a preposterous annual rate" of 1,440 per 1,000 per year. Raul Hilberg also notes the futility of offering annualized infant mortality rates of over 1,000 per 1,000 in the ghetto experience. At Auschwitz between July 1942 and March 1943, even among those Jews and non-Jews not immediately killed on arrival, the "annualized" death-rate was more than 2,400 per 1,000. It would be even more absurd to speak of the series of mass slaughters during the early months of the Nazi sweep through the various regions of the Soviet Union in terms of "annual" mortality.[18] What is clear is that in this opening phase of the Final Solution in the East, the primacy of on-the-spot maximum annihilation was manifest in the documentary reports making their way back up through the Nazi chain of command.

For the millions of Jews who resided elsewhere in Nazi-dominated Europe, the Holocaust proceeded rapidly, from late 1941 to early 1945, through stages of identification, concentration, and deportation.[19] Short of death for victims of the Atlantic slave trade, one peak of collective suffering came early in the process of enslavement: the trauma of uprooting, family disintegration, and physical restraint (shackling). A fresh set of afflictions accompanied the march to the sea, including attrition from epidemic disease, hunger, and thirst. In this African side of the process, large numbers of slaves were siphoned off into local populations. Others, however, were added to the enslaved caravans along the line of travel as criminal and "tribute" slaves. Captives were sometimes used as beasts of burden, carrying other commodities down to the coast, thereby offsetting some of the costs of transportation for their captors. At the coast there would be some respite from shortages of food and water experienced en route. However, the slave would have exchanged the conditions of forced marches in shackles for the dangers and discomfort of sedentary imprisonment. Concentrations of people from different disease environments increased the appalling toll of disease. The "slave pens" in Benguela, Angola, "were about 17 meters square with walls three meters or more in height." With "two square meters per individual," the barracoons contained 150 to 200 slaves, often enclosed together with pigs and goats.[20]

Few aspects of the trade expressed the valuelessness of dead slaves more clearly than the slave merchants' habit of dumping bodies of the dead in a heap in a small cemetery or depositing them in shallow graves in great numbers as food for scavenging birds and animals. On the western shore of the Atlantic in Rio de Janeiro, slave traders heaped up their decomposing losses in a mountain of earth awaiting weekly burials. On those occasions when slaves died too quickly for burial, the decomposing corpses were partially burned, giving off a terrible odor.[21]

Transit

For those captives not retained in Africa who survived the barracoons, the most distinctive part of the Atlantic slave trade was the transoceanic journey. The Middle Passage was a voyage lasting from weeks to months in an environment that none of the enslaved had ever experienced in their lives. In the Holocaust, there is no precise counterpart to the Middle Passage. For European Jews, a completed *seaborne* voyage actually represented redemption. During the Nazi period, one transatlantic voyage of Jews illustrates the contrasting contexts of the two systems. In the famous case of the aborted journey of the *Saint Louis* to Cuba and the United States in 1939, passengers' forced return to the Old World meant captivity and destruction.

For enslaved Africans, the boarding process often signaled their transfer to the authority of Europeans. The state, the church, and the owners might affix their own seals of ownership upon each boarding victim through the repeated application of hot irons to their bodies. Europeans branded slaves as marks of ownership exactly as they branded their cattle or horses or as goods clearing customs. In addition to the marks of capitalist ownership, some states might add their separate brand of royal arms, denoting vassalage to the crown. Representatives of the Church could add a cross branding to the royal arms as a mark of baptism. Under certain jurisdictions, the branding process might continue in the Americas where slaveowners affixed their own signs and renamed their new human properties or designated them as runaways.[22]

For deported Jews, the passage to the death camps in boxcars was also like nothing they had ever experienced before. Lack of food, water, heat, or sufficient air circulation created a human environment rife with futile disputes—by "curses, kicks and blows . . . a human mass extended across the floor, confused and continuous, sluggish and aching, rising here and there in sudden convulsions and immediately collapsing again in exhaustion." The journey of two or three days ended when the crash of opening doors and barked orders forced the passengers out onto platforms.[23] The closest analogue to the branding of Africans was the tattooing of inmates at Auschwitz after selection. They were not renamed but numbered, signifying their transition to the condition of anonymous state property. Only by showing one's "baptism" (number) could an inmate get his or her daily ration of soup.[24]

For Africans, the ordeal of oceanic transit could last from weeks to months. Many of the Africans were sick, and all must have been terrified boarding an object that they had never seen, heaving upon a medium they had never experienced. The passengers were arranged in tightly packed horizontal rows lying shoulder-to-shoulder along the length of the ship and were even curled around the mast. The males were linked together in irons, making it difficult for them to "turn or move, to attempt to rise or lie down," without injuring each other. The collisions and curses that accompanied the crowding were further intensified by fights at feeding times and during attempts to relieve themselves. Overflowing lavatory buckets and the effluvium of digestive tract diseases added to the discomfort of stifling air. From the beginning of the voyage, the holds were covered with blood and mucus and were so hot that the surgeons could visit the slaves only for short periods at a time. To the many incubating intestinal diseases that the slaves had brought on board with them were added the nausea of seasickness.[25] Accounts of the pervasive sensory impact of excrement on the slave ships correspond to Holocaust reports of the wall of feces three feet high in one ghetto lavatory and a concentration camp latrine at Auschwitz where a system with a capacity for 150 was used each morning by 7,000 people. With many inmates stricken with diarrhea and dysentery and with no more than ten minutes allowed for bodily functions, people were knee-deep in excrement.[26]

Cruelty and arbitrary abuse added to the toll of hunger, thirst, and disease in both systems, but most slaves who died of hunger and thirst did so as the consequence of unanticipated long voyages. The railroads to Auschwitz moved relatively close to a schedule, the precision of which was the pride of the German railway bureaucracy. Trains rolled when they had been cleared for through passage to their destination. What one historian calls the "floating tombs" of the African trade had their literal equivalents during the Holocaust. Trucks in transit to death camps sometimes served as gas chambers.[27]

Crews of African ships were at much greater risk than were the Nazi guards and their auxiliaries. Slave crews faced considerable danger from tropical disease, hunger, and thirst. They had no recourse to reinforcements in the event of a slave uprising when slaves were released from their hold below deck for daily exercise. Above all, ship's captains in the slave trade had a stake in the survival of their human cargo. Every sale at the end of the voyage meant revenue for the state and profits for the traders. Every dead body meant some loss on invested capital.

Nothing better illustrates the legal difference between the two systems than one of the most bizarre slave trade cases ever heard in an English Court—the *Zong* case, argued in Britain in 1783. The slave ship *Zong* had sailed from Africa to the Caribbean in 1781 loaded with 470 slaves bound for Jamaica. After twelve weeks under sail, it had already lost over sixty Africans and seventeen crew members. In order to preserve the rapidly dwindling water reserves, save the remaining "cargo," and allow the investors to claim a loss under their insurance policy, the captain threw 131 of the sickest slaves to their deaths. (Unlike losses due to capture or insurrection, losses of slaves due to death by suicide or sickness were routinely uninsurable.) Designated victims were selected in daily batches by the *Zong*'s crew. They were pushed overboard in sight of the remaining slaves. Consequently, ten more slaves, witnessing the selections, threw themselves overboard.

The underwriters refused to pay for those cast into the sea. A civil suit was brought by the investors. The case was argued in the court of Lord Chief Justice Mansfield, famous for having declared in 1772 that colonial slave law did not apply within England. Counsel for the slavers logically brushed aside the whole question of murder, on the ground that in terms of the suit the *Zong* slaves were goods and property. The only question before the court was whether some property had been rationally jettisoned at sea in order to preserve the rest. Mansfield agreed: "Though it shocks one very much . . . the case of the slaves was the same as if horses or cattle had been thrown overboard."[28]

Nothing like the *Zong* case came before a German court over the disposal of captive Jews—nor could it in Nazi "actions" or shipments. No one who engaged in either the authorized killing of or who *refused* to kill Jews was the object of legal action. There was no property over which such a case could have arisen— no acknowledgment of the monetary value of persons, no contract for the sale of persons, no description of the sex and age of the deceased at the point of loading, no lawful insurance upon the human cargo, and no inquest into reasons for the deaths of any or all of a transported group. The passengers' fares were payable to the railway system whether or not they arrived alive (one-way for Jews, round-trip for their guards). The fares were paid for by funds previously confiscated from the victims themselves. No suits were filed for uncompleted journeys due to death en route. There was literally no "interest" in the survival of the passengers en route.

Both captive Africans and Jews were designated as "pieces," but Africans were more highly differentiated goods because an African's status was derived from the exchange value of an adult male for a piece of imported textile. A set of categories designated slaves who were less than full "pieces," in order to indicate their lower exchange value, ranged according to age, health, and strength. The "use-value" of the ideal African piece was clear. By contrast, all Jews who were not deemed of "full" immediate labor value were immediately sent to the furnace. Their only use-value was that of certain "pieces" of their bodies.[29]

Divergence

At journey's end, the fate of the captives diverged. In the transatlantic slave trade, landfall marked the end of the seaborne horrors. Slaves very often arrived disabled, covered with sores, and suffering from fevers, but the sight of land and the removal of shackles excited a transient feeling of joy. The captives were offered fresh food. They were bathed, "bodies cleansed and oiled," and given gifts of tobacco and pipes. In some ports, a priest might come aboard to reassure the terrified passengers that they had not been transported in order to be eaten on disembarkation. The next stage of the process involved further psychological humiliation. Captives had to endure long and repeated physical inspections by prospective buyers. Slaves were offered for sale almost naked to prevent deception. The healthiest and strongest went first. The remaining ("refuse") slaves were sometimes taken on to other ports or sent onshore to taverns and public auctions. Further separations from relatives or shipboard companions at this point added to the trauma of sale. If slaves survived this series of traumas, they might enter a period of relative recovery ("seasoning"), along with the imposition of a new name, instruction in a new language, and coercion in a new work discipline.[30]

For Jews in transit, the moment of arrival marked not a lessening but the most dangerous, single moment of their collective suffering. As they arrived, they were unloaded onto a vast platform. Compared to the purchase of African slaves, the railside inspection of Jews was extraordinarily casual. SS men or other agents of the state moved quickly through the silent crowd interrogating only a few: "How old? Healthy or ill?" Mothers who did not wish to be separated from children were told to remain with their children. The SS decided, often in a fraction of a second, between life and death. In a few minutes from the opening of a railway car, the overwhelming majority were on their way to the gas chamber. A mentality of superfluity enveloped the whole process. Only in this context can one fully appreciate Primo Levi's opening phrase in *Survival at Auschwitz*: "It was my good fortune to be deported to Auschwitz only in 1944, that is, after the German

Government had decided, owing to the growing scarcity of labor, to lengthen the average life span of the prisoners destined for elimination."[31]

The slave trade was always predicated on the value of the captives as potential laborers. Well before the decision for the "Final Solution" to the "Jewish question" by mass murder in 1941, the Nazi regime had also realized the potential utility of coerced Jewish labor following the captives' pauperization. In Germany, a series of decrees between 1938 and 1941 mobilized all able-bodied Jewish labor within the Reich and occupied Poland, sustained at a standard of remuneration and nutrition far below that of the non-Jewish populations around them. On the eve of the invasion of Russia, more than 100,000 had been conscripted in Germany alone.[32] In the occupied Polish territories between 1939 and 1941, a running debate ensued between attritionists (favoring accelerated starvation) and utilitarians (favoring temporary use of Jewish labor for producing at least the equivalent of their temporary upkeep). The debate revolved around local policy options while awaiting decisions from above about the disposition of the Jewish population. Some ghettos briefly succeeded in achieving the status of short-term economic (not long-term demographic) viability. By the end of 1941, a portion of ghettoized adult able-bodied Jews was contributing to the Nazi economy and war production at minimal survival levels. Had the Nazis decided in favor of exploitation rather than liquidation of the Warsaw ghetto in the summer of 1942 and had the harsh living conditions and the high death rate remained at levels of the first half of that year (i.e., over 1,000 percent of the prewar monthly rate), "it would have taken eight years for all of Warsaw's Jews to die out."[33]

The German invasion of Russia was accompanied not only by a moving frontier of massacre to its east but by the creation of death camps. The decision for mass annihilation in the already conquered territories was taken at a moment when the Nazis looked forward to total victory in the East. In such a context, the Slavic populations under Nazi control were also perceived to be superfluous— one more obstacle to the movement of an Aryanized frontier to the east. Enormous numbers of Russian prisoners of war were allowed to starve to death during this early period of the Holocaust. The Nazis, therefore, anticipated no major economic impediments to their twin ideal of general racial reorganization and accelerated Jewish annihilation. By stressing the parasitic concept in relation to both economic and racial development, the Nazis could also formulate the annihilation of Jews in terms of accelerated economic modernization. In addition to its public health dimension, the Final Solution would eliminate petty bourgeois impediments to the growth of large-scale industrial organization. This "imagined economy" of some Nazi bureaucrats drew on both capitalist and Communist visions of the industrial future.[34]

The division of "visions of labor" between slave traders and Nazi officials illustrates another divergence between the Holocaust and the transatlantic slave trade. Jews were of demographically negative value to the Nazi New Order. To the sponsors of the slave trade, Africans were indispensable, or at least optimal, to economic and imperial development. The failure of slaves to achieve a positive reproduction rate in the tropical Americas (thereby requiring continuous infusions of Africans for sustained economic growth) was perceived as a shortcoming, not a virtue, of the Atlantic system.

Labor

In policy terms, these divergences between the two systems are even more marked for the period of the Holocaust after the stalling of the German blitzkrieg against the Soviet Union. By the end of 1941, the conflict had settled into an extended struggle. German economic mobilization for war was intensified. As more Germans were required for military service, massive inputs of new labor were needed to fuel the German war machine. At that critical moment, the Nazis finalized the Final Solution into a rational bureaucratic annihilation. German industrialists began scrambling for alternative sources of labor, including the remnants of the Russian prisoners of war. The moment that killing operations against the Jews accelerated, the economic pressure increased. Thus, by 1944 there were more than 7.5 million coerced laborers in the heart of Europe, compared with less than 6 million African slaves in the Americas in 1860 after more than three centuries of the Atlantic slave trade.[35]

However, the rising number of Germany's slave laborers failed to boost productivity. The disciplinary habits and indifference to human suffering, developed during the era of superfluity, hindered the introduction of rationalized allocation or management of labor and precluded the development of incentives among prisoners. "Until the very end the Nazis pursued the policy of maximum results with minimum investments." The system was most effective not in raising productivity but "in squaring the economic postulates of German industrial circles with the plans to exterminate the Jews and certain categories of slaves, which had been outlined in the first years of the war by Nazi leaders and put into practice by the SS."[36] Primo Levi's opening phrase about his own "good fortune" in arriving at Auschwitz in May 1944 was, therefore, also an obituary on the fate of his fellow Jews. When Levi was arrested, the overwhelming majority of Jews in Nazi-controlled Europe had already been murdered.

The labor shortage caused a small slowdown in the killing process. For three years, individual Jews engaged in desperate attempts to ensure themselves against deportation to the death camps by retaining their status as slaves. Even small children grasped the significance of labor qualification as a final, frail barrier between death and brief survival. "How deeply this labor-sustained psychology had penetrated into the Jewish community is illustrated by a small incident observed by a Pole. In 1943 when an SS officer (Sturmbannführer Reinecke) seized a three-year-old Jewish girl in order to deport her to a killing center, she pleaded for her life by showing him her hands and explaining that she could work. In vain."[37]

The comparative figures on enslavement and annihilation between 1941 and 1945 show that the ideology of Jewish elimination took precedence over the ideology of production in Nazi policy. Time and again Jews were deported before requested replacements arrived. At the highest political levels, economic reasoning was treated with condescension or contempt. Even when grudging concessions were made to urgent requests for the temporary retention of Jewish slave labor, it was understood that "corresponding to the wish of the *Führer* the Jews are to disappear one day."[38] Hitler personally overruled a request by the bureaucrat responsible for labor supply to postpone the removal of Jews from German soil in vital armaments factories. Josef Goebbels rejoiced that the arguments of "economic experts and industrialists, to the effect that they cannot do without so-called Jewish precision work, do not impress him [Hitler]."[39]

In Nazi Europe, it was usually capitalists and bureaucrats in direct control of Jews who tried to rationalize labor mobilization on the road to elimination. This underlines the difference between the two historical processes that we emphasized at the outset. In the Atlantic system, political rulers—both African and European—tapped into and tried to manipulate a competitive market that they could never hope to fully master. They failed in their attempts to control the flow of slaves to or at the coast or to monopolize the seaborne transit of slaves. If they succeeded temporarily, the effect was either to stifle the slave trade to their own zones of power, to draw new competitors into the trade, or to stimulate the formation of new networks of trade and production.[40] In the Holocaust, the power relationship between state and capitalists was reversed. It was the political leadership that literally controlled the switches governing the flow of captive populations into war industry or death factories.

Europeans in both systems converged in acquiring adult males as slaves. This group was heavily overrepresented among those boarded on the African coast. It also was overrepresented among those selected for survival at Auschwitz and elsewhere. (One must note, however, that adult males were the *first* group targeted for mass killing by the Nazi *Einsatzgruppen* in the East during the summer of "superfluity" in 1941.)[41] The Nazis, however, chose their labor force from a full demographic range of human beings. Mothers, children, and the aged were transported in the same shipments as young males and were usually designated for death on arrival. In the slave trade, African captors and traders substantially altered the sex and age distribution of captives offered for sale to European traders. Among Africans, captive women and children had considerable value.[42] Women and children in the slave trade who died from hunger, nutritional deficiencies, thirst, exposure, and disease perished for reasons beyond the determination of their captors. Under the Nazis, Jewish children who died in large numbers for these same reasons perished because of Nazi decisions to withhold food and medicine available to the surrounding population.

If one turns from victims to perpetrators, one professional group appears to have played a significant role in both processes. Doctors in the British slave trade were rewarded for saving lives en route to the Americas. A recent economic historian specializing in the medical history of the slave trade has concluded that doctors, for all of their limitations, succeeded in reducing mortality on the slave ships. Moreover, in the end, the greatest contribution to Africans by some "Guinea surgeons" in the Atlantic system was their testimony about conditions aboard slave ships. Physicians enjoyed quite a different role in the Holocaust. In Auschwitz, conclude two historians, doctors presided over the killing of most of the 1 million victims of that camp. They chose between labor and death, decided when the gassed victims were dead, rationalized the selection and cremation process, and lent the prestige of their profession to the whole operation, converting mass murder into a medical procedure. Nazi doctors rationalized the public health ideology of annihilation. They spent more time and care in examining some of the dead than most of the living. They conducted ferocious experiments on the bodies of the living. Jews who never saw a Nazi doctor during the years of the Holocaust stood a far better chance of survival than those who did.[43]

Racism

Justification for the two systems also overlapped. "Race" was used as a rationale for sustaining both processes. "No other slave system," writes one recent historian of British slavery, "was so regulated and determined by the question of race."[44] Historians of slavery might make an equally strong claim about the rationale for collecting vast numbers of coerced laborers at work sites throughout Nazi-dominated Europe. Jews, Gypsies, and Slavs were not only ranked in racial "value" but their bodies were at the disposal of the state for experiments, as well as for labor brigades and brothels.

Ironically, race may have played a limited role as a justifying concept in the launching and early expansion of the Atlantic slave trade. This finding has generated a long and inclusive debate on the role of antiblack racism as a cause or consequence of the enslavement of Africans.[45] Slavery was hardly synonymous with Africans nor were Africans with slaves when the Portuguese first began to purchase Africans in the mid-fifteenth century. Africans did not regard themselves as a unitary "race," and Europeans continued to enslave people from other portions of the world well into the age of exploration. From their earliest transoceanic voyages down to the eighteenth century, various European groups continued to enslave people in the Mediterranean, Africa, the sub-Sahara, America, and Asia. At the beginning of the Atlantic slave trade, only peoples of European descent were considered nonenslavable in the full sense of becoming inheritable reproductive property. Many non-European groups were only gradually exempted from enslavement by Europeans. By 1750, sub-Saharan Africans and their descendants constituted the overwhelming majority of slaves in the Americas and the exclusive source of slaves for the transatlantic trade. As the African slave trade persisted, the racial link embedded itself ever more deeply in the ideological fabric of European consciousness, especially in the Americas. In the process of dehumanization, European holders of African slaves intrinsically linked them to domestic animals or pets. Inventories consistently listed the value of slaves first and that of livestock second. Unlike Jewish captives, however, Africans "were not generally likened to predators, or to vermin," or to invisible carriers of disease.[46]

At no time, moreover, was the linkage between Africans and slaves fully congruent. European states and slave traders were fully aware that their slave-trading partners in Africa (princes, warriors, and merchants) possessed some of the same distinctive physical features as the enslaved. Treaties were signed and contracts were made by Europeans with Africans. Europeans paid tribute and customs to Africans. Military, economic, and marital alliances were formed with Africans. Africans were educated in European schools. Legal and administrative precautions were taken against wrongful seizures or enslavements of Africans. General characterizations of Africans as being more uncivilized or barbarous than Europeans, therefore, did not preclude an enormous range of political, economic, family, and cultural exchanges with Africans as equals in those relationships.[47]

Whatever the constraints against enslaving non-Africans, the identification of slavery with Africans in the Americas was a residual result of centuries of experimentation with various African and non-African groups, not the outcome of an imagined racial selection before the beginning of the Atlantic slave trade. Considerations of race came to define the outer limits of enslavability, not the designated status of Africans as slaves. The color-coded racial hierarchy was designed by Europeans to stabilize an asymmetrical distribution of transatlantic power over the long term. Given the indispensability of the slaves, renegotiations of master-slave relationships began almost from the moment slaves arrived in the New World. If racism undergirded the African slave trade, it was an effect rather than a cause of that system.[48]

Ironically, the closest analogue in European culture to a "racially" defined fear of contamination during the early period of the transatlantic slave trade was the Iberian obsession with "purity of blood." For two centuries after 1500, Spanish and Portuguese authorities conducted ongoing hunts for "Judaizing" descendants of Jews converted to Christianity. Such *conversos* or "New Christians" were indefinitely branded by their ancestral link to the Jewish tradition. In the Iberian settler societies, racial legislation was primarily concerned with the regulation of nonslave groups, including New Christians, Indians, and free people of "mixed" race. For slaves, legal codes inherited from *pre-Atlantic* Roman law constituted the primary juridical nexus for grounding master-slave, free-slave, and slave-slave relationships.[49]

Racism fulfilled a different systemic function during the Holocaust. The difference was not that Jews were defined primarily by the religious affiliation of their grandparents rather than by ancestral geographic origin or by color. For the Nazis, a racial revolution was needed to unravel past legal and social integration. Racial legislation also prescribed a new system of individual classification in order to unravel the results of religious intermarriage. The regime intended that one precisely designated group would, one way or another, disappear. Nazi racial policy was, in this sense, committed to *a* final solution—a policy of "disappearance"—long before the particular physical implementation that began in 1941.[50] Thus, if European statesmen and merchants measured success in the slave trade in terms of ships and colonies increasingly filled with aliens, success for National Socialists was measured in terms of body counts and empty horizons. Rudolf Höss, the commandant of Auschwitz, not only arranged to return to his killing center in 1944 so that he could personally oversee the destruction of Hungarian Jewry but claimed credit for annihilating 2.5 million, rather than the 1.25 million, people actually murdered there.[51]

The slave trade and the Holocaust are characterized by another striking difference. For the first three centuries of the transatlantic slave trade, only isolated voices—no government—attempted to prohibit slaving by its own citizens. There was no need for concealment and no international declaration against the Atlantic slave trade until more than three centuries into the duration of the system. Every European state with ports on the Atlantic participated in the trade at one time or another. Participants in the Atlantic system operated within the comforting context of doing or seeing ordinary and customary things, even at times when they expressed personal revulsion or reservation about some particularly brutal action within that system.

The Holocaust differed from the slave trade in that it was not described by its perpetrators as conforming to some ancient and universal practice. The Nazis were cognizant that they were radical innovators and directors of an operation that they themselves had begun and that they alone were capable of seeing through to completion. Their commitment was crucial to the process. Indeed, they knew that they had bet their lives on a project that would be considered a war crime were they to be defeated.

Conclusion

This brief overview emphasizes the difficulty of comparing two events so disparate in space, time, intention, duration, and outcome. Yet the urge to find analogues to one's suffering is unquenchably human. What could be more encouraging than to see the recent surge of historical interest in the Holocaust as a model for calling attention to other human catastrophes? The African slave trade had, in its turn, served Jews as a means of making sense of catastrophic oppression, for apprehending the disorienting cruelty of the world. It was reflexive for Anne Frank to draw upon Europe's dark chapter in Africa in order to come to terms with her own terrifying present: "Every night people are being picked up without warning and that is awful particularly for old and sick people, they treat them just like slaves in the olden days. The poor old people are taken outside at night and then they have to walk . . . in a whole procession with children and everything. . . . They are sent to Ferdinand Bolstraat and from there back again and that's how they plague these poor people. Also they throw water over them if they scream." Beyond the evocation of comprehensible and distant past horrors lay only fragments of other incomprehensible and distant present horrors: "If it is as bad as this in Holland whatever will it be like in the distant and barbarous regions they are sent to? We assume most of them are murdered. The English radio speaks of their being gassed perhaps the quickest way to die."[52]

Anne Frank's successive entries should serve as a caution to scholars. In comparing historical catastrophes, there is a temptation to argue as though one could arrive at a hierarchy of suffering or cruelty or radical evil such that only one such process reaches the apogee of uniqueness. Systems of human action are like Tolstoy's happy and unhappy marriages, all alike in some ways but each different in its own.

NOTES

I wish to thank Stanley L. Engerman, George Mosse, and Alexander Orbach for their helpful comments.

1. James Walvin, *Black Ivory: A History of British Slavery* (Washington, D.C.: Howard University Press, 1994), p. ix. For a parallel and much more ambitious claim for the Holocaust, see Steven T. Katz, *The Holocaust in Historical Context*, 3 vols. (New York: Oxford University Press), vol. 1, p. 1.

2. *New York Times*, April 2, 1995, p. 1.

3. See Stanley Elkins, *Slavery: A Problem in American Institutional and Intellectual Life* (Chicago: University of Chicago Press, 1959), pp. 104–115; Earle E. Thorpe, "Chattel Slavery and Concentration Camps," *Negro History Bulletin* (May 1962):171–176; republished in *The Debate over Slavery: Stanley Elkins and His Critics*, ed. Ann J. Lane (Urbana: University of Illinois Press, 1971), pp. 23–42; Sidney W. Mintz, "Slavery and Emergent Capitalisms," in *Slavery in the New World*, ed. Laura Foner and Eugene D. Genovese (Englewood Cliffs, N.J.: Prentice-Hall, 1969), pp. 27–37; Laurence Mordekhai Thomas, *Vessels of Evil: American Slavery and the Holocaust* (Philadelphia: Temple University Press, 1993), esp. pp. 117–147. See the introduction to Martin A. Klein, *Breaking the Chains: Slavery, Bondage, and Emancipation in Modern Africa and Asia* (Madison: University of Wisconsin Press, 1993), pp. 11–12. In a reappraisal, Elkins did not seem inclined to defend the heuristic value of the analogy in comparison with other institutions such as asylums and prisons. See Elkins, "Slavery and Ideology," in Lane, *Debate over Slavery*, pp. 325–378; John Thornton, *Africa and the Africans in the Making of the Atlantic World, 1400–1680* (Cambridge: Cambridge University Press), pp. 152–182, 206–253.

4. See, most recently, the essays in Larry E. Hudson Jr., ed., *Working Toward Freedom: Slave Society and Domestic Economy in the American South* (Rochester, N.Y.: University of Rochester Press, 1994), p. viii; and Stanley L. Engerman, "Concluding Reflections," in ibid., pp. 233–241. See also the essays in *The Slaves' Economy: Independent Production by Slaves*

in the Americas, a special issue of *Slavery and Abolition* 12(1) (May 1991); and Robert W. Fogel, *Without Consent or Contract: The Rise and Fall of American Slavery* (New York: Norton, 1989), pp. 154–198.

5. See Raul Hilberg, *The Destruction of the European Jews*, rev. and definitive ed., 3 vols. (New York: Holmes and Meiers, 1985).

6. See Paul E. Lovejoy, "The Impact of the Atlantic Slave Trade on Africa: A Review of the Literature," *Journal of African History* 30 (1989):365–394, esp. p. 387.

7. Patrick Manning, "The Slave Trade: The Formal Demography of a Global System," in *The Atlantic Slave Trade: Effects on Economics, Societies and Peoples in Africa, the Americas, and Europe*, ed. J. I. Inikori and S. L. Engerman (Durham, N.C.: Duke University Press, 1992), pp. 117–141, esp. pp. 119–120; Philip D. Curtin, *The Atlantic Slave Trade: A Census* (Madison: University of Wisconsin Press, 1969); David Eltis, *Economic Growth and the Ending of the Transatlantic Slave Trade* (New York: Oxford University Press, 1987); idem., "Free and Coerced Transatlantic Migrations: Some Comparisons," *American Historical Review* 88(2) (1983):251–280; J. D. Fage, "African Societies and the Atlantic Slave Trade," *Past and Present* 125 (1989):97–115; David Eltes, David Richardson, and Stephen Behrendt, "The Structure of the Atlantic Slave Trade, 1597–1867" (unpublished typescript).

8. See, inter alia, Thornton, *Africa and the Africans;* Inikori and Engerman, *The Atlantic Slave Trade*; Herbert Klein, *The Middle Passage: Comparative Studies in the Atlantic Slave Trade* (Princeton: Princeton University Press, 1978); David Brion Davis, *Slavery and Human Progress* (New York: Oxford University Press, 1984); Orlando Patterson, *Slavery and Social Death* (Cambridge: Harvard University Press, 1982).

9. See Paul Lovejoy, *Transformations in Slavery: A History of Slavery in Africa* (Cambridge: Cambridge University Press, 1983); idem., "Impact of the Atlantic Slave Trade"; and Patrick Manning, "The Impact of Slave Trade Exports on the Population of the Western Coast of Africa, 1700–1850," in *De la Traite à l'esclavage*, ed. Serge Daget (Nantes, France: Société française d'histoire d'outre-mer, 1988), pp. 111–134. Compare, with David Eltis, *Economic Growth*, pp. 64–71; John Thornton, "The Slave Trade in Eighteenth Century Angola: Effects on Demographic Structures," *Canadian Journal of African Studies* 14(3) (1980):417–427; and Martin A. Klein, "The Impact of the Atlantic Slave Trade on the Societies of the Western Sudan," in Inikori and Engerman, *Atlantic Slave Trade*, pp. 25–47.

10. William A. Darity, "A General Equilibrium Model of the Eighteenth Century Atlantic Slave Trade: A Least-Likely Test for the Caribbean School," *Research in Economic History* 7 (1982):287–326; Hilary McD. Beckles, "The Economic Origins of Black Slavery in the British West Indies, 1640–1680: A Tentative Analysis of the Barbados Model," *Journal of Caribbean History* 16 (1982):35–56; Raymond L. Cohn and Richard A. Jensen, "The Determinants of Slave Mortality Rates on the Middle Passage," *Explorations in Economic History* 10(2) (1982):173–176; David W. Galenson, "The Atlantic Slave Trade and the Barbados Market, 1673–1723," *Journal of Economic History* 42(3) (1982):491–511; Herbert S. Klein, "Novas Interpretaoes do trafico de Escravos do Atlantico," *Revista de Historia* 120 (1989):3–25.

11. See, inter alia, Inikori and Engerman, *Atlantic Slave Trade*; Barbara L. Solow and Stanley L. Engerman, eds., *British Capitalism and Caribbean Slavery* (Cambridge: Cambridge University Press, 1987); Barbara L. Solow, ed., *Slavery and the Rise of the Atlantic System* (New York: Cambridge University Press, 1991); David W. Galenson, *Traders, Planters, and Slaves:*

Market Behavior in Early English America (New York: Cambridge University Press, 1986); Janet J. Ewald, "Slavery in Africa and the Slave Trades from Africa," *American Historical Review* 97 (1992):465–485; Julian Gwyn, "The Economics of the Transatlantic Slave Trade: A Review," *Social History* 25 (1992):151–162. On the contrasting meaning of humans as "things" in the Atlantic system and in the Nazi system, see Claudia Koonz, "Genocide and Eugenics: The Language of Power," in *Lessons and Legacies: The Meaning of the Holocaust in a Changing World*, ed. Peter Hayes (Evanston, Ill.: Northwestern University Press, 1991), pp. 155–177; David Brion Davis, *The Problem of Slavery in Western Culture* (Ithaca, N.Y.: Cornell University Press, 1966), ch. 2, pp. 31–35; and Sidney Mintz, ed., *Esclave = facteur de production: l'economie politique de l'esclavage* (Paris: Dunod, 1981).

   12. See Henry A. Gemery and Jan S. Hogendorn, eds., *The Uncommon Market: Essays in the Economic History of the Atlantic Slave Trade* (New York: Academic Press, 1979), on the "Western" transoceanic trade; and *The Economics of the Indian Ocean Slave Trade in the Nineteenth Century* (Special Issue), *Slavery and Abolition* 9 (December 1988).

   13. See, above all, Hilberg, *The Destruction*, vol 2, pp. 543–860.

   14. See Claudia Koonz, "Genocide and Eugenics," pp. 162ff; Robert Jay Lifton and Amy Hackett, "Nazi Doctors," in *Anatomy of the Auschwitz Death Camps*, ed. Michael Berenbaum (Bloomington: Indiana University Press, 1994), pp. 301–316.

   15. See David Eltis, "Free and Coerced Transatlantic Migrations: Some Comparisons," *American Historical Review* 88(2) (1983):251–280; Stanley L. Engerman and Kenneth L. Sokoloff, "Factor Endowments, Institutions and Differential Paths of Growth Among New World Economies: A View from Economic Historians of the United States," in *Why Did Latin America Fall Behind?*, ed. Stephen Haber (Stanford: Stanford University Press, forthcoming 1996). On depopulation in Africa, compare Manning, "The Slave Trade," in Inikori and Engerman, *Atlantic Slave Trade*, pp. 117–141, and Eltis, *Economic Growth*, pp. 64–71.

   16. See Joseph C. Miller, *Way of Death: Merchant Capitalism and the Angolan Slave Trade, 1730–1830* (Madison: University of Wisconsin Press, 1988), p. 439, figure 11.1. Miller's data base is quite small and lower estimates have been suggested by other authors. For example, Miller estimates an average loss of 35 percent from the point of capture to arrival at the coast, with a further loss of 10–15 percent in the port towns, yielding a total depletion in Africa of 45 percent (ibid., p. 440). Patrick Manning estimates an interior loss of about 15 percent ("The Slave Trade," p. 121); as does John Thornton, "The Demographic Effect of the Slave Trade on Western Africa 1500–1850," in *African Historical Demography*, vol. II, *Proceedings of a Seminar* (Edinburgh: University of Edinburgh, 1977), pp. 693–720. Manning notes that population loss in Africa, though relatively less serious than the depopulations of the Americas and Oceania, was caused in large part by human agency. This characteristic would bring the slave trade closer to the Holocaust in terms of agency than other population catastrophes; Manning, *Slavery and African Life: Occidental, Oriental, and African Slave Trades* (Cambridge: Cambridge University Press, 1990), p. 87.

   17. See Yitzhak Arad, "The Holocaust of Soviet Jewry in the Occupied Territories of the Soviet Union," *Yad Vashem Studies* 21 (1991):1–47.

   18. Compare Miller, *Way of Death*, p. 401, n. 89, with Raul Hilberg, "Opening Remarks: The Discovery of the Holocaust," in *Lessons and Legacies*, pp. 11–19, esp. pp. 15–16; Yisrael Gutman, "Auschwitz–An Overview," in *Anatomy of the Auschwitz Death Camp*, ed. Yisrael Gutman and Michael Berenbaum (Bloomington: Indiana University Press, 1994), pp. 5–33. It is important to note that the Auschwitz mortality figure applies only to the 400,000

(of 1.5 million) who were given inmate status, registered, numbered, and left alive for some time. The majority of arrivals were killed immediately. See Franciszek Piper, "The System of Prisoner Exploitation," in *Anatomy of the Auschwitz Death Camp*, pp. 34–49; and "The Number of Victims," ibid., pp. 61–76.

19. Hilberg, *Destruction*, vol. I.

20. Miller, *Way of Death*, pp. 379–401; Philip Curtin, *Economic Change in Precolonial Africa: Sengambia in the Era of the Slave Trade* (Madison: University of Wisconsin Press, 1975), pp. 168–173, 277–278.

21. Miller, *Way of Death*, pp. 391–392.

22. Miller, *Way of Death*, pp. 404–406; Walvin, *Black Ivory*, pp. 250–251, 284–292; see also Herbert S. Klein, *The Middle Passage: Comparative Studies in the Atlantic Slave Trade* (Princeton: Princeton University Press, 1978).

23. Levi, *Survival in Auschwitz*, pp. 17–20.

24. Ibid., pp. 27–28.

25. See Thornton, *Africa*, pp. 153–162. For eyewitness accounts by a slave and a surgeon, see Olaudah Equiano, *The Interesting Narrative of the Life of Olaudah Equiano*, 2 vols. (London, 1789), vol. 1, pp. 78–80; Alexander Falconbridge, *An Account of the Slave Trade on the Coast of Africa* (London: J. Phillips, 1788), p. 25.

26. Robert-Jan Van Pelt, "A Site in Search of a Mission," in *Anatomy of the Auschwitz Death Camp*, pp. 93–154, esp. pp. 130–132. See also Terrence Des Pres, *The Survivor: An Anatomy of Life in the Death Camps* (New York: Oxford University Press, 1976), p. 60, describing the "excremental assault" on the inmates. See also Hilberg, *Destruction*, p. 490.

27. Arad, "Holocaust of Soviet Jewry," p. 14.

28. Walvin, *Black Ivory*, pp. 16–20.

29. That captive Jews were more readily imagined to be criminals than slaves may also be inferred from the case of the Ukrainian who consented to find refuge for two Jewish children whose father feared an imminent Nazi "action" in his ghetto. When the children were discovered, Bazyli Antoniak was accused of complicity in harboring "criminals," not stolen goods. He was convicted and sentenced to death, despite the fact that the children, aged six and seven, were too young to be charged as criminals. Ingo Müller, *Hitler's Justice: The Courts of the Third Reich*, trans. Deborah Lucas Schneider (Cambridge: Harvard University Press, 1991), p. 164. Jews under Nazi control were, however, of value to Jewish groups outside the range of Nazi power. For details of the futile negotiations on the ransoming of Jews, see Yehuda Bauer, *Jews for Sale? Nazi-Jewish Negotiations, 1933–1945* (New Haven: Yale University Press, 1994). On the value of corpses, see Andrzej Strzelecki, "The Plunder of the Victims and Their Corpses," *Anatomy of the Auschwitz Death Camp*, pp. 246–266. Under the auspices of Breslau University, a doctoral dissertation was published in 1940, "On the Possibilities of Recycling Gold from the Mouths of the Dead"; Miller, *Way of Death*, pp. 66–69; Levi, *Survival*, p. 16.

30. Thornton, *Africa*, pp. 162–182; Walvin, *Black Ivory*, pp. 59–66; Miller, *Way of Death*, pp. 445ff.

31. Levi, *Survival*, pp. 9–21. See also Paul Hoedeman, *Hitler or Hippocrates* (Sussex England: Book Guild, 1991), pp. 187–193; Franciszek Piper, "Gas Chambers and Crematoria," in *Anatomy of the Auschwitz Death Camp*, pp. 157–182.

32. Konrad Kwiet, "Forced Labour of German Jews in Nazi Germany," in *Leo Baeck Institute: Year Book*, vol. 36 (London: Secker and Warburg, 1991), pp. 389–410, esp. p. 393.

33. Isaiah Trunk, "Epidemics and Mortality in the Warsaw Ghetto, 1939–1942," in *The Nazi Holocaust: Historical Articles on the Destruction of European Jews,* ed. Michael R. Marrus, 9 vols. (Westport, Conn.: Meckler, 1989), vol. 6; vol. 1, p. 43; Christopher R. Browning, *The Path to Genocide: Essays on Launching the Final Solution* (Cambridge: Cambridge University Press, 1992), pp. 34–51, 130–141. For an alternative and detailed account of the Warsaw ghetto, see Charles G. Roland, *Courage Under Siege: Starvation, Disease, and Death in the Warsaw Ghetto* (New York: Oxford University Press, 1992).

34. Browning, *Path,* pp. 59–61; 111–122.

35. Ibid., pp. 73–74; Ulrich Herbert, "Labour and Extermination: Economic Interest and the Primacy of *Weltanschauung* in National Socialism," *Past and Present* 138 (1993): 144–195; Peter Hayes, "Profits and Persecution: Corporate Involvement in the Holocaust," in *Perspectives on the Holocaust: Essays in Honor of Raul Hilberg,* ed. James S. Pacy and Alan P. Wertheimer (Boulder: Westview Press, 1995), pp. 51–73.

36. Franciszek Piper, "The System of Economic Exploitation," p. 47. For an extended discussion of the role of utilitarian and nonutilitarian rationalizations of the Holocaust, see the essays by Susanne Heime and Götz Aly, Dan Diner, David Bankier, and Ulrich Herbert, in *Yad Vashem Studies,* vol. 24, ed. Aharon Weiss (Jerusalem: Yad Vashem, 1994), pp. 45–145. However configured, the Holocaust frame of reference assumed a "surplus" of people. The slave trade frame of reference assumed a deficit of laborers.

37. Hilberg, *Destruction,* p. 529.

38. Himmler, quoted in Kwiet, "Forced Labour," p. 403 (October 1942).

39. From J. Goebbels, *Tagebuck,* 2 March and 30 September, 1943, quoted in Kwiet, "Forced Labour," pp. 403–404.

40. Thornton, *Africa,* pp. 53–71.

41. Arad, "Holocaust of Soviet Jewry," p. 23.

42. Miller, *Way of Death,* pp. 159–163. On attitudes toward women and children in the African slave trade and in Auschwitz, compare Claire C. Robertson and Martin A. Klein, eds., *Women and Slavery in Africa* (Madison: University of Wisconsin Press, 1983), esp. the introduction, "Women's Importance in African Slave Systems," pp. 3–25; Irena Strzelecka, "Women," in *Anatomy of the Auschwitz Death Camp,* pp. 393–411; and Helena Kubica, "Children," ibid., pp. 412–427.

43. See Richard B. Sheridan, "The Guinea Surgeons on the Middle Passage: The Provision of Medical Services in the British Slave Trade," *International Journal of African Historical Studies* 14 (1981):601–625; idem., *Doctors and Slaves: A Medical and Demographic History Slavery in the British West Indies, 1680–1834* (Cambridge: Cambridge University Press, 1985), pp. 108–126; Robert Jay Lifton and Amy Hackett, "Nazi Doctors," p. 303. On the role of Nazi medicine in the process of mass murder, see also Robert Jay Lifton, *The Nazi Doctors: Medical Killing and the Psychology of Genocide* (New York: Basic Books, 1986); Götz Aly, Peter Chroust, and Christian Pross, *Cleansing the Fatherland: Nazi Medicine and Racial Hygiene* (Baltimore: Johns Hopkins University Press, 1994); Paul Hoedeman, *Hitler or Hippocrates* (Sussex, England: Book Guild, 1991).

44. Walvin, *Black Ivory,* p. ix; Anna Pawelczynska, *Values and Violence in Auschwitz: A Sociological Analysis* (Berkeley: University of California Press, 1979), pp. 54–55.

45. See, inter alia, William A. Green, "Race and Slavery: Considerations on the Williams Thesis," in Solow and Engerman, *British Capitalism,* pp. 25–50; Thornton, *Africa,* pp. 137–138; 143–151.

46. Winthrop D. Jordan, *White Over Black: American Attitudes Toward the Negro, 1550–1812* (Chapel Hill: University of North Carolina Press, 1968); David Eltis, "Europeans and the Rise and Fall of African Slavery in the Americas: An Interpretation," *American Historical Review* 98 (1993):1399–1423; Philip D. Morgan, "Slaves and Livestock in Eighteenth-Century Jamaica: Vineyard Pen, 1750–1751," *William and Mary Quarterly* 52 (1995):47–76.

47. See, inter alia, Philip D. Curtin, *The Image of Africa: British Ideas and Action, 1780–1850* (Madison: University of Wisconsin Press, 1964); William B. Cohen, *The French Encounter with Africans: White Response to Blacks, 1530–1880* (Bloomington: Indiana University Press, 1980).

48. Magnus Morner, *Race Mixture in the History of Latin America* (Boston: Little Brown, 1967).

49. Albert A. Sicroff, *Les Statutes de pureté de sangre en Espagne, au XVI, et XVII siècles* (Paris, 1955).

50. Koonz, "Genocide and Eugenics"; George L. Mosse, *Toward the Final Solution: A History of European Racism* (New York: Harper and Row, 1978), pp. 215–231.

51. Franciszek Piper, "The Number of Victims," an essay in *Anatomy of the Auschwitz Death Camp*, pp. 61–76, esp. p. 64.

52. *The Diary of Anne Frank: The Critical Edition* (New York: Doubleday, 1987), pp. 265, 273, 316: entries of October 6, 9, and November 19, 1942.

The Armenian Genocide
as Precursor and Prototype of
Twentieth-Century Genocide

ROBERT F. MELSON

Twentieth-Century Genocide

*D*uring this century, the world has experienced four tidal waves of national and ethnic conflict and genocide in the wake of collapsing states and empires. These were punctuated by the First and Second World Wars and by the postcolonial and post-Communist eras. During the First World War and its aftermath the Ottoman empire collapsed, and it committed the first total genocide of the twentieth century against its Armenian minority.[1] In the same period, the disintegration of the German and Austro-Hungarian empires set off *Volkisch*, nationalist and fascist movements that repressed minorities and precipitated the Second World War. In the context of that war, the Nazis attempted to exterminate the Jews and Gypsies and committed partial genocide against other peoples. Following the Second World War, as former European colonial empires—notably Britain and France— withdrew from their possessions, they left behind fragile regimes that lacked legitimacy. Such "Third World" governments frequently ruled over culturally plural societies and tried to impose the hegemony of one ethnic group over the rest. In reaction, minorities rebelled and sought self-determination. This led to ethnic wars and genocide in places like Indonesia, Burundi, Sri Lanka, Nigeria, Pakistan, Ethiopia, Sudan, and Iraq. In the wake of the recent collapse of Communist regimes in the Soviet Union and former Yugoslavia, we are experiencing the fourth wave of nationalist upsurge, ethnic conflicts, and genocide. Meanwhile, as in contemporary Rwanda, it should be noted that the third wave of postcolonial genocide has not yet spent its force.

This chapter puts forth the position that the Armenian genocide was not only the first total genocide of the twentieth century but that it also served as the prototype for genocides that came after. In particular, the Armenian genocide approximates the Holocaust; but at the same time its territorial and national aspects, which distinguish it from the Holocaust, make it an archetype for ethnic and national genocides in the Third World, as well as in the post-Communist states.

This chapter offers a brief historical overview of the Armenian genocide, then compares that event first to the Holocaust and also to the Nigerian and Yugoslav genocides. The second set of cases represents contemporary instances of genocide in the Third World and the post-Communist states, respectively. The chapter concludes by raising a number of questions about the Armenian genocide and about genocide in general.

The Armenian Genocide

In traditional Ottoman society, Armenians—like other Christians and Jews— were defined as a *dhimmi millet*, a non-Muslim religious community of the empire. Their actual treatment by the state varied to some extent with the military fortunes of the empire, with the religious passions of its elites, and with the encroachment upon their land of Muslim refugees from the Balkans and the Caucasus and of Kurdish pastoralists.

Although by and large *dhimmis* (religious minorities) were free to practice their religion, they were considered to be distinctively inferior in status to Muslims.[2] However, in the nineteenth century, the Armenians challenged the traditional hierarchy of Ottoman society as they became better educated, wealthier, and more urban. In response, despite attempts at reforms, the empire became more repressive, and Armenians, more than any other Christian minority, bore the brunt of persecution.[3]

Throughout the nineteenth century, the Ottoman sultans were caught in the vise between great power pressures on the one hand and the demand for self-determination among their minorities on the other. By the time Abdul Hamid II came to power in 1876, he had set a course of political and social repression and technological modernization. Nevertheless, he could not halt the military and political disintegration of his regime, and he was replaced in 1908 by a political revolution of Young Turks with new and radical ideas of how to address the Ottoman crisis.

In the first instance, the Committee of Union and Progress (CUP), the political organization formed by the Young Turks, attempted radically to transform the regime following liberal and democratic principles that had been embodied in the earlier constitution of 1876. They hoped for the support of the Great Powers for their reforms, but neither the European powers nor the minorities reduced their pressures. On the contrary, they took the opportunity of internal Ottoman disarray and revolutionary transformation to press their demands, and between 1908 and 1912 they succeeded in reducing the size of Ottoman territory by 40 percent and its population by 20 percent.[4]

Concluding that their liberal experiment had been a failure, CUP leaders turned to Pan-Turkism, a xenophobic and chauvinistic brand of nationalism that sought to create a new empire based on Islam and Turkish ethnicity. This new empire, stretching from Anatolia to western China, would exclude minorities or grant them nominal rights unless they became Turks by nationality and Muslim by religion.

This dramatic shift in ideology and identity, from Ottoman pluralism to an integral form of Turkish nationalism, had profound implications for the emergence of modern Turkey.[5] At the same time, Pan-Turkism had tragic consequences for Ottoman minorities, most of all for the Armenians. From being once viewed as a constituent *millet* of the Ottoman regime, they suddenly were stereotyped as an alien nationality. Their situation became especially dangerous because of their territorial concentration in eastern Anatolia on the border with Russia, Turkey's traditional enemy. Thus, the Armenians, at one and the same time, were accused of being in league with Russia against Turkey and of claiming Anatolia, the heartland of the projected Pan-Turkic state.

This was the situation even before the First World War. When war broke out, however, the Young Turks, led by Talaat Pasha, the minister of interior, and Enver Pasha, the minister of war, joined the German side in an anti-Russian alliance that would allow Turkey to expand at Russia's expense. It was in this context of revolutionary and ideological transformation and war that the fateful decision to destroy the Armenians was taken.

By February 1915, Armenians serving in the Ottoman army were turned into labor battalions and were either worked to death or killed. By April, the remaining civilians were deported from eastern Anatolia and Cilicia toward the deserts near Aleppo in an early form of ethnic cleansing. The lines of Armenian deportees were set upon again and again by Turkish and Kurdish villagers who were often incited and led by specially designated killing squads, *Teshkilat-i Makhsusiye*. These units had been organized for their murderous purposes at the highest levels of the CUP.[6] Those Armenians who escaped massacre were very likely to perish of famine on the way. In this manner, between 1915 and the armistice in 1918, some 1 million people—out of a population of 2 million—were killed. Later, a half-million more Armenians perished as Turkey sought to free itself of foreign occupation and to expel minorities. Thus, between 1915 and 1923 approximately one-half to three-quarters of the Armenian population was destroyed in the Ottoman empire.

The Armenian Genocide and the Holocaust

The Armenian genocide and the Holocaust are the principal instances of total domestic genocide in the twentieth century. In both cases, a deliberate attempt was made by the government of the day to destroy in whole an ethno-religious community of ancient provenance. When one compares the situation and history of the Armenians in the Ottoman empire to the Jews in Europe, a pattern leading to genocide becomes apparent. It is a pattern that also reveals some significant differences, and it is those differences that link the Armenian genocide not only to the Holocaust but to contemporary instances of that crime. Let us first consider the similarities between the Armenian genocide and the Holocaust:

1. Under the prerevolutionary regimes in the Ottoman empire and Germany, Armenians and Jews were ethno-religious minorities of inferior status that had experienced rapid social progress and mobilization in the nineteenth century. These circumstances helped to create what came to be known as the "Armenian question" and the "Jewish problem." Armenians raised a "question" and Jews created a "problem," because neither the Muslim Ottoman empire nor Christian Europe were prepared to deal with low-status religious minorities that had become increasingly assertive and successful in the modern world.

2. Under the prerevolutionary regimes, Armenians may have suffered massacres, and Jews may have experienced discrimination in Germany as well as pogroms in Russia; but in none of these cases was a policy of total destruction formulated or implemented to resolve "questions" or to solve "problems." Genocide followed in the wake of revolutions in the Ottoman empire and Germany.

3. Following the reversals of 1908–1912, the CUP rejected Pan-Islam and Ottomanism as legitimating ideologies linking state to society and turned to Turkish nationalism and Pan-Turkism. The CUP identified the Turkish ethnic group as the authentic political community on which the Turkish state could and should rely, and by implication it excluded the Armenians from the Turkish nation.

The Armenians were in danger of being conceived as enemies of Turkey and of the Turkish revolution once Ottoman Turks came to view themselves not in religious terms but in ethnic terms. What made the Armenian situation significantly more dangerous than that of other minorities was the Armenian *millet*'s concentration in eastern Anatolia, an area that Turkish nationalists claimed to be the heartland of the Turkish nation. Moreover, the eastern *vilayets* (provinces) of Anatolia were on the Russian border, Turkey's traditional enemy, casting the Armenian presence in a sinister light.

In a similar fashion, a revolutionary situation in Germany allowed the Nazis to recast German identity and ideology. The German revolution destroyed the Weimar Republic, undermined democratic and socialist conceptions of legitimacy, and enabled the Nazis to come to power. Once the Nazis controlled the apparatus of the state, they set about recasting German political identity in terms of their racial and antisemitic ideology. They did this by excluding and expelling those whom they defined as "non-Aryans" and "Jews" from the newly valued and invented "Aryan" community.

4. When the First World War broke out, the CUP enthusiastically joined the Ottoman empire to the Germans against the Russians. This permitted Talaat and Enver to claim that the internal Armenian enemy was in league with the external

Russian foe. Wartime circumstances then were used to justify the deportation and destruction of the Armenian community.

Similarly, the Nazis launched the Second World War in order to carve out an empire for Germany, and it was under wartime circumstances that they implemented their policies of partial genocide against Poles, Russians, and others and their extermination against the Jews. In particular, they viewed the Soviet Union as their principal foreign foe, and they assumed that it was ruled by a "world Jewish conspiracy." Thus, in 1941, at the same time that they invaded the Soviet Union, they launched the "Final Solution."

Thus did ideological vanguards use the opportunities created by revolution and war to destroy ancient communities that had been judged to be "problematic" under the prerevolutionary regimes and "enemies" under revolutionary and wartime circumstances. These elements—the prerevolutionary statuses of the victims and revolutionary and wartime circumstances—may be said to account for some of the essential similarities between the two genocides. There were, however, significant differences as well.

The perpetrators of the Armenian genocide were motivated by a variant of nationalist ideology, the victims were a territorial ethnic group that had sought autonomy, and the methods of destruction included massacre, forced deportation, and starvation. In contrast, the perpetrators of the Holocaust were motivated by racism and antisemitism and ideologies of global scope; the victims were not a territorial group, and so, for the most part, they had sought integration and assimilation instead of autonomy, and the death camp was the characteristic method of destruction. A word needs to be said about these factors that differentiate the Armenian genocide from the Holocaust. It will be shown, however, that it is precisely these differences that link the Armenian genocide to contemporary events.

Differences Between the Armenian Genocide and the Holocaust

Like these similarities, the differences between the Armenian genocide and the Holocaust may be plotted along the same dimensions: Jews and Armenians differed in status in the two empires; Nazi racist antisemitism differed significantly from the Pan-Turkist nationalism of the Young Turks; and the killers of the Armenians relied mostly on massacre and starvation rather than the death camps.

Like the Armenians in the Ottoman empire, the Jews were an ethno-religious community of low status in Christian Europe. Unlike the Armenians, however, who were the subject of contempt for being non-Muslims, the Jews of feudal Europe became a pariah caste stigmatized as "killers of the Son of God." Thus,

Jews were not only despised in most parts of Europe, they were also hated and feared in a way the Armenians in the Ottoman empire were not.

In the nineteenth century, to the extent that the state became bureaucratic, the society meritocratic, and the economy capitalistic, Armenians and Jews began to advance in status and wealth. Indeed, it has been suggested that Armenian and Jewish progress was viewed as illegitimate and subversive, which precipitated antagonistic reactions both in the Ottoman empire and in imperial Germany.[7]

Here at least two variations may be noted. Whereas Armenians were a territorial group that increasingly made known its demands for greater autonomy and self-administration within the Ottoman system, Jews were geographically dispersed and thus, with the exception of the Zionists who sought a Jewish state in Palestine, most made no territorial demands on the larger societies in which they lived.[8] Instead, to the extent that they accepted the modern world, most Jews sought assimilation to the culture and integration into the wider society.

The reaction against Jewish progress, assimilation, and attempts at integration became a wide movement of European antisemitism, a form of racism that set up unbridgeable obstacles to Jewish inclusion. According to antisemites, Eugen Dühring, for example, not even conversion would allow Jews to become the equals of Germans or other Europeans. Already in 1881, he wrote:

> A Jewish question would still exist, even if every Jew were to turn his back on his religion and join one of our major churches. Yes, I maintain that in that case, the struggle between us and the Jews would make itself felt as ever more urgent . . . It is precisely the baptized Jews who infiltrate furthest, unhindered in all sectors of society and political life.[9]

According to Wilhelm Marr (another nineteenth-century antisemite), for example, Jews were not only an alien race, they constituted an international conspiracy whose aim was the domination of Germany, Europe, indeed, the whole world. Thus, antisemites founded not only a movement that opposed Jewish progress and assimilation, they formulated a far-reaching ideology that helped them to explain the vacillations and crises of the modern world. It was an ideology that came to rival liberalism and socialism in its mass appeal.

By way of contrast, no such ideology of anti-Armenianism developed in the Ottoman empire. Armenians may have been popularly despised for being *dhimmis*, or *Gavur* (infidels), and later, under the Young Turks, they may have been feared as an alien nation supposedly making claims to Anatolia, the heartland of the newly valued "Turkey." However, even Pan-Turkism left the door open to conversion and assimilation of minorities, something that racism and antisemitism explicitly rejected.

Moreover, though the Young Turks may have claimed that the Armenians were in league with their international enemies, especially the Russians, there was no equivalent in the Pan-Turkish view of the Armenians to the Nazis' hysterical struggle against the "Jewish spirit" that was said to linger in Germany and Europe even after most of the Jews had been murdered. Saul Friedländer has noted:

> It was the absolutely uncompromising aspect of the exterminatory drive against the Jews, as well as the frantic extirpation of any elements actually or supposedly linked to the Jews or to the "Jewish Spirit" . . . which fundamentally distinguished the anti-Jewish actions of the Nazis from their attitude toward another group.[10]

Thus, the Holocaust became centered not only in Germany but evolved into an international policy of mass murder and cultural destruction that included Europe and even the whole world. Finally, the death camp, a conception of the Nazi state, was an extraordinary organization, not seen before or since. It was a factory managed by the SS but staffed at all levels by the inmates themselves. Its primary aim was to dehumanize and kill its prisoners after confiscating their property and making use of their labor. Although Jews, like Armenians, perished in massacres and by starvation, the use of the death camp as a method of extermination differentiates the Holocaust from the Armenian genocide.

At the same time that these differences—the nationalist ideology of the perpetrators, the territoriality of the victims, and the methodology of destruction, especially expulsion and starvation—differentiate the Armenian genocide from the Holocaust, they link that earlier genocide to contemporary destructions in the Third World and in the post-Communist states. In that sense, as has already been noted, the Armenian genocide predates and partly encompasses both kinds of genocide and is, thereby, a prototype for genocide in our time. We now turn to an examination of the Nigerian and Yugoslav genocides and to their comparison to the Armenian prototype.

Nigeria

Genocide has been committed throughout the Third World. Following are a few examples: Indonesia, Burundi, Rwanda, Sudan, East Pakistan, and Iraq. In all of these instances, a shaky and hardly legitimate postcolonial state ruling over a culturally plural society attempted to establish the hegemony of a leading ethnic group over other ethnic segments of society. This attempt at domination provoked movements of resistance and self-determination, which the postcolonial state then tried to halt by force, including massacre and partial genocide.

Nigeria gained its independence from Great Britain in 1960. It was organized as a federation of three states, each centering on a major ethnic group. The northern state was dominated by the Hausa-Fulani, the western by the Yoruba, and the eastern by the Ibos. The major ethnic groups jockeyed for power at the federal level, but each had its "minorities" that felt discriminated against at the state level of the federation. The postindependence government, dominated by Hausa-Fulani Muslims, was resisted by southern, largely non-Muslim groups, especially the Ibos. In 1966, after a failed military coup, thousands of Ibos were massacred in northern Nigeria. In 1967, a year after the massacres, the Ibos tried to secede. They called eastern Nigeria "Biafra" and fought a war of self-determination until 1970, when their secession attempt collapsed.

During the war, over 1 million Biafrans starved to death as a result of the deliberate Nigerian policy of blockade and disruption of agricultural life. Thus, between 1966 and 1970, a "genocide-in-part" occurred in Nigeria, following the United Nations (UN) definition. It is important, however, to recall that what happened in Biafra differed from the Holocaust and the Armenian genocide in that the policies of the Nigerian Federal Military Government (FGM) did not include extermination of the Ibos.

Yugoslavia

A definitive history of the recent conflict in former Yugoslavia does not yet exist, but it is possible to render a provisional sketch. The Yugoslav disaster stems from the failure of the Communist regime to establish legitimate political institutions, a viable economy, and a compelling political culture. After Marshal Tito's death in 1980, ethnically based nationalist movements started to mobilize and to demand greater autonomy if not yet self-determination. The process of dissolution and disintegration was drastically accelerated with the rise of Slobodan Milosevic, who articulated an integral form of Serbian nationalism and irredentism that called for the creation of a Yugoslavia dominated by Serbia such as had existed after the First World War. This frightened the other nationalities and encouraged intransigent elements.

Milosevic's integral Serbian nationalism, in a context of Yugoslav and Communist institutional decay and insecurity, helped to sharpen ethnic enmities, strengthen centrifugal forces throughout the federation, and accelerate the processes of disintegration. Thus, on September 27, 1989, the parliament of Slovenia adopted amendments to its constitution giving the republic the right to secede from Yugoslavia. Thousands of Serbs demonstrated in Novi Sad, fearing for their status in an independent Slovenia. On July 3, 1990, the Slovenian parliament declared that the laws of the republic took precedence over those of Yugoslavia; on December 22, 1990, Slovenia reported that 95 percent of the voters supported a plebiscite on independence; and on June 25, 1991, Slovenia declared its independence from Yugoslavia.

A similar march of events occurred in Croatia, which declared its independence on the same day. The big difference between Slovenia and Croatia, however, was the presence of a large Serbian minority in the latter. Moreover, no sooner was independence declared in Croatia than the Franjo Tudjman regime launched an anti-Serb campaign that would have alarmed the Serbs, even if nationalist elements among them had not been earlier mobilized by Milosevic. Now that their kin were being threatened in Croatia, Milosevic and other Serbian nationalists could call forth the terrible history of the Ustasha genocide of the Second World War to mobilize the Serbs against Croatian independence and in support of Serbian irredenta.

After June 25, 1991, when Slovenia and Croatia, in declaring their independence, thereby created Serbian minorities—especially in Croatia—the Serb radicals, using the cover of the Yugoslav army, launched an attack intended to incorporate Serbian-populated Croatian territory. To this end, Serbian forces not only initiated hostilities but set out on a path of terrorism and massacre in order to drive Croats out of areas that they desired to incorporate into Greater Serbia.

This policy of terrorism and ethnic cleansing accelerated with even greater ferocity against Bosnia when it declared independence on March 3, 1992. Indeed, in time, both Serb and Croat forces descended on Bosnia with the clear intention of carving up and destroying a state that initially had tried to stand aside from ethnic nationalism and had opted for a pluralist society. However, both Serb and Croat nationalists were intent on either carving up and destroying Bosnia or making it a rump state that would in time collapse. To this end, the Bosnian Serbs, led by their leader, Radovan Karadzic, a psychiatrist of Montenegrin origin, especially practiced massacre, ethnic cleansing, and cultural destruction against those they called the "Turks." Taken together, such policies of destruction on a wide scale are called genocide.[11]

Keeping Nigeria and Yugoslavia in mind, it is also important to note the great fear and insecurity that possess everyone when a government is challenged and a state begins to disintegrate. This great fear, especially in culturally plural societies, leads people to seek the shelter of families and kin and persuades various groups to band together for protection and to view one another as potential enemies.

Indeed, before a culturally plural state like Nigeria or Yugoslavia disintegrates, its politics may revolve about various ethnic issues of group status and the distribution of scarce goods; but once a state crashes, for whatever reasons, ethnic groups begin to fear for their lives, as well they should. Once a political order disintegrates, who can guarantee an ethnic group that its mortal enemies won't come to power and try to dominate it or even destroy it? It is this great fear that has seized all the groups in Yugoslavia, including those Serbs who are the main perpetrators of partial genocide.

The Armenian and Nigerian Genocides

In both the Nigerian and Bosnian cases, we can see some parallels to the Armenian genocide. A dominant ethnic group in a culturally plural society attempted to establish its hegemony. It was resisted by minorities that attempted to gain some form of autonomy or self-determination. In reaction, the dominant group perpetrated repression and genocide. Yet there are significant differences that may be even more instructive.

The crucial difference between a total domestic genocide, as occurred in the Armenian case, and a partial one, as occurred in Nigeria, can also be seen by comparing the two. Unlike the Armenians, once Biafra was defeated and the danger of secession passed, the Ibos were not massacred or further expelled from Nigeria. On the contrary, there was a genuine attempt to reintegrate the Ibo population into Nigeria when the war ended.

This difference may be due to two reasons. First, although the FGM was dominated by Hausa-Fulani elements, it included minorities in its leadership; indeed, General Yakubu Gowon, its commander, was a Christian from the north. Thus, the FGM never developed an ideology of "northernization" or "Muslimization" the way the Young Turks relied on Turkification and sought to create an ethnically homogeneous Turkey.

Second, the territorial issue, a crucial element in the Armenian case, was present in the Biafran case, but it worked in favor of the Ibos. The Ibos of the north were "strangers" and not "sons of the soil"; thus, they could not make a legitimate claim to northern territory.[12] Moreover, it is significant that the Ibos had their own area, which, except for its oil, the north did not covet. Once the Ibos were driven from the north back into their space and the Biafran secession was defeated, the northern elements in the army and elsewhere had succeeded in their major aims. Further massacre and starvation of the Ibos was unnecessary for ideological, territorial, or any other reasons, and the partial genocide ceased.

The Biafran state was never claimed as the "homeland" of the Hausa-Fulani in the manner that Anatolia had been staked out by the Turks. Thus, a federal solution to ethnic conflict could be implemented in Nigeria the way it could not in the Ottoman empire. The Armenians could not be driven back to "their" lands, since their lands were claimed to be the heartland of Turkey. Indeed, it may be suggested that this Turkish claim to Armenian lands was a major reason why the Armenian genocide, unlike the mass death of Biafra, became total in the manner of the Holocaust.

The Armenian and Bosnian Genocides

Two major similarities between the Armenian genocide and the partial genocide occurring in Bosnia should be apparent. Like the Young Turks, the Serbian—and to some extent the Croat—nationalists are also dreaming of a large state that would include their peoples and exclude other ethnic and national groups. Like the Armenians, the Bosnian Muslims, an ethno-religious community making claims to land, were being massacred and driven out by Serb and Croat nationalist movements that sought to incorporate their lands, "cleanse" the area of their presence, and destroy their culture.[13]

However, the status of Bosnia as an independent state recognized by the international community marks a significant difference between the situations of Ibos in Nigeria and of Armenians in the Ottoman empire. Neither Armenians nor

Biafrans were widely recognized as members of independent states while their destructions were in process.[14]

Armenians were largely abandoned to their fate, in part because the genocide occurred in the midst of a world war. During the cold war, both the Eastern and Western blocs discouraged movements of self-determination, fearing superpower involvement; and the African states did the same, fearing their own disintegration along ethnic lines. This may explain, in part, why Ibos, like Armenians, were also abandoned, except for some humanitarian relief.

That "partial" and not "total" genocide occurred in Bosnia, unlike Armenia, should be very cold comfort for the world community. Eighty years after the Armenian genocide and fifty years after the Holocaust, a European state practiced genocide while Europe, the United States, and the United Nations seemed unable or unwilling to halt the slaughter. If genocide cannot be halted in Europe, it cannot be stopped or prevented anywhere else, certainly not in places like Rwanda or Burundi. This, then, is the "New World Order" we face as we stand at the threshold of the third millennium.

Conclusion

The Armenian genocide was a precursor and prototype for the Holocaust in that a minority of traditionally low status that had successfully begun to enter the modern world was set upon and nearly destroyed in the context of revolution and war. However, the Holocaust was not an identical replay of the Armenian genocide. The Armenian case differed from the Holocaust in three dimensions: First, the Young Turks were largely motivated by an ideology of nationalism, whereas the Nazis were moved by an ideology heavily influenced by social Darwinism and racism. Second, the Armenians were a territorial group concentrated in the eastern *vilayets* of the empire, and they had historical claims to the land. In contrast, the Jews were not a territorial group. To destroy the Jews, the Nazis had to formulate a policy of genocide that transcended Germany and even Europe. Lastly, the method of destruction of the Armenians centered on their deportation, shooting, and starvation, whereas in the Holocaust the majority of Nazi victims perished in death camps. This is not to deny that a large percentage of Nazi victims also perished by shootings and starvation in the manner of their Armenian predecessors.

It should be noted, however, that it is precisely these differences that enable the Armenian genocide to be a precursor and prototype for contemporary genocide. Indeed, one conclusion we can draw from this analysis is that the Armenian genocide is a more accurate archetype than is the Holocaust for current mass murders in the postcolonial Third World and in the contemporary post-Communist world. In Nigeria and Yugoslavia, for example, as in the Armenian case and unlike the Holocaust, the perpetrators were driven by a variant of nationalism, the victims were territorial ethnic groups aiming at some form of autonomy or self-determination, and the methods of destruction involved massacre and starvation.

I have tried to show that the Armenian genocide was a precursor and proto-type both for the Holocaust and for contemporary nationalist genocides. In no case was it an exact template for later genocides, nor were these duplicates of the Armenian case; nevertheless, the Armenian pattern of destruction set a terrible precedent for our century and for the future.

NOTES

This chapter was first delivered as a paper at "The Armenian Genocide: An Eighty Year Perspective, 1915–1995," a conference held at the University of California–Los Angeles, April 7–8, 1995. An earlier version of this paper was presented at "Remembering for the Future International Conference on the Holocaust," held at Berlin, Germany, March 13–17, 1994.

1. On the basis of the United Nations definition, it is possible to distinguish between "genocide-in-whole" and "genocide-in-part." In this chapter, a "total domestic genocide" is a genocide-in-whole directed against a group of a state's own society, whereas "partial" genocide is a genocide-in-part. Total genocide implies extermination and/or massive death of such order that a group ceases to continue as a distinct culture and collectivity. Partial genocide stops at extermination and the annihilation of culture. For further discussion concerning these distinctions, see Robert F. Melson, *Revolution and Genocide: On the Origins of the Armenian Genocide and the Holocaust* (Chicago: University of Chicago Press, 1992), pp. 22–30.

2. See Roderic H. Davison, "Turkish Attitudes Concerning Christian-Muslim Equality in the Nineteenth Century," *American Historical Review* 4 (1954):844–864.

3. See Melson, *Revolution and Genocide,* pp. 43–69.

4. See Feroz Ahmad, *The Young Turks* (Oxford: Clarendon Press, 1969), p. 153.

5. See Bernard Lewis, *The Emergence of Modern Turkey* (New York: Oxford University Press, 1961).

6. See Vahakn N. Dadrian, "Genocide as a Problem of National and International Law: The World War I Armenian Case and Its Contemporary Legal Ramifications," *Yale Journal of International Law* 2 (Summer 1989):221–334.

7. See Melson, *Revolution and Genocide,* p. 137.

8. For discussions of the ideological crosscurrents that affected Jews in this period, see Jonathan Frankel, *Prophesy and Politics: Socialism, Nationalism, and the Russian Jews, 1862–1917* (Cambridge: Cambridge University Press, 1981), and Ezra Mendelsohn, *The Jews of East Central Europe Between the World Wars* (Bloomington: Indiana University Press, 1983).

9. Cited in Paul R. Mendes-Flohr and Jehuda Reinharz, *The Jews in the Modern World: A Documentary History* (New York: Oxford University Press, 1980), p. 273.

10. See Saul Friedlander, "On the Possibility of the Holocaust: An Approach to a Historical Synthesis," in *The Holocaust as Historical Experience,* ed. Yehuda Bauer and Nathan Rotenstreich (New York: Holmes and Meier, 1981), p. 2.

11. According to a Helsinki Watch *Report,* genocide is taking place in Bosnia and other former areas of Yugoslavia. Although all sides have been accused of atrocities, it is the

Serbian side, especially in Bosnia, that is charged with genocide. See *War Crimes in Bosnia-Hercegovina* (New York: Human Rights Watch, 1992), p. 1.

12. See Donald L. Horowitz, *Ethnic Groups in Conflict* (Berkeley: University of California Press, 1985), for discussions of how groups validate their claims to status and power. A basic distinction lies between those who have historically dominated an area and migrants who are new arrivals. The first, the "sons-of-the-soil," make their claims on the basis of ancestral privilege; the second cannot. Thus, Armenians in Anatolia could make a claim to the land, the way Ibos in the north could not.

13. As of this writing (January 1996), Bosnian Muslims and Croats are part of a shaky confederation. In the recent past, however, Croat and Bosnian Croat troops, like their Serbian counterparts, were equally intent on dismembering Bosnia and expelling Muslim populations from territories they claimed for Croatia.

14. See Richard G. Hovannisian, *Armenia on the Road to Independence* (Berkeley: University of California Press, 1967), and John J. Stremlau, *The International Politics of the Nigerian Civil War* (Princeton: Princeton University Press, 1977).

❀ 8 ❀

The Comparative Aspects of the Armenian and Jewish Cases of Genocide: A Sociohistorical Perspective

VAHAKN N. DADRIAN

Introduction

*T*his chapter is an attempt to interrelate, within the confines of a few written pages, the two principal genocides of this century in order to encourage emerging efforts to shift attention from case studies to comparative studies of genocide. Case studies by nature are narrowly conceived undertakings, no matter how unusual the event they may cover. They are self-contained discourses, and as such they have limited value for science and scholarship. Yet nations that have been victimized by genocide tend, by the very nature of that victimization, to inflate their experiences to the level of historical uniqueness. Actually, there is some validity to this stance. Wholesale and exterminatory massacres do constitute unique experiences, but they are not necessarily exclusive experiences. It is this aspect of the argument that renders the issue problematic; the idea of uniqueness does not need to be entwined with that of exclusivity.

The reason for this is as logical as it is simple. Although genocidal victimization may be a unique experience for the victim group in question, in a broader perspective, one that transcends the confines of the victim experience, that uniqueness may be superseded by conditions of comparability, that is, elements suggesting commonality in relation to the experience of other victim nations. Moreover, the sense of uniqueness belongs to the domain of emotive self-images intruding into the functions of analysis. It is in the nature of things that the universal significance of a case of genocide becomes diminished to the extent that it may be portrayed as a singular case. This inverse relationship is intrinsic to the canons of analytical reasoning and methodology; in principle, singularity simply precludes universality.

In the case of genocide, unlike other crimes, the ramifications are global and devastating for humanity at large. Therefore, the importance of the task of analyzing genocide is matched and even exceeded by the importance of the task of preventing it. But the notions of singularity and exclusivity impede rather than facilitate such analysis, which is a prerequisite for prevention. The pitfalls of this emphasis on singularity were recently underscored by a noted author in the field of genocide studies, who also happens to be a Holocaust survivor. I refer to Robert Melson, who wrote:

> Some of us who have turned to the Holocaust as a reference point for comparison have done so in order to keep its message alive. Indeed, I would suggest that if the Holocaust is not compared to past and contemporary instances of genocide, its message and significance will wither. In time, its history will become like the Crusades or the Chmielnitski massacres, for example, the preserve only of Jewish mourners, narrow specialists, and Holocaust deniers.[1]

Comparison is essentially an analytical task, whereas case studies, in their general thrust, are descriptive because their texture disallows the depiction of common denominators among several cases. The determinants of genocide are to be discerned in the interplay of such common denominators. In brief, only comparative studies can yield carefully delimited generalizations about the nature and mechanics of genocide as a general problem of humanity. Generalizations of this type constitute the core of scientific endeavor affording progress toward the ultimate goal of averting genocidal cataclysms. The conditions under which Auguste Comte, the founder of the modern discipline of sociology, relinquished his involvement in mathematics and statistics and initiated that new discipline are instructive in this respect. As a contemporary of the French Revolution, he was aghast at the explosion of brutality and lethal violence under its banner ideals; as he acutely felt the need to avert such explosions in the arena of human conflict, he postulated his maxim about social engineering, *Voir pour prévoir, prévoir pour prévenir.* Translated broadly, it means, "It is necessary to understand in order to be able to anticipate, and it is necessary to anticipate in order to be able to prevent."

Even though generalizations, which are distilled from comparative studies, reflect the common features and characteristics among the cases being compared, their elaboration does not need to exclude other features that are not common. One may not limit oneself to the quest for common denominators in order to do justice to the comparative method. By taking into account those factors that are rather uncommon, one may in fact underscore the importance of the common features. In other words, the depiction of certain dissimilarities among two or more cases of genocide may serve to enhance the significance of the similarities yielding a set of generalizations. Precisely for this reason and in preface to our discussion, below I single out and review a number of dissimilarities between the Armenian and Jewish cases of genocide.

I

The Incidence of Dissimilarities in the Two Cases

Important dissimilarities come to the fore when one tries to apply the victimological perspective. How did Armenians and Jews become victims for dissimilar rather than similar reasons? The first thing to consider is their status as victim populations, for it is here that they emerge as victims for opposite reasons. The Armenians were destroyed in their natural homeland—their ancestral territories—in historic Armenia. Consequently, the devastation enveloped the very fabric of the Armenian nation in terms of its social, religious, and cultural institutions. An indigenous civilization with its legacy of antiquity was torn asunder by a nation that had secured possession of these territories through invasion and conquest. In the Jewish case, the victims were destroyed as an immigrant population by the rulers of the host country. The cultural losses sustained thereby involved the treasures of a diasporan subculture.

A similar condition of victimization for dissimilar reasons concerns the matter of the religious status of the two victim groups. The Armenians were essentially destroyed on account of their identification with Christianity in general; the Jews were mainly destroyed for a diametrically opposite reason, namely, for their dissociation from Christianity and for all that such dissociation implied. Granted that neither the Nazis nor the Young Turks, the Ittihadists, were in any significant way religious people, but vast segments of the populations they controlled allowed themselves to be swayed by the animus of religion and, accordingly, either assisted in the process of destruction or condoned it.

One should not underestimate the ballast of Martin Luther's legacy of anti-Jewish animosity in Protestant and even Catholic Germany. In the Turkish case especially, Muslim fanaticism was ignited through the manipulation of religious hatred that reached its acme by the proclamation of "holy war" against "the infidels." As in the case of Nazi Germany, so in the case of the Turks, the exterminatory massacres were somehow an extension of the legacy of religiously fueled anti-Armenian sentiment prevalent in the era of Sultan Abdul Hamit. The massacres of this period were framed in terms of Muslims pitted against infidel Armenians. There was hardly any reference to Turks being described as confronting Armenians. It may be argued in this context that another significant difference is this very fact of antecedent massacres. Whereas the Armenian genocide may be considered as the culmination of a cumulative process of decimation of the Ottoman Armenian population through episodic massacres, there are no comparable antecedents in the history of German-Jewish relations. The historical evolution of antisemitism in modern Germany never found expression in pogroms that erupted, for example, in tsarist Russia in the decades preceding World War I.

This very fact of a history of past massacres in the case of the Armenians is another dissimilarity. Total helplessness had rendered the Armenians exceedingly vulnerable in the 1894–1896 and 1909 massacres, thereby amplifying the scale of their decimation, which is estimated to involve about 200,000 victims. Consequently, small bands of Armenian patriots—identified with Armenian political parties—had stockpiled arms and ammunition in the years following these massacres in anticipation of future massacres against which they intended to defend themselves and their communities. This condition, coinciding with the conditions of World War I, in which Turkey had intervened, particularly aggravated the plight of the general Armenian population targeted for destruction. At the rudimentary stages of the genocide, the leadership of the Armenian nation throughout the length and breadth of the Ottoman empire was subjected to an array of tortures as their tormentors held them responsible for the creation of these stockpiles. In his memoirs, U.S. Ambassador Henry Morgenthau describes the fiendishness of the methods used to torture the victims.

> One day I was discussing these proceedings with Bedri Bey, the Constantinople Prefect of Police. With a disgusting relish Bedri described the tortures inflicted. He made no secret of the fact that the Government had instigated them, and, like all Turks of the official classes, he enthusiastically approved this treatment of the detested race. Bedri told me that all these details were matters of nightly discussion at the headquarters of the Union and Progress Committee. Each new method of inflicting pain was hailed as a splendid discovery, and the regular attendants were constantly ransacking their brains in the effort to devise some new torment. Bedri told me that they even delved into the records of the Spanish Inquisition and other historic institutions of torture, and adopted all the suggestions found there. Bedri did not tell me who carried off the prize in this gruesome competition, but common reputation throughout Armenia gave a pre-eminent infamy to Djevdet Bey, the Vali of Van, whose activities in that section I have already described. All through this country Djevdet now became known as the "marshall blacksmith of Bashkale," for this connoisseur in torture had invented what was perhaps the masterpiece of all—that of nailing horseshoes to the feet of his Armenian victims.[2]

Obviously there was no comparable resort by the Jewish victims to such stockpiling of weapons, as they had no reason to anticipate comparable massacres and, hence, felt no need. This Armenian resort to anticipatory defense measures was and still is being used by the advocates of "the Turkish viewpoint" as a principal ground for justifying governmental anti-Armenian measures. These are portrayed as intended to quash rebellion while blaming the victims as guilty of stabbing Turkey in the back in her struggle of life and death.

Another dissimilarity relates to the diverseness of the mechanics of genocidal mass murder. Given the primitive conditions and level of technology in Turkey in World War I, in the Armenian case the operations of mass murder were particularly harrowing, as dying was made a prolonged and agonizing experience for most of the victims, especially the old, the women, and the children that made up the deportee convoys. In his narration of the mechanics of the Armenian genocide, Ambassador Morgenthau gives an example of a massacre in which a "mob of Turkish peasants" used "clubs, hammers, axes, scythes, spades and saws."

> Such instruments not only caused more agonizing deaths than guns and pistols, but, as the Turks themselves boasted, they were more economical, since they did not involve the waste of powder and shell. . . . Bodies, horribly mutilated, were left in the valley, where they were devoured by wild beasts. After completing this destruction, the peasants and gendarmes gathered in the local tavern, comparing notes and boasting of the number of "giaours" that each had slain.[3]

As if to emphasize the inordinate significance of this mode of killing the victims, Morgenthau decried "the utter depravity and fiendishness of Turkish nature, already sufficiently celebrated through the centuries."[4] Despite diverse circumstances, even though victims of mass murder share a common fate, the incidence of dissimilarity in the use of techniques of killing has some significance in itself. It not only brings into relief the disparities of the levels of culture and civilization of the perpetrator groups but may differentially accentuate the memories and the pain of remembrance of future generations identified with the victim populations.

Closely allied to this notion is the issue of the implementation of the genocide as distinct from such other issues as decisionmaking, supervision, and control. In the Jewish case, the bulk of the victim population was destroyed within the confines of concentration camps where the killing operations were streamlined, mechanized, and systematic through the use of advanced technology. Therefore, through the method of division of labor, special cadres were selected and trained to carry out the actual killing operations. In the case of the Armenians, however, there was no similar specialization of perpetrator groups. By Turkish admissions, large segments of the provincial population in particular willingly participated in regional and local massacres.[5] These acts were made relatively easy because the killing fields were not concentration camps but the remote valleys, gorges, hills, mountaintops, rivers, and lakes of Turkey and the Black Sea littoral.

Two types of mass murders especially punctuate the harrowing character of the Armenian genocide. Tens of thousands of Armenians, by special maritime arrangements, were taken to and drowned in the high seas that enveloped the many districts of the province of Trabzon constituting a narrow littoral on the Black Sea.[6] Similar drowning operations were conducted in areas through which run the Euphrates River and its tributaries. As Ambassador Morgenthau wrote, "The most terrible scenes took place at the rivers especially at the Euphrates.

. . . In a loop of the river near Erzinghan . . . the thousands of dead bodies created such a barrage that the Euphrates changed its course for about a hundred
yards."[7] The other type of mass murder underscores the holocaustal dimensions
of the Armenian experience. Nearly the entire population of Muş city, Muş plain,
in Bitlis province, consisting of about 100 villages with a total population of
80,000–90,000, was burned alive in stables, haylofts, and farm yards. The commander of the Ottoman 3rd Army, one General Mehmed Vehib, in his testimony
to the Inquiry Commission that was attached to the Turkish military tribunal investigating the wartime massacres, described the procedure involved with particular reference to Tchreeg, one of those villages.[8] There were many instances of
such holocaust in the provinces of Van and Aleppo. A case in point is the holocaust at Deir-Zor. "On October 9, 1916, Moustafa Sıdkı [Deir Zor's police chief
from 1914 to 1918] ordered great stocks of wood to be piled and 200 cans of pe-
troleum spilt on to the whole stock; he then lit it and had 2,000 orphans with
bound hands and feet thrown into the pyre." This is the statement of an Armenian
lawyer, a surviving eyewitness who, in a memorandum dated January 31, 1921,
informed the Armenian patriarch of Istanbul of this instance of a holocaust.[9] In
his postwar memoirs, German Colonel Ludwig Schraudenbach, the commander
of the 14th German-Turkish Division fighting in the area of these massacres, con-
firms this "most shocking atrocity. . . . Children pressed between wooden planks,
tied to them, and burnt to death."[10]

The types of atrocities detailed in the memorandum sent to the Armenian patriarch represent the memories and images that Armenians continue to harbor,
assigning to their genocide the attribute of singularity. But types of atrocities belong to the category of the mechanics of genocide; they are but details in the overall scheme of genocide in which the experience of victimization is lethal, massive,
and terminal insofar as the process of extermination is concerned. In this process,
victim differences involving nationality, gender, socioeconomic class, and age dis-
sipate and collapse as the engine of genocidal mass murder functions to level
these differences with swift finality. The degree of importance one may attach to
the method of destruction is, therefore, eclipsed by the overriding significance of
the genocidal character and outcome of that destruction. Singular or unique
deaths do not necessarily yield a singular or unique genocide. Victim nations may
be drawn and, therefore, respond primarily to these particular aspects of the
genocide, defining it as a unique experience. But as far as scholarship is concerned, what matters most is the common genocidal fate in which these particular aspects of such victim nations tend to configure.

A signal dissimilarity attaches to the level of genocidal decisionmaking involving actual intent. Even though Holocaust literature is dominated by the argument
that Hitler and his cohorts were totally and unconditionally committed to the extermination of the Jewish race immediately upon their seizure of power in inter-
war Germany, the historical evidence is indicative of a different pattern of behavior by these Nazi leaders. What is discernible in this pattern is the gradual

evolution of an attitude where actual genocidal intent appears developmentally to be crystallizing itself.

Apart from sporadic and general statements advocating the destruction of the Jews, by all accounts there is no definite and firm decision at the outset to exterminate them wholesale; there seems to be no clear sign of focusing on a signal lethal option, preempting all other options, to "solve" the "Jewish question." In fact, evidence demonstrates that the Nazis eventually opted for the Holocaust largely by default. In the initial stages of the initiative to get rid of the Jews, the Nazi concern was mainly economic. Indeed, as the plenipotentiary of the Four-Year Plan, Hermann Göring, in November 1938, assumed control of the planning and implementation of Jewish policy, and that policy was defined as "the Elimination of Jews from the German *Economy*" (emphasis added). In relaying Hitler's respective order, Martin Bormann, head of the Nazi Party Chancellery, chose to define the respective measures as "the beginning of the final solution to this problem."[11]

The subsequent draft plans revolved around the central issue of Jewish immigration from Germany, Austria, and other incorporated areas. The coercive aspects of this policy reduced emigration to expulsion, which, however, at times was staggered to allow the victim émigrés and their families to join the workforce and integrate into the economy of the host countries, even though they were being subjected to thorough expropriation by the Nazis themselves. After the German invasion and victory in Poland, emigration gave way to organized deportations to various localities in the newly formed *Generalgovernment* in the occupied center of Poland. Yet this was considered an intermediary stage for the long-range plan of resettling "millions of Jews," perhaps in Madagascar, a jungle island lying in the Indian Ocean about 250 miles off the southeastern coast of Africa.

Involved in all these arrangements were the Jewish Emigration Section of the Gestapo, Section III of the Foreign Office, and the central security bureau of the SS (the *Reichssicherheitshauptamt*, or RSHA), all eager to streamline the procedures for purging Germany of the Jewish element through emigration rather than extermination. Moreover, as late as September 21, 1939, Reinhard Heydrich, the head of the RSHA, defined the "ultimate goal" as the "emigration of the Jews [which] must be completed later." The absence of a genocidal policy—as distinct from genocidal thought—in the treatment of the Jews by the antisemitic Nazis up to the period ushering in the war against the Soviet Union is described by Raul Hilberg:

> As a plan for administrative actions, the idea [of genocide] was not yet obvious or even feasible; but as a thought of something that could happen, it was already ingrained in German minds. . . . Hitler did not order the annihilation of the Jews immediately upon the outbreak of the war. Even Hitler shrank from such a drastic step. Even Hitler hesitated before the "final solution." Even Hitler had to be convinced that there was no other choice.

. . .

From 1938 to 1940, Hitler made extraordinary and unusual attempts to bring about a vast emigration scheme. The biggest expulsion project, the Madagascar plan, was under consideration just one year before the inauguration of the killing phase. The Jews were not killed before the emigration policy was literally exhausted.[12]

Notwithstanding the sporadic pronouncements of Hitler (including those in *Mein Kampf*) and of his cohorts, it is clear that Nazi antisemitic activities were not necessarily on a genocidal track. However coercive and brutal, the measures of expropriation and expulsion were not exterminatory. In a recently publicized document, it is revealed that even beyond the year 1940 the Nazis, led by Hitler, were intent on resettling rather than literally exterminating the Jews. Here is a portion of that document explained; the event described refers to December 1941.

Heydrich revealed that the Führer had authorized Himmler to resettle Jews from all German-controlled territories into certain Russian areas in the northeast. Bühler believed that Heydrich had spoken of eleven million Jews. To accomplish this task, Heydrich said, Himmler would need exclusive control of resettlement, and he would forbid any interference with the task given him by the Führer. Bühler wanted to know if this new policy meant that there would be no more dumping of Jews into the *Generalgouvernement*, and that those Jews already brought there would soon be removed. Heydrich said that he hoped so. Apparently mollified, Bühler agreed to report this information to Frank.[13]

No such options were considered by the Young Turk Ittihadists for the emigration of the Armenian population. In discussing the doom of "two million or more Armenians" slated for wholesale "deportation," Ambassador Morgenthau observed, "As a matter of fact, the Turks never had the slightest idea of reestablishing the Armenians. . . . When the Turkish authorities gave the orders for these deportations, they were merely giving the death warrant to a whole race; they understood this well, and, in their conversation with me, they made no particular attempt to conceal the fact."[14] In other words, at the very outset the genocidal intent was there; the respective decision was firm and implacable. The German state archives, containing a vast amount of wartime confidential and secret reports from German ambassadorial, consular, and military officials stationed in Turkey during the war as that country's allies, amply and unmistakably attest to this fact.[15]

This feature of dissimilarity is critical in the sense that it allows an examination into the conditions under which Nazi measures against the targeted Jewish population changed direction, ultimately acquiring a genocidal thrust. In other words, the Holocaust was an emergent rather than a firmly shaped and prefixed undertaking; it evolved and became a by-product of the dynamics of war and its consequences. Involved here are such developments as intensification of the existing conflicts, new opportunities to reduce inhibitions and increase the temper for boldness in action, and a significant change in the nature, dimension, and composition of the potential victim population. These developments were due to both the swift military successes of the Wehrmacht in the initial stages of the campaign against the Soviet Union and the attendant, vast aggregation of the potential victim population. The inclusion in that population of millions of eastern Russian Jews, as opposed to European and German Jews, qualitatively and quantitatively altered the equation as far as Nazi designs of victimization of the Jews were concerned.

There is another aspect to this problem that arises out of the contentions of most, if not all, Holocaust scholars who insist on the exclusivity of the tragedy of the Holocaust. In differentiating the Armenian genocide from the Holocaust, many of these noted Holocaust scholars assert, for example, that even though the Armenian genocide comes closest to the Holocaust, still, in one major respect, it cannot be compared to it. The core of their assertion is the argument that the Nazi genocide against the Jews was not only total and unconditional but also had a generic thrust in that it aimed at the obliteration of the Jewish race on a global rather than on a regional scale. In support of this argument, these scholars invariably refer to the fate of the Armenian populations of Istanbul and Smyrna, who are portrayed as people who, in fact, were spared and, therefore, escaped deportation and eventually survived. In recently rejecting the inclusion in a text describing the Armenian genocide (intended for Israeli high school students slated to be educated about other cases of genocide), the commission in charge of examining that text, with a view to making appropriate recommendations to the Israeli Ministry of Education, added to these cities Jerusalem and Aleppo. In other words, since so many Armenians escaped destruction, there could not be a design to eradicate the Armenian people as a whole. Hence, or so goes the argument, it is even questionable whether the term "genocide" applies to the Armenian experience. The inaccuracies and misinterpretations associated with these contentions epitomize the pitfalls of cursory or defective knowledge on the subject.

First of all, Istanbul Armenians were not spared deportation and destruction, as has been maintained for so long by Turks and non-Turks alike. In addition to the 2,345 intellectuals, businessmen, clergymen, teachers, and others who had been rounded up and mostly destroyed at the initial stage of the genocidal enactment,[16] subsequently, and in stages, 30,000 other Istanbul Armenians were quietly but systematically seized and eliminated, as indicated by confidential German reports. Ambassador Morgenthau further stated that the Ittihadists had plans to eliminate the rest of the Armenian population of Istanbul. Only the Turkish military setbacks and ancillary handicaps prevented the perpetrators from completing this task. As to Smyrna (Izmir), here again faulty information led to the inaccurate belief that the Turkish authorities, on their own volition, spared the Armenians of that port city. The fact is, however, that Liman von Sanders, the German general in charge of the military security of that zone, threatened the Ittihadist governor of the province with the use of military force to block the deportation of the rest of that city's Armenian population after one contingent was already deported; as the German Foreign Office in Berlin supported the stance of the German general, the Turkish governor felt constrained to oblige.[17]

This raises the issue as to how thorough or complete the Nazi sweep was of the destruction of the targeted Jewish population. Were there no clusters of Jewish groups that escaped or were allowed to escape the lethal clutches of that sweep? In other words, is it warranted for students of the Holocaust to differentiate the Jewish victims from other victim groups, such as the Armenians, by the yardstick of the optimal scale of destruction avowedly characterizing the Holocaust? Given the vastness of the subject, only a few illustrations may be offered to question this line of thought. Out of the total 515,000 German Jews, the Nazis allowed 165,000 of them to emigrate to other countries. In 1939, the combined German-Austrian Jewish population had "shrunken to half of its original size" for the same reason.[18] In the Armenian case no person was allowed to emigrate or to leave the country under any circumstances following the initiation of the empire-wide anti-Armenian measures. Moreover, out of a total population of 330,000 Jews in France, "around 80,000 were victims of the Final Solution."[19]

Do these facts on incomplete instances of mass murder diminish the severity of the Holocaust taken in its totality as a genocidal undertaking? If mitigating circumstances are adduced to explain away these instances of incomplete mass murder or to call them mere aberrations, do they only apply to the Holocaust? The leeways through which the Nazis allowed exceptions to certain categories of Jews to be exempt from mass murder are evident. Hilberg cites Heydrich's "old-age ghetto" in Theresienstadt as a "reservation for old and sick Jews." However dubious in purpose this arrangement was, the old and sick Armenians, slated for destruction, were afforded no such exemption, not even on paper. As late as February 1943, Himmler ordered his subordinates "to permit the Jews in the old people's ghetto of Theresienstadt to live and die there in peace." Change of administrative personnel and dramatic changes in the fortunes of war were factors, however, to the aggravation of the plight of these Jews, many of whom subsequently ended up being transported to death camps to share the fate of their co-nationals.[20] There were similar cases of aberrations with respect to children and young females in the Armenian victim population. They escaped destruction through compulsory proselytizing, induced conversions, adoptions, concubinage, slave labor, bribery, and isolated instances of pity and compassion by individual Turks, Kurds, and other Muslims. As in the case of the Young Turks, so in the case of the Nazis, as far as official policy was concerned, exceptions and exemptions were more often than not either indulgences meant to deflect from the capital crime of genocide or tactical adaptations to pressing needs and exigencies. One can afford to neglect certain parts of an organism after having targeted and succeeded in destroying the core of that organism. In this sense, it is the ultimate outcome of the operation that counts, not the aberrant details of the operation.

Finally, reference may be made to the aftermaths of both genocides, marking diametrically opposite end results. In the Jewish case, there was retributive justice to a significant degree; it was attended by widespread German contrition, the payment of indemnities on a massive scale, and correlative atonement. The entire process culminated in a new drive for political regeneration that ushered in the establishment of the state of Israel. In a macabre yet auspicious way there was an attempt at redemption for all the losses and ordeals the Holocaust entailed for the victim population. One may say that, obversely, all these measures of remorse, reparation, and redemption were denied the surviving Armenian population, whose genocidal victimization is still being denied with persistence and truculence by the perpetrator camp. This can only serve to compound the effects of the genocide. Instead of the appearance on the scene of a residual and liberated new Armenian nation, the surviving Armenian population was in part dissolved in a number of host nations through dispersal or endured seven decades of new hardships under the heels of an oppressive Communist regime. In terms of future developments, this is perhaps the most crucial aspect of the problem of dissimilarity under review here.

II
The Elements of Convergence of the Two Cases

As stated in the introduction to this chapter, the primary purpose of comparing cases of genocide is to distill from them certain common characteristics on the basis of which one may be able to offer some limited generalizations. Such a methodology requires, however, a statement in which genocide is defined as a concept. For the present purposes, it may, therefore, be suggested that three major components are discernible in the definition of genocide. First and foremost, genocide presupposes an intergroup conflict with a history of growth and escalation. Second, genocide serves as a radical device to resolve that conflict; in this sense, genocide is functional. Third, genocide is afforded by a critical disparity of power relations obtaining between the parties to the conflict. In the final analysis, genocide is, therefore, an exercise of power with lethal consequences for the weaker party being victimized by the overwhelming power of the perpetrator group. Within this framework, the mutual relations between a potential perpetrator and a potential victim group—and especially the conflictual aspects of these relationships—emerge as the central problem in the occurrence of genocide. Accordingly, the discussion below focuses on these relationships in the quest for similarities that may lend themselves to the drafting of a modest set of generalizations.

The Historical Ballast of Persecution

Jews and Armenians are two distinct peoples of antiquity. Their histories span millennia punctuated by episodes of sustained persecution. The cumulative effect of this exposure to persecution could not fail to impact upon the collective psyche of these peoples and contribute to the cultivation of defense mechanisms geared to the need for survival as ethnic-national entities. As a result, there developed an ethos of submissiveness intended to mollify the agents of persecution and, thereby, avoid confrontation and peril. With respect to Jewish survival techniques, Hilberg calls this phenomenon "compliance" syndrome, which is anticipatory and often automatic. "The Jews anticipated the force and complied . . . in advance."[21] Extending this notion to his explanation of Jewish behavior during the Holocaust, Hilberg refers to "a two-thousand-year-old experience. In exile . . . the Jews had always been in danger; but they had learned that they could avert danger and survive destruction by placating and appeasing their enemies."[22] Identical patterns developed among the Armenians as a subject people. Yielding completely to their subjugators was a technique for ethnic-national survival, but such submissiveness had consequences that thrust the condition of survival to the threshold of permanent peril. Indeed, when submissiveness becomes predictable for a potential perpetrator group, the submissive group automatically becomes a potential target for abuse; it becomes fair game for victimization because its submissiveness can be taken for granted.

Throughout their histories it is in this sense that Jews and Armenians earned a reputation as tested targets for an assortment of methods of victimization. In a perverse twist of labeling, both peoples acquired a notoriety as ideal objects of persecution, akin to the notoriety of some perpetrator groups. By the same token, both peoples developed an inner toughness that served to preserve their sense of ethnic identification but that was masked by their functional submissiveness. The cultivation of ethnocentrism under such circumstances was conducive to the maintenance by both peoples of a minority status among a host of dominant groups, a status that was portentous in several respects.

The Ramifications of a Minority Status

In sociological terms, the concept of minority has less to do with the criterion of numbers of people and has more to do with that of domination; in this sense, it has reference primarily to quality of status rather than to quantity of people. The logical counterpart to minority is, therefore, not majority but the dominant group. In some instances, a numerically inferior group may have the status of dominant group, and a numerically superior group may be relegated to a minority status. In the genocidal victimization of the Armenians and the Jews, their unchanging minority status in relation to the perpetrator groups, possessing a dominant status, played a major role. It is, therefore, important to understand the specifics of the relevance of this dominant group-minority relationship.

One of the by-products of minority status in societies that have no democratic tradition, are nonpluralistic, or are mainly nominally pluralistic, is the exposure of a given minority to the practice by the dominant group of prejudice and discrimination. Such a practice, as a rule, entails a variety of disbarments, exclusions, and even legal disabilities imposed upon the minority directly or indirectly, overtly or covertly. No minority can escape the psychological and social-psychological effects of such an exposure. Interactive mechanisms in the evolution of mutual relations begin to shape up in such a way as to reflect the consequences of such prejudice and discrimination. In important respects, the behavior of the minority is conditioned by the treatment it is accorded by the dominant group. In this sense, such behavior becomes a function of that treatment. In a pilot study of German Jews who were confined to a ghetto in Frankfurt am Main in the pre–World War II years in Germany, Louis Wirth, one of the pioneers of the Chicago School of Sociology, came up with the following conclusion: When a group of people is treated differentially over a period of time, in due course they will begin to think of themselves as being, in fact, different and may even end up acting differently.[23]

This is an allusion to the by-products of ghettoization and to the rise of an allied ghetto mentality. As such, it is an allusion to obstacles of assimilation through the creation of walls of separation from the mainstream of society. The transition from a condition of denial of the means of assimilation to that of eventual unassimilability is one of the major issues straining dominant group-minority relations. The more the Armenians were degraded by the dominant Muslims for their Christian faith and debarred from many spheres of social and national life, the more they clung to that faith and to all that is implied by it. The ethnocentrism of the Armenians that developed as a result in no small way contributed to the aggravation of the Turko-Armenian conflict, which always existed in an embryonic form. The same argument more or less applies to the Jews. One can hardly separate Jewish ethnocentrism from the tribulations that the Talmudic faithful endured throughout the centuries.

In both cases, the legacy of religion not only in some way preconditioned the minority status but, in the process, left its imprint upon the ethnic consciousness and subdued ethnic assertiveness of both peoples.[24] In brief, the religious identities of both peoples were pregnant with the rudiments of conflict, with a potential to erupt in major conflagrations. As Richard L. Rubenstein observes in this connection, "It is my conviction that the Holocaust can be understood with least mystification if we do not ignore the abiding elements of conflict characterizing the relations between the Jews and their neighbors throughout the entire period of their domicile in the European Christian world."[25] But the consummation of intergroup conflict involves power relations in which the factor of disparity in strength and leverage is likely to determine the outcome. Given the minority status of the Jews and the Armenians, their disadvantage emerges here as a structural problem. Their position of weakness or relative impotence was determined by the arrangements of the sociopolitical system in which they were pitted against dominant groups equipped with most of, if not all, the resources of power. This fact leads to the consideration of another common denominator.

The Vulnerability Factor

As minorities, Jews and Armenians have been frequent targets of persecution throughout history but especially in modern history. As noted above, this is a known fact. What needs to be emphasized, however, is the related fact that their having been recurrent targets, without the ability to counteract or retaliate, proved to be an experience that compounded their condition of vulnerability. When a group is subjected to repeated acts of victimization and the victimizers are not held accountable, for one thing the vulnerability of the victim group is confirmed through the fact of impunity accruing to the perpetrator. But beyond that, and all things being equal, the confirmation yields for the perpetrator, or other potential perpetrators, prospects of new levels of victimization; that confirmation, in fact, becomes a source of new incentives for victimization by way of sheer extrapolation on the part of the potential victimizer.

From a well-known fact, one does draw inferences and projects them into the future. In other words, the impunity accruing to a victimizer functions to amplify the vulnerability of the victim. Armenian and Jewish histories are punctuated by episodes of this type. The anti-Jewish pogroms of 1881–1882 and the 1903 Kishinev massacre in tsarist Russia in the decades preceding World War I are two such examples. They not only confirmed the vulnerability of the Jews, they portended developments capable of compounding that vulnerability. By the same token, one may argue that both the Abdul Hamit–era massacres in the 1894–1896 period and the 1909 Adana massacres dramatically exposed the vulnerability of the Armenians in the Ottoman empire.

The absence of any significant measure of retributive justice in the aftermath of all these massacres immensely aggravated the plight of the Ottoman Armenian population, rendering it an easy target for optimal destruction. In fact, one may even assert that the World War I Armenian genocide is foreshadowed in this series of untamed massacres. Two authors who personally examined the 1894–1896 massacres, by way of on-the-spot investigations, prophetically foretold at that time the demise of Ottoman Armenians through a major holocaust. One of them was an American—a student of the Civil War—who boasted of his "rather keen appetite for facts."[26] The other was noted British ethnographer William M. Ramsay, who in 1897 predicted the genocidal fate of the Armenians with these words: "The Armenians will in all probability be exterminated except the remnant that escapes to other lands."[27]

In discussing tsarist intentions about the Jews, Rubenstein allows that "the ultimate aim of Russian policy in the aftermath of the events of 1881 was the total elimination of the Jews."[28] He recognizes even a transfer of the condition of vulnerability from the Jews to the Armenians by the establishment of precedents, such as the tsarist pogroms that preceded the Abdul Hamit–era massacres. The impunity of one perpetrator group by way of contagion impinged upon the deadly motivations of another, thereby bringing into acute relief the vulnerability of Ottoman Armenians. It is in this sense that Rubenstein observes the existence of "an eerie parallel between the beginnings of the process which led to the destruction of European Jews and the one leading to the destruction of another 'elite minority,' the Armenians."[29]

Another aspect of the vulnerability syndrome has a paradoxical twist and is an extension of the effects of the structural barriers imposed upon the Jews and the Armenians. As degraded and often despised minorities, they were debarred from certain occupations and offices, most notably the military, the government, and the civil service. As preemptive and exclusionary as such arrangements were, they impelled—if not compelled—these two peoples to pursue other alternatives and forego the military and the government. The result was that appreciable numbers among them cultivated skills and aptitudes through which they prospered. Instead of being confined to the limited incomes of salaried employment in government, the military, and the civil service, they expanded and opened up new vistas offering possibilities for unlimited riches through the vehicles of trade, commerce, and industry.

The economic ascendancy that many of them thereby achieved and the wealth they had acquired proved a liability, however, especially in times of economic crises affecting the respective dominant groups. It did not matter that this type of ascendancy was made affordable in default, that is, mainly as a result of debarments described above. The ability to harness to advantage such debarments and attain relative affluence proved a liability in relation to the resentment of the dominant groups that might be struggling economically. In democratic and pluralistic societies, economic preponderance is a distinct source of power, impinging upon all spheres of life, including polity. But the societies enveloping the Armenians and Jews as minorities were apt to consider such preponderance as an unwarranted anomaly calling for remedies. It may, therefore, be proposed that when economic ascendancy is attended by political impotence, in times of acute national crises, the combination may prove perilous for the minorities. This represents an aberrant form of vulnerability that has plagued Armenian and Jewish efforts to coexist with antagonistic dominant groups. The vulnerability stems from the cardinal fact that because of their minority status they were denied access to resources of power within the sociopolitical systems of which they were a part.

The critical significance of this economic factor in the vulnerability syndrome of both peoples was cast in stark relief in the course of their genocidal victimization. It not only aroused the inveterate cupidity of the manifold casts of perpetrators, but, in several respects, economic considerations became codeterminants in genocidal decisionmaking and genocidal enactments involving both victim groups. (Hilberg has an entire chapter on this subject, subsumed under the title "Expropriation.")[30] This was even more so in the Armenian case. Not only German, Austrian, and American but authentic Turkish sources attest to the incidence of a genocide that was largely based on economic calculations, projections, and designs. The goal was to invest Muslim Turks with economic power and promote the formation of Turkish commercial classes to supplant those among the non-Muslim minorities, particularly the Armenians. It was a violent form of enacting a massive redistribution of wealth.

This fact was implicitly acknowledged by Halide Edib, a prominent Turkish feminist writer who had close ties to Ittihadist leaders. She wrote, "Besides this political argument . . . there was a strong economic one, morally supported by the Germans. This was to end the economic supremacy of the Armenians, thereby clearing the markets for the Turks and the Germans."[31] In his August 19, 1915, report to Ambassador Morgenthau, Aleppo's veteran American consul, J. B. Jackson—whose district was the scene of untold acts of plunder, robbery, and pillage by the Turks—characterized the ongoing Armenian genocide as "a gigantic plundering scheme as well as a final blow to extinguish the race."[32] In his memoirs, Morgenthau describes the economic animus in the enactment of the genocide. In the narration of one particular encounter with Mehmed Talât, the architect of the Armenian genocide, the latter is portrayed as having impetuously demanded that two American life insurance companies, New York Life Insurance and Equitable Life of New York, "send us a complete list of their Armenian policy holders, they are practically all dead now. . . . It of course all escheats to the State. The Government is the beneficiary now." This "most astonishing request . . . was too much, and I lost my temper," wrote the ambassador.[33]

There was one more element of vulnerability afflicting these two victim groups in particular. Neither the Armenians nor the Jews had a parent state to warn, threaten, counteract, or retaliate against the perpetrator groups. They had been, and at the time of their demise they were, virtually orphan nations. The perpetrators could, therefore, afford to discount a direct confrontation with any state entity with a high stake in their fates. This element of vulnerability was further accented by the passive attitude of the world powers. Pleading intense preoccupation with warfare and with the objective of ultimate victory, they allowed both genocides to run their course without any significant measure of preventive intervention on their part. This fact reinforced the assessment of the Nazis and the Young Turk Ittihadists that their targeted victims were fair game. Passivity and inaction by these powers were conditions that, in the minds of the perpetrators, were converted into a license for mass murder.

The inclination for such an inference is explained in American sociologist W. I. Thomas's notion of "definition of the situation." According to this notion, if men define situations as real, they are real in their consequences. The dismal failure of the Nazi efforts to induce the Western powers, especially France, to help resettle the Jews of Germany and Austria in their territories is underscored by the attitude of French Foreign Minister Georges Bonnet, who, in an exchange with German Foreign Minister Joachim von Ribbentrop in December 1938, rebuffed the latter on this issue. In fact, Bonnet asked Ribbentrop to prevent German Jews from coming to France, adding that France was thinking of shipping 10,000 Jews somewhere else, probably Madagascar; concluded Ribbentrop, "No country wished to receive them."[34] This kind of attitude prompted even Hitler to lament in January 1939 the plight of the Jews with these words: "It is a shameful example to observe today how the entire democratic world dissolves in tears of pity, but then, in spite of its obvious duty to help, closes its heart to the poor, tortured Jewish people."[35] Three years later, when the destruction process was in high gear, Dr. Joseph Goebbels, a top Nazi leader, made the following entry in his diary on December 13, 1942: "At bottom . . . I believe both the English and the Americans are happy that we are exterminating the Jewish riffraff."[36] All this led to the suspicion "in the Jewish ranks" that "the Allies secretly approved" the Nazi campaign of annihilating the Jews.[37]

As to the Ittihadists, based on past experiences, they were convinced that they would again have a more or less free hand in bringing into play their anti-Armenian scheme, which this time involved the introduction of a "final solution" with regard to the Armenian population of the Ottoman empire. The exigencies of the war, in which practically all the Great Powers were embroiled, fortified that conviction. So much so, in fact, that they completely ignored the formal and ostensibly solemn warning of the Allies—England, France, and Russia—who, on May 24, 1915, when the genocide was being initiated, declared they would hold responsible all Turkish officials and other people implicated in the mass murder of the Armenians.[38] If anything, however, the tempo of the genocide was intensified and accelerated in the wake of this proclamation. The significance of the spirit of disdain and defiance, implicit in this sequential response, was exceeded only by the significance of the patent failure of the Allies to live up to their commitment when Turkey lay prostrate at the end of the war and sued for armistice.

In holding Turkey accountable for the atrocities against the Armenians, the Allies in 1915 had introduced the concept of "crimes against humanity," which was later adopted by the prosecutors at Nuremberg and subsequently incorporated into the Preamble of the United Nations (UN) Convention on Genocide.[39] The legal condemnation of the Holocaust and the conviction and sentencing of the Nazi perpetrators were acts that were essentially predicated upon this concept of "crimes against humanity." One of those who was thus convicted in Nuremberg allowed in his memoirs that the Holocaust and the related crimes were afforded due to the failure of the victors to exact retribution from those guilty of crimes against humanity in World War I. He maintained that such prosecution "would have encouraged a sense of responsibility on the part of leading political figures [i.e., Nazis] if after the First World War the Allies had actually held the trials they had threatened."[40] Nowhere is this more patently attested to than in a famous statement attributed to Hitler, who is quoted as saying, "Who after all is today speaking of the destruction of the Armenians" *(Wer redet heute noch von der Vernichtung der Armenier).*[41] In other words, the impunity associated with the perpetration of the Armenian genocide not only highlighted the abiding vulnerability of the Armenians but had such repercussions as to bring into relief the analogous vulnerability of the Jews.

This is one instance where the principle of common features entwines with the principle of common links. In this sense, the Armenian genocide is not only a precedent but also a source of instigation for the enactment of the Holocaust; it incited the criminal instincts of the Nazi perpetrators by exciting their unbridled racist and nationalist ambitions.

For all these reasons, one should not underestimate this third element of vulnerability so gravely imperiling the survival of the Jews and Armenians. And that perilousness demonstrates how the internal vulnerability of a minority can be immeasurably magnified when combined with external vulnerability. It may best be described as the absence of external deterrence in face of internal threats of destructive designs against a vulnerable minority. That peril is aptly articulated by Hilberg who, speaking of the doom of the Jews, states, "The Jews of Europe had no allies. In its gravest hour Jewry stood alone."[42] Yet this is a statement that accurately describes a condition, without placing it in a context where one can relate to analogous phenomena, in order to achieve a deeper level of penetration. As noted at the outset, this is a problem intrinsic to all case studies, which are self-contained discourses lacking a transcendental, analytical bent by the exploration of the comparative method. The pathos for exclusive singularity undergirds the entire framework of Hilberg's monumental treatise, which, accordingly, ends with a lamentation reflecting that pathos. In explaining why the Jews became the prime targets of the Nazis, Hilberg maintains that "historical precedents . . . determined the selection [of the Jews], which for centuries had been the standby victim of recurring destruction" and prepossessingly concludes that "no other group could fill this role so well. None was so vulnerable."[43]

The Opportunity Structure

However motivated, tempted, or eager, no potential perpetrator can proceed from contemplation to action without suitable opportunities. This is a basic law of criminology encompassing many forms of criminal behavior. More often than not, the greatest restraining force for criminally inclined individuals or groups is not the penal codes of criminal justice but, instead, want of suitable opportunities. It is no coincidence that the two major genocides of this century were consummated in the vortex of two global wars. There is, therefore, an intrinsic, acute relationship between the concepts of modern warfare and the opportunity structure, in the sense that the exigencies and emergencies of warfare are pregnant with uncommon opportunities for illicit behavior by state apparatuses, governments, monolithic political parties, or military juntas. The utilization of vehicles for such behavior calls, therefore, for a brief revue.

The nature of warfare is such, for example, that as a rule it allows legislative authority to subside, if not to vanish entirely, with the executive branch of the government as the main beneficiary of the "emergency powers" accruing to it. In a war, the bastion of power is usually the executive branch. As the authority of the legislative branch either subsides or vanishes altogether, the power of the executive increases substantially. Emergency powers are expressive of the supreme opportunities that a war yields in this regard. In both systems, the Nazi and the Young Turk Ittihadists—the principal agents of these powers—have been the so-called "security forces" comprising a vast network of outfits; they were invested with levels of power that in most cases bordered on license for criminal abuse.

Perhaps the greatest source of power in an oppressive society in times of war is the military establishment that is identified with the authorities in charge. To the extent that the outcome of the war hinges on military performance, military authorities will acquire inordinate power and, accordingly, will be catapulted into relative predominance. Genocide not only requires opportunistic decisionmaking, its execution depends on functional efficiency. In addition to planning and administering the logistics involved, there has to be a command-and-control setup to ensure a reasonably smooth operation. The goal is optimal destruction at minimal cost. This is a task for which the specialized skills of the military are needed.

In both cases of genocide, the military played a crucial role. Involved were not just regular officers but officers who were intensely committed to the respective ideologies and goals of the Nazis and Ittihadists. Within this framework of loyalty and dedication, they performed critical staff work, maintained secrecy and discipline, and participated in field operations as commanders of killer bands. Such terms as "Nazi officers" and "Ittihadist officers" are descriptive of the potentially lethal process of indoctrinating military officers with political party credos and teachings and, in general, of politicizing the military or segments of it. War emerges here as an ideal opportunity for harnessing political power into military power as an instrument of genocide.

The dynamics of such a process of power amplification were such that the vulnerabilities of the Jews and Armenians as minorities increased in proportion to this growth of power; the stronger the victimizers became, the weaker became the victims. This is a mechanism that ultimately leads to what might be called "victim entrapment."

In the Armenian case, the Turks used four devices to amplify their power while increasing the vulnerability of the Armenians. First, they suspended the parliament; it was prorogued just before the initiation of the genocide and was reconvened when that genocide had all but run its course. Second, they introduced a system of temporary laws, the framing of which became the prerogative of the executive, that is, the Ittihadist power-wielders. Third, armed with these powers, they launched a program of massive arrests in all parts of the Ottoman empire. Nearly all community leaders, intellectuals, educators, ranking clergymen, and political activists were simultaneously rounded up in nightly surprise raids, deported; most of them were subsequently liquidated. Finally, in order to further

emasculate the victim population and reduce it to easy prey for eventual annihilation, all able-bodied Armenian males were conscripted in three stages as part of
the general mobilization. Very few of them survived the ensuing operations of
summary executions or extirpation through other lethal measures. The resort to
these measures was considerably facilitated by the continuation of the state of
siege and martial law.

In the Jewish case, similar procedures were adopted. The emasculation of the
Jewish community in Germany was more progressive in its course, as its initiation dated back to the interwar years. Its first stage—the promulgation of the
March 23, 1933, Enabling Act—had a general thrust and was not specifically directed against the Jews. As in the case of the Ittihadist initiative described above,
the Nazis managed to institute an act through which they would be empowered
to make laws without the approval of the German parliament, the *Reichstag*. The
five articles of the act all but destroyed the German constitution. As in the case of
the Young Turk Ittihadists, the Nazis subsequently embarked upon their deadly
scheme of *Gleichschaltung*, whereby they substituted Nazi power for parliamen-
tary power. With the outbreak of World War II, however, the Enabling Act acquired special significance for the Jews, as it was renewed in 1939 and 1942 in
conformity with its article 5, which required renewal every four years. These re-
newals imparted a semblance of legitimacy to the array of anti-Jewish measures
adopted by the various agencies of the Nazi-dominated government.

The principal rationale for targeting the Jews and Armenians during these two
global wars was the designation and the decrial of both groups as "internal foes."
This way, they could be considered as legitimate targets for destruction; after all,
enemies in warfare are meant to be destroyed in pursuit of victory. Genocide thus
becomes an integral part of warfare, an extension of the external war—internally.
Here, the social-psychological mechanism of interactive behavior described
above, involving the reliance on the mechanism of "definition of the situation,"
came into play. No matter how inaccurate, misperceived, or distortive, when a dis-
cordant or potentially harmful minority is defined as an "internal foe" by a dominant group waging an exhaustive war, the subsequent treatment accorded to that
minority will be attuned to that definition. Definitions of situations, no matter
how unreal or misleading, do indeed have consequences, and the standards used
to fashion such definitions are determined by the more powerful party to the conflict, that is, the dominant group. Such power, indeed, yields manifold latitudes
to contrive and impose arbitrary definitions, affording abusive or criminal actions against the group denounced, degraded, and targeted within the framework
of the definition in question.

The exigencies of war provided another set of opportunities for the perpetrators. There is a need for methods and instruments geared to facilitating the
process of destruction. In other words, as already noted, there is a need for functional efficiency. The standard mechanism in all these definitions that applied to
the Armenians and Jews was the act of labeling them as actual or potential "trai-

tors," "enemies of the state." For victimization to have an appearance of validity, if not legitimacy, the victims have to be stigmatized first; labeling is intended to serve that purpose.

At the level of actually implementing a scheme of genocide, the opportunity factor emerges as pivotal. The maxim employed here by the perpetrator is "optimal results at minimal losses." To achieve such a goal, the victim population must be trapped by methods of deception, deflection, and, when necessary, coercion. The element of surprise is part of this procedure. The most striking and, at the same time, the most functional method of trapping the targeted Jewish and Armenian populations was the reliance on the use of the term "deportation." The term was easy to explain and defend in the context of wartime exigencies. It allowed the victims to acquiesce to what it denoted, without much pondering as to what it might connote to the perpetrators. To reinforce the imagery of a temporary inconvenience, the perpetrators contrived such ancillary terms as "relocation" (*Aussiedlung, Evakuierung, Wohnsitzverlegung, Umsiedlung*); in Turkish, the Ittihadists used the words *tehcir, tebdili mekân*.

In the Nazi case, if one disregards the operations of the *Einsatzgruppen*, the mobile killer bands, there were mostly the death camps. In the Ittihadist case, there were no such camps but open-ended traps of all kinds of death and destruction. Thus, the reliance on euphemisms, involving code words for genocidal killing operations, had a definite function. Once dislocated and removed from their cities, towns, and villages, the victim populations were totally defenseless. Coercive hardships, despair, and physical isolation combined to render them an easy prey for disposal. Deportation had the additional function of creating a condition where destruction became substantially facilitated; it created a temporary concentration and density of population that, for purposes of targeting, is an ideal condition. The cycle of trapping thus reaches its terminal and lethal stage.

This process of destruction by way of deportation was attended by a host of auxiliary measures endemic to wartime emergency conditions. They included control of nearly all channels of internal and external communications of those in the targeted victim populations who were placed under clandestine surveillance. The victim populations underwent fragmentation in the manner in which they were subjected to deportation, especially in the Armenian case. As a result, clusters of populations were kept in the dark as to one another's conditions and the overall fate of the entire population. Again, in the Armenian case, the process of destruction was immensely facilitated by two types of procedures. Due to a general mobilization, most able-bodied men were conscripted and removed from the fold of their families. As already described, they were then handled separately by military authorities. At the first opportunity, those remaining—the young and the old males—were separated from the deportee convoys and were then promptly liquidated, often in front of their female relatives.

The ultimate weapon that was forged and amply used by the Nazis and Ittihadists in connection with the opportunities afforded by the two global wars was the type of outfit most suited for the performance of inexorable killing operations. The Young Turk Ittihadist leadership called it the "Special Organization" (*Teşkilâtı Mahsusa*), which was largely, almost entirely, comprised of felons, convicts, and repeat criminals. They were released from the prisons of the Ottoman empire and carefully examined by teams consisting of medical experts, War Ministry staff officers, and representatives of the Justice Ministry in charge of the Ottoman prison system. After one week of training at the camp grounds of the War Ministry, they were put in special brigand (*çete*) uniforms and sent to the interior of the country to carry out their secret missions. They were deployed at remote and strategic spots through which the multitudes of deportee convoys were expected to pass. The standard procedure was to set upon these convoys and slaughter them on the spot, after robbing and plundering them. These killer bands were led by select army staff officers. The logistics and related aspects of planning were arranged by Department II at the Ministry of War and Ottoman General Headquarters in close cooperation with the secret Directorate of the Ittihad Party, often portrayed as the Central Committee of the party.[44]

The creation of special units to destroy the Jewish victim population is meticulously detailed by Hilberg.[45] The roles of *Einsatzgruppen* are of particular significance, underscoring the paramount role of the SS and police units affiliated with it, especially in occupied Russia.[46] But superseding in importance these roles, relative to this discussion, is the involvement in killing operations of convicts, mobilized and directed by the SS. This organization was branded a criminal organization by the International Military Tribunal in Nuremberg. Foremost in this connection were some of the units operating under the command of Erich von dem Bach-Zelewski, SS *Obergruppenführer*, and general of the Waffen SS and Police. The number of troops under his command was greater than that of the *Einsatzgruppen*. Von dem Bach had up to two divisions at his disposal. These divisions included the Dirlewanger Brigade, "which was composed of habitual criminals." Dirlewanger, the commander, was a convict in his own right. Among the victims of the von dem Bach killer bands were 363,211 Jews.[47] For his part, noted author Robert Jay Lifton emphasizes the role at Auschwitz of "hardened criminal psychopaths" joining the SS personnel there in killing operations.[48]

All these arrangements raise the question as to specifically how and by whom they were made. What is the source of authority in terms of ultimate instances and intermediary instances of authority involving a hierarchical structure? By what criteria and at what level have these authorities claimed legitimacy and, accordingly, tried to legitimize the entire lethal undertaking? These issues are addressed below.

The Decisive Roles of Two Monolithic Political Parties

Holocaust and genocide literature is dominated by a central theme about the fundamental problem as to who the ultimate authors of genocidal initiatives are. Due to the application of massive and lethal state force and the complex organization needed to mobilize such force through institutional channels, the vast majority of scholars involved in genocide studies depict the state as the supreme author in this respect. After all, the sovereign state is the embodiment of legitimate power that, at will, can be converted into coercive force by simply applying and exerting that power. Moreover, the levers of state organization are equipped to handle the task of streamlining the genocidal enactment. The works of noted author Irving Louis Horowitz epitomize this conceptual orientation.[49]

The flaw in this approach is that it issues from a perspective in which the relationship of formal authority to informal authority is not properly assessed. By definition, the state is simultaneously the locus and the expression of formal authority. Under more or less normal circumstances, that authority is predicated upon the principle of legitimacy, which not only serves to sanction the authority of the state but also circumscribes the parameters of that authority while conditioning the terms of its application. Even in times of war, there are limits as to the extent to which these parameters may be enlarged and the conditions—under which force may be used—may be relaxed. In other words, in origin, structure, and function, the state is not geared to conceiving, organizing, and implementing a monstrous crime such as genocide represents. As a rule, formal authority precludes such a recourse to criminality. In order for a state to get involved in the business of genocidal enactments, it has to undergo structural changes and transform itself into an engine of destruction. In other words, it has to be criminalized.

The only instrument capable of generating such a transformation is a type of informal authority that is in ascendance and in rivalry with the authority of the state. Driven by an inveterate urge for power, the agents of such authority compete for the resources of the state. In the two genocides under review here, these agents were none other than the combative and daring leaders of two monolithic political parties that were animated with revolutionary and radical designs. I refer, of course, to the Nazis (the National Socialist Party) and the Young Turk Ittihadists (the Committee of Union and Progress).

As they proceeded to entrench themselves in their respective positions as monolithic parties—in the course of which they had to overcome obstacles, resistance, and threats—they drifted into progressively more radical ideologies and postures. Their drive for supreme domination culminated in the seizure of the reins of power over the respective states. In the modern history of sovereign states, this is perhaps the most dramatic and portentous juncture, where the bearers of informal authority overwhelm the formal authority of the state apparatus. What is even more critical, however, is the fact that with seizure of power the informal authority of the party does not evaporate or subside. Merging with the formal authority of the state organization that the party now controls, it emerges in a reinforced mold of informal authority, holding sway over the key agencies of the government identified with that state. This is a process of intrusion in and permeation and domination of the state apparatuses, as a result of which the functions of the state are subverted for the benefit of the party and party programs and ideologies are superimposed upon governmental agencies. In brief, for all practical purposes, the state is reduced to a tool of the party and its ideological interests.

These considerations suggest, therefore, that the focus of attention be shifted from states to political parties capable of displacing state power and substituting for it party power and leverage. A state, thus divested of or impaired in the free use of its means of authority, can hardly be considered a determinant in the conception and enactment of the crime of genocide. It is a historical fact of paramount import that the architects of the genocides of the Jews and Armenians were placed in the highest leadership strata of the Nazi and Ittihadist parties. This means that in order to examine and comprehend the overt as well as covert aspects of both genocides it is necessary to examine the leadership, ideology, structure, and inner workings of the two political parties that, in fact, became substitutes for the governments they supplanted and usurped. As Ambassador Morgenthau observed, "The Young Turks were not a government; they were really an irresponsible party, a kind of secret society, which, in intrigue, intimidation, assassination, had obtained most of the offices of state."[50] Commenting on the Nazis in the same vein, a German author recently noted that the German "state apparatus was controlled by the staff of Hess and the party-chancellery of Martin Bormann."[51]

Nowhere is the convergence of the Jewish and Armenian cases of genocide so dramatically revealed as in the exposure of the crucial, initiatory roles the two parties played. The act of initiation was intimately connected with two analogous top-secret conferences in the course of which a final decision was reached to liquidate the two victim populations. The January 20, 1942, Wannsee Conference is a well-known fact. What is less emphasized, however, is that even though there were some professional civil servants and servile bureaucrats attending that conference it was the purest form of party decision reached by those potentates of the party whose prime and exclusive loyalty was not to the German state but to the *Führer*, Adolf Hitler. The deliberations took place in the central office of National Security, run by the SS.[52] The idea was to render Germany "free from the Jews" (*Judenfrei*).

An almost identical conference took place in Istanbul, then the Ottoman capital, shortly after Turkey unilaterally intervened in the war. It was a major link in the chain of secret party enclaves meant to radically resolve the Armenian question. As in the case of Wannsee, the five participants included the highest ranking party leaders, such as party boss Mehmed Talât; doctors Mehmed Nazım and Behaeddin Şakir, the most powerful two members of the party's Supreme Directorate; Seyfi Düzgören, the head of counterintelligence and guerrilla war at the Ottoman General Headquarters; and Ismail Canbolat, head of the National Security office (*Emniyeti Umumiye*). The blueprint that resulted from this conference outlined the measures to be taken and the methods to be used for the liquidation of Ottoman Armenians.[53] What is so remarkable about this document is the fact that the actual process of destruction and its outcome confirm the authenticity and operativeness of the blueprint, serving as it did as a basic directive for the organization of the Armenian genocide.

The distinct and nearly exclusively genocidal roles of the two political parties are underscored by the fact that the party executioners had sworn their oath of allegiance not to the state, nation, country, or any other symbol but to Adolf Hitler and national socialism, on the one hand, and to Ittihad and its mission on the other. In interpreting this ritual, Robert Jackson, chief counsel for the United States at Nuremberg, wrote this:

> The membership took the Party oath which in effect, amounted to an abdication of personal intelligence and moral responsibility. This was the oath: "I vow inviolable fidelity to Adolf Hitler; I vow absolute obedience to him and to the leaders he designates for me." The membership in daily practice followed its leaders with an idolatry and self-surrender more Oriental than Western.[54]

Likewise the Ittihadist operatives, agents, and killer-band leaders were sworn party loyalists and felt hardly any obligation to the state. Their oath included the commitment that should they ever reveal a party secret or disobey a command of the central authorities of the party they would be targeted for destruction. Special Organization Chieftain Major Yakub Cemil, who played a major role in the Armenian genocide, openly declared: "If the party ordered me to kill my father, I would not hesitate for a moment."[55] Informal authority has optimal scope for exercise, because, unlike a state organization, it does not have to observe fixed or preordained rules and regulations. Precisely for this reason, it can afford to be irresponsible and dispense with the need for accountability. These are conditions that not only allow but stimulate, if not encourage, deviant or criminal behavior. The genocidal enterprises reviewed here were essentially the by-products and consequences of the exercise of informal authority by political parties that held the levers of power of a state but also had covert genocidal agendas.

The organizational makeup of the two parties was such as to allow the leadership strata to rely on a level of discipline on the part of the committed party faithful that exceeded the functionality of the most dutiful bureaucrats engaged by the two respective states. Some illustrations are in order. The Third Reich of the Nazis was administered and controlled by a network of *Gauleiters*, all of whom were devoted—if not fanatic—party luminaries. The entire system of internal security, police, intelligence, and the rest was run by select and trusted party zealots. These were the essential components of the gigantic machinery through which the destruction process was consummated with the help of a network of co-opting or submissive functionaries of the state representing formal authority.

Similar patterns obtained in the Armenian case. Ittihad engineered and supervised the destruction process through three types of representatives who were sent to the provinces to serve as party provincial commissars overseeing the details of the massacres. There were first the so-called Responsible Secretaries (*Kâtibi Mes'ul*); then there were the delegates (*Murahhas*); and then the Inspectors (*Müfettiş*). Many of these party commissars were former army officers of different ranks who had resigned from the military to dedicate themselves to the goal of serving the party. In the implementation phase of the genocide, they proved themselves as most efficient executors of the covert party designs targeting the provincial Armenian population. All of them were invested with a level of power that surpassed that of the provincial governors-general over whom they exercised veto power.

Nor can one underestimate the reward system set up by the party organization to promote its designs and goals. As in the case of the Nazis, so in the case of the Ittihadists, a system of adroitly arranged rewards elicited a high level of compliance from party members to requests and commands that were such as to compromise the integrity of the latter, reduce their capacity for compunction, and obviate guilt feelings. When guilt is shared with fellow partisans within the context of pressing party desiderata, inhibitions tend to attenuate themselves and guilt feelings are more or less smothered. There arise so-called emergent norms that elicit from the party faithful a deviant form of conformity.

To sum up, in the course of the genocides under review here, the state organizations in the Third Reich and the Ottoman empire were almost reduced to irrelevance as the Nazis and the Ittihadists gained optimal control of these organizations, including the key governmental agencies, such as cabinet ministries and legislative bodies. The analysis of the two genocides, therefore, has to be primarily anchored on the genesis, structure, leadership, reward system, and overt and covert designs of these two parties, considered to be the actual authors of these twin genocides.

Genocide as a Function of Social Restructuring

I stated at the beginning of this chapter that genocide presupposes an intergroup conflict that defies nonviolent settlement with a tendency to escalate and intensify. In line with this view, genocide can be regarded as a device to resolve that conflict radically and terminally. But the scrutiny of the two genocides in question clearly indicates that the resolution of the conflict itself may be considered as a means to still another end. The clue to this phenomenon is contained in the nature of the conflicts at issue. When a dominant group is bent on purging an ethnic minority from the fabric of its mainstream society, this is a reflection of a perception by that dominant group that there is an unacceptable incompatibility between itself and the minority; the conflict is expressive of this perceived incompatibility. The Nazis wanted to rid Germany of the Jews; the Ittihadists wanted to rid Turkey of the Armenians. The watchwords, "Germany for the Germans" and "Turkey for the Turks," encapsulated these sentiments. The implied common objective here was to reduce the heterogeneous complexion of German and Turkish societies toward the goal of optimal homogeneity. In other words, the underlying urge was to alter, for a variety of reasons, the ethnic-national makeup of the German and Turkish societies. This is a type of alteration that is best described as social restructuring.

This line of reasoning warrants a final conclusion with respect to the issue of the comparative similarities of the Armenian and Jewish cases of genocide; namely, in its ultimate thrust genocide is a function of social restructuring.[56] The destruction of the two victim populations was a means to the superordinate goal of recasting German and Turkish societies in the projected mold of integral nations. That function was afforded by conditions and developments in which the factors of minority status, vulnerability, opportunity, and the dictatorial ascendancy of monolithic political parties configured and pushed the genocidal process into channels for consummation. In recognizing the functional character of genocide, these factors need to be taken into account as contingency factors.

The Sweep Beyond Domestic Genocide

One of the misconceptions of a number of holocaust scholars venturing to evaluate the Armenian genocide is revealed in their common argument that the Turkish drive to destroy the Armenians applied only to the Armenians of Ottoman Turkey. As such, so goes the argument, that drive was geographically confined as it was circumscribed by the territorial boundaries of Ottoman Turkey. In other words, it had a limited compass of destructiveness as compared with the Nazi drive culminating in the Holocaust. The facts are, however, at variance with this notion.

Following the outbreak of the Bolshevik Revolution in 1917 and the ensuing collapse of the Russian army that had occupied vast tracts of land in eastern Turkey, the Ottoman 3rd Army, which was on the verge of total defeat, was unexpectedly relieved of the perils of such defeat; it received a new lease on life. Taking advantage of this lifesaving opportunity, that army, after replenishing itself, launched a new offensive in the spring of 1918 and ended up occupying substantial portions of Russian Armenia in the Transcaucasus. As a result, the genocidal engine of destruction unleashed by the Young Turk Ittihadists was once more activated to decimate and destroy the other half of the Armenian population living beyond the established frontiers of Turkey. The horrors of this new drive of genocide were such that two German generals and a staff colonel, allies of Turkey and, at the time, on duty in the Transcaucasus, felt compelled to send to their superiors in Berlin a string of reports decrying the Turkish methods of annihilating the new victim population.

Major General Otto von Lossow, the German military representative at the Batum Conference, on May 15, 1918, informed Berlin that the Turks had embarked upon "the total extermination of the Armenians in Transcaucasia also" (*völlige Ausrottung der Armenier auch in Transkaukasien*).[57] On June 3, 1918, he sent a warning to the effect that "Talât's government party wants to destroy all Armenians [*alle Armenier ausrotten will*], not only in Turkey, but also outside Turkey."[58] For his part Major General Kress von Kressenstein, chief of the German imperial delegation in the Caucasus, on July 13, 1918, reported to Berlin about "the Turkish resolve to annihilate the Armenians" (*der Vernichtungswille der Türkei gegenüber dem armenischen Element*).[59] On July 31, the same general declared that "the Turks have by no means relinquished their intention to exterminate the Armenians" (*ihre Absicht . . . auszurotten*).[60] Colonel Ernst Paraquin, at the time the chief of staff of General Halil Kut (the commander-in-chief of the Turkish Army Groups East, which had invaded Russian Armenia) angrily declared, "With hypocritical indignation the Turkish government denies all barbarous conduct against the Armenians. The evacuation of Anatolia by the Russians furnished the desired opportunity to clear out also the Russian Armenians. . . . The annihilation campaign against the Armenians proceeded . . . with inexorable ruthlessness" (*mit geheuchelter Entrüstung jedes barbarische Verfahren gegen Armenier bestritt*).[61]

The two foremost military leaders of wartime Germany in their memoirs corroborate these charges of organized mass murder against Armenians in the Caucasus. General Erich Ludendorff, chief of staff in the German High Command, for example, declared, "Turkey plunged into a war of murder and looting in the Caucasus" (*Mord und Beutekrieg*).[62] Field Marshal Paul von Hindenburg likewise wrote: "Turkey wants to annex the Caucasus entirely and exterminate [*ausrotten*] the Armenians with all means available, massacres and bloodbaths are in the order of the day."[63] All these indictments and condemnations were formally and officially verified by Richard von Kühlmann, former ambassador to Turkey (1916–1917) and Germany's foreign minister at the time of the Turkish invasion of the Caucasus. He denounced the authorities, declaring "In violations of their promises the Turks systematically are pursuing their plan of annihilation of the Armenians in the Caucasus" (*die Vernichtung planmässig betreiben*).[64]

As if these exterminatory operations were not enough,[65] the new Kemalist regime, which on every occasion publicly had distanced itself from the previous Ittihadist regime on account of its criminal activities, after a lapse of sixteen months resumed the genocidal onslaught against the Armenians. Without declaring war, Turkish General Kâzım Karabekir in September 1920 attacked the fledgling Republic of Armenia in the Transcaucasus after having secured the formal authorization from Mustafa Kemal and his government in Ankara. Ill-equipped, ill-trained, and ill-prepared, and additionally fractured by the infusion of bolshevik propaganda that described the invading Turks as comrades and liberators, the untested army of the Republic folded rather quickly. Two factors considerably influenced the new Turkish élan to resume the genocidal drive. The victorious Allies were set to punish vanquished Turkey for wartime crimes, especially for the massacres against the Armenians, and concomitantly compensate the Armenians. They proceeded to redraw Turkey's boundaries for the benefit of a new Armenian state entity to be created in such a way that it was to bestride eastern Turkey and Russian Armenia in the Transcaucasus. More important, many of the leaders of the invading Kemalist army were those Special Organization leaders who during the war had played a key role in organizing and executing the genocide in Turkey proper. They were now reengaged as "freedom fighters" but actually resumed their genocidal task performance in the new occupied territories.[66] By all accounts that performance yielded what might be called a mini-genocide against the Armenians in the region of Gümrü (Leninakan). According to Soviet and Armenian sources, in five months of Turkish conquest and occupation about 200,000 Armenians of the region perished.[67]

That mini-genocide was enacted in compliance with top-secret instructions issued by Ankara. Turkish General Karabekir was ordered to initiate measures aiming at "the political and physical obliteration of Armenia" (*siyaseten ve maddeten ortadan kaldırmak*).[68] Only the prompt intervention of the 11th Red Army, stationed nearby, and the concomitant sovietization of Armenia averted the all but certain extirpation of the remnants of the Armenian nation by preventing the occupation of the rest of Armenia by Karabekir's troops.

The similar aspect of the two cases in terms of the Nazi and Turkish Ittihadist drives to go beyond domestic genocide has within its structure, however, a very important dissimilar element. In contrast to their periodic indulgencies through which the Nazis vowed to destroy the Jews as a race, the Young Turk Ittihadists rarely, if ever, allowed themselves to lapse into such indulgencies. For them, the destruction of the Armenians was and remained a hidden agenda, a top-secret plan. They skillfully conspired for it, knew how to bide their time, and, when the opportunity presented itself, that plan was carried out swiftly and implacably. Turkish archival documents demonstrate, for example, that this pattern was followed in the execution of the 1920 mini-genocide in the Transcaucasus described above. On the very same day that Ankara, through a cipher telegram, secretly ordered General Karabekir to wipe out Armenia through appropriate means (November 8, 1920), it sent to the Armenian government in Yerevan a parallel telegram. In it the Kemalist government expressed its "profound and genuine friendship" (*amik ve samimi*) toward the Armenian people, invoked the ideals of "humanity" (*insaniyet*), and promised assistance to help Armenia recover economically and achieve "complete independence and security."[69] Consistent with this proclivity for cunning and trickiness, Ankara, in its order to obliterate Armenia, had advised the Turkish general to "deceive the Armenians" (*Ermenileri iğfal*) and "fool the Europeans through an appearance of peacelovingness. In reality, however, [*fakat hakikatde*] the purpose of all this is to achieve the objective [stated above]."[70]

In trying to interpret the parallel character of the Nazi and Ittihadist mass-murder sweeps beyond domestic genocide, one is struck with a paramount fact that may be viewed as a condition transcending in significance the factors of perpetrator ideology and an allied perpetrator motivation. In both cases, the decisive motor force was military conquest resulting from warfare. In conditions of military occupation, associated with an ongoing war, it is far more easy to sustain the momentum of a successfully launched initial genocide than under almost any other condition. The objective element of opportunity and the subjective element of opportunism combine here to generate an inveterate urge in the mind-set of a perpetrator to be consequential in task performance; it is most tempting to try "to complete the job." In this sense, it may be argued that the extension of a domestic genocide beyond territorial boundaries is primarily a function of military conquest resulting from warfare. By virtue of such a conquest, the dispersed elements of the original victim population can be readily targeted as well, especially in the aftermath of such a conquest and occupation, absent changes in the leadership of the perpetrator group or the onset of new domestic or external impediments or constraints.

The postulate that emerges from this comparative perspective is that the evolution and transformation of a domestic genocide into a territorially transcendental holocaust is not an intrinsic process but one that depends upon the effects of extrinsic factors acting as catalysts. No matter how powerful the ideological animus of such a transcendental drive may be, the actualization of the ideology hinges on the operational effectiveness of such catalysts. In brief, the phenomenon of holocaust, contrary to prevailing assumptions, is not a sui generis phenomenon but one bound up with extra-ideological contingencies.

NOTES

This is a revised and expanded version of a lecture delivered at the University of California–Los Angeles, on October 31, 1993.

1. Robert Melson, "Response to Professor Dadrian's Review," *Holocaust and Genocide Studies* 8(3) (Winter 1994):416.

2. Ambassador Henry Morgenthau, *Secrets of the Bosphorus* (London: Hutchinson, 1918), p. 202. It is significant that, in the American edition of this book, the name of Bedri, the chief of police in the Ottoman capital, whose position and rank were comparable to that of minister of police, is deleted. Instead, he is described as "a responsible Turkish official." Henry Morgenthau, *Ambassador Morgenthau's Story* (Garden City, N.Y.: Doubleday, Page, 1918), p. 307.

3. Ibid., p. 312.

4. Ibid., p. 328.

5. In using the general term "deportation," which, in practice—more often than not—meant massacres, wartime Turkish Foreign Minister Halil Menteşe (in his postwar memoirs) stated that "there are very few Turks in Anatolia who were not involved in this business of deportation" (*tehcir meselesi*) of the Armenians. "The Memoirs of Halil Menteşe: The Exile to Malta," *Hayat Tarih Mecmuası* 9(2) (September 1973):22. In his report to the

State Department in Washington, D.C., Lewis Heck, the U.S. High Commissioner in the Ottoman capital from November 1918 through April 1919, declared that the deportation and massacre of the Armenians "were heartily approved at the time by the vast majority of the Turkish population of the country." The January 9, 1919, report, U.S. National Archives, R.G. 256. 867.4016/2, p. 2. The same statement is repeated in the January 20, 1919, report, R.G. 256. 867.00/59, p. 3.

6. For details on these drowning operations in and around the Black Sea port city of Trabzon, see the special issue of *Journal of Political and Military Sociology* 22(1) (Summer 1994), which contains collected essays by this author. The drownings are discussed at pp. 40–49.

7. Morgenthau, *Ambassador* [n. 2], pp. 317, 318.

8. The text of General Vehib's affidavit in original Ottoman script is deposited in the archives of the Jerusalem Armenian Patriarchate, Series H. 17, File nos. 171 and 182.

9. Ibid., Series L. 13, File nos. 323–239. Following is another portion of the Armenian lawyer's affidavit (pp. 5–6):

II. THE BEHEADING OF 500 CHILDREN

Only few days had passed from the burning of the 2,000 orphans, when Moustafa Sıdkı and his men tried to devise other means of torture.

They took 500 children to a part of the desert near the German Wireless Telegraph Station. He had them tied two by two by their feet and afterwards had them placed in a line on the ground. Then Moustafa Sıdkı sat in a heavy cart which was driven on this line of lying children in such a way that the wheels crushed the necks of these unfortunate children. Their heartrending shrieks resounded in the whole vicinity.

III. 2,000 ORPHANS DROWNED IN THE EUPHRATES

The annihilation of these helpless orphans was giving Moustafa Sıdkı and his accomplices such profound joy that soon other means of torture were found. On October 24, 1916, 2,000 orphans were carried to the banks of the Euphrates hands and feet bound. Moustafa Sıdkı after having sitted himself at ease, ordered to throw the orphans into the water two by two and enjoyed thoroughly the sight of their drowning.

IV. THE VICTIMS OF THE BRIDGE

On August 10, 1916 a caravan set on its journey to Mossoul. While passing over the bridge on the Euphrates, Moustafa Sıdkı, who was waiting there, ordered to bring the prettiest girls under the bridge. There these poor girls served to the lusts of Moustafa Sıdkı and his accomplices and were after that thrown into the Euphrates.

10. Ludwig Schraudenbach, *Muharebe* (War) (Berlin: Drei Masken Verlag, 1924), p. 352.

11. K. A. Schleunes, *The Twisted Road to Auschwitz: Nazi Policy Toward German Jews, 1933–1939* (Chicago: University of Illinois Press, 1970), pp. 215 and 225.

12. Raul Hilberg, *The Destruction of European Jews* (Chicago: Quadrangle, 1969), pp. 230–232.

13. Jerry Sawicki, *Vor dem Polnischen Staatsanwalt* (Berlin: Deutscher Militaerverlag, 1962), p. 198, quoted in Richard Breitman, "Additional Remarks," to Yehoshua Büchler's "Document: A Preparatory Document for the Wannsee 'Conference,'" trans. Yehuda Bauer, *Holocaust and Genocide Studies* 9(1) (Spring 1995):128. See also Yehuda Bauer's review of Richard Breitman, *The Architect of Genocide: Himmler and the Final Solution* (Hanover,

N.H.: University Press of New England, 1992), in *Holocaust and Genocide Studies* 6(3) (1991):307–312.

14. Morgenthau, *Ambassador* [n. 2], p. 309.

15. See Vahakn N. Dadrian, "Documentation of the Armenian Genocide in German and Austrian Sources," *Widening Circle of Genocide: A Critical Bibliographic Review*, ed. Israel Charny, vol. 3 (New Brunswick, N.J.: Transaction, 1994), pp. 104–107.

16. Esat Uras, *Tarihte Ermeniler ve Ermeni Meselesi* (The Armenians and the Armenian Question), 2d ed. (Istanbul: Belge, 1976), p. 612.

17. In the case of Constantinople the facts are as follows: In the key indictment of the Turkish Military Tribunal, investigating the wartime massacres against the Armenians, there are repeat references to the sweeping compass of the deportation scheme, *Takvimi Vekâyi* No. 3540, pp. 6, 7; on p. 4 of the same document the procuror-general makes an allusion to the design of the Ittihadists involving a Final Solution of the Armenian question, and on p. 8 the same idea is expressed through an attribution to Dr. Nazım who uses a broader term, the "eastern question." In the ancillary indictment addressed against the responsible secretaries of the Young Turk Ittihad Party, the document makes a similar allusion about the empire-wide range of the anti-Armenian measures (*Memaliki Osmaniyenin hemen her tarafında*). *Takvimi Vekâyi* No. 3571, p. 130.

The German documents found in the state archives of Bonn are corroborative in this respect. In a major report on December 7, 1915, German Ambassador to Turkey Count Paul von Wolff-Metternich informed his chancellor in Berlin that

A. already 30,000 Armenians have been deported from Istanbul;

B. 4,000 of them were dispatched only recently;

C. plans are made to remove the remaining 80,000 Armenians from the Ottoman capital;

D. the source of his information was the chief of the Istanbul police;

E. these bits of information should be kept secret (*die ich bitte geheim zu halten*) (this part of the report is deleted from the massive documentary tome compiled by J. Lepsius, *Deutschland und Armenien* [Potsdam: Tempelverlag, 1919], p. 202), German Foreign Ministry Archives (Bonn) A.A., Türkei 183/40, A36184. U.S. Ambassador to Turkey Henry Morgenthau, in a report to Washington on August 11, 1915, stated that Talat "hints at drastic measures against all [Armenians] in Constantinople." U.S. National Archives. R.G. 59. 867.4016/90.

In a subsequent report on October 4, 1915, the same ambassador declared: "The greatest wealth of the Armenians is centered in Constantinople and I fear that it is but a question of time when the cupidity of some of the Turkish leaders and the desire of others to complete their nefarious scheme of practically destroying Armenians in Turkey will be to treat Constantinople Armenians as they have the others. Delay is being secured but entire escape of Constantinople Armenians is doubtful if present general political conditions here remain unchanged." Ibid., 867.4016/159. For a variety of reasons, that time was not to come as Turkey was busy completing the exterminatory work in the provinces and subsequent military setbacks ultimately compounded the problems her leaders faced in the task of completing the removal and annihilation of Istanbul Armenians. The documentary thrust of this study leaves very little doubt about what Melson has called "total domestic genocide." Robert Melson, *Revolution and Genocide. On the Origins of the Armenian*

Genocide and the Holocaust (Chicago: University of Chicago Press, 1992), pp. 2–4, 247–257. Even more authoritative in this regard is the characterization of Tarık Zafer Tunaya, the late dean of Turkish political scientists. When discussing the criminal proceedings against the Ittihadist leaders in his third volume on the Turkish political parties, he saw fit to translate the Ottoman word *taktil* into the modern Turkish equivalent of "genocide" ("*soykırım*"). The word *taktil* is the standard word the Turkish court-martial regularly used to describe the thrust of the empire-wide massacres. Tarık Z. Tunaya, *Türkiyede Siyasal Partiler* (Political Parties of Turkey), vol. 3, *Ittihad ve Terakki* (Istanbul: Hürriyet Vakfı, 1989), page 281.

As to Smyrna (Izmir), as stated in the text, the Turkish governor-general was personally and directly threatened by the German General Liman von Sanders, who was then commander-in-chief of the Ottoman Fifth Army and whose zone of command encompassed Smyrna and its environs. Upon the first act of deportation of 300 Armenians, signalling subsequent wholesale deportations, General von Sanders informed Rahmi, the governor-general, that in the case of any further act of deporting the city's Armenian population he would use military units to arrest the teams of policemen assigned to deportation duties. Von Sanders's objection to "massive deportations" was not meant to protect the Armenians, he said, but to secure and protect military interest, which, he argued, might be jeopardized by the turmoil the deportation measures were likely to create; and he prevailed. There were no further deportations from Smyrna. German Foreign Ministry Archives, Türkei 183/45, A31127, No. 703; Austrian Foreign Ministry Archives, P.A. 12/463, No. 89/P.-A; U.S. National Archives, RG.59.867.00/802.5. General von Sanders was supported in his move by then German Foreign Affairs Minister Arthur Zimmermann. German Foreign Ministry Archives (Bonn) Türkei 183/45, A30700. No. 1301.

18. Hilberg, *The Destruction* [n. 12], pp. 98 and 258.

19. Michael R. Marrus, "Coming to Terms with Vichy," *Holocaust and Genocide Studies* 9(1) (Spring 1995):24.

20. Hilberg, *The Destruction* [n. 12], pp. 278, 283, and 284.

21. Ibid., p. 62.

22. Ibid., p. 666.

23. Louis Wirth, *The Ghetto* (Chicago: University of Chicago Press, 1928).

24. Vahakn N. Dadrian, "The Convergent Aspects of the Armenian and Jewish Cases of Genocide: A Reinterpretation of the Concept of Holocaust," *Holocaust and Genocide Studies* 3(2) (Summer 1988):151–154.

25. Richard L. Rubenstein, *The Age of Triage* (Boston: Beacon Press, 1983), p. 130.

26. George H. Hepworth, *Through Armenia on Horseback* (New York: E. P. Dutton, 1898), pp. 146–147, 263, and 339–140.

27. William M. Ramsay, *Impressions of Turkey During Twelve Years' Wanderings* (New York: G. P. Putnam's Sons, 1897), pp. 156–157.

28. Rubenstein, *The Age of Triage* [n. 25], p. 142.

29. Ibid., p. 144.

30. Hilberg, *The Destruction* [n. 12], ch. 5, pp. 54–105.

31. *Memoirs of Halide Edib* (New York: Century, 1926), p. 386.

32. U.S. National Archives, R.G. 59. 807.4016/148.

33. Morgenthau, *Ambassador* [n. 2], p. 339.

34. Hilberg, *The Destruction* [n. 12], p. 259.

35. Ibid.

36. *The Goebbels Diaries*, ed. L. Lochner (New York: Doubleday, 1948), p. 241.

37. Hilberg, *The Destruction* [n. 12], p. 672.

38. Vahakn N. Dadrian, "Genocide as a Problem of National and International Law: The World War I Armenian Case and Its Contemporary Legal Ramifications," *Yale Journal of International Law* 14(2)(Summer 1989):262.

39. United Nations War Crimes Commission, *History of the United Nations War Crimes Commission and the Development of the Laws of War* (London: H.M.S.O., 1948), pp. 188–189; M. C. Bassiouni, *Crimes Against Humanity in International Criminal Law* (Dordrecht, Holland: Martinus Nijhoff, 1992), pp. 168–169 and 184–187.

40. Quoted In J. Willis, *Prologue to Nuremberg: The Politics of Diplomacy of Punishing War Criminals of the First World War* (Westport, Conn.: Greenwood Press, 1982), p. 173.

41. E. L. Woodward, R. Butler, and A. Orde, eds., *Documents on British Foreign Policy, 1919–1939*, 3d series, vol. 7, 1939 (London: H.M.S.O., 1954), Doc. No. 314, enclosure, pp. 258–260; Kevork Bardakjian, *Hitler and the Armenian Genocide* (Cambridge, Mass.: Zoryan Institute, 1985), pp. 3–24.

42. Hilberg, *The Destruction* [n. 12], p. 671.

43. Ibid., p. 641.

44. Vahakn N. Dadrian, "The Role of the Special Organization in the Armenian Genocide During the First World War," in *Minorities in Wartime: National and Racial Groupings in Europe, North America and Australia During the Two World Wars*, ed. P. Panayi (Oxford: Berg, 1993), pp. 50–82. See also Ahmed Refik (Altınay), *Iki Komite–Iki Kıtal* (Two Committees–Two Mass Murders), Ottoman script (Istanbul: Orhaniye Press, 1919), p. 23; Falih Rıfkı Atay, *Zeytindağı* (Mt. Olive) (Istanbul: Ayyıldız, 1981), pp. 35–36. See also the respective testimonies (at the Turkish court-martial trials) of defendants Colonel Cevad Kıanlıklı, the wartime military commandant at the Ottoman capital, and Atıf Kamçil, one of the chief directors of the Special Organization headquartered in Istanbul. See *Takvimi Vekâyi*, the official gazette of the Ottoman government whose supplements (*ilâve*) published select portions of the proceedings of the military tribunal in the period from 1919 to 1921, No. 3543, pp. 26–30. Page 28 contains additional documents from Colonel Behiç Erkin, the deputy director in Department I of the Ministry of War in charge of the Bureau of Procurement (*Ikmal Şubesi*). During the war, when the legal authorization of the release of the convicts was being sought by the Ministries of War and Justice, the same Colonel Behiç testified in the Ottoman Upper House (the Senate) about the necessity for and usefulness of the Special Organization relative to special task performances. *Meclisi Âyan Zabıt Ceridesi*, 3d period, 3d sess., 15th sitting, December 12, 1916, vol. 1, p. 187. As to the testimony before the Chamber of Deputies' Fifth Committee investigating the wartime misdeeds of cabinet ministers, wartime Justice Minister Saib Mollazade Ibrahim stated that the number of convicts released from the empire's prisons for such a mission "amounted to a significant sum total" (*mühim bir yeküna balig*). *Harb Kabinelerinin Isticvabı* (The Hearings on Wartime Cabinets) (Istanbul: Vakit Publications, 1933), p. 537.

45. Hilberg, *The Destruction* [n. 12], ch. 7, "Mobile Killing Operations," pp. 177–256, ch. 9, "Killing Center Operations," pp. 555–635.

46. Ibid., pp. 242–243.

47. Leo Alexander, "War Crimes and Their Motivation: The Socio-Psychological Structure of the SS and the Criminalization of a Society," *Journal of Criminal Law, Criminology, and Police Science* 39 (September-October 1948):309.

48. Robert Jay Lifton, *The Nazi Doctors: Medical Killing and the Psychology of Genocide* (New York: Basic Books, 1986), pp. 224 and 388.

49. Irving Louis Horowitz, *Genocide, State Power, and Mass Murder* (New Brunswick, N.J.: Transaction, 1976); *Taking Lives, Genocide and State Power*, 3d ed. (New Brunswick, N.J.: Transaction, 1980), p. 11.

50. Morgenthau, *Ambassador* [n. 2], p. 11.

51. Peter Longerich, *Hitler's Stellvertreter: Führung der Partei und Kontrolle des Staatsapparates durch den Stab Hess und die Partei Kanzlei Bormann* (Münich: Saur, 1992).

52. The participants were: Reinhardt Heydrich and Alfred Meyer, Drs. Georg Leibbrandt, Wilhelm Stuckart, Roland Freisler, and Joseph Bühler, and Martin Luther, Karl Schöngarth, and Otto Lange; other security potentates, likewise present, were Erich Neumann, Gerhard Klopfer, Wilhelm Kritzinger, Otto Hoffmann, and Heinrich Müller. Hilberg, *The Destruction* [n. 12], p. 264.

53. Vahakn N. Dadrian, "The Secret Young-Turk Ittihadist Conference and the Decision for the World War I Genocide of the Armenians," *Holocaust and Genocide Studies* 7(2) (Fall 1993):173–201.

54. Robert H. Jackson, *The Nürnberg Case: Together with Other Documents* (New York: Cooper Square Publishers, 1971), p. 40.

55. Special Organization Chieftain Major Yakub Cemil. Quoted by Secret Service Administrator Galip Vardar, *Ittihad ve Terakki İçinde Dönenler* (The Inside Story of Ittihad ve Terakki), ed. N. Tansu (Istanbul: Inkilâp, 1960), pp. 279–280.

56. Vahakn N. Dadrian, "Towards a Theory of Genocide Incorporating the Instance of Holocaust: Comments, Criticism and Suggestions," *Holocaust and Genocide Studies* 5(2) (1990), pp. 129–143.

57. A.A. Türkei 183/51, A206981.

58. *Deutsches Zentralarchiv*, or DZA (Potsdam). Bestand Reichskanzlei, or BRK. No. 2458/9. Bl. 202.

59. A.A. Türkei 158/20. A31679.

60. DZA. BRK. No. 2458/9. Bl. 287.

61. Ernst Paraquin, "Politik im Orient," *Berliner Tageblatt* (January 24 and 28, 1920). See also A.A. Türkei 158/24, A1373 for a summary of the contents of this two-part article. The quotation is from part 1.

62. Erich Ludendorff, *Urkunden der obersten Heeresleitung über ihre Tätigkeit, 1916–1918* (Documents of the High Command on its Activities, 1916–1918) (Berlin: Mittler und Sohn, 1922), p. 500.

63. Paul von Hindenburg, *Aus Meinem Lebel* (From My Life) (Leipzig, Germany: S. Hirzel, 1934), p. 168.

64. A.A. Türkei 183/51, A28533. No. 1178. June 3, 1918.

65. For a full reproduction of these and other comments by German military and civilian officials on these operations, see Dadrian, "Documentation" [n. 15], pp. 122–125.

66. Vahakn N. Dadrian, *The History of the Armenian Genocide: Ethnic Conflict from the Balkans to Anatolia to the Caucasus* (Providence: Berghahn, 1995), pp. 367–370.

67. Ibid., p. 361. See also Dadrian, "Genocide as a Problem," [n. 38], p. 332.

68. Ibid., p. 358.

69. Ibid., p. 386.

70. Ibid.

❀ 9 ❀

Stalinist Terror and the Question of Genocide: The Great Famine

BARBARA B. GREEN

The question of whether Stalin's terror was genocidal in intent has focused largely on the famine of 1932–1933 and the assertion that it was not only artificial and man-made but was an intentional act of genocide directed against the Ukrainian people. Although a thorough consideration of this question must take into account the fate of the Kazakhs during collectivization and the deportation of entire nations—the "punished peoples"—this essay will consider questions surrounding the 1932–1933 famine.[1]

What was perhaps the greatest social and economic revolution in history—the industrialization of the Soviet Union—was carried out from above against opposition not only from the masses but from much of the elite. It required the concentration of an enormous amount of power in the hands of one man, Stalin, and the unleashing of unprecedented terror. Every effort was expended to prevent the development of any autonomous centers of power that could act independently of the state. Stalin instituted a relentless struggle for rapid industrialization and total collectivization, which he carried out with unbridled coercion. Collective and state farms put the rural population under state control, thereby simplifying the task of extracting grain both to feed the workers and for export.

There is no question but that a famine of enormous proportions took place in 1932–1933, primarily in Ukraine, in which millions died of starvation and disease. Most U.S. and British reporters at the time failed to report the nature or extent of the famine.[2] The British, Canadian, and U.S. governments, though aware of the famine, took no action because of the impact of the Great Depression in their own countries and because of international considerations.[3] It is through the relentless insistence of Robert Conquest, James E. Mace, Marco Carynnyk, and others that the famine has been brought to public attention.

These writers have argued that Ukraine was a deliberate and intended target because the loyalty of all Ukrainians was suspect. They maintain that the famine of 1932–1933, in which millions died, was deliberately engineered by Stalin to crush the Ukrainian people, eliminate the peasantry as a force upholding Ukrainian national ideals, stifle Ukrainian culture, and eliminate any manifestation of independence. Charging Stalin with genocide, Mace has called the famine "a means used by Stalin to impose a 'final solution' on the most pressing nationality problem in the Soviet Union."[4]

In contrast, Robert Tucker, Adam Ulam, Martin Malia, and other scholars, in discussing the devastating impact on the peasantry of Stalin's forced collectivization and extraction of grain, speak more to the transformation of Russian society and the impact on Russian peasants. For the most part, they merge Ukrainians with Russians and then label them all "Russian." They tend to consider the famine as an outcome of Stalin's obsession with power or as a consequence of the effort to transform a backward peasant society by extracting a surplus from the peasantry in order to invest in rapid industrialization.[5] When Hannah Arendt writes of the liquidation of the Soviet peasantry—the "most powerful class in the Union"—she says that it "was more thorough and more cruel than that of any other group and was carried through by artificial famine and deportation." However, Arendt makes no reference to Ukrainians as the intended victims.[6]

In direct opposition to Mace and Conquest, Stephen Wheatcraft argues that the famine was not created to weaken Ukrainian nationalism. Rather, Ukrainian nationalism was weakened as a consequence of the famine.[7] The fact that nationality policy changed in the early 1930s does not in itself prove that the change in nationality policy was the impetus for Stalin to impose a "final solution" by means of an artificial famine. It is important to bear in mind that Stalinist measures, when viewed only in terms of their impact on Ukraine, may appear as if they were directed specifically at Ukraine and Ukrainians. These measures were, however, intended as a means of transforming peasant society and solving the Soviet Union's serious grain problem, rather than as a policy directed at Ukrainians for genocidal reasons. Millions died during the famine of 1932–1933, but not all mass deaths are genocide.

Collectivization was bound to have a particularly cruel effect on the population of the borderlands. The urban population of the Soviet Union was largely clustered in the center, whereas the periphery was populated by peasants and herdsmen. Even in the borderlands, Russian or Russian-speaking cities were surrounded by non-Russian countryside. Collectivization and the Five-Year Plan were intended to put the burden of industrialization on the peasantry and this meant that there would be a disparate impact on nationalities on the periphery. Collectivization, directed primarily by Russians, was implemented despite opposition—even open rebellion—from the nationalities of the periphery.[8] A policy designed to forcibly extract grain from peasants to feed urban workers was bound to be perceived as a policy directed against the nationality that was dominant in the countryside. In the case of Ukraine, forced collectivization was seen as a war by the non-Ukrainian urban population against the Ukrainian villagers. As peasants and as Ukrainians, they resisted collectivization by whatever means they could. Resistance was met by increased force. There was a disparate impact on Ukrainians—not because they were Ukrainians but because they were peasants.

In this chapter I will argue that the deaths of millions of Ukrainians and other Soviet peoples in the famine of 1932–1933 are directly attributable to Stalin's attempt to totally reconstruct society through rapid industrialization, an effort in which he was determined that nothing would stand in his way. In the process, he instituted a totalitarian system permeated by terror. There were mass deaths and overwhelming suffering as a result of excessive grain procurement, but this was not genocide. I will trace the reasons for the excess grain procurement in the context of Stalin's Five-Year Plan and forced industrialization. My intent is to establish that this effort to totally reconstruct society can in itself account for the excess grain procurement that led to mass deaths and the famine.

Genocide Defined

Before it is possible to discuss whether genocide has occurred in a particular case, a clear understanding of the meaning of *genocide* is essential. Michael Ignatieff argues:

> "Genocide" is a worn and debased term, casually hurled at every outrage, every violence, even applied to events where no death, only shame or abuse, occurs. But it is a word that does mean something: the project to exterminate a people for no other reason than because they are that people. Before the experience of genocide, they may believe it a matter of personal choice whether they belong or believe. After genocide, it becomes their fate.[9]

An article in *Economist*, after noting that the Ukrainian terror-famine of 1932–1933 may have claimed as many victims as the Holocaust, has this to say:

> Yet the peculiar circumstances of the Holocaust do make it unique. Never has the extermination of an entire people, coupled with the technology of industrialisation . . . been attempted so systematically as an end in itself. Never has mass murder been so efficiently, so scientifically, perpetrated. Never has the annihilation of a race been so central to an ideology.[10]

The meaning of genocide and the uniqueness of the Holocaust are revealed in a few characteristics. The Holocaust was aimed at the extermination of an entire people because they were that people. The extermination was not a means toward an end; it was an end in itself. It was not an act of demonstrative violence in which some were killed in order to terrify the other members of the people into submission. It was not intended to affect behavior. It was not a pogrom or the result of uncontrolled mass violence. It was, rather, an intentional, systematic effort to exterminate an entire people utilizing modern technology to ensure efficiency.

The Question of Numbers

There has been a great deal of debate over the number of people who died in the 1932–1933 famine from starvation or from diseases resulting from widespread malnutrition. When the population totals in the All-Union Census of 1937 fell far short of expectations, the three statisticians directly responsible for the census were arrested as "enemies of the people," and the entire census was suppressed. M. Maksudov uses 1939 census data to argue that not less than 4.4 million, or one-tenth of the population of Ukraine, perished between 1927 and 1938.[11] Mace asserts that the figure of 5–7 million deaths in the famine for Ukraine alone is a conservative figure.[12] Conquest gives a figure of about 11 million premature deaths between 1926–1937, of which approximately 7 million can be attributed to the 1932–1933 famine. He claims that 5 million of the famine deaths were in Ukraine.[13]

During the Mikhail Gorbachev era, materials from the 1937 census were published, and these confirm that millions of lives were lost. Between 1926 and 1936, the total population of the Soviet Union increased by slightly over 10 percent, from 147 million to 162 million, considerably less than predicted. The Russian population increased from 77.8 million in 1926 to 94 million in 1937, but the Ukrainians decreased from 31.2 million to 26.4 million. Population decreases or failures to increase at the expected rate, of course, cannot be attributed solely to excess deaths caused by the famine. These changes were also a consequence of changing birthrates, migration, and assimilation.[14] A Russian writer recently attempted to calculate the number of victims using data from the files of the USSR Central Statistical Administration and National Economic Records. She estimates that the total number of deaths in the USSR in 1933 was 6.7 million, of which half were victims of the famine. In 1933, the only year in which statistics reveal a net population loss for the Soviet Union, the European part of the USSR lost 1.7 million people, of which 1.5 million were in Ukraine. A slow recovery began only at the end of the summer in 1933, after crops were harvested.[15] Wheatcraft, using the 1937 census figures, argues that the scale of excess mortality for the Soviet Union as a whole in 1932–1933 might be as high as 4–5 million.[16] Alec Nove, using figures cited by V. Tsaplin, a Soviet scholar, in the April 1989 issue of *Voprosy istorii*, estimates that in 1933 there were 3.1–3.2 million famine deaths in Ukraine alone.[17]

The controversy over the number of Ukrainians killed in the 1932–1933 famine continues. The subtext of the controversy is the assumption that if it can be established that the Ukrainian terror-famine claimed as many victims as the Holocaust, then an equivalence between the two events will have been established.

Mace is explicit on this. After discussing census figures, he states, "The point is that the Ukrainian famine was a deliberate act of genocide of roughly the same order of magnitude as the Jewish Holocaust of the Second World War, both in the number of its victims and in the human suffering it produced."[18] However, the question of numbers, though it has provoked high levels of controversy, cannot resolve this issue.

War Communism and the New Economic Policy

Tracing the development of Soviet agricultural policy from 1917 to 1932 illuminates the conditions that led, tragically and inexorably, to the Great Famine of 1932–1933. War communism, the attempt to build communism and serve practical needs during the civil war, was prompted by ideological idealism and cold necessity. Faced with the task of feeding the army and the workers, the Bolsheviks had no choice but to institute "forcible requisitions," which amounted to sending raiding parties into the countryside to seize food. With money worthless and no consumer goods to purchase, there was no incentive for peasants to sell their produce—they produced only enough to feed themselves and their families. Although the raiding parties were supposed to take only surplus food, this was usually not adhered to. War communism, however, was not just a policy of necessity. There was a determined effort to destroy the market economy.

Once the civil war was over, Bolsheviks faced severe domestic problems. The country's industry, transportation system, and agriculture were in ruins after six years of war. The disastrous harvest of 1921 produced a famine costing 4–5 million lives and was alleviated only through Western assistance.[19] The half-starved workers and peasants were turning against the Bolsheviks. At the Tenth Party Congress of 1921–1922, Lenin introduced the New Economic Policy (NEP), intended as a temporary retreat from building communism. NEP involved abandoning the policy of forced requisitions and the encouragement of private farming. It allowed small private or cooperative industries to produce consumer goods, permitted private trade, and encouraged a free labor market. Although economic reality necessitated reliance on peasants, traders, and small-businessmen, Lenin had no intention of permitting them to block the advance of socialism. He envisaged only a temporary retreat in the economic realm, but a retreat that might last one to two decades.

The introduction of NEP improved agricultural production as peasants responded to incentives. By substituting a tax in-kind for forced requisitions and enabling peasants to dispose of their surplus on the free market, peasants had reason to produce a surplus. In 1924, as the country stabilized, the tax in-kind was replaced by a money tax. A mixed economy developed as agriculture and petty trade were conducted by private individuals and a new entrepreneurial class of Nepmen (private traders) emerged.[20] In 1925, peasants were even permitted to hire farm workers and lease additional land. However, the Bolsheviks were not reconciled to dependency on the peasantry. Adam Ulam speaks of the "superstitious and deep-seated fear of the peasantry as a whole, the feeling on the part of the Communists that a vast, inert, and yet somehow threatening mass of people barred Russia's path to industrialization, modernity, socialism; that a kingdom of darkness must be conquered before the Soviet Union could become the promised land."[21]

Economic differentiation developed during NEP, although the lines between strata were not clear. The Communists divided the peasant class into three ill-defined groups. Poor peasants, or *bedniaks,* were those with no land or insufficient land to support their families. Middle peasants, or *seredniaks,* were those who were able to meet the needs of their families through their own work and that of their families; they accounted for about 63 percent of the peasantry. *Kulaks* were the so-called rich peasants, who hired farm laborers. Although most of the peasantry lived at bare subsistence level, it was the kulaks who produced most of the farm surplus to feed the cities and for export. The prerevolutionary, prosperous kulaks had been eliminated by revolution and civil war. These were peasants who, through ability, luck, and hard work, became somewhat better off than their neighbors. They might own two or three cows, a plow horse, and about 25 acres of farmland. They accounted for less than 4 percent of the peasantry and produced about one-fifth of the grain.[22] In order to recover from the effects of war and famine, the kulaks had to be indulged. However, this risked putting control of the Soviet economy in the hands of the despised kulak, "*the class enemy . . .* the personification of evil on the social scene." Ulam states, "For many Communists the kulak was a demonic force," and he adds that Stalin was "abundantly endowed with the Communist obsession about the kulak."[23]

The Procurement Crisis

The "procurement crisis" of 1927–1928 was a critical step in the march toward the disaster of 1932–1933. The price of food fell while consumer goods were in short supply. Although the harvest was normal, peasants began to hold back their surpluses, refusing to meet their quotas for sale to the state at low, state-determined prices. From October to December peasants sold official collection agencies only half as much grain as they had during the same months in the previous year. To get cash, peasants sold their surpluses on the free market at higher prices or sold industrial crops for which the state paid fairly high prices. Peasants also earned money through seasonal work in towns. They tried to keep their grain until spring in the expectation that procurement prices would rise; this endangered food supplies to urban areas as well as the army.[24] Grain exports virtually ceased, foreign currency earnings fell, and the government was unable to import machinery to industrialize. Stalin saw "not peasants trying to earn a few more rubles, but millions of class enemies trying to ruin his benevolent designs and overthrowing Soviet power."[25] He refused to capitulate to the kulaks by raising procurement prices. He was convinced that class enemies were carrying out deliberate sabotage. Stalin announced the policy of "liquidating kulaks as a class."

Although he denied that he was ending NEP or restoring forced requisitions, in a January 6, 1928, directive Stalin instituted a program of forced confiscation of grain. His primary concern was short-range: He was determined to make the peasants turn over their surpluses. Local officials were threatened if they failed to improve grain procurement. Thirty thousand party activists were sent to the countryside. Even members of the Central Committee and the Politburo went to Ukraine, North Caucasus, the Volga region, and Siberia to supervise procurement operations. Fixed delivery quotas were set for each individual household. House-to-house searches were conducted to find hidden grain, and any grain discovered was confiscated.

All peasants were required to hand over surplus grain, but kulaks were subjected to especially harsh treatment. Local authorities set arbitrary quotas; if these were not delivered by a fixed date, the offender was subject to fines, confiscation, and prison sentences. Kulaks who refused to sell their surplus grain at official prices could be treated as speculators and have their surplus confiscated. Since most grain was in the hands of the middle peasants, they too were subjected to arbitrary procedures. In an effort to secure the support of the poor peasants and drive a wedge between them and the better-off peasants, one-quarter of the grain confiscated from kulaks was sold to poor peasants at reduced prices. Private individuals were forbidden to buy from peasants, and most free markets in rural areas were closed. Militias were posted at district boundaries to prevent grain smuggling.[26] By April, the deficit in grain procurement had been largely made up. This confirmed Stalin's belief that the peasants had sufficient grain to feed the country and to export. The problem was to extract it from them. This experience helped to shape Stalin's actions in 1932–1933.

Peasants concluded that since surplus production would be confiscated it made no sense to sow as much grain as they had in the past. In short, their economic incentive was destroyed. Many kulaks, the most productive peasants, "liquidated themselves" by selling their farms, mills, machinery, and draft animals and hiding their money and valuables. Well-to-do middle peasants produced less out of fear of being labeled as kulaks. When the sale of grain to the state dropped off sharply during the spring of 1928, the government renewed its emergency measures, including house-to-house searches. Fedor Belov describes how the committees of the poor raided victims' households, seizing grain, agricultural implements, harnesses, livestock, furniture, and clothing.[27] When the grain they had stored for spring sowing and to feed their animals and their families was seized, peasants retaliated with violence against party agents with arson and looting of shops and warehouses. Even poor peasants turned against the regime. The sale of bread was restricted in most regions, and rationing was introduced in the Urals and several grain-consuming regions. Despite Stalin's vow not to give in to the peasants, procurement prices were raised 15 to 20 percent, the supply of manufactured goods in the countryside was increased, and searches and seizures of grain were halted. The Soviet Union imported 250,000 tons of grain during the summer of 1928. The fall 1928 grain procurement plan was underfilled, the regime had not ensured the necessary minimum grain reserves, and peasant mistrust and hostility were heightened.[28]

Stalin became increasingly certain that class enemies were out to wreck the Soviet economy. He declared that as the country got closer to socialism, the resistance of the class enemy would grow stronger and the class struggle more intense. From May to July 1928, Stalin staged the Soviet Union's first show trial, the Shakhty affair, a public trial of fifty-two "wreckers," primarily members of the old technical intelligentsia, charged with participating in a foreign-controlled conspiracy to wreck the coal-mining industry in the Donbas. Stalin used the trial to emphasize the dangers from hostile capitalist countries and the need to build an industrial base for defense of the country.

The regime introduced the "Ural-Siberian" or "social influence" method of grain collection in March 1929. The *skhod*, or village assembly, with kulaks excluded, levied grain quotas on peasant households, thereby putting the main burden on kulaks and well-to-do middle peasants. Thousands of party activists infiltrated the skhods and manipulated them to suit the regime's purposes. Both social pressure and severe economic penalties were exerted to ensure delivery. Those who failed to deliver the quota were subject to the *piatkratnika*, a fine equal to five times the quota. If this fine was not paid, a kulak could be imprisoned and subject to confiscation of tools and property. The intent was to mobilize the rural poor to assist the state in grain procurement.[29] This effort to create class struggle in the countryside was not entirely successful, as village solidarity often prevailed.

Industrialization and the First Five-Year Plan

Stalin became convinced of the need for rapid industrialization to overcome the Soviet Union's backwardness in the shortest possible time. In order for the Soviet Union to survive in an increasingly hostile international environment, a modern industrial economy was essential. Rapid industrialization would require huge expenditures to import foreign technology and machinery. Therefore, the Soviet Union needed to greatly expand exports, primarily grain. Stalin concluded that the free market in grain presented the regime with an unpredictable, expensive, and inefficient food supply that made it impossible to accumulate the capital needed for industrialization. For Stalin, collectivization was intended not only as a means to transform the countryside but as a means to carry out an industrial revolution from above. Since long-term foreign loans were not available for investment, the only alternative was to extract a surplus from the agricultural sector. This would necessitate lowering prices paid to peasants for agricultural goods, increasing the tax on peasants, and taxing kulaks more heavily. Stalin said industrial expansion had to be paid for by "tribute" exacted from agriculture. An independent peasantry would react to such measures by cutting output. This would make collectivization imperative, though by this time Stalin was also stressing the need for increasing the productivity of individual farms. The onset of the world economic depression would make achievement of Stalin's goals increasingly difficult. The Soviet Union launched its program of rapid industrialization requiring the importation of manufactured goods precisely when the price of grain, its principal export, was about to fall on the world market.

The introduction of the First Five-Year Plan reflected Stalin's determination to move toward rapid industrialization and put increased demands on the countryside. Nothing would be permitted to stand in the way. *Gosplan*, the State Planning Commission, developed two versions of the First Five-Year Plan. The Sixteenth Party Conference of April 1929 endorsed the optimal variant, which depended on a totally unrealistic set of assumptions. Fulfillment of the Plan depended upon an increase in agricultural productivity, despite the fact that it was inaugurated in the middle of a grain crisis and that grain procurement was below that of the previous year. It called for sizable increases in resources to be made available to the agricultural sector for mechanization and fertilizer. The main thrust was for an ambitious expansion of heavy industry, but it assumed that heavy and light industry could expand together and that both investment and consumption could increase. These assumptions proved overly optimistic.[30]

The Plan called for partial voluntary collectivization but assumed continued long-term reliance on the private sector. It was hoped that the collective sector would demonstrate its economic superiority and, thus, win over peasants for the collective sector. Twenty-three percent of peasant farms were to be collectivized in the following five years. Collective and state farms, which had accounted for less than 2 percent of grain production between 1927 and 1928, were to cover 17.5 percent of the total cultivated area and account for 43 percent of grain production for the market by 1932–1933. Although 23 percent of peasant households were to be collectivized over the life of the Plan, in the first year the level of collectivization was to be raised only from 1.7 to 2.2 percent.[31] There were three forms of *kolkhoz* (collective farm). The loosest form of collective, the *toz*, was to predominate during this period. In the toz, peasants retained their individual holdings but joined together to buy or rent tools and machinery and worked some land cooperatively. In the *artel*—which eventually became the standard form of collective farm—all land, except for small garden plots, was owned and worked in common. In the *kommuna*, the highest type, private property was completely abolished, and peasants worked and lived communally.[32]

The Plan was based on the expectation that the 1929 harvest would be substantially larger than that in 1928. Large increases were expected in grain collections without any increase in the prices paid to peasants by the collection agencies. However, a severe drought hit parts of Ukraine and areas of the North Caucasus in July 1929. Losses in the Ukrainian harvest exceeded the entire amount of grain procured by state collection agencies the previous year. At the end of July, compulsory grain delivery quotas were allocated to districts and villages, not as an emergency measure but as regular policy. Essentially, this meant a return to the grain requisitioning policies of the civil war period.

The peasants' first priority in sale of grain was in fulfillment of state obligations as determined by skhods acting on instructions received through party channels. Penalties were imposed for refusal to deliver grain, even if there was no evidence the peasant actually had any. Grain collection officials and kolkhoz chairmen could be tried if they failed to take adequate measures to ensure grain delivery. Peasants felt cheated when they were forced to sell to government procurement agencies for less than they could get on the free market. They hid grain in pits to avoid the procurement or sold it on the black market. Speculators bought bread on the free markets of towns and resold it in areas short of bread. The price of food on the free market soared. By November 1929, the peasant population of large areas of Ukraine moved north in search of food. James Hughes states that "the specter of famine" endangered Ukraine and the industrial heartland. As the price of food increased in cities and towns, worker dissatisfaction grew. Although the regime had spent hard currency reserves to import grain the previous year, the commitment to rapid industrialization made the regime unwilling to repeat this. Nor was it willing to moderate the pace of industrial development.[33]

The regime reacted by sending in large numbers of party members and government officials to enforce grain collection. Merle Fainsod describes the actions of these special emissaries in the Western Oblast of Russia. Although they were supposed to enlist poor and middle peasants in requisitioning grain from the kulaks, many kulaks were respected village leaders. Often the villagers maintained solidarity with the kulaks. Even local soviet and party officials often protected kulaks from the emissaries. Under pressure to procure grain, the emissaries often seized grain not only from kulaks but from middle and even poor peasants. The collection campaign thus undermined the official policy of driving a wedge between the kulaks and the rest of the village. When kulaks failed to meet their quotas, "workers' brigades" or village soviet forces raided households and confiscated grain. Kulaks hid grain, offered bribes, and retaliated. Reports of killings and arson multiplied and the emissaries pleaded for Unified State Political Administration (OGPU) reinforcements.[34] The entire campaign was confused; the railroads had difficulty in transporting grain, and quotas were changed arbitrarily. Grain continued to be collected in regions that had already fulfilled their plans.[35] Despite warnings by Nikolay Bukharin and other party moderates that continued use of forceful measures would lead to catastrophe, Stalin was convinced that peasants were hoarding grain and deliberately sabotaging the regime.[36]

Rapid Collectivization

The tempo of collectivization began to accelerate rapidly during this period. By July 1, more than 1 million households—nearly double the number anticipated—

had joined kolkhozes, but this still amounted to only 4 percent of all peasant households.[37] In August, the party approved rapid collectivization of entire regions and a stepped-up campaign of dekulakization. The already heavy tax burden on kulaks was sharply increased, and any resistance led to total expropriation. Kulaks were assigned high quotas for grain delivery. Although local practices varied, kulaks who failed to meet quotas were deprived of their property and expelled from villages. Part of the intent was to terrorize middle peasants into joining collectives rapidly to avoid the risk of being thrown in with the kulaks.[38] By September, a new slogan, "The Five-Year Plan in Four," was being proclaimed. By October 1, 7.5 percent of all households were collectivized, the figures for the major grain-producing regions being considerably higher.[39]

In November 1929, the party's Central Committee met to congratulate itself on its success on the agricultural front. Grain had been collected more rapidly and in larger quantities than in previous years. And though the socialized sector had failed to fulfill its plan, collections from individual peasants had more than made up the difference, leading to overfulfillment of the plan. Grain collection was 50 percent over that of the previous year. Not only was the government able to export substantial amounts of grain, it was able to create a grain reserve of more than 1.5 million tons to ensure that spring sowing would be favorable for collectivization. Vyacheslav Molotov spoke of the need for immediate collectivization to provide the state with agricultural products at low prices, thus enabling the state to finance industrialization.[40] The Central Committee emphasized the need for a new decisive offense against the kulak. This produced a profound shift in party policy from the attempt at gradual transformation to the establishment of whole villages, districts, and even regions in which collectivization would be completed within a short time span. Party members believed that the goals of the Five-Year Plan could be achieved, that industrialization could be accomplished and agriculture transformed. However, for this to occur, the power of the kulaks would have to be broken.[41]

Brigades of party activists, worker battalions, Komsomol (the Communist Union of Youth), and OGPU detachments were sent to villages. The party mobilized 25,000 urban members, the so-called Twenty-Five Thousanders, to go to the countryside to "liquidate the kulaks as a class" and create collective farms. Party workers were supposed to ally with poor peasants, oust kulaks from the villages, and try to win over the middle peasants for the kolkhozes. In practice, any peasant who resisted was labeled a kulak and treated as an enemy. Party activists closed village churches, burned icons, and arrested priests.[42] From October to December 1929, collectivized households increased from 7.5 percent to 15 percent.[43]

Stalin now determined to move even more rapidly. A Central Committee decree of January 5, 1930, called for completing collectivization in all grain-producing areas by the fall of 1931, but the process moved much faster once it got under way. Machine Tractor Stations (MTS) were established to service the collective farms. In less than two months, the number of collectivized households doubled. The effort was to collectivize most peasants before sowing started in mid-April. To supervise local dekulakization and collectivization, special *troikas* were established, consisting of the first secretary of the district party committee, the chairman of the Soviet executive committee, and the head of the local OGPU. These local authorities were under unremitting pressure from the center to fill collectivization targets. Factory workers poured into the countryside along with party and local government officials. More than a quarter of a million agents were sent from the cities and towns. Mass terror and coercion were used against peasants reluctant to join collective farms.[44] In some areas, peasants' land and draft animals were expropriated for the collective, as were cows, pigs, and chickens. In other areas, even peasant homes and garden plots were merged into communes. The Central Committee declared that the artel, by now the dominant form of kolkhoz, was to serve as a transitional form toward a full kommuna, in which peasants would have no individual property. Kulaks, except for those with sons in the army, were not permitted to join collective farms.[45]

Dekulakization

Expropriation of kulaks was carried out simultaneously with collectivization. A reign of terror was unleashed in large areas of the countryside. Many kulaks were expelled from their homes, their land, and often their villages. A top-secret letter of February 12 divided all kulak households into three groups based on the danger they presented and the severity of the punishment they should suffer:

1. Active counterrevolutionaries who organized terror and counterrevolution: these were to be shot or sent to prison or corrective labor camps; their families were to be banished to remote regions. Fifty thousand households were to be included in this category.
2. Politically active rich kulaks: they and their families were to be banished to remote regions. About 112,000 households were to be included in this category.
3. Less powerful kulak households who would be permitted to remain in their own district but would be resettled outside the collectivized villages on the worst land. These kulaks, numbering approximately 5 million, were to be required to perform communal duties.

The letter prohibited deportation or resettlement of poor or middle peasants, but in practice, many more peasants than the recommended numbers were banished, sent to corrective labor camps, or shot.[46]

The definition of "kulak" was so broad that few were safe. A peasant could be deemed a kulak for once having hired a laborer. Any peasant who was uncooperative could be labeled a *podkulachnik*, or kulak henchman, and treated as a kulak.

Raiding parties took clothing, warm underwear, hats, and shoes from the bodies of members of kulak and even seredniak households. Often the goods were shared out among members of the raiding party who ate the food and drank the alcohol on the spot. Fear became pervasive among well-to-do peasants. There was a wave of suicides. Kulaks orchestrated fictitious divorces in hopes of saving the lives of their wives and children. Some abandoned their property and went into hiding.[47] Peasants resisted in the only way they could: destroying crops and slaughtering and eating their livestock. Four million horses were slaughtered. But it was not just draft animals that were killed. In February and March 1930, one-fourth of all cattle, one-third of all pigs, and more than one-fourth of the sheep and goats were destroyed. Riots, arson, and terrorist killings of officials multiplied. The majority of attackers were peasant women wielding pitchforks, spades, and axes. When heads of households were imprisoned, wives and children were left with no means of support. Bands of beggar children roamed the countryside and wandered into towns. Although some poor peasants used dekulakization to pay off scores against kulaks and to share in the spoils, most sympathized with the fate of their neighbors. Armed peasant revolts broke out. Violent reprisals were taken against the peasants. Chaos threatened.[48]

Some estimates suggest that approximately 1.1 million households were expropriated and that about one-half of the resulting 7 million dislocated citizens were packed into unheated boxcars and deported to special settlements or labor camps in the far north and other distant areas of the country where, if they survived the trip, they provided forced labor for road building, lumbering, construction, and mining. The number in labor camps grew from about 30,000 in 1928 to nearly 2 million in 1931.[49]

A Respite

Stalin's article, *Dizzy from Success,* published in *Pravda* on March 2, called a temporary retreat to prevent the breakdown of spring sowing. Stalin blamed local party and government officials for violating the voluntary principle of collectivization. Fifty-eight percent of all peasant farms had been collectivized on March 1, but many were only paper organizations. Peasants began leaving collective farms in such numbers that by June 30 the bloated collectivization figure was down to 23.6 percent. More than half of those leaving were in Ukraine and the North Caucasus. The mass exodus from the collectives threatened to disorganize the spring sowing.

The Great Depression had caused grain prices to fall 49 percent in 1930, but the price of machinery that the Soviet Union needed to import remained stable. This meant that the country had to export twice as much grain per unit of machinery imported as it had in 1928.[50] There were highly optimistic expectations for the harvest of 1930–1931 and an ambitious grain collection plan. The village quota took absolute precedence over all other needs. Peasants who failed to meet individual quotas were fined or imprisoned and their property was sold. Relentless pressure stripped the individual peasants of their grain. Although less grain was collected than anticipated in the plan, it was 6 million tons over the 1929–1930 collection and double the 1928–1929 collection. No less than 83.5 million tons of grain were harvested, 26.5 percent of which was procured by the state through obligatory deliveries at low prices. The country exported 4.8 million tons, but because of the depression, the price received on the world market in early 1931 was only 36 percent of that received the previous year. Since the prices for cotton and timber had not fallen as badly, grain was supplied to cotton- and timber-producing areas of the country so they could export their production, enabling the Soviet Union to import the machinery and industrial materials needed for industrialization. Although agricultural supplies to towns increased more slowly than did the urban population, workers in large capital goods factories received higher bread rations than those in less important industries. The rural population had an absolute decline in consumption per head in 1930.[51]

Renewed Collectivization

After the successful harvest of 1930, Stalin pushed for collectivization with renewed vigor and determination, particularly in the major grain-growing regions. This time, however, peasants were permitted to keep homes, garden plots, and some domestic animals. More farm machinery was available, concentrated in the MTS, each of which had a Communist Party police unit, the "political section," charged with supervising the countryside. The MTS became centers of power in the countryside. Many middle peasants who refused to enter collective farms were reclassified as kulaks. By June 1931, the number of households in collective farms was back to the March figure. By September, 60 percent of peasant households were collectivized. This time around, compared to the first collectivization drive, there were more instances of destruction of property and slaughter of draft animals.[52]

The harvest of 1931 was poor, especially in Ukraine, but Stalin was relentless. The proportion of the gross yield procured by the state increased from 27 percent in 1930 to 33 percent in 1931. Procurement quotas had to rise because of the increase in the urban population. In 1930, there were 26 million urban workers being provisioned by the state. This rose to 33.2 million by 1931.[53] Under collective farm rules, the first obligation of a kolkhoz after a harvest was to deliver grain to the state in accord with procurement quotas. The second priority was to create seed reserves, supplies of fodder, and grain reserves and to pay the MTS for work performed. Only then was grain distributed to collective farmers. About 10 to 15 percent of the *kolkhozniks'* anticipated earnings were distributed in advance, but the peasants had to wait until December for final distribution. The poor harvest and high procurements left little grain for the kolkhozes to distribute to their members in 1931. In some areas, as much as 60 percent of the harvest was taken, leaving the peasant with little incentive to produce.[54] Archives recently discovered at the Ukrainian Communist Party's Institute of Party History document severe food shortages in the Ukrainian countryside during the winter of 1931–1932.[55]

The 1932 Harvest and Grain Procurement

Proponents of the view that the Great Famine of 1932–1933 constituted an officially directed genocide—accomplished through procurement quotas—against the Ukrainians argue that the grain harvest of 1932 was not particularly low and should have been adequate to feed the population. However, Mark B. Tauger points out that recent data from Soviet archives demonstrate that the 1932 harvest was considerably lower than official statistics indicate, aggravating the serious food shortage that had struck the country in 1931 and making "famine likely if not inevitable in 1933." His calculations give a total Soviet harvest of 50.06 million tons, nearly 30 percent below the official figure of 69.87 million tons. He argues that the famine was primarily the result of a genuine shortage.[56]

The 1932 harvest, as Sheila Fitzpatrick points out, was only the third since collectivization, so there was no backlog of experience to draw on. The state was not yet sure how much it could extract from the peasantry. The peasants, for their part, were trying to figure out how little they could deliver. When the government established procurement quotas, it had to guess the size of the future harvest and then announce the quotas. At all levels of agricultural production, from the peasant up, all were motivated to argue that the quota was impossible to meet; and, at all levels of party and government, every official knew or suspected the others were exaggerating the difficulties of meeting the quota. The pressures of the Five-Year Plan and the demands of industrialization pushed Moscow to impose unrealistically high quotas. The urban population was growing rapidly, and the government wanted to increase grain exports to pay for foreign technology and machinery. And whereas unrealistic quotas for industrial output could mean unfortunate results, in agriculture the result could be fatal, leaving peasants without food to survive the winter.[57]

The procurement plan for 1932 was initially fixed at 29.5 million tons, though it was later reduced to 18 million. As the regime encountered difficulties in grain procurement, pressure was increased. In June 1932, raions (districts) in the Western Oblast of Russia were informed that grain supplies, even for basic industries, would be exhausted by July 1. No reserves were left to meet July commitments. In a desperate attempt to feed the cities and towns, additional emergency grain-delivery quotas were imposed. An additional 4–5 percent was added to the grain delivery plans for each raion to ensure plan fulfillment. Militia and OGPU units prevented all sale of bread in bazaars until the peasants had met delivery quotas.[58] Peasants went on "grain strikes," refusing to work unless advance grain payments were increased. Raids on kolkhoz fields and thefts of grain, often by members of the kolkhozes themselves, became increasingly common. Much of the stealing was a result of hunger, but some was out of anger and resentment.[59] Desperately hungry peasant women called "barbers" scissored off spikes of grain from unripened fields to feed their children. Peasants carried off in their pockets small amounts of grain from threshing stations. Others slaughtered pigs and cattle. Seed grain set aside for sowing, fodder for draft animals, and grain already distributed to collective farmers were requisitioned to meet quotas. Thousands of collective farm chairmen, specialists, and even party and state officials were arrested and convicted of "connivance in kulak sabotage."[60] The main centers of resistance were in Ukraine, the North Caucasus, and parts of the Volga region.

Famine spread across the country, primarily in rural areas but affecting towns as well.[61] Urban workers deserted factories, and millions of peasants fled collective farms in search of food. Internal passports were issued to registered town dwellers to control movement. Since peasants were not given passports, they were prevented from moving to towns without authorization, even to take seasonal work. Starving bands of children roamed the streets of towns. Hungry peasants crowded railroad stations and begged in the streets, even in Moscow and Leningrad. In July 1932, All-Union Party Politburo members Vyacheslav Molotov and Lazar Kaganovich appeared at the Third All-Ukrainian Party Conference to take the Ukrainian leadership to task for jeopardizing fulfillment of the agricultural plan.[62] The Ukrainian party leadership argued that the plans imposed on Ukraine were unrealistic. They pleaded for lower quotas but to no avail.[63]

Reprisals Against Peasants

An August 7, 1932, decree declared kolkhoz property "sacred" and "inviolable." Those who pilfered it were labeled "enemies of the people." The stealing of kolkhoz property, even of crops in the fields, was punishable by a death sentence or, in mitigating circumstances, by a minimum sentence of ten years in a labor camp and confiscation of property. Police, military, paramilitary, and Komsomol patrols were established in the countryside to protect the grain against the peasants who had grown it. Harvesting now took place under armed guard. Zhores Medvedev states that even this draconian law had little effect. Grain collections continued to be low. To add to the pressure, the government set up roadblocks in parts of Ukraine, North Caucasus, and the Don region to prevent grain being smuggled out for sale and to prevent the delivery of salt, kerosene, and cloth until quotas had been fulfilled.[64]

Grain exports continued, albeit at a reduced rate. Exports fell from 4.8 million tons in 1930 and 5.1 million tons in 1931 to 1.8 million in 1932 and 1 million in 1933. Tauger argues that as a result of the fall in world market prices for grain the Soviet Union's indebtedness increased while its potential ability to pay decreased. The West contemplated seizing Soviet assets and denying future credits if the Soviet Union defaulted. This would have undermined fulfillment of industrialization plans.[65] Exports could not be halted without scrapping the Five-Year Plan, which Stalin was not willing to do.

Stalin believed that the peasants suffered as a consequence of their own misdeeds—their earlier opposition to collectivization, their stealing of grain, and their slaughtering of animals. If grain procurement quotas could not be filled, Stalin assumed that this had to be the result of deliberate efforts by enemies to undermine Soviet socialism and him personally. Stalin blamed local party workers and kolkhoz chairmen for attending to the needs of collective farms before fulfilling obligations to the state. He blamed local authorities for their lack of vigilance in uncovering the kulaks who were responsible for the disaster. Feeding the army, OGPU troops, and urban workers and exporting grain took priority over alleviating the starvation of peasants.[66]

Ruthless reprisals were taken against peasants, particularly in the North Caucasus and Ukraine. In the fall of 1932, a special Politburo commission headed by Kaganovich was sent to the North Caucasus to quell a strike of Kuban Cossacks who refused to cultivate their land. The entire populations of sixteen Cossack villages in the North Caucasus were deported to Siberia.[67] When grain procurements in Ukraine failed to meet the goals, procurement brigades were sent back again. These procurement brigades, which included members of OGPU, the local militia, and armed activists, moved from village to village threatening the peasants.[68] At the end of December, Moscow sent instructions that kolkhozes that had not met their quotas were to give up all their grain, including seed funds.[69] Fedor Belov speaks of the "red brooms," the name given to groups of party members, primarily from the cities, who searched kolkhozes and individual plots for food peasants might have hidden, taking "surplus" grain from barns and corncribs.[70]

A Ukrainian decree of December 6, 1932, assigned six villages to a *chorna doshka*, or black list, for sabotaging grain procurements. Other villages were soon added to the list. This came close to constituting a collective death sentence. All state and cooperative stores were closed and all goods removed from the villages. All trade, including that in bread, was banned. Warehouses containing food grain were sealed and even seed grain was seized. All credits and advances, including bread, had to be repaid immediately. The kolkhozes were threatened with dissolution if they still failed to deliver their quotas. Collective farms and state apparatuses were purged of those who argued that failure to meet quotas was a consequence of famine and urged the retention of seed grain to ensure spring sowing from collective farms. A special system of local prosecutors was established to impose criminal penalties for nonfulfillment of quotas.[71]

Agricultural Disaster: The Winter of 1932–1933

By the end of 1932, it was clear that Ukraine and North Caucasus, the lower and middle Volga region, the southern Urals, and Kazakhstan were in the grip of a catastrophic famine. The famine was not restricted to only these areas, however.

Fainsod reports that the food crisis in the Western Oblast "reached a climax of desperation during the bitter Winter of 1932–1933."[72] Peasants left their villages in search of food, but roadblocks and military cordons prevented movement. Peasants had been in the habit of finding temporary work in towns in the winter, but this was now forbidden. Collective farmers were not allowed to leave their villages. Although some peasants managed to reach the towns, this failed to alleviate their desperate situation since all food was rationed and they lacked ration cards. Corpses lay in the streets of cities and towns until collected by special trucks.[73]

Once the true dimensions of the famine were evident, the regime realized that the lack of seed grain for spring sowing could endanger the next year's harvest. Some grain quotas were lowered and some grain reserves were opened. On February 25, 1933, a Central Committee decree allotted 320,000 tons of seed to Ukraine and 240,000 to the North Caucasus.[74] Minimal food rations were distributed to peasants who actually worked in the fields. The planting took place under the direct supervision of political departments of the MTS. In many places, the army guarded the seed grain from hungry peasants.[75] On May 8, 1933, Stalin and Molotov sent secret instructions to halt the "saturnalia of arrests" and curtail the scale of repression in the countryside. Maximum deportation quotas were established. Arrests and deportation could still occur on an individual basis against those who carried on active struggle against collective farms or organized refusals to sow and deliver produce.[76]

Impact on Ukraine

The agricultural disaster put Stalin's entire plan at risk. He could not accept the fact that the famine was the culmination of previous policies; scapegoats had to be found. Stalin attributed the catastrophe to recalcitrance on the part of peasants and disloyalty on the part of local leaders, especially in Ukraine. The Ukrainian party organization was assailed for failure to meet production quotas. Pavel Postyshev, a non-Ukrainian member of the All-Union Party Secretariat and close associate of Stalin, was sent to Ukraine as second secretary of the Ukrainian Communist Party with broad authority to reorganize and purge the party. Party personnel from outside Ukraine were transferred in, and urban cadres were transferred to rural areas. In February, a new OGPU chief was sent to Ukraine. On February 28, announcement was made of the uncovering of an alleged major anti-Soviet conspiracy to undermine agriculture. Seventy members of the agricultural commissariat were put on trial. Others lost their posts and were deported or imprisoned.[77]

Mykola Skrypnyk, a strong supporter of Ukrainization and boss of Ukraine since 1927, was demoted from his post as commissar of education and assigned to a less sensitive post in charge of the Ukrainian Gosplan. Orchestrated attacks against Skrypnyk followed, leading to his suicide on July 6, 1933. After Skrypnyk's death, the party campaign against Ukrainian nationalism accelerated. Henceforth, Russification would be imposed in politics, economics, and culture throughout the non-Russian areas of the Soviet Union. Decisions would be made in Moscow. Robert Sullivant contends that the pressures of collectivization and industrialization led the central leaders to regard any expression of independence in culture as an attack on the party. Their suspicions were exacerbated by the rebirth of German militarism, since Germany had earlier been the sponsor of Ukrainian nationalism. This led them to regard all nationalist manifestations as signs of subversion. He states that, therefore, it was not unreasonable for party leaders to conclude that, for both security reasons and the success of Soviet programs, Ukrainian nationalists had to be restricted or destroyed.[78]

In support of the conclusion that the famine resulted from the regime's determination to use grain procurements as an instrument to crush the Ukrainian people, Mace and Conquest point to the fact that the famine stopped at the Byelorussian-Ukrainian border in the north and the Russo-Ukrainian border in the northeast. The Russo-Ukrainian border was closed by security troops to prevent Ukrainian peasants from getting out to find food. If they did manage to leave, they were not allowed to return with food. However, the border with Byelorussia apparently was not closed. Many Ukrainians went there seeking food since the famine was much less severe.[79] Fitzpatrick writes that the flight of starving peasants toward the towns in the winter led to a crisis. The towns were already overcrowded from the influx of previous years and were unable to cope. The urban rationing and supply systems threatened to break down. Steps were therefore taken to cordon off the towns. Those not engaged in productive work were given ten days to leave. About 300,000 were deported from Moscow alone.[80]

On April 22, 1933, Stalin and Molotov circulated a directive in response to mass exodus from the North Caucasus and Ukraine to the central regions of Russia and Byelorussia. The directive insisted that the exodus was organized by Polish agents and enemies of the Soviet regime in order to agitate against collective farms and the Soviet system. Local authorities and the OGPU were ordered to prevent mass departures and to immediately arrest the "peasants" of the Ukraine and North Caucasus who made their way north and, after the counter-revolutionary elements had been separated, to return the remainder to their place of residence.[81] An order banned the sale of railroad tickets in the Ukrainian countryside to anyone without travel authorization from local authorities. OGPU guards inspected all trains at the border to search for peasant stowaways. About 220,000 fleeing peasants were caught and returned to their villages in the spring of 1933.[82]

Conclusion

The government could have relaxed procurement, eliminated grain exports, and even imported grain and encouraged famine relief; but its failure to take these measures does not justify the charge of Ukrainian genocide. J. Arch Getty stresses that objective effect is not the same as subjective intent.[83] Similarly, David R. Marples, after reviewing recent publications by the Institute of History of the Ukrainian Academy of Sciences, concludes:

> It is more logical to perceive Stalinist agricultural policies, for example, as motivated by a desire for the acquisition of grain rather than by an aversion to Ukrainians as an ethnic or national group. . . . Because the effects of Soviet policies have been so tragic, the worst motives on the part of the perpetrators are often assumed.[84]

Unlike the Holocaust, the Great Famine was not an intentional act of genocide. The purpose was not to exterminate Ukrainians as a people simply because they were Ukrainians. Extermination was not an end in itself. The famine was the result of Stalin's effort to totally reconstruct Soviet society through rapid industrialization. The burden of industrialization, of necessity, fell most heavily on peasants. Since Ukrainians were overwhelmingly a peasant people, they suffered disproportionately. The deaths of millions of Ukrainians and other Soviet peoples in the famine were not the intent but rather the consequence of a ruthless economic policy. When the famine put Stalin's plans at risk, Stalin attributed the disaster to disloyalty, particularly in Ukraine, where resistance to forced procurement was strongest. Ukrainian nationalism was attacked because it was perceived as a threat to Stalin's procurement policies, thus endangering rapid industrialization.

A multitude of interconnected factors contributed to the Great Famine. An unrealistic procurement and pricing policy eliminated incentives for peasants to produce more than they and their families consumed. When their surpluses were taken away at low, state-imposed prices, they sowed less the next year. Kulaks, the hardest-working and most ambitious peasants, were eliminated, and middle peasants were discouraged from producing more, lest they be labeled kulaks. To ensure control over grain collection, the regime introduced forced collectivization when adequate machinery and management were not available. In protest, peasants slaughtered draft animals. Grain confiscation efforts took seed grain, fodder, and even the necessary minimal food from peasants. Increasing urbanization meant that grain-producing regions could not keep all they produced, even in a famine, lest the cities starve. The world economic depression lowered agricultural prices in relation to industrial prices, meaning that the country had to increase exports to obtain the same amount of imports. The most important factor, the one that overrode all other considerations, was Stalin's determination that nothing would stand in the way of forced, rapid industrialization.

After the famine, peasants no longer had the will to resist. By 1936, over 90 percent of peasant households were collectivized. Almost 250,000 kolkhozes replaced the 25 million inefficient, primitive, small individual peasant farms tying up labor needed for industrialization. The peasant was eliminated as an independent force standing in the way of modernization. The average rate of increase in large-scale industrial output from 1928 to 1937 was about 15–16 percent per year. The gross national product rose 6.5–7 percent annually. In 1926, more than 80 percent of the Soviet Union's workers were in the agricultural sector. During the next thirteen years, 25 million people moved to cities, doubling the urban population.[85]

The Soviet Union, through forced collectivization and the relentless struggle for industrialization, created a powerful industrial state; but Stalinism ultimately left the Soviet Union with an inefficient and distorted system of production. Heavy industry, especially defense, had absolute priority. The planning process itself distorted production, as industries strove to meet production targets rather than producing what the economy needed. Consumer goods were sacrificed. There was a housing shortage as more workers poured into the cities. The chaos of collectivization, peasant resistance, the lack of incentives for the individual peasant, and the low investment in agriculture continued to plague the Soviet economy. Ultimately the Soviet people discovered that their enormous sacrifices produced an economy that no longer worked.

NOTES

1. See Aleksandr M. Nekrich, *The Punished Peoples*, trans. George Saunders (New York: W. W. Norton, 1978); Bohdan Nahaylo and Victor Swoboda, *Soviet Disunion: A History of the Nationalities Problem in the USSR* (New York: Free Press, 1989), pp. 79–106; Helene Carrere d'Encausse, "When the 'Prison of Peoples' Was Opened," in *The Soviet Nationality Reader,* ed. Rachel Denber (Boulder: Westview Press, 1992), pp. 88–91; Shirin Akiner, *Islamic Peoples of the Soviet Union* (Boston: Kegan Paul International, 1983). For an account of the Kazakh tragedy, see Robert Conquest, *The Harvest of Sorrow: Soviet Collectivization and the Terror-Famine* (New York: Oxford University Press, 1986), pp. 189–198.

2. Marco Carynnyk, "The Famine the 'Times' Couldn't Find," *Commentary* 76 (November 1983):32–40; Marco Carynnyk, "Making the News Fit to Print: Walter Duranty, the *New York Times,* and the Ukrainian Famine of 1933," in *Famine in Ukraine, 1932–1933,* ed. Roman Serbyn and Bohdan Krawchenko (Edmonton: Canadian Institute of Ukrainian Studies, University of Alberta, 1986), pp. 67–95; Eugene Lyons, *Assignment in Utopia* (New York: Harcourt, Brace, 1937, republished, New Brunswick: Transaction Publishers, 1991), pp. 541–577; Conquest, *Harvest of Sorrow,* pp. 308–321.

3. Marco Carynnyk, "Blind Eye to Murder: Britain, the United States, and the Ukrainian Famine of 1933," in Serbyn and Krawchenko, *Famine in Ukraine,* pp. 109–138; the eighty-five documents collected in Marco Carynnyk, Lubomyr Y. Luciuk, and Bohdan S. Kordan, eds., *The Foreign Office and the Famine* (New York: Vestal, 1988), present contemporary descriptions of the famine sent to the West in British diplomatic pouches. These communications were largely ignored or suppressed at the time. See also Mark B. Tauger, "Reviews: The Foreign Office and the Famine/Investigation of the Ukrainian Famine, 1932–1933," *Slavic Review* 48 (Winter 1989):680.

4. James E. Mace, "Famine and Nationalism," *Problems of Communism* 33 (May-June 1984):37. See also Nahaylo and Swoboda, *Soviet Disunion,* p. 70; Conquest, *Harvest of Sorrow*; Commission on the Ukrainian Famine, *Investigation of the Ukrainian Famine, 1932–1933: Report to Congress* (Washington, D.C.: Government Printing Office, 1988). It should be noted that James E. Mace was the staff director for the congressional commission. For a sharp attack on Conquest's hypothesis, sources, and evidence, see J. Arch Getty, "Starving the Ukraine," *London Review of Books,* January 22, 1987.

5. See Robert C. Tucker, *Stalin in Power: The Revolution from Above, 1928–1941* (New York: W. W. Norton, 1990), as well as his "Stalinism as Revolution from Above," in *Stalinism: Essays in Historical Interpretation,* ed. Robert C. Tucker (New York: W. W. Norton, 1977); and Robert C. Tucker, *Political Culture and Leadership in Soviet Russia* (New York: W. W. Norton, 1987); Adam Ulam, *Stalin: The Man and His Era* (New York: Viking, 1973); Martin Malia, *The Soviet Tragedy: A History of Socialism in Russia, 1917–1991* (New York: Free Press, 1994), pp. 139–227.

6. Hannah Arendt, *The Origins of Totalitarianism,* 2d ed. (New York: Meridian Books, 1958), p. 320.

7. Stephen Wheatcraft, "Correspondence: Ukrainian Famine," *Problems of Communism* 33 (March-April 1985):134.

8. Nahaylo and Swoboda, *Soviet Disunion,* pp. 60–65.

9. Michael Ignatieff, *Blood and Belonging: Journeys into the New Nationalism* (New York: Farrar, Straus, and Giroux, 1993), pp. 194–195.

10. *Economist,* January 28, 1995, p. 18.

11. M. Maksudov, "Ukraine's Demographic Losses, 1927–1938," in Serbyn and Krawchenko, *Famine in Ukraine,* pp. 34–37.

12. James E. Mace, "The Famine of 1933: A Survey of Sources," in Serbyn and Krawchenko, *Famine in Ukraine,* p. 50. In "Famine and Nationalism in Soviet Ukraine," *Problems of Communism* 33 (May-June 1984):39, Mace concludes that 7.5 million people in Ukraine died prematurely from famine.

13. Robert Conquest, *Harvest of Sorrow,* pp. 299–307.

14. Robert E. Johnson, "Introduction," *Russian Studies in History* 31 (Summer 1992):2–7; Iurii Aleksandrov Poliakov, Valentina Borisovna Zhiromshaia, and Igor' Nikolaevich Kiselev, "A Half-Century of Silence: The 1937 Census," *Russian Studies in History* 31 (Summer 1992):53.

15. Elena Aleksandrovna Osokin, "The Victims of the Famine of 1933: How Many?" *Russian Studies in History* 31 (Fall 1992):5–18.

16. Stephen Wheatcraft, "More Light on the Scale of Repression and Excess Mortality in the Soviet Union in the 1930's," *Soviet Studies* 42 (April 1990):355–367.

17. Alec Nove, "How Many Victims in the 1930's?" in *Soviet Studies* 42 (April 1990):369–373. "Research Materials," *Journal of Soviet Nationalities* 1 (Winter 1990–1991):158–159, argues that data from the 1937 census indicate that more than 5 million Ukrainians died in the famine and that millions more were not born or died in collectivization and the Great Purge between 1926 and 1937. It suggests a total population loss for this period of about 10 million.

18. James E. Mace, "The Man-Made Famine of 1933 in Soviet Ukraine," in Serbyn and Krawchenko, *Famine in Ukraine,* p. 11.

19. For an analysis of the 1921 famine, see Roman Serbyn, "The Famine of 1921–1923: A Model for 1932–1933?" in Serbyn and Krawchenko, *Famine in Ukraine,* pp. 147–178. Serbyn argues that whereas the 1921 famine in Russia was a result of natural calamities, in Ukraine it was caused "primarily by excessive taxation and outright plunder" and served as an effective means to crush Ukrainian peasant resistance to the Soviet regime.

20. Malia, *The Soviet Tragedy,* p. 146.

21. Ulam, *Stalin: The Man and His Era,* p. 295.

22. Tucker, *Stalin in Power,* p. 72.

23. Ulam, *Stalin: The Man and His Era,* pp. 294, 249.

24. R. W. Davies, *The Socialist Offensive: The Collectivization of Soviet Agriculture, 1929–1930* (Cambridge, Mass.: Harvard University Press, 1980), p. 39; Roy A. Medvedev, *Let History Judge: The Origins and Consequences of Stalinism,* trans. Colleen Taylor (New York: Alfred A. Knopf, 1972), p. 77; Moshe Lewin, *Russian Peasants and Soviet Power* (New York: W. W. Norton, 1967), p. 216.

25. Ulam, *Stalin: The Man and His Era,* p. 355.

26. Lewin, *Russian Peasants and Soviet Power,* pp. 217–230.

27. Fedor Belov, *The History of a Soviet Collective Farm* (New York: Praeger, 1955), p. 6.

28. Lewin, *Russian Peasants and Soviet Power,* pp. 239–244; Davies, *Socialist Offensive,* pp. 46–56.

29. James Hughes, "Capturing the Russian Peasantry: Stalinist Grain Procurement Policy and the 'Ural-Siberian Method,'" *Slavic Review* 53 (Spring 1994):76–78.

30. Lewin, *Russian Peasants and Soviet Power,* pp. 344–352.

31. Roy Medvedev, *Let History Judge,* p. 83; Lewin, *Russian Peasants and Soviet Power,* pp. 353–354.

32. Ulam, *Stalin: The Man and His Era,* pp. 322–323.

33. Hughes, "Capturing the Russian Peasantry," pp. 81–102; Davies, *Socialist Offensive,* pp. 63–76; Lewin, *Russian Peasants and Soviet Power,* pp. 382–87; Tucker, *Stalin in Power,* pp. 131–132.

34. Merle Fainsod, *Smolensk Under Soviet Rule* (Cambridge, Mass.: Harvard University Press, 1958), pp. 239–241.

35. Davies, *Socialist Offensive,* pp. 82–103.

36. Roy Medvedev, *Let History Judge,* pp. 80–81.

37. Ibid., p. 83.

38. Ulam, *Stalin: The Man and His Era,* pp. 324–325; Tucker, *Stalin in Power,* pp. 130–132, 138–141.

39. Davies, *Socialist Offensive,* p. 133.

40. Tucker, *Stalin in Power,* pp. 134–135; Davies, *Socialist Offensive,* pp. 105–107.

41. Davies, *Socialist Offensive,* pp. 172–173.

42. Sheila Fitzpatrick, *Stalin's Peasants: Resistance and Survival in the Russian Village After Collectivization* (New York: Oxford University Press, 1994), p. 6.

43. Lewin, *Russian Peasants and Soviet Power,* p. 514.

44. Davies, *Socialist Offensive,* pp. 204–230.

45. Ulam, *Stalin: The Man and His Era,* pp. 327–329.

46. Fainsod, *Smolensk,* pp. 242–244; Roy Medvedev, *Let History Judge,* p. 98.

47. Fainsod, *Smolensk,* pp. 245–247.

48. Davies, *Socialist Offensive,* pp. 246–251; Malia, *The Soviet Tragedy,* p. 197; Tucker, *Stalin in Power,* pp. 176–182; Roy Medvedev, *Let History Judge,* pp. 85–87; Lewin, *Russian Peasants and Soviet Power,* pp. 494–505.

49. Tucker, *Stalin in Power,* pp. 138, 173–175, 180–181.

50. Davies, *Socialist Offensive,* p. 107.

51. Ibid., pp. 350–371.

52. Malia, *The Soviet Tragedy,* p. 198.

53. Conquest, *Harvest of Sorrow,* p. 168.

54. Fitzpatrick, *Stalin's Peasants,* p. 72; Zhores A. Medvedev, *Soviet Agriculture* (New York: W. W. Norton, 1987), pp. 87–88.

55. Sergei Tsikora, "The Truth About the 1930's Famine," *Izvestia,* February 8, 1990, in *Current Digest of the Soviet Press* 42 (March 14, 1990):30–31.

56. Mark B. Tauger, "The 1932 Harvest and the Famine of 1933," *Slavic Review* 50 (Spring 1991):70–84. The quotation is on page 71. See also Mark B. Tauger, "Reviews: The Foreign Office and the Famine/Investigation of the Ukrainian Famine, 1932–1933," *Slavic Review* 48 (Winter 1989):678–679. He cites the Soviet publication *Istoriia krest'ianstva SSSR: Istoriia sovetskogo krest'ianstva* t.2, *1927–1937* (Moscow: Nauka, 1986) for his statistical information.

57. Fitzpatrick, *Stalin's Peasants,* pp. 70–71; Zhores Medvedev, *Soviet Agriculture,* p. 87.

58. Fainsod, *Smolensk,* pp. 259–260.

59. Fitzpatrick, *Stalin's Peasants,* p. 72.

60. Tsikora, "The Truth About the 1930's Famine," pp. 30–31.

61. The reports of Andrew Cairns, a Canadian wheat expert, provide contemporary graphic descriptions of conditions at this time. See "*Mr. Cairns' Investigations in Soviet Union*: William Strang (Moscow) to Sir John Simon, 12 August 1932, and John Cairns to E.M.H. Lloyd, 3 August 1932," in Carynnyk, Luciuk, and Kordan, *The Foreign Office and the Famine,* pp. 104–165, and "*Description of a Tour in the Volga Region*: Report by Andrew Cairns (Moscow)," p. 22, August 1932 in ibid., pp. 174–194.

62. "*Conditions in Ukraine*: Sir Esmond Ovey (Moscow) to Sir John Simon, 18 July 1932," in Carynnyk, Luciuk, and Kordan, *The Foreign Office and the Famine,* pp. 79–81.

63. Hryhory Kostiuk, *Stalinist Rule in the Ukraine* (New York: Praeger, 1960), pp. 22–23.

64. Zhores Medvedev, *Soviet Agriculture,* pp. 89–90.

65. Tauger, *The 1932 Harvest,* pp. 88–89.

66. Ulam, *Stalin: The Man and His Era,* pp. 345–349.

67. Nikita Khrushchev, *Khrushchev Remembers,* trans. Strobe Talbott (Boston: Little, Brown, 1970), p. 73.

68. Zhores Medvedev, *Soviet Agriculture,* pp. 90–91.

69. Fitzpatrick, *Stalin's Peasants,* p. 74.

70. Belov, *History of a Soviet Collective,* p. 28.

71. Fitzpatrick, *Stalin's Peasants,* pp. 76–77; Mace, *Famine and Nationalism,* p. 46.

72. Fainsod, *Smolensk,* p. 262.

73. Zhores Medvedev, *Soviet Agriculture,* pp. 91–92.

74. "Sir Esmond Ovey to Sir John Simon, 27 February 1933," in *The Foreign Office and the Famine,* p. 214. See also "*Conditions in Northern Caucasus in Spring of 1933*: Report by Otto Schiller, German Agricultural Attache in Moscow, 23 May 1933, Forwarded to Anthony Eden by the Duchess of Atholl, July 1933," in ibid., pp. 258–268.

75. Lyons, *Assignment in Utopia,* p. 577.

76. Leonard Schapiro, *The Communist Party of the Soviet Union* (New York: Vintage Books, 1964), pp. 386–387; V. P. Danilov and N. V. Teptsov, "Kollektivizatiia: Kak eto bylo," *Pravda,* September 16, 1988, in *The Stalin Revolution,* 3d ed., ed. Robert V. Daniels (Lexington, Mass.: D. C. Heath, 1990), p. 122.

77. Robert S. Sullivant, *Soviet Politics and the Ukraine, 1917–1957* (New York: Columbia University Press, 1962), pp. 192–194.

78. Ibid., pp. 195–203; for a contemporary report, see "William Strang (Moscow) to Sir John Simon on the Suicide of Mykola Skrypnyk, 10 July 1933," in *The British Foreign Office and the Famine,* pp. 253–254.

79. James E. Mace, "Correspondence," *Problems of Communism* 34 (March-April 1985):137; Nahaylo and Swoboda, *Soviet Disunion,* p. 70.

80. Fitzpatrick, *Stalin's Peasants,* pp. 92–95.

81. The directive is cited in Nikolai Ivnitsky's June 18, 1993, article in *Moscow News,* in which he includes excerpts of recently declassified documents from the archives of the Politburo of the Soviet Communist Party.

82. Fitzpatrick, *Stalin's Peasants,* p. 95.

83. Getty, *Starving the Ukraine,* pp. 7–8.

84. David R. Marples, "New Interpretations of Ukrainian History," *RFE/RL Research Report* 2 (March 12, 1993):60.

85. A. F. K. Organski, *The Stages of Political Development* (New York: Alfred A. Knopf, 1965), pp. 103–105.

❧ 10 ❧

The Holocaust and the Japanese Atrocities

KINUE TOKUDOME

Two Doctors

*W*ith his eyes glued to the TV screen, eighty-three-year-old Dr. Yuasa listened to my translation intently as we watched *The Last Days* together. In that film, another octogenarian doctor, Dr. Münch, was confronted by an Auschwitz survivor, Renee Firestone, whose sister had died in the clinic at Auschwitz where various medical experiments were carried out. With a paper she had just found at the Auschwitz archives in her hand, Renee asked, "Can you tell me what this is? What kind of experiments were these?" Dr. Münch admitted that the paper showed that it was at his clinic that Renee's sister had died, but kept saying that he saw nothing unusual written on the paper. "Why did she die?" Renee pressed on. Trying to maintain his composure he asked, "How long did she stay?" Equally calm Renee answered, "Six months." Dr. Yuasa shook his head as he listened to Dr. Münch's next words, "Well, that is the normal period. Do you understand? You were in Auschwitz as well. Well, then you should know."

These two doctors, although having lived their entire lives a world apart, had one thing in common. They both participated in medical experiments on human beings even though they were members of a profession whose dedication should have been for the well-being of patients.

Dr. Yuasa was a young army doctor of the Japanese Imperial Army when he was sent to China in 1942. Between then and Japan's defeat in 1945, he regularly participated in medical experiments and operation exercises using live Chinese civilians. Having always been a good student in a society that placed supreme value on total devotion to the emperor, Dr. Yuasa took his responsibility as an army doctor very seriously. He believed that he had to improve his skills so that he would be capable of taking care of as many wounded Japanese soldiers as possible. Moreover, he was ready to do anything to win the war, including waging a biological warfare.

Dr. Yuasa remembered that Army Medical Lieutenant General Shiro Ishii, the director of infamous Unit 731, visited his hospital often. Under Ishii, hundreds of Japanese scientists engaged in research and development of viable biological weapons using humans, mostly Chinese, as the guinea pigs. After the war, Dr. Yuasa remained in China working for the Nationalist Army. In 1951, he was arrested and detained as a war criminal in the People's Republic of China and spent the next five years in a prison at Taiyuan, Shanshi where he confessed everything he had done during the war. He came back to Japan in 1956 after having been set free by the Chinese military courts. For the past forty-three years, Dr. Yuasa has worked at a small clinic for needy families and spent much of his free time talking to young people about what he had done in China so that they would never again repeat his crimes.[1]

After watching the exchange between Dr. Münch and Renee, Dr. Yuasa started to talk with a deep sigh, "I myself had a similar experience." I stopped the VCR and began recording his story:

> It was almost at the end of my five years in the Chinese prison that a prison guard showed me a letter. It was written by the mother of the Chinese victim who I ordered to be brought in for an operation practice. Having studied Chinese in high school, I could read her letter and was completely devastated by what she had written to me. She wrote, "I saw my son with his hands tied behind his back being transported from the Kempeitai (Japanese secret police) station on a truck. I followed the truck as far as I could with my bound feet, but it disappeared from my sight quickly. The next day, I was told by people in my village that my son had been brought to your hospital and used by doctors for practice. I cried and cried until I thought my eyes were crushed. I could not eat a thing. I now know that you are in a prison. I asked the authorities that you be given the maximum sentence."

You see, before I read this letter I had felt that I had been deeply repentant. I had confessed every crime I had committed in China and expressed my utmost remorse. But No, I was not even close to a true, I mean, true realization of what I had done. Somewhere in the back of my mind, I was still saying to myself, 'It could not be helped. That was war after all.' I had never understood the suffering from the standpoint of the victims. It took me the image of this mother with her tiny feet running after the truck to finally realize that I had committed the most unforgivable crime—taking the precious life of her son. The guilt I felt was unbearable. It was as if I was being dragged into the abyss. I became convinced that I should be given a death sentence. Even that would not be enough. You know how I felt for the mother who wrote the letter? I was glad that she found the person who had killed her son. I was happy for her because, you see, although the Japanese Army killed millions of Chinese people, for us they were not human beings. We didn't keep records that such and such a Chinese person was killed by such and such a Japanese soldier. So it was very rare that the victim's family could track down their killer. But this mother found me. I felt relieved that she had, at least, some actual figure, not a faceless soldier of the Japanese Imperial Army, to be responsible for her son's death."

I then shared with Dr. Yuasa the conversation I had had with Renee Firestone just a few days earlier in Los Angeles:

I had no idea how old this man was, I had no idea how this man looked, so I did not know how I was going to react to this person who was going to greet me. You know, and I saw this elderly nice gentleman reaching for my hand. I just automatically put my hand out. And as I was holding his hand, I looked up the wall behind him and there was a picture of him in a Nazi uniform. And I began to shake.

I was very upset. And I did not know how to react after that. Then I kept telling myself, "Well, he is now haunted. So just keep calm. And I promised myself that there were two things that I would never do in front of him. I will never cry no matter what he would do or say, I will not cry. I just did not want him to see me vulnerable. And the other thing is that I did not want him to see me angry. I wanted to be in control and I wanted to be calm.

He pointed to the seat next to him and I sat down. I immediately started to attack. I asked, "I understand you have two children. When you came home from work and sat at the dinner table did you tell your children what kind of work you did? Or when you put them to bed did you tell them bedtime stories about the kind of work you did all day? He got really angry and said, "No, I did not tell bedtime stories to my children because I had an aunt who would tell me bedtime stories and after she told me her bedtime stories I used to have nightmares." And I calmly turned to him and said, "Well imagine what kind of nightmares your children would have had if you had told them about your work."

At this point he was very angry. But I did not want him to get up and walk out on me. So I immediately went back to my paper. I said, "Dr. Münch, I just came from Auschwitz," and showed him the paper. He recognized his signature. I wanted him to explain the paper and the experiments. He was really vague and didn't want to do that. When he kept saying, "This means nothing, nothing. She was fine," I asked him, "Well if she was fine why did she die?" He asked how long my sister stayed in Auschwitz and I answered six months. Then he said, "Well, that is the normal period. Do you understand? You were in Auschwitz as well. Well then, you should know." At that point, I knew that if he said one more word to me I was going to get his throat and choke this man. So I just got up and walked out of the room.

I did want him to show some remorse. I wanted him to say to me, "I am really sorry for your sister. I am sorry for what happened to your sister." I don't know if that would make me feel better. But maybe it would make me feel that he was a human. Maybe it was better that this was how he came across on the film. If he had shown some remorse people would have felt sorry for him in some way. I am now glad that he didn't show remorse. These people are robots. I don't know if I should feel sorry for them or whether I should be angry with them. It was probably one of the most difficult things I did for the film. I am very glad that I did it because it showed, after all those years, who this man really was. And it may be that he was a sample of who they all were. We have to show these people for who they were so that future generations realize that these people are dangerous.

The Rape of Nanking: Another Holocaust?

Are the crimes committed by these two doctors the same? Should we compare the Holocaust and the Japanese atrocities of which Dr. Münch and Dr. Yuasa respectively were a part? By comparing them, can we broaden our understanding of each crime and gain some insights that would better prepare us in our efforts to create a more humane world? Or do we even know the whole history of what the Imperial Japanese Army did in Asia during the 1930s and 1940s to make a meaningful comparison of it to the Nazi Holocaust? If not, why don't we know about it? Should we know about it? And how?

In the following pages, I will examine these questions within the context of events that followed the publication of *The Rape of Nanking: The Forgotten Holocaust of World War II*, (New York: Basic Books, 1997).

In this book, Chinese-American author Iris Chang depicted the barbaric acts of mass executions of soldiers and the slaughtering and raping of tens of thousands of civilians by the Japanese Imperial Army in the city of Nanking within a few weeks after its fall in December 1937. Presenting the death toll in the killing ranging from 260,000 (the estimation by the International Military Tribunal of the Far East) to well over 300,000, Chang wrote, "Indeed, even by the standards of history's most destructive war, the Rape of Nanking represents one of the worst instances of mass extermination."[2] She went on to say, "The Rape of Nanking should be remembered not only for the number of people slaughtered but for the cruel manner in which many met their deaths."[3] She then described many graphic examples of such cruelty. She also wrote about the second rape—Japan's alleged cover-up, denial and whitewashing of the history of the Nanking massacre. Chang concluded, "At a minimum, the Japanese government needs to issue an official apology to the victims, pay reparations to the people whose lives were destroyed in the rampage, and, most important, educate future generations of Japanese citizens about the true facts of the massacre."[4]

The book received overwhelmingly favorable reviews in the U.S. media. It was on the New York Times' best seller list for several months in early 1998. In addition to receiving extensive media coverage on her and her book, Chang traveled to more than sixty cities across the U.S. and Canada to talk about her book.

There were some critical responses to her equating Nanking with the Holocaust, however. Jacob Heilbrunn, associate editor of *The New Republic*, wrote in the *Wall Street Journal*, "Ms. Chang and her publisher refer to the massacre as a Holocaust. This is unfortunate since the massacre was not—for all its murderous horror—an attempt to wipe out the Chinese as a race."[5] To this, the editor of *The Rape of Nanking*, herself Jewish, responded, "The word 'holocaust,' an old word meaning 'firestorm,' does not require a sense of genocide . . . If those who have suffered grievously at the hands of others start bickering over whose suffering is entitled to be characterized by which words, justice will be ill-served."[6]

David Kennedy, a history professor at Stanford University, also wrote in *The Atlantic Monthly*, ". . . despite Chang's shocking description of the events in Nanjing, she gives the reader little reason to conclude that what happened there should be compared to the systematic killing of the Holocaust, an episode that was surely the loathsome spawn of Hitler's purposeful policy—not an incident of war or the mere excrescence of individual cruelty or the result of a poorly disciplined army run amok. The Holocaust entailed a methodical application of all the apparatus of the modern bureaucratic state and all the most advanced technologies of killing to the cold-blooded business of mass murder."[7]

When I interviewed Chang for the article I was preparing for a Japanese monthly magazine she responded to this criticism in the following way:

"When I was invited to speak at the United States Holocaust Memorial Museum, I was told that it drew the largest audience ever in the history of the museum. I spoke there twice, one for general audience and the second for scholarly audience. Not one person there, Jewish or non-Jewish, objected my usage of the word 'Holocaust.' The response was overwhelmingly positive in the question and answer session. In fact, one gentleman who worked at the Holocaust Museum said that he was very excited about what was happening in the Chinese community because what the Pacific Holocaust studies were at this point reminded him of what the Jewish Holocaust studies were at twenty or twenty-five years ago. He said that for a long time the Jewish Holocaust studies were not taken seriously and many of the survivors often refused to speak about it. Later, there was a big flowering of literature of the Holocaust. He predicted that there would be a similar kind of flowering of literature on the Sino-Japanese war."[8]

These responses by the editor of *The Rape of Nanking* and Chang herself might not be direct answers to the criticism on their equating the Japanese atrocities with the Nazi Holocaust. But their responses did suggest that they were more concerned about the accountability imposed on the perpetrator rather than about the uniqueness of the individual crimes. And their concern might be justified given the very hostile response *The Rape of Nanking* received in Japan.

Ever since the book became a best seller in the U.S., hardly a month went by without it being attacked by Japanese conservative and right wing monthly magazines.[9] Pointing out what they alleged to be "errors" in the book, including the number of victims killed and some of the picture captions, Japanese right wing writers declared that the book was an anti-Japan propaganda.[10] They also dismissed Chang's accusation of Japan of having tried to cover-up the massacre. As for an official apology and reparations, they insisted that Japan already had apologized and that the issue of reparations had been settled by the 1951 San Francisco Peace Treaty, the same stance the government of Japan maintained.

Publication of the Japanese edition of *The Rape of Nanking* was canceled due to the publisher's concern over these issues. While the publisher believed that "Chang's indictment of Japan's wartime atrocities and the country's postwar attempts to cover up and distort history will help raise public awareness of the incident and of how Japan's behavior is perceived abroad,"[11] they feared that any error in the book would be used by the various right wing groups in their attempt to deny the massacre itself. Chang maintained, ". . . virtually none of these errors had anything to do with the historical description of the Nanking massacre itself."[12]

The usage of the word "Holocaust" also became ammunition for the Japanese right wing writers in their attacks on *The Rape of Nanking*. They welcomed every opportunity to introduce the critical views on this issue expressed by Americans. Heilbrunn's criticism was wildly reported in Japan by these groups.[13] Those who were eager to introduce Heilbrunn's point—Nanking massacre was not a holocaust—were the very people who insisted that the Nanking massacre never happened or who tried to play down the massacre as a small incident. The Japanese translation of Professor Kennedy's article also appeared in a monthly magazine that had by then become the regular forum for those who attacked *The Rape of Nanking*.[14] Incidentally, the publisher of this magazine had been strongly protested by the international Jewish community a few years earlier for its publication of an article entitled, "The Greatest Taboo of Postwar History: There Were No Nazi Gas Chambers."[15] One historian who maintained that victims of the Nanking massacre were somewhere from 40,000 to 60,000 wrote, "When 'holocaust' is coupled with 'rape,' neither Americans nor Japanese of any sensitivity can help lapsing into silence. Skillfully using this psychology, Chang has built up a strong anti-Japanese presentation and turned her book into a long-running bestseller."[16] There was even a suspicion expressed by one Japanese writer that Chang's equating the Nanking massacre with the Holocaust was her scheme to mobilize Jewish groups into the united front against Japan.[17]

It was unfortunate that the appropriateness of comparing the Holocaust with the Japanese atrocities was not debated in Japan with the intellectual honesty and sensitivity that such a discussion deserved. Moreover, those Japanese who insisted that the Holocaust and the Nanking massacre should not be compared were not particularly interested in disclosing historical facts about other crimes committed by the Japanese Imperial Army. While severely denouncing Chang's equating Nanking with the Holocaust, they were mostly silent on other Nazi-like crimes such as those of Unit 731 or "Three-all" policy ("Loot all, kill all, burn all") in Northern China. This was in spite of the fact that Chang herself wrote, "The Rape of Nanking was only one incident in a long saga of Japanese barbarism during nine years of war"[18] As much as the Holocaust encompassed the atrocities committed by Nazi Germany between 1933 to 1945, the appropriate comparison, if it should be made, would be with all the Japanese atrocities against civilians in Asian countries during the 1930s and 1940s.

Taking this Japanese situation into consideration, the response by Chang and her editor to the criticism for their using the word "Holocaust"—emphasizing more on accountability imposed on the perpetrator—might be on target. Her reference to the enthusiastic response she received at the Holocaust Memorial

Museum in Washington, DC. during my interview was also a clear message to the Japanese right wings—Those people for whom this issue mattered most did not object to my usage of the word "Holocaust."

Do We Know the Whole History of Japanese Atrocities?

Iris Chang recalls that she could not find a single book on the Nanking massacre in the local public library when she was in grade school. It took her own book to introduce a wider audience in the English speaking world to the subject of the Japanese atrocities during World War II. Indeed, while there have been thousands of books written on the Holocaust,[19] until recently there were very few books on the Japanese atrocities written in English including those that were translated from Japanese. There are several reasons that could explain this huge gap between the amount of works done on these two equally atrocious histories. The most obvious one is the availability of relevant information. Unlike in Germany, some crucial documents are still not available in Japan today for those who try to write about its wartime history. First of all, Japan had a couple of weeks after its formal surrender to destroy wartime documents before the U.S. troops arrived. Secondly, the occupation of Japan by the Allied Powers, which was practically the U.S. occupation, was an indirect one with the Japanese bureaucracy carrying out General MacArthur's policy. Japan could somehow find the way to deal with the occupation authorities regarding handing over whatever wartime documents were still intact, something Germany could not do. By the time the occupation ended, Japan was firmly incorporated into the Western camp in the Cold War and the history of Japanese atrocities slipped away from people's consciousness.[20] For many years since then, the former victims of Japan were not in a position to call the world's attention to their sufferings. As far as the history of Japanese atrocities was concerned, there was no similar phenomenon as the blossoming of the Holocaust literature in the West.

Another reason why there are very few books on the Japanese atrocities, particularly those that are translated from Japanese, may be the way these types of books are written in Japan. With the end of the Cold War and the death of the Showa emperor, some Japanese historians and journalists started to write impressive books on Japan's wartime atrocities. Today, at any large bookstore in Japan, one can find scores of titles dealing with this subject. Yet, many of these books give an impression that they were written with a clear mission of refuting the nationalistic interpretation presented by conservative and right wing scholars. Although based on meticulous researches, writing only for a small audience could be one of the reasons that not many of their works are translated into English. Yuki Tanaka, one of the very few Japanese historians who has his work *Hidden Horrors: Japanese War Crimes in World War II* (Boulder, CO: Westview Press, 1996) published in English wrote, "Critical Japanese historians have effectively demolished the self-serving analysis of the nationalists, but the effect of their critiques has been limited by an inability to analyze effectively both specific and universal elements. Caught up in a polar opposition with the conservatives, they have tended to focus exclusively on the unique and timeless features of Japanese aggression and inhumanity."[21]

Focusing on only what took place under the Japanese Imperial Army also kept Japanese scholars from probing deeper into the more fundamental and universal issue of "why it happened?" or "how could it happen?" Professor Kennedy wrote, "She (Chang) offers little that is comparable to the carefully nuanced analysis of the motives behind Nazi brutality that one finds in works like Christopher Browning's *Ordinary Men* (1992) and Omer Bartov's *The Eastern Front, 1941–1945* (1985) . . . "[22] It was ironic then that those Japanese who were so eager to use his article to attack *The Rape of Nanking* were often the same people who dismissed the confessions of repentant veterans, saying that these veterans had been brainwashed in Communist China and that their confession could not be trusted. Today, while hundreds of thousands of copies of the books written by the Japanese right wing writers are being sold, the group of repentant veterans, of which Dr. Yuasa is a member, is struggling to sell just a few thousand copies of their seasonal journal carrying their personal testimonies. In addition, these veterans, most of whom are now in their 80s and late 70s, grew up in a culture that never encouraged them to express their feelings. To go beyond confessing the crimes they committed and to plead to young listeners not to repeat the same mistakes again is not easy for them. It took me three meetings and hours of listening to have Dr. Yuasa finally express his feeling upon receiving the letter from the victim's mother.

So it was not only Chang's book that did not fully explore the human personality of those who committed atrocities. Until the publication of *Senso To Zaiseki* (*War and Responsibility*) (Tokyo: Iwanami Shoten, 1998) written by psychiatrist Masaaki Noda, there had been very few books in Japan that dealt with the psychology of war criminals. In this book, Dr. Noda interviewed several repentant veterans of the Japanese Imperial Army. While acknowledging their courageous efforts in publicly expressing their remorse, he still found that even these veterans had not had their humanity completely destroyed by their guilt. To prevent similar atrocities from ever happening again, Dr. Noda believes that each individual, when put into the role of a perpetrator, must have deep enough compassion so that he/she would face the prospect of being completely destroyed by the sadness of hurting others. The subtitle of his book is, "*To Regain the Capacity to Feel the Sadness*." Dr. Noda concluded that the Japanese people could start that process by trying to know honestly what their peers or their parents did during the war.[23]

Efforts to Know the History

Iris Chang refused to have her "errors" in *The Rape of Nanking* corrected in its Japanese edition. The request for such corrections by the publisher, whose past publications included the Japanese edition of Raul Hilberg's *The Destruction of the European Jews*, was based on their sincere desire to publish a book that would withstand the criticism from the right wing groups. But Chang's suspicion that the publisher was under the pressure from the same groups was understandable given the relentless attacks on her book from them. But during my interview, she did say:

If the Japanese Foreign Ministry and the rest of the Japanese government truly care about historical truth, then they should open up all their wartime archives to the rest of the world. . . They shouldn't mind inviting an international task force of historians—historians from the US, China, Japan, Korea and other countries—to review all the high-level Japanese records from that era and publish them for general and scholarly consumption. Trust me, if the newly released archival records disprove any of the facts in my book, I would be the first person to acknowledge this in the next edition of *The Rape of Nanking*. Moreover, I would help the Japanese government publicize the new facts to the world media and find prestigious publishers in the US to translate the documents into English.[24]

Setting up of such an international commission by the Japanese government was indeed proposed by Rabbi Abraham Cooper, the associate dean of the Simon Wiesenthal Center, a Los Angeles based international human rights organization. Rabbi Cooper was with me when I first met Dr. Yuasa and other repentant veterans in Tokyo in 1997. But it was his meeting with another veteran of the Japanese Imperial Army, a former member of Unit 731 that convinced him that the world must know about the horrific crimes his unit had committed. This unrepentant veteran told Rabbi Cooper that he would do it again under the same circumstances. "An international historic commission convened by Tokyo," Rabbi Cooper wrote in an op-ed piece published in *Los Angeles Times*, "would replace revisionism and propaganda with an honest quest for history. It would also go a long way toward reassuring Japan's Asian neighbors that it has learned the lessons of the past and deserves their trust."[25]

Rabbi Cooper also learned that the U.S. Department of Justice's Office of Special Investigations could not obtain the cooperation of the government of Japan in identifying a list of Japanese war criminals, including those implicated in Unit 731, so that they could be barred from entering the U.S. He sent a letter to Foreign Minister Masahiko Komura urging him to take quick action to assist the United States in this matter.[26]

A similar letter was also sent by California Congressman Tom Lantos, the only survivor of the Holocaust ever elected to the U.S. Congress, to the Japanese Prime Minister Keizo Obuchi. In his Oct. 27, 1999, letter, Congressman Lantos warned, "The failure of the government of Japan to cooperate with the Department of Justice as well as its refusal to open the World War II archives to the public will prove an ongoing irritant to U.S.-Japan relations."[27] At the time when this essay was written, neither Rabbi Cooper nor Congressman Lantos has received a satisfactory response from the Japanese government.

While the government of Japan remained unresponsive, activist groups in the U.S. took the issue to the U.S. Senate. In November of 1999, California Senator Dianne Feinstein introduced a bill called "Japanese Imperial Army Disclosure Act" that would, like the "Nazi War Crimes Disclosure Act" passed in the previous year, require the disclosure under the Freedom of Information Act classified records and documents in the possession of the U.S. Government regarding chemical and biological experiments carried out by Japan during the course of the Second World War.[28] This bill has a significant meaning because of the situation under which these documents were handed over to the U.S. occupation. Senator Feinstein asked to be printed in *Congressional Record*, "Japan's Biological Weapons: 1930–1945—A Hidden Chapter in History" written by Robert Gomer, John Powell, and Burt Roling (*The Bulletin of The Atomic Scientists*, October 1981) which revealed how the U.S. occupation had obtained these records and documents. The article quoted a confidential memo sent from two occupation officials in Tokyo to the State Department saying that "the value to U.S. of Japanese BW data is of such importance to national security as to far outweigh the value accruing from war crimes prosecution."[29] The U.S. government granted blanket immunity to those who engaged in these horrific crimes in exchange for data on their experiments on human beings.

Senator Feinstein also asked that the letter she had received from Professor Sheldon Harris, the author of *Factories of Death: Japanese Biological Warfare, 1932–45, And the American Cover-Up* (New York: Routledge, 1994), be printed in *Congressional Record*. The letter reads in part:

> I discovered in the course of my research for this book, and scholarly articles that I published on the subject of Japanese biological and chemical warfare preparations, that members of the Japanese Imperial Army Medical Corps committed heinous war crimes. These included involuntary laboratory tests of various pathogens on humans—Chinese, Korean, other Asian nationalities, and Allied prisoners of war, including Americans. Barbarous acts encompassed live vivisections, amputations of body parts (frequently without the use of anesthesia), frost bite exposure to temperatures of 40–50 degrees Fahrenheit below zero, injection of horseblood and other animal blood into humans, as well as other horrific experiments. When a test was completed, the human experimented was 'sacrificed,' the euphemism used by Japanese scientists as a substitute term for 'killed.'

In my capacity as an academic Historian, I can testify to the difficulty researchers have in unearthing documents and personal testimony concerning these war crimes. I, and other researchers, have been denied access to military archives in Japan. These archives cover activities by the Imperial Japanese Army that occurred more than 50 years ago. The documents in question cannot conceivably contain information that would be considered of importance to 'National Security' today. The various governments in Japan for the past half century have kept these archives firmly closed. The fear is that the information contained in the archives will embarrass previous governments.

Here in the United States, despite the Freedom of Information Act, some archives remain closed to investigators. At best, the archivists in charge, or the Freedom of Information Officer at the archive in question, select what documents they will allow to become public. This is an unconscionable act of arrogance and a betrayal of the trust they have been given by the Congress and the President of the United States. Moreover, 'sensitive' documents—as defined by archivists and FOIA officers—are at the moment being destroyed. Thus, historians and concerned citizens are being denied factual evidence that can shed some light on the terrible atrocities committed by Japanese militarists in the past.[30]

Senator Feinstein went on to say that Professor Harris's letter had cited three examples of the destruction of documents relating to chemical and biological warfare experiments that he was aware of: At Dugway Proving Grounds in Utah, at Fort Detrick in Maryland, and at the Pentagon.

Efforts to investigate the history of Japan's war crimes have also been made in the Japanese Diet. A bill to create a bureau within the Library of Diet to investigate the extent of the damage caused by the Japanese military was introduced in August of 1999. The bill specifically mentioned the chemical and biological warfare experiments by the Japanese Army.[31] One hundred and eighteen Diet members, mostly from opposition parties, supported the bill that needs 256 votes to pass. With only a few members of the Liberal Democratic Party, Japan's conservative ruling party, supporting the bill, it is still pending in the Lower House of the Japanese Diet.[32]

In addition, several lawsuits seeking an apology and compensation from the Japanese government have been filed in Tokyo by a group of Japanese lawyers on behalf of Chinese victims of Japan's biological warfare program.[33]

Should We Compare the Japanese Atrocities with the Holocaust?

We hear that the Holocaust was unique because of the scale of the killings, the technology that was used for the killings, the bureaucracy that was involved, and the intent to annihilate every member of the Jewish people. We will never know how many millions of innocent people in Asia were killed by the Japanese forces during the period of its colonial rule and aggression in the 1930s and 1940s. We do know, however, that the number of victims of the Japanese human experiments were twelve times as many as those who were killed by the Nazi doctors in a similar way.[34] We do know that the best and the brightest of the Japanese medical profession were recruited and engaged in the crimes that could be only possible under the most elaborate bureaucratic structure. Not a single person was prosecuted for having participated in this crime against humanity because of the blanket immunity the U.S. government gave. Many of these doctors came to occupy prominent positions in the medical field in postwar Japan. There might have been no express purpose to annihilate all the Chinese people in Japan's policy to create a Greater East Asia Co-Prosperity Sphere, but we do know that many documents are still not available for historians to determine the true extent to which the highest authority, including the Showa emperor, was involved in these crimes.

At a personal level, it is almost impossible for me not to compare these atrocities. I knew Dr. Yuasa was comparing himself to Dr. Münch when he said, "If I were him, I would just beg her apology for killing her sister. That's the only thing I could do even if she would never forgive me." When Rabbi Cooper and I met the group of repentant veterans in Tokyo, the first thing that hit me was the realization that any one of them could have been my father. They are my fathers in the sense that they were the ones who worked hard to rebuild Japan so that our generation could grow up in prosperity and enjoy everything that they could not enjoy. And now these elderly men were confessing with tears in their eyes. It was not easy for me to see my father's generation in that situation. But listening to their confessions with someone whose people experienced unspeakable sufferings gave me a proper perspective—we all bear the responsibility for our efforts to know what happened and have a true compassion toward the sufferings of our fellow human beings. It was my profound experience of learning about the Holocaust and the devotions of those who tried to learn from this enormous tragedy, that awoke me to the realization of my own country's dark history. If more Japanese people can share an experience similar to mine by learning about the Holocaust, then I believe that we should be allowed to compare these two histories.

NOTES

1. See Haruko Taya Cook and Theodore F. Cook, *Japan at War: An Oral History* (New York: The New Press, 1992), p. 145 for more information about those Japanese veterans who were detained in the Chinese reeducation prison after the war.

2. Iris Chang, *The Rape of Nanking: The Forgotten Holocaust of World War II* (New York: Basic Books, 1997), p. 5.

3. Ibid., p. 6.

4. Ibid., p. 225.

5. Jacob Heilbrunn, "Savagery in the East," *The Wall Street Journal*, December 29, 1997.

6. Susan Rabiner, "Rape of Nanking Was a Holocaust," *The Wall Street Journal*, January 13, 1998.

7. David M. Kennedy, "The Horror," *The Atlantic Monthly*, April, 1998.

8. Kinue Tokudome, "Why I Wrote '*The Rape of Nanking*': Interview with Iris Chang," *Ronza*, October, 1998.

9. See "The Nanking Massacre in Print: A Recent Bibliography," *Japan Echo*, August, 1998, p. 58 for a list of related articles appeared in Japan.

10. See, for example, Kazuyuki Hamada, "'*The Rape of Nanking*' Chugoku no Inbo o Mita" (In "*The Rape of Nanking*" I see a Chinese Conspiracy), *Bungei shunju*, September, 1998, pp. 180–89.

11. "War Again Is Raging Over Japan's Role in 'Nanking'," *Los Angeles Times*, June 6, 1999.

12. Ibid.,

13. See, for example, "The Impact of '*The Rape of Nanking*'," *Sankei Shimbun*, December 11, 1999. This conservative newspaper also wrote when the publication of the Japanese edition of *The Rape of Nanking* was cancelled, "It is fortunate that many Japanese will not be misled by its erroneous historical description."

14. David M. Kennedy, "Nanking massacre was not a Holocaust," *Shokun!*, August, 1998, pp. 170–77.

15. "Tokyo Publisher Regrets 'pain' to Jews," *Los Angeles Times*, February 3, 1995.

16. Ikuhiko Hata, "The Nanking Atrocities: Fact and Fable," *Japan Echo*, August, 1998, p.55.

17. "Nanking Is Not A Holocaust," *Sankei Shimbun*, December 13, 1999.

18. Chang (1997), p. 215.

19. Michael R. Marrus, *The Holocaust in History* (New York: Meridian Book, 1987), p. 6.

20. See John W. Dower, *Embracing Defeat: Japan in the Wake of World War II* (New York: W.W. Norton & Company, 1999) chapter 15 for the prosecution of Japanese war criminals by the Occupation.

21. Yuki Tanaka, *Hidden Horrors: Japanese War Crimes in World War II* (Boulder, CO: Westview Press, 1996), p. 6.

22. Kennedy, *The Atlantic Monthly*.

23. Masaaki Noda, *Senso to Zaiseki* (Tokyo: Iwanami-shoten, 1998), p. 356.

24. Tokudome, *Ronza*, p. 86.

25. Abraham Cooper, "Tokyo Must Address the Actions of Its Wartime Killing Machine," *Los Angeles Times*, April 26, 1999.

26. November 17, 1998 letter to the Japanese Foreign Minister Masahiko Komura sent from Rabbi Abraham Cooper.

27. October 27, 1999 letter to the Japanese Prime Minister Keizo Obuchi sent from Congressman Tom Lantos.

28. *Congressional Record*, November 10, 1999, p. 14542.

29. Gomer, Powell and Roling, "Japan's Biological Weapons: 1930–1945—A Hidden Chapter in History," *The Bulletin of the Atomic Scientists*, October, 1981, pp. 47–48.

30. *Congressional Record*, November 10, 1999, p. 14542.

31. "Senso Higai Chousakai Ho o Kangaeru," Senso Higai Chousakai Ho o Jitsugen Suru Shiminkaigi, September, 1999, p. 52.

32. On February 17, 2000, the bi-partisan group of Japanese Diet members who supported this bill invited Rabbi Abraham Cooper to address them and other Diet members on the importance of facing one's own history honestly.

33. List of war-related lawsuits prepared for *International Citizen's Forum on War Crimes ands Redress* held in Tokyo, December 10–12, 1999.

34. Sheldon H. Harris, "Japanese Biological Warfare," a paper presented at *International Citizen's Forum on War Crimes and Redress*, December 11, 1999.

❀ 11 ❀

Applying the Lessons of the Holocaust

DR. SHIMON SAMUELS

*T*he 1996 edition of *Is the Holocaust Unique?* set the lines for an acrimonious debate between specifists and universalists. The former fear debasement of the Holocaust by invidious comparison.[1] The latter place the Holocaust alongside non-Jewish experiences of mass extermination as part and parcel of the global context of genocide.

This writer views that debate, ipso facto, as dishonoring the memory of the respective victims of each genocide. Each case is specific as a threshold phenomenon, while each also adds its unique memory as signposts along an incremental continuum of horror.

We focus here on the *relevance* of the Holocaust as a preventive instrument against its recurrence, that is, a benchmark for minorities, a yardstick for contemporary atrocity, and an early-warning system for mass murder.

The Holocaust's uniqueness within Jewish history is only a question of degree. Two thousand years of antisemitism—successively political, theological, and racial—climaxed in the Final Solution. The durability, persistence, and pervasiveness in time and space of ever-mutating Jew-hatred have made the Holocaust a unique baseline among genocides. Nevertheless, the steps to the Final Solution provide a paradigm. Its stations proceed from incitement to an ideology of hate, its dissemination from a political power base, its inculcation bound together with paramilitary training, the delegitimization of targeted enemies, legislation to validate their social exclusion and incarceration, their deportation and eventual extermination.

For two millennia of exile, Jewish history was characterized by constant precariousness. The decade 1938–1948 represented the extremes of nadir to apogee along the Jewish timeline—from utter powerlessness and almost extinction to a return to sovereignty and history.

A lachrymose interpretation of these 2000 years may be a prescription for para-noia. Yet, whether acknowledged or not by the Diaspora, the Jewish State is a psy-cho-political shattering of the image of marginalization in the communities of exile. For the first time since the Second Temple, "Let My People Go" is a reality, from the Soviet Gulag to the Rivers of Babylon. To be a Jewish victim of oppres-sion today is an act of choice.

The battle for Jewish survival is a function of power politics. The fiddler may still be astride the roof, but, rather than pathos and precariousness, he now sym-bolizes the next round—the battle for Jewish identity.

Our sages have long debated two distinct modes for interaction with the world:

- "Am Levadad Yishkon"—a people that dwells alone, i.e., ostracized, mar-ginalized, ghettoized, victimized, introverted, etc.
- "Or Lagoyim"—a light unto the nations, i.e., a barometer, an alarm bell, a participant and even a role model.

At the 1938 Evian conference on refugees, the world was not silent. Each na-tion's representative explained why Jewish fugitives from Nazism were unwel-come. Only the Ambassador of the Dominican Republic offered places for Jewish agriculturists.

In 1971, I drove the 150 miles across this Caribbean island from the farm co-operative established by Jewish refugees of the Holocaust at Sosua[2] in the North, to an Israeli rural training project at Azua in the South. To have joined with the Israeli technical assistance team in building the village church for Dominican "campesinos" was, for me, a dramatic and personal act of transition between the modes from object to subject, from voyeur to actor.

Pastor Martin Niemöller confessed a betrayal of personal responsibility: *When they came for the Jews, I was not a Jew, so I did not protest. When they came for the Communists, neither was I a Communist. When they came for the Trade Unionists, nor was I a Trade Unionist. When they came for me, there was no one left to protest...* He might have said, "What starts with the Jews does not end with the Jews, for hatred is indivisible." So too with the Holocaust.

For the last twenty years, curricula development and research into the Holocaust have been accepted into mainstream academic programs in North America and Western Europe. Should we not now move the emphasis to defin-ing, drawing and applying its lessons to a practical global agenda focussed upon, inter alia, language, memory, jurisprudence, restitution, and technology?

Language

In the immediate postwar, the images of the Holocaust acted as protective "teflon" against blatant expressions of antisemitism in the West. Indeed, open identification with such positions became distasteful and even legally actionable. For the past twenty years, this "teflon" has been eroding.

- Remaining pangs of conscience for active or passive collaboration in countries occupied by the Nazis have been assuaged by a projection of guilt mechanism, i.e., the use of Holocaust language by European media to describe Israel during the 1982 Lebanon war. West Beirut became the "Warsaw Ghetto," South Lebanon "the Sudetenland," talk of "the Israeli Luftwaffe," "a Palestinian Holocaust," "pogroms" by Jews. A Portuguese caricaturist reversed roles, by portraying Stars of David on the Nazi helmets and a Arab "Kefiyya" headdress on the child whose arms are raised, in the unforgettable photo of the Warsaw Ghetto's fall. A German Green Party calendar of 1983 called for a boycott of Jaffa oranges (redolent of "Kaufen Nicht bei Juden" as "Germans now pass on the burden of their history to the new Jewish Nazis of Israel").[3]
- Rabbi Abraham Joshua Heschel has said that "Auschwitz was built not with stones, but words." The torrent of Holocaust language, now turned against Jews, could be directly correlated with a dramatic growth in antisemitic incidents and especially terrorist acts against Jewish institutions.[4] The victims were often portrayed by government officials as Middle East imports (e.g., French Minister Raymond Barre's description of the casualties of the Copernic synagogue bombing as including foreigners and "innocent French citizens"). This extraterritorialization of the Jewish victims was a precursor for Moslem nationals who fell in later inter-necine Arab terrorist attacks across Europe.

The Israeli operation in Lebanon had an unintended by-product: the flight and repatriation of European terrorists from their Palestinian training camps in the Bequ'a Valley. Terrorism thus became a general scourge, no longer focussing only Jewish targets and, consequently, a central issue for intergovernmental counteraction. "What started with the Jews. . . "

- The 1989 fall of the Berlin wall and the end of the Soviet empire released the pent-up ghosts of classical antisemitism in countries where the Holocaust has succeeded, i.e., "an antisemitism without Jews" or "a phantom pain syndrome" (the limb has been amputated but the body still seeks to scratch it). The last vestiges of the ravaged communities of Eastern Europe are often the scapegoats for the pain of withdrawal from the central economy and the transition to market capitalism.
- Yet East European antisemitism has less to do with "real Jews" than with the abstract image of "the Jews"—an euphemism or code-word for "imported," "foreign," "Western," etc. For instance, the International Monetary Fund, the scapegoat for unemployment and inflation, is portrayed by

ultra-nationalists as the tool of a Jewish plot manipulated by both Washington, D.C. and Tel Aviv. *The Protocols of Zion* have resurfaced in every post-Communist country, feeding a persistent disposition to hate that which is most feared—the unknown! To make sense of it, a conspiracy theory of invisible enemies of the nation is the line of least resistance. Antisemitism in almost "Judenrein" post-Holocaust Eastern Europe is a diagnostic code to undemocratic conditions and behavior and a threat for all minorities.

A Solidarnosc leader interpreted to me Polish Primate Cardinal Glemp's 1989 Auschwitz monastery speech, claiming it was "not a Jewish issue."[5] Indeed, he insisted, "Glemp's talk of Jewish control of the world's media does not target the remaining 4,500 elderly Jews of Warsaw and Crakow, nor was he objecting to renewed relations with Israel, nor Western Jewish tourism to Holocaust sites. . . He was simply indirectly attacking Solidarnosc and signaling that he, not the Pope, was the head of the Polish Church"! In other words, in the absence of real Jews, antisemitic prejudice still persists as a vital element of political discourse.

The 1990 newly reconstituted Slovak Hlinka Guard was, in equal measure, anti-Jewish, anti-Czech, anti-Hungarian, anti-Russian, and anti-Roma. Despite only 1,000 Jews remaining in Slovakia, Hlinka's nationalist graffiti were expressed in the language of antisemitism. Ironically, it was the self-styled Mischlinge[6] Sports Club of Bratislava that took responsibility for cleaning up the graffiti.

The word "Jew" represented anything alien to the "Volk," from Western media to pop music, human rights to technology. Ignorance, frustration, envy, rancor, fear of the new and the different are the bases for the conspiracy theories that are the building blocks of xenophobia. Post-Kosovo Serbs explain their situation as the result of American/NATO interventionism, German revanchism, Islamic fundamentalism, the Vatican and even Zionism. Remove German revanchism and the Vatican for the Croat. The litany has its variants throughout East-Central Europe. There may be no Jewish presence, but the default page for each conspiracy is still *The Protocols of the Elders of Zion* in every vernacular.

Memory

"Zachor"—Thou shalt remember!—is Judaism's categorical imperative. Instrumental memory draws lessons for survival. "Memoricide" is an abomination. Holocaust denial or so-called "revisionism" is genocide compounded by memoricide. A political tranvestitism has focused extremist agendas on the Holocaust, e.g., the French denier Robert Faurisson, though identified with the extreme right, published his denials of the gas chambers in Trotskyite publications:

- The far right aimed to absolve Germany: "if the Holocaust was a Jewish lie, then Germany was its first victim."

- The far left argued that "if the Holocaust was a lie, but due to conscience the world gave the Jews a state, then its first victim was the Palestinians."

Holocaust denial is increasingly strident in the new media, as an obscene challenge to the debate on freedom of expression. It pales, however, when compared to State "de-Judaization" of the Holocaust in the Soviet official version or in the post-Soviet revisionist rehabilitation of anti-Bolshevik Nazi collaborators in East-Central Europe. Memorials to these nationalist heroes and the rehabilitation of war criminals expose the fragility of these post-Communist societies.

Even in France, it took the personal campaign of New Jersey lawyer, Stephen Draisin,[7] together with the Simon Wiesenthal Centre, to obtain a plaque in memory of the 87 Jews brought west from Auschwitz to Struthof-Natzweiler. There, they were gassed to supply skeletons at the request of the Anatomy Department of nearby Strasbourg University. The campaign for integrity to history will not be over until plaques are erected at Struthof for all its other victims: Algerian Moslems, Soviets, Spanish Republicans, Roma, and homosexuals.

Memory is to be applied:

At the inauguration of the Lyons Museum of Resistance and Deportation, Suzanne Lagrange, recounting her deportation to Auschwitz and the murder of her father before her eyes on arrival, was interrupted by a young German in the audience who wished to apologize for Nazi Germany. "Sit down, we do not believe in trans-generational guilt," she said. He took his seat, whereupon Mme Lagrange turned on him. "Now apologize," she rebuked him. "I don't understand. You said. . . ," protested the young German. "I said you bear no responsibility for the crimes of Nazi Germany, but you share responsibility for the neo-Nazi crimes of young Germans today! Germany is not the bearer of collective guilt. But it must acknowledge its collective shame, thus endowing it with a special sensitivity."

The opening of both World War Two and Communist-period archives are, for a new generation of political leadership and opinion molders, a painful crisis of memory with perceptual withdrawal symptoms (what is termed in psychology "cognitive dissonance"). Absorption of new and contradictory information, resulting in the deconstruction of anchored myths, predispositions and prejudices, require the reformulation or reinterpretation of collective memory, i.e., "cognitive dissonance."

This can take two forms:

- Negative: neurotic grappling to unreality, a search for scapegoats, further denials and an entrenchment of extreme positions;
- Positive: exposure of truths to lance a long-festering boil, thus allowing the pus to drain. The cleansing of the wounds is an act of catharsis and a rejection of revisionist escape-routes, which were constructed to assuage conscious or unconscious scars of guilt.

Such transparent fine-tuning of the psychological underpinnings of national collective memory may be excuses for conflict resolution based directly upon the lessons of Holocaust denial.

At the 1994 Buenos Aires inauguration of the Wiesenthal Center's Holocaust exhibit, **The Courage to Remember,** journalists asked its relevance to Argentina's recent "dirty war" and its "disappeared" victims. I spoke of the same exhibit's successful tour of China, where visitors, who knew nothing of Jews or Nazis, viewed it through the prism of their own experience: the Tanaka Plan, the Nanking massacre, Japanese war crime medical experiments, etc. **The Courage to Remember** acts as a memory trigger to whomever peers into its mirror. The same applied to the Argentine visitor.

Jurisprudence

We are witnessing an evolving jurisprudence on genocide, war crimes, crimes against humanity, and human rights. Real-time media reporting, shrinking world village market interdependence and the ineluctable imperative towards transparency are telescoping time and space. Scenes of families forcibly on the move, snaking lines of lame and elderly, homes burning, refugee camps are all too familiar. These may not be genocides, but each is a posthumous failure in drawing the lessons of World War Two and the reference points of the Nuremberg Trials.

Despite the political obstacles along the path to the International Criminal Court, there is growing international understanding that conflict resolution requires psychological closure which, in turn, is conditioned upon collective satisfaction that justice is seen to be done. Sleeping dogs must not be left to lie, for sleeping dogs are not dead dogs. The conviction in Britain of Nazi collaborator, Sawoniuk, for his crimes in Belarus, was simultaneous to the detention of Chilean General Pinochet. Britain took two steps against collective oblivion, signaling that, for the greatest of human crimes, there could be neither immunity nor statute of limitations.

A newly established British NGO, *Justice Action,* has defined its objectives as filling the judicial gaps in international mechanisms for war criminal prosecutions by:

- Identifying significant cases and investigating their crimes
- Tracking and inhibiting their movements
- Assisting their delivery to a court or tribunal
- Increasing public awareness of their actions
- Shaming those who offer safe haven to suspects
- Locating their assets and seeking to seize and advertise them
- Devising a strategy for prosecution and passing on evidence to prosecutorial authorities

- Matching individual suspects to individual prosecutors in favorable jurisdictions
- Pressuring governments to live up to their commitments
- Shaming them when they do not.

They promise to make the world a small and unpleasant place for those who commit war crimes, and to send a powerful signal to future perpetrators that they will be pursued and held to account.

Justice Action's founder, Tim Sebastian, explained his initiative as "based upon the lessons of Holocaust perpetrator trials and the model of Simon Wiesenthal's work."[8]

In the same spirit, the Wiesenthal Center was invited to join the Helsinki International Federation on Human Rights as a consultant on the documentation of war crimes in the ex-Yugoslavia. The Holocaust, as the most documented of genocides, provides examples to the perils and pitfalls in constituting and analyzing archives and determining rights to access them. In the former Yugoslavia, the murder of witnesses has acted as a deterrent to testimony. The very existence of a war-crime document can endanger its owner or researcher and target an archive for arson or terrorism.[9]

Restitution

Organizing a 1996 conference in Geneva on "Loot and Restitution—The Moral Responsibility to History," I could not imagine the volume over the next four years of World War Two assets restitution enquiries, claims, and negotiation. Media and judicial pressure demanded transparency, and most combatant and neutral nations successively established national archival research commissions to investigate banks, insurance companies, museums and private industry.

The Washington, DC, conference on Holocaust Assets in December 1998 defined the array of problems and set the scene for the final phase—that of enforcing settlement, the close of commitments, the fulfillment of promises. In the spirit of the Biblical injunction of Leviticus, Chapter 25, verse 10: "In the fiftieth year . . . thou shalt restitute to each . . . his property. . . "

Why over fifty years till Pandora's emergence? Most Holocaust survivors, for self-rehabilitation, had closed a curtain. Those returnees who submitted claims were met, at worst, with Kielce-style violence, or, at a poor best, with Swiss banker obscurantism. The prevailing exigencies of resettlement in lands of freedom, the establishment and support of a Jewish state and, for those who stayed behind, the new challenges of survival under Communism, vitiated immediate postwar indemnification demands.

The weakness of the Jewish lobby, and its ideological divisions over reparations from the new Germany, was to limit strategic approaches to the issue. With the onset of the Cold War, Jewish material claims from the West were frozen as energy was devoted to the needs of their brethren under Communism and in other lands of oppression. The fall of the Berlin Wall and the consequent rollback of the Soviet Empire led to the opening of archives, first throughout Eastern Europe, with an imperative to transparency which moved ever westwards.

From 1989 to 1995, the focus of fiftieth anniversaries drew, from the mouths of survivors, belated testimonies for the grandchild generation. Holocaust museums, *Schindler's List*, global village communications technology, real-time genocidal reporting and a fascination with the accoutrements of the 1930s set the scene and the tone. The catalyst was the political and juridical clout of the U.S. Congress and Federal class action suits against American affiliates of European holders of looted assets.

Were this to have remained a uniquely Jewish issue, the price might have invalidated its purpose by leading to a fomenting and intensification of structurally dormant antisemitism. The restitution campaign had not only its own intrinsic justice, but served as the springboard for a moral pedagogy, including the caveat that the targets of research, World War Two neutrals and combatants, are not the bearers of collective intergenerational guilt. Indeed, the enquiry process requires the co-optation of all elements in societies eager for the truth.

The restitution issue is not exclusive to Jewish claimants, but of concern to a community of World War Two victims, now evident in Slavic forced/slave labor and Sinti and Roma claims processes. Indeed, in 1995, I conducted research on the Tripartite Gold Commission in the French Finance Ministry archives. This revealed Nazi "mix and melt" of "monetary gold" (looted from occupied Central Banks) and "non-monetary gold" (stolen from Holocaust victims and mainly comprising "tooth gold"). Following the release of those findings, I was asked for information on lost gold by officials from Hungary, Italy, Spain and Turkey. Such claims are also a contribution to an evolving jurisprudence in the war crime of looting. A CNN financial analyst emphasized this during Kabila's march on Kinshasa. "It took a Holocaust bank scandal to open Mobutu's accounts . . . "

Based on this precedent, a study of Swiss and German bank support for the apartheid regime in South Africa is leading to demands for compensation and reconsideration of that country's current debt. The British Society of Black Lawyers is campaigning for both a high school curriculum on the history of colonialism and compensation for slavery by forgiving African debt. Similarly, Ethiopian refugees have approached New York Holocaust Class Action lawyers to consider restitution action for their lost assets. The restitution campaign has shaken to the core national myths of World War Two neutrality and resistance, questioning human behavior and disestablishing collective memories.

Technology

At a 1988 anti-racist conference in the Netherlands, migrant workers' groups attacked me for holding a seminar on "The Holocaust Experience as an Early

Warning System." They claimed that the Holocaust only served Zionist interests and was irrelevant to their needs. I shared with them a number of neo-Nazi computer games that I had just obtained from Germany. These included "The Aryan Test," "The Führer Lives" and "KZ Manager." The latter game required the player, normally of high-school age, to select among a series of victims: Jews, Turks, North Africans, Pakistanis, homosexuals, handicapped, Communists or Jehovah's Witnesses. Given an initial 2500 deutschemarks, the child would choose victims according to a tariff, purchase Zyklon-B gas canisters, proceed to exterminate them, sell the hair and gold-teeth fillings to recoup capital and buy new victims, etc.

The language and modalities of the Holocaust were now addressed to contemporary targets and the Netherlands migrant groups were shocked into a new mindset regarding cooperation with Jews. In fact, these very groups, in 1998, elected me to the Board of the European Network Against Racism (ENAR) and, at its 1999 meeting in Helsinki, endorsed the Wiesenthal Center's call for "German industry to compensate their former slave and forced laborers."[10]

The child player of these games is also a victim. Desensitized to hate, he becomes vulnerable recruit potential for neo-Nazi circles. My exposure of these games led to an international conference at UNESCO in 1992 on "Educating Against Prejudice," as also to an Istanbul television debate on "The Turkish Victim of neo-Nazism in Today's Germany."

Two thousand floppy disks of "Race War," a game produced by the Nebraska-based American Nazi Party's Gary Lauck, were held by Amsterdam airport Customs in 1992. Twenty years of Lauck's mailings and postage-stamp licking can now be downloaded in five minutes over the World Wide Web.

In 1999, the Wiesenthal Center issued its CD-ROM, *Digital Hate 2000*, with interactive access to 1426 hate sites, a figure that is growing exponentially from *Stormfront*, the first such site, launched in 1995. These are the addresses for over 500 self-proclaimed hate groups in the United States, now linked with racist sympathizers globally. By a mouse click, the surfer jumps from Nazi ideology to Skinhead music, from Holocaust denial to bomb-making formulae. Thus a swastika-chained young Internet nerd, in July 1999, shot up a Chicago synagogue and an Asian Church worshipper, having been inspired by the homepage of the racist and anti-Christian *World Church of the Creator*.

Simon Wiesenthal characterized the Holocaust as the meeting point between ideology and technology. Perhaps an important lesson is to base the battle against recurrence upon the same combination. Thus the Los Angeles-based Museum of Tolerance of the Simon Wiesenthal Centre is a hi-tech human rights laboratory directed to the Internet generation. The Museum's "Tools for Tolerance" programs provide sensitization to pluralism courses for law enforcement agencies and the military.

Technology has empowered the forces of hate. Terrorists, political extremists, racists and Holocaust deniers have invaded cyberspace to sow the seeds of prejudice with impunity. Hate is indivisible. For the hate-monger, the Jew is only a tactical target; his strategic objective is democracy itself.

The murdered civil rights champion, Martin Luther King, Jr., is the latest victim of revisionism. An Internet site, www.mlking.org displays his photos and quotes, but, with great sophistication, subtly denigrates his memory. It was Holocaust denier and Ku Klux Klan leader, Don Black, who had founded *Stormfront* (the very first Internet hate site, in 1995), who had now posted this site.

The Wiesenthal Centre's Associate Dean, Rabbi Abraham Cooper, who is one of the greatest authorities on the insidious abuse of this technology, points out that "it stunts critical capacity by the theft of historic truth. Technology, however, is neutral—it may be abused or productively and creatively used." This technology is, in fact, an agent for both Holocaust education and the application of its lessons to cutting-edge dilemmas and challenges.

Conclusion

The experience of the Holocaust has endowed the Jewish people with a unique responsibility. For 2,000 years the lightning-rod, the "universal otherhood" must become the "universal example" as a weather vane or windsleeve, to sound the alarm and train society's ears to the sounds of impending danger.

"What starts with the Jews . . ." is an instrument of measure, a barometer for democratic health, and the lessons of the Holocaust provide an early-warning system to combat contemporary intolerance.

The Simon Wiesenthal Center has defined this engagement on three levels:

- "monitoring" of the trans-ideological and international linkage between all actors that threaten the democratic condition
- "counteraction" through coalition-building, networking, exposure through the media, legislative, judicial and governmental authorities and international organizations
- "prevention" through contributing to an expanding moral pedagogy on human rights.

The examples drawn in this paper from the lessons of the Holocaust point to demands for greater media responsibility, more humane treatment of refugees, improved professional accountability of insurance companies towards beneficiaries, an exercise in prudence for art dealers and museum curators, a reminder of client-first good practice for the banking industry, and more acute governmental sensitivity to the posterity power of archival transparency.

Simon Wiesenthal conditioned the granting of his name, in his lifetime, to an institution that would guard memory and employ vigilance to assist in preventing the Holocaust's recurrence for any people.

Following the "machete genocide," the Rwandan government of reconciliation sought advice from three Jewish experts, respectively in regard to the rehabilitation of survivors, the apprehension of criminal perpetrators and the establishment of mechanisms for commemoration and education. The Holocaust has taught us that no closure can be possible without serving rehabilitation, justice, and memory.

At the November 1999 "Holocaust Phenomenon" conference in Prague, Yehuda Bauer was quoted to have said, "even as the mass murder of Jews was ended by the defeat of the Nazis, the source of the Holocaust remains the same. It is a scorpion who changed its outer appearance but inside, the poison remains the same. . . "

The Wiesenthal Center's Latin American office has produced a Clio-winning one-minute Public Service Announcement entitled "SkinHitler." It portrays Adolf Hitler shaving himself into the image of a contemporary Skinhead to the beat of techno music. It is captioned: "The monster is not dead. It is mutating. We must not let it grow."

In looking back at 2,000 years of exile, the Israeli anthem, "Ha Tikva" (The Hope), evokes the millennium: "The hope of 2,000 years is yet to be realized . . ." Fifty years of Jewish sovereignty have not ended antisemitism nor normalized the Jewish condition among the comity of nations. The millennium has ushered in a communication revolution that should break asunder every barrier in our global village. Yet, this same technology now serves the cause of hate.

There are two doors into the Museum of Tolerance. One is marked "With Prejudice." The other, signposted "Without Prejudice," is locked. By judicious application of the lessons of the Holocaust to the treatment of prejudice—the true Y2K bug—we hope that the new millennium will see us enter through that other door.

NOTES

1. To accommodate the banalization of the term "Holocaust" (as in such obscenities as the title of a pornographic movie, *The Naked Holocaust*), or even political-agenda amalgams, as raised in this paper (such as "Palestinian Holocaust"), there is an increasing use of the Hebrew "Shoah," to replace the pagan-rooted "Holocaust."

2. S. Samuels, "Sosua—Moshav in the Caribbean," *The American Jewish Yearbook*, New York, 1972.

3. Here was a pan-European media attack on the Jewish State (called by French scholars at that time "The Jew among the Nations") and through Israel, Jewish citizens of the very countries of these media. Content analysis later presented this as a crisis in media responsibility, which, in turn, led to "mea culpae" and apologies, e.g., from Norwegian television and the Italian press. See:

Demonization of Jews in the Italian Media (The Green Book), CDEC, Milan, 1983

Shimon Samuels, "West European Media Antisemitism in the Lebanon War: Political Campaign or Mimetic Effect?" presented at the International Society of Political Psychology 1983 conference at St. Catherine's College, Oxford.

4. Shimon Samuels, "Antisemitic Incidents and Anti-Jewish Terrorism in Western Europe 1980–1982—The Dam Breaks," *ADL Eurobriefs*, Paris, September 1982, Anti-Defamation League of B'nai B'rith.

5. In a conversation with Sewerin Blumsztajn

6. "Mischlinge" was the Nazi term for mixed-race half or quarter Jews

7. "One Person's Commitment to Never Forget" *Response*, p.4, September 1989, Simon Wiesenthal Center, Los Angeles

8. Based on a discussion between the author and Tim Sebastian in Paris on 14 November 1999.

9. Based on a seminar held by the Soros Foundation at the Central European University in Budapest in 1997, which the author attended.

10. ENAR is an umbrella body for over 600 anti-racist NGOs in the fifteen member States of the European Union, established in cooperation with the European Commission.

❀ 12 ❀

The Rise and Fall of Metaphor: German Historians and the Uniqueness of the Holocaust

WULF KANSTEINER

$\mathcal{R}$eviewing concentration camp research in 1998, the German sociologist Wolfgang Sofsky concluded that "historiographical academic discourse avoids irritation and destruction of historical meaning by rigidly concentrating on facts. Skeptical against large-scale interpretations it tends to focus on research of single case studies."[1] As a result, historians sidestep typological and comparative research projects and are ill equipped to deal with transnational comparisons of camp systems, genocides, and other forms of modern violence which represent the most important challenge to Holocaust studies in the new century. In the case of the Holocaust, German historians could not completely avoid interpretive irritation, but they have worked tirelessly to regain historiographical equilibrium and have succeeded in recent years in containing the Holocaust's disruptive potential within conventional historiographical methods and strategies of representation. The process took five decades and several generations of scholars. In addition, at the height of internal strife and methodological insecurity in the 1980s, this surprisingly speedy resolution of the crisis of interpretation must have appeared highly unlikely to all participants.

The history of Holocaust studies in Germany is divided in four, relatively clearly defined phases. From the end of World War II until 1957 the "Final Solution" was not a central reseach topic for German historians. Subsequently, for a over a decade, German historiography produced an impressive record of empirical work about the Nazi genocide of European Jewry, especially its administrative implementation. During the third phase, from 1972 through 1980, the topic was again marginalized and only surfaced in very few publications before it became the subject of heated theoretical debates and, commencing in the mid-1980s, the focus of a new and still ongoing wave of Holocaust research.[2]

The notion of the Holocaust's singularity played a crucial role in the tumultuous debates of the early 1980s. In other national settings the overdetermined notion of the Holocaust's uniqueness has been employed to provide cohesion and purpose to a whole range of Jewish causes,[3] to help frame ambitious, yet misguided research projects,[4] or to defend the discipline of Holocaust studies against non-academic revisionists as well as academic critics.[5] None of these objectives were decisive when German historians temporarily adopted the notion of the Holocaust's uniqueness in the early 1980s before it was effectively dismantled after the Historians' Debate of 1986/87. Faced with unusual and harsh methodological and political disagreements in a discipline which tended to share a common mission, German historians imported the uniqueness concept as a metaphorical crutch; it helped them define common ground despite severe internal divisions and align themselves with interpretive tastes in other Western countries, especially Israel and the US. At the same time, at least in Germany, the theoretical debates, including debates about the singularity of the Holocaust, "represented a sustained refusal to confront the events [of the Holocaust] directly and unprotected."[6] Unfortunately yet understandably, the generation of German historians who dominated the profession during the 1970s and 1980s and who had themselves been adolescents in the Third Reich could not bear to study the Nazi atrocities with the same detachment and the same ability to look into the abyss of genocide as their younger colleagues today.

Judging from the perspective of the year 2000 the history of German Holocaust studies reflects a cumbersome and protracted process of rhetorical and methodological normalization. The exceptional efforts required for this process are ingrained in the very langage of German Holocaust historiography. Before German historians concluded their historiographical reconstuction process in the 1990s, they went through phases of rigid empiricism, during which they ignored doubts about the adequacy of their methods for the study of the Holcaust, as well as periods of ruthless self-criticism of the very foundations of their discipline. The notion of the Holocaust's uniqueness is one of the most visible signs of this identity crisis. It called into question traditional linguistic protocols for doing history and the referential illusion sustained by conventional historiographical prose.

The effect of historical verisimilitude depends on successfully merging past historical contexts with present historical writing by way of ordinary prose composition. To this end, historical discourse is constructed on the principle that its language and topics reflect actual existential contiguities of past worlds, or at least contemporary perceptions of such contiguities. The objects, persons, actions, and themes under description, as well as the language used for the description, have to share a certain historical proximity; they have to appear to be part of the same narrative universe. Therefore, for instance, we do not expect to encounter anachronisms or poetic comparisons in the narrative reconstructions of past events. For this linguistic strategy which informs ordinary referential discourse, Roman Jacobson has used the term metonomy which he differenciates from the other basic linguistic construction principle of metaphor. Metaphorical texts are not driven by real or perceived contiguity but by imagined similarity; they combine and compare themes and expressions which might share certain semantic or formal characteristics but they do not necessarily occur together in any given prelinguistic situation. The results are much more subjective texts which potentially defy comprehension, as for instance in the case modernist prose or some types of poetry. For Jacobson, metaphor and metonomy are not mutually exclusive but complementary strategies which occur, to varying degrees, in any given text.[7]

German historians rarely deviate from the straight path of metonomy in the body of their texts. We find modest metaphorical ambition primarily in the margins of their writings, when they spell out the significance of their endeavors and discuss methodology and theory. In the case of the Holocaust, however, metalinguistic concerns and search for symbols have taken center-stage, albeit only briefly. Considered from this perspective, the prominent discussions about historical theory in the 1970s and the temporary acceptance of the negative simile, that the Holocaust is unlike any other event in history, amounted to a structural scandal. It marked the disturbing intrusion of metaphor into a decidedly metonymical discursive environment.

Postwar Silence and the Prototypes of Holocaust Studies

When a new generation of university professors in unified Germany surveyed the works of their teachers and predecessors in the 1990s they inevitably came to the conclusion, as Ulrich Herbert stated in 1992, that, "taken as a whole, the West German contribution to empirical research about the persecution and destruction of European Jewry is quite small."[8] Much more work had been undertaken in Israel, Poland, and the US. This situation has changed in recent years, primarily due to the impressive achievements of this new generation whose members have diligently combed the archives for new insights about the origins and development of the "Final Solution." In contrast, the historians of the immediate postwar era faced a relative dearth of archival material, but also in other respects they were singularly ill prepared for a thorough and sustained empirical analysis of the history of the Holocaust. As we know now, many academics, including many historians, who returned to their jobs after 1945, had heavily invested in the "Nazi revolution" and were part of the functional elite which organized and implemented the military occupation, the economic exploitation, and the ethnic cleansing of occupied Europe.[9] In addition to such personal/ideological legacies, which stood in the way of historiographical inquiry into the Nazi crimes, German historians also lacked the necessary methodological and philosophical prerequisites. As Martin Broszat put it, "for the language and thought style of historicism, permeated with elevated notions about History, . . . the mass executions and gas chambers represented a serious lapse in style, which one tried to leave behind as quickly as possible."[10] But even intellectuals and academics who clearly acknowledged the terrible legacy of the Nazi period felt that the best response and most urgent task consisted of building democratic institutions. Therefore, they also refrained from further inquiry into the history of the Holocaust. As a result of all these factors, the academic publications of the postwar period present a very unbalanced picture. German historians addressed the history of the "Final Solution" primarily in collections of sources and short essays.[11] On the other hand, they spent considerable efforts on researching the history of the bourgeois resistance against Hitler to counter any real or alleged charges of German collective guilt.[12]

The historians' initial unwillingness to inquire about the Holocaust reflects a similar reluctance in West Germany's public sphere. While academics limited themselves to the production of marginal texts, the wider public engaged with the Nazi crimes through two important books, i.e., the *Diary of Anne Frank* and Eugen Kogon's *Der SS-Staat*.[13] However, the former never touches upon the abyss of the death camps and the latter focuses primarily on the concentration camp universe and dedicates only a few pages to the Nazi genocide of European Jewry. This tacit agreement between academics and the educated public should not simply be construed as repression or denial; after all, the facts of the "Final Solution" had been very well publicized through the media in the immediate postwar years.[14] The general avoidance of the topic in the late 1940s and early 1950s is more accurately described as a desire not to engage with the details of a shameful legacy which was quite well known in more general terms.[15] In subsequent decades, as historians probed more deeply into the history of the Nazi genocide, they frequently developed explanations and theories which did not penetrate into the public discourse about the Nazi past. Nevertheless, in terms of timing, academics and the public appeared to be quite in sync. The two most fruitful phases of Holocaust studies in Germany, in the 1960s and 1980s respectively, coincided with intense public concern about the Nazi legacy in the Federal Republic.

The few scholarly texts which address the Nazi crimes in the postwar years attest to the profound helplessness of its authors who tried to extract some meaning from the crimes at a time when West German society had not even found a common linguistic denominator for Nazi genocide. Their quest for moral repair work certainly fit the climate of the times. In the political realm the extraordinary nature of the Holocaust was only very indirectly reflected in a self-indulgent pathos of national moral crisis. Politicians primarily concerned themselves with the extraordinary challenge which the Nazi past represented for the recovery of Germany's moral and political standing in the world. Even the few political leaders and intellectuals, who honestly reflected about the Nazi crimes or had themselves survived the camps, shared this hope for national revival.[16] Kogon, for instance wished that his study of the concentration camp universe may help "Germany to recognize itself: its noble as well as its horrible traits so that its contorted, disfigured face regains equilibrium."[17] In a similar vain, Alexander Mitscherlich and Fred Mielke, who edited an important collection of documents about Nazi "euthanasia" and human experiments in the camps, declared that their objective was "not indictment but enlightenment, not ostracism but the blazing of a new trail—a common path into the future that may, in all our misery, at least spare us from self-abasement."[18] Such metaphorical excursions are rare exceptions in otherwise strictly scholarly texts but they illustrate that the events under description retained a surplus of meaning which could not be expressed in conventional academic prose.

Like all subsequent Holocaust scholars, the authors of these two extraordinary texts emphasized the need for extensive, truthful inquiry into the Nazi crimes as the only possible path towards redemption: "Only the truth can liberate us."[19] In this respect, especially in the case of Kogon, the texts reflect the very origins of all histories of the Nazi crimes. For decades the history of the camps was primarily written by survivors, not historians: "[A]lready during their time of incarceration the inmates had felt strongly about their responsibility to inform posterity about the monstrous events which surpassed common experience and conventional morality."[20] This experience motivated the first texts about the camps, but it also represents the closest empirical equivalent to the notion of uniqueness.

Even in other respects, the texts already anticipated future strategies for scholarly *Vergangenheitsbewältigung* (coming to terms with or mastering the past). Speaking as a sociologist, Kogon already stressed in 1946 that research about the camps should not deal with "parts, experiences, and this and that, but the *whole system*"—a dictum which could serve as a motto for most of the research undertaken in the 1960s.[21] Mitscherlich/Mielke, even more ahead of their times, concluded that the deeds of doctors without mercy represented "the alchemy of the modern age, the transmogrification of subject into object, of man into thing against which the destructive urge may wreak its fury without restraint."[22] This insight into the pathology of the modern era contains in a nutshell the critical impetus which has informed much of German Holocaust research since the late 1980s.

A closer look into the first laboratories of West German academic memory work reveals 'prototypes' of future rationalizations and research strategies but it also reveals severe terminological and conceptual helplessness vis-à-vis the Nazi crimes. Completely unselfconsciously Kogon still heralded the "extermination [Ausmerzung] of methodological mistakes" in his third edition and Mitscherlich/Mielke tried to capture Auschwitz' specificity by declaring it to be "on a cosmic scale, like a shift in the climate."[23] In subsequent decades the quest for language commensurate with the events would produce more symbolic language and occasionally involve the whole discipline, as, for instance, during the Historians' Debate. However, although German historians finally found names for the genocide of European Jewry—first "Auschwitz" and later "Holocaust"— their more ambitious attempts to agree about its historical meaning and philosophical significance proved unsuccessful. Due to its inherent structural limitations historiography never found appropriate metaphorical language which could do justice to the feelings of the contemporaries of Nazism. Therefore, historiographical normalization could only conclude after the generations' departure from the profession.

The Historiography of Sobriety

The silence of the postwar era ended in the late 1950s and early 1960s when the legacy of the Nazi crimes and the question of postwar German anti-Semitism was raised through a number of scandals and trials. A wave of anti-Semitic graffiti in 1959/60, the Eichmann-Trial in Jerusalem in 1961, and later the Auschwitz-Trial in Frankfurt in 1964/65, among other incidents, caused and indicated important transformations in West Germany's historical culture. For the first time since the immediate postwar years the question of how to come to terms with Nazism topped the national political agenda.[24] A new generation of historians, who had been young adults at the end of the war, participated in this turning point. Several specialists in the area of contemporary history, mostly associated with the Institut für Zeitgeschichte in Munich, wrote expert opinions for German courts to assist in legal disputes about restitution to victims of the Nazi regime and about reinstating former civil servants who had lost their positions during the Allied occupation. In addition, especially in the 1960s, they supported renewed efforts to bring Nazi perpetrators to trial.[25] Their research for the courts formed the core of the first systematic German inquiries into the development of the "Final Solution" and the concentration camp universe. Although many results of their work have been confirmed and remain valid to this date, the research of 1960s was restricted by the needs of the courts. In their efforts to help determine guilt and innocence historians focused on administrative decision making processes and especially the role of the highest echelon of the Nazi leadership. As a result, the victims of the Holocaust never appeared on the historiographical field of inquiry and the close connections and interdependencies between the various Nazi campaigns of ethnic cleansing, racial warfare, and mass killings eluded historical scrutiny. Nevertheless, in comparison with the previous and the following decade, the 1960s were exceptionally productive: "Until the early 1980s very little was published which displayed the same thoroughness and analytical sophistication."[26]

The historians who initiated research about the Holocaust in Germany in the 1960s hoped that their work would help "restore our people's moral integrity not only in the eyes of the world but also and especially in our own eyes."[27] But this interest in furthering collective "cartharsis" for the purposes of improved "national self-respect" was only very rarely spelled out in the margins of their texts.[28]

In principle, they decidedly condemned "general, moralistic and cultural critical reflections" after Auschwitz which they identified as the deplorable, "popular style of emotional *Vergangenheitsbewältigung*."[29] Instead they declared categorically that "for the intellectual confrontation with National Socialism and its era we in Germany require neither emotions nor moralistic revival movements but rational work based on reason and common sense." For this purpose they wholeheartedly embraced the "rigor of legal proceedings" because it offered the "necessary standard for rationality."[30] In their desire to understand the political and organizational preconditions for genocide, and to reveal the anatomy of the SS-State and its mechanisms of power, the historians produced texts which were superficially devoid of any emotions but which, in terse language and in close reading of the documents, inadvertently reproduced the style of said documents and its rationality of genocide. They revealed more historical empathy for the mechanisms of power which facilitated genocide than for its victims. This style of engagement is illustrated by Uwe Dietrich Adam's path-breaking study of 1972 which ends with the awkward, tautological conclusion that "the forces and tendencies which characterized Hitler's totalitarian state can only be explained—as the catastrophe of Germany and of Jewry prove—through the internal tensions and dynamics of said state."[31] Occasionally, however, the texts reveal how many questions remained unaddressed and unanswered in the rational historiography of the Nazi era. The texts inadvertently illustrate the uncomfortable proximity between genocidal rationalization and rational historiographical explanation. In his 14-page introduction to Rudolf Höss's memoirs Martin Broszat helplessly and obsessively admonishes Höss's propensity for "book-keeping, terse and exacting," "shocking," "apathetic," "unbearable," and "shameless rationality" (Sachlichkeit) without being able to counter it with anything else but terse, exacting, historical prose.[32]

Through their contributions to the court proceedings the historians helped establish Auschwitz as the first generally accepted name for the Nazi genocide. However, committed to a "pathos of sobriety" they declined to participate in the search for suitable metaphors and philosophical concepts.[33] As a result, the scholarship of 1960s unraveled the mechanisms of power but had nothing to say about the uniqueness of the Holocaust, let alone the emotional aspects of its legacy. For historians, the 'natural' flight into historical objectivity had effectively cut them off from other realms of German historical culture. Kogon could still be scholar and popular author in one; the scholars of the 1960s communicated largely among themselves and the courts. But even for the contemporaries of Nazism who had embraced the discourse of sobriety there remained an emotional surplus lodged within the legacy of the Holocaust; they still perceived an incommensurability between the methods of representation and the subject matter of their work. This discrepancy explains the historians' subsequent flight into metaphor, first through thoeretical skirmishes and then through a temporary adoption of the negative simile of uniqueness.

Flight into Theory

In the wake of the student movement West German historiography about the Nazi past took a theoretical, non-empirical turn. The student activists "attempted to effect a break with the National Socialist past which was cultural as well as political, one which also affected those value spheres and areas of life that had not been transformed fundamentally following 1945."[34] To this end they emphasized and criticized the lines of continuities that linked the Third Reich and the Federal Republic, especially in terms of personnel and economic structure. They denounced that the German elite had persevered after 1945 and that the capitalist order, especially 'big business,' had survived unscathed. On the basis of this Marxist inspired consensus about the persistence of German fascism the theorists of the student movement engaged in increasingly esoteric, divisive, and confusing discussions about the precise nature of the fascist phenomenon.[35]

The debates among the student activists had little direct impact on German historiography, but a number of younger professional historians, who had finished their university training in the 1960s, shared some of the political concerns and theoretical reference points with the student rebels. These historians were only slightly younger than the first group of Holocaust historians; they belong to the age cohorts of the Hitler Youth generation. As young academics in a rapidly expanding university system they wanted to partake in sociocultural reforms by transforming West German academia from the inside out. In their attempts to break with the methodological and philosophical traditions of the discipline they and their older colleagues spent considerable time discussing the merits and limitations of competing historiographical models for the study of Nazism. As a result, the historiography of the 1970s remains memorable for the heated debates, including *ad hominem* attacks, among academics who subscribed to different theoretical frameworks, methodologies, and philosophies of history.

One topic of discussion was the question whether Nazism is best understood as a brand of fascism, and should be studied within the context of the history of other fascist regimes, or whether it is more accurately categorized as a totalitarian system and should be compared to the Soviet Union.[36] These questions had already been discussed in other countries before they were addressed in Germany. In all these settings the debates served the purpose to displace the theory of totalitarianism which had been the dominant view of 20th century history in the West and "the official ideology of the Federal Republic from 1955 to 1975."[37] In addition, as a result of attempts to reform their conservative discipline, German historians came to interpret the political history of Nazism and its prehistory from incompatible philosophical vantage points. The majority camp followed the conventional notion that 'Men make history' and therefore studied the motives, ideologies and actions of the Nazi leadership. But a very vocal minority, mostly members of the Hitler Youth generation, developed an alternative research agenda which was based on an eclectic assemblage of neo-Marxist theory, sociological classics, and Anglo-American social history. The new paradigm can be somewhat simplistically summarized by the slogan 'not men but structures make history.' This 'functionalist' approach, as it came to be known, proved particularly productive for the study of 19th century Germany and the prehistory of the Nazi era.[38] Applied to the political history of the Third Reich it yielded detailed studies of the power structure of the Nazi bureaucracy. Its authors emphasized time and again that political outcomes were primarily the result of competition and cooperation between a multitude of state and party agencies. In their eyes the catastrophic policies of the Nazi government could not be satisfactorily explained through the intentions of the leaders—even if their intentions fit some of the outcomes very nicely. Rather, each statement and document had to be interpreted according to its position and 'career' within the complex, polycratic governmental structures of the Third Reich.[39] This structuralist or functionalist view of history has been labeled social history by its practitioners. However, at least with regard to the history of Nazism the new paradigm provided little insight into the social fabric of Nazi society but offered a very productive, alternative understanding of political processes and political history before and during Nazism.

Flight into Exceptionality

The theoretical turn in German historiography during the 1970s produced little empirical, comparative work and, at least initially, offered no new insights into the history of the "Final Solution." In fact, German historians engaged in "wars of interpretations on an outdated, thin empirical basis."[40] Like the work of the 1960s, the abstract debates about fascism and totalitarianism, and intention and structure, rendered invisible the victims. In addition, unlike earlier historiographical efforts, the theoretical discussions obstructed the view of the perpetrators of the Nazi crimes.

In the context of the theoretical discussions of the 1970s, German historiography underwent a process of trifurcation. A steady production of monographs about the history of the "Final Solution" continued the tradition of the historiography of sobriety. As new sources became available and as German historians spent less time studying the collapse of the Weimar Republic and the first years of the Nazi regime, and focused instead on the period of World War II, new publications about the *Einsatzgruppen*, the death camps, and the war of extermination on the Eastern front considerably advanced the German historiography of the Holocaust.[41] On a second historiographical scene academic historians were effectively challenged by the rise of the history of everyday life (*Alltagsgeschichte*). Its practitioners, located in the margins or even outside academia, rewrote the history of Nazism from the perspective of the postwar generations. Finally, the public debates about the appropriate definition of Nazism quickly evolved into a semi-independent, third arena of historiographical practice. Especially for Germany's established academics the participation in political and polemical exchanges became a frequent, even routine undertaking. Not surprisingly, the rise of metaphor began and ended on this third level of historiographical practice. The public struggles provided the perfect outlet for representational interests which remained unaddressed in more conventional historiographical texts. In the early 1980s the debates focused again on the divide between functionalists and intentionalists, but this time specifically applied to the "Final Solution."

During the increasingly hostile exchanges of the 1970s the opposing camps seemed to agree on little more than "the central role of anti-Semitism in National-Socialist ideology and politics."[42] Despite radically different ideas about political practice and decision-making processes in the Third Reich the consensus was reflected in monographs and handbooks at the time. But the consensus about the centrality in the "Final Solution" was merely stated in passing; with few exceptions the Nazi crimes were not the subject of original research.[43] This equilibrium might have continued for a while if the academic experts had not been shaken by the broadcast and reception of the television mini-series *Holocaust* in 1979. Leading representatives of the profession conceded that the historians "may have paid too little attention to the problem of the "Final Solution" and the task of distributing their insights to the wider public."[44] The surprising popular interest in Holocaust history was met with a surge of publications which powerfully illustrated that academic self-criticism was quite appropriate. The ensuing flood of books "consisted only of old classics and rapidly penned Holocaust products."[45] At the same time the publications also played an importat role in introducing the concept of the Holocaust's uniqueness to Germany.[46] As a result of such unusual public scrutiny at home and abroad Germany's historians went to work. However, instead of hitting the archives, they did what they had done best for over a decade; they focused on one of the few original contributions to German Holocaust studies in the 1970s and began a theoretical discussion about the merits of functionalist and intentionalist interpretations of the origins of the "Final Solution."[47]

In two programmatic essays Martin Broszat and Hans Mommsen stressed that the Holocaust was the outcome of the gradual radicalization of Nazi anti-Jewish policies in response to the failure of alternative plans for the removal of European Jewry.[48] They maintained that genocide resulted from a combination of general central policy decisions and local *ad hoc* initiatives by competing agencies which tried to 'solve' the increasingly chaotic conditions in the ghettos and camps in occupied Eastern Europe. According to their assessment, Hitler was kept informed and supported the radicalization towards mass murder—often *post factum*—but he did not design nor micro-manage the Holocaust himself as historians had conventionally assumed. For both authors, these conclusions indicated that the political and moral responsibility for the "Final Solution" was shared by many officials, including many members of traditional elites, and could not be limited to Hitler and the top Nazi leadership. These ideas were vigorously debated and resulted in important transitions in the German historiography of the "Final Solution."

When the different methodological perspectives were brought to bear on the decision-making processes concerning the Holocaust, it became quickly apparent that the prior formulaic consensus about "the central role of anti-Semitism in National-Socialist ideology and politics" would not survive close examination. Not surprisingly, the representatives of the opposing schools of thought could not agree on the role of Hitler, Nazi ideology, and German bureaucracy in the Holocaust. In this situation of increasing division and public scrutiny the German professoriate enlisted help from their Israeli colleagues and appropriated the idea of the Holocaust's uniqueness as a temporary, politically correct abstract consensus. Both the recognition of irreconcilable differences and the adoption of new metaphorical common ground were illustrated by an important international conference in Stuttgart in 1984. As the participants from Germany, Israel, and the US engaged in fruitless discussions of smaller and smaller minutiae in hopeless attempts to resolve larger philosophical and methodological differences, some of the scholars from Israel became increasingly skeptical about this particular style of academic *Vergangenheitsbewältigung*. Yehuda Bauer asked the assembled experts: "Don't we run away from ourselves? Don't we try, albeit of course subconsciously, to look away from the cruel reality of the most terrible mass murder in history and focus instead on easily digested, abstract conceptualizations?"[49] and Saul Friedlander voiced uneasiness about the surreal efforts to deal with the mechanics of mass murder in strictly academic fashion over the course of several days.[50] It is not incidental that these two scholars have provided two of the best, albeit very different, definitions of the Holocaust's singularity and have played an important role in relating this notion to their German colleagues.

In the late 1970s and early 1980s the Holocaust became a cornerstone of American Jewish identity and was enlisted for a whole range of Jewish and non-Jewish political objectives. As a result, the idea of the Holocaust's uniqueness was embraced by the Jewish community while it was simultaneously employed and contested by other ethnic groups in their struggles for publicity and self-validation. Bauer "was the most prominent and outspoken proponent of uniqueness in this period"[51] and he has forcefully stated his position ever since: "[N]ever before in human history has a well-organized state, representing a social consensus, tried to murder, globally, every single member of an ethnic or ethno-religious group as defined by the perpetrator, for purely ideological reasons that bore not the slightest relation to reality."[52] This empirical definition has to be differentiated from Friedlander's insistence on the Holocaust's incomprehensibility: "Paradoxically, the 'Final Solution,' as a result of its apparent historical exceptionality, could well be inaccessible to all attempts at a significant representation and interpretation. Thus, notwithstanding all efforts at the creation of meaning, it could remain fundamentally irrelevant for the history of humanity and the understanding of the 'human condition.'"[53] Elaborated over the years with "a peculiarly authoritative custodial voice" Friedlander's "defense of the historical and moral centrality, as well as the ultimate inexplicability, of the Holocaust" has proven particularly appealing to German historians.[54]

Since the early 1980s the notion of the Holocaust's uniqueness has become a standard framing device in German historiography, at least for one generation of scholars. Especially members of the Hitler-Youth generation, the German contemporaries of Bauer and Friedlander, have habitually introduced their publications by acknowledging their belief in the historical singularity of the "Final Solution." The metaphor is used on both sides of the intentionalist/functionalist divide. Scholars who approach the study of the Holocaust from such different vantage points as Hans Mommsen and Eberhard Jäckel nevertheless consistently agree on its exceptional nature.[55] In addition, the status of the Holocaust as "the singular most monstrous crime in the history of human kind" is also routinely stated in new surveys.[56] But the agreement was never unanimous. Andreas Hillgruber repeatedly suggested that the large number of perpetrators and more or less informed bystanders gives us reason "to think beyond the historical singularity of the events" and Martin Broszat had doubts about the usefulness of metahistorical categories stipulating the singularity of any event, including the "Final Solution."[57] Very soon after being adopted by German historians under exceptional circumstances, the notion of uniqueness was exposed as little more than a useful political tool during the Historians' Debate and, finally, quite unceremoniously discarded by Germany's most recent crop of professional historians.

The Historians' Debate

In mid-1986, the philosopher Jürgen Habermas delivered a frontal attack against a number of well-established conservative historians. Habermas argued that conservatives had violated the prior consensus stipulating that "after Auschwitz we can only create national self-confidence by selectively appropriating our more suitable traditions" through rigorous self-critical examination.[58] Instead, he claimed, conservative historians now engaged again in "reviving a sense of identity naively rooted in national consciousness," an aim that Habermas found clearly expressed in the programmatic editorial essays of the historian Michael Stürmer.[59] For Habermas, such efforts of national identity construction were supported by Stürmer's colleagues, Ernst Nolte and Andreas Hillgruber, who advanced the cause in a number of short texts addressed to lay audiences. Nolte helped by denying the historical singularity of Auschwitz, which he characterized as a reaction to and imitation of similar events in the Soviet Union and thus "a mere technical innovation."[60] Hillgruber lent support to the conservative campaign by considering the last phase of war on the eastern front exclusively from the viewpoint of the German troops, which, he argued, resisted heroically to save the German population from the Red Army's wrath. For Habermas such histories amounted to apologetic tendencies toward the Third Reich.

The criticized historians responded quickly and dismissed the charges in equally personal attacks. With short delay Habermas's supporters, especially prominent liberal historians, joined the battle and restated his critique. In his initial intervention Habermas argued that the criticized historians supported each other's efforts, yet he never clarified whether he alleged any conscious conspiratorial activity, or if he merely described a disconcerting discursive formation. His supporters were less circumspect. For many commentators on the left, the scandal, as defined by Habermas, fit their favorite paranoid fantasy of a right-wing conspiracy at the center of West Germany's conservative establishment. They therefore joined the battle against the "new revisionism" without much ado. After the initial exchange of polemics, both sides ceased to engage in further debate, let alone any constructive discussions. Since the conservative camp, with few exceptions, refused to continue the debate, the great majority of the articles reflected the liberal point of view.

Although the question of the Holocaust's historical singularity was not Habermas's single or even primary focus (he spent more time and effort on the critique of conventional national forms of historical identity), the uniqueness and comparability question became the overriding concern of most commentators.[61] Very few of the commentators were in any position to add new material to the discussion concerning, for instance, new research about the Soviet Union and other genocidal regimes. Therefore, the Historians' Debate soon turned into a repetitive acclamation of the historical singularity of the Holocaust.[62] The tacit agreement about the central importance of anti-Semitism had become an explicit, widely shared metaphorical dictum. On the basis of this result it is not surprising that the liberal camp declared victory. It seemed as if the conservative cultural trend had been resoundingly defeated. However, with hindsight, the Historians' Debate is much better understood "as the protracted political farewell—abruptly ended by German unification—of a generation of researchers and individuals who had a specific autobiographical agenda and were facing retirement at the start of the 1990s."[63]

While liberal historians and their supporters enjoyed this success, the relativization of the concept of exceptionality was already well under way. A number of initiatives and research strategies called into question the simplistic notion of singularity which had triumphed during the Historians' Debate. These initiatives included the social historians' own emphasis on the importance of modern social structures and bureaucracies which was continued by younger historians in their own research about the interdependence of Nazism and modernity, and new research on the perpetrators of the Holocaust. However, most important was the rise of *Alltagsgeschichte*. Increased interest in the history of everyday life, both within and outside academia, produced a wave of publications which provided vivid and tangible details about life in the Third Reich to generations whose members had no personal memories of the period. Designed as critical antidotes to abstract debates and lofty discussions about high politics and administrative structures, many contributions to the history of everyday life inadvertently overemphasized the seemingly normal, unproblematic daily routines of the contemporaries of Nazism.[64] On the other hand, *Alltagsgeschichte* also illustrated the pervasiveness of racism and anti-Semitism in Nazi Germany. Although Alltagsgeschichte was initially not focused on the Holocaust, many local and regional studies finally gave voices and faces to the victims of the Nazi policies of persecution and extermination, including its Jewish victims. A fitting example is the work of Monika Richarz who edited autobiographical writings of German Jews about life in Nazi Germany and broke with the historiographical convention which had represented "the Jews as nameless, passive victims of an all-powerful machinery of destruction".[65]

At the end of a long phase of theoretical discussions and a short phase of the reign of metaphor, the notion of uniqueness received a last enthusiastic, over-the-top endorsement of truly epic (and epigonic) proportions: "Auschwitz is a no-mansland of understanding, a black box of explanation, a vacuum of transhistorical significance which absorbs all historiographical attempts of interpretation. Only ex negativo, only through constant efforts to understand the futility of understanding, can we begin to grasp the break in civilization that this event represents. As a radical extreme case and absolute measure of history this event can very likely never be historicized."[66] Dan Diner's metaphorical firework might be the most elegant and self-confident endorsement of the incomprehensibility claim but it does not ring true any longer, precisely because it misses the element of self doubt which had accompanied the language of his predecessors.

Self-Confident Empiricism

In the late 1980s and 1990s, partly in response to earlier overly theoretical discussions, a new generation of historians returned to the search of historical evidence, especially, but not exclusively in the recently opened archives of Eastern Europe. Many of the younger historians had absorbed or even participated in the wave of everyday history and they studied the Holocaust from a similar methodological vantage point. In addition to their interest in concrete empirical data, they resurrected conventional historiographical research and writing strategies which had been dismissed by the first generation of social historians. Some of the best works of the late 1980s and 1990s provide regional studies of the origins of the "Final Solution" in occupied Eastern Europe. The authors seek to understand what concrete, local factors contributed to the development of genocidal policies and how these local factors interacted with political directives from Berlin.[67] In addition to this methodologically conventional regional emphasis, historians have frequently chosen traditional biographical approaches and narrative formats.

These trends and recent advances in Holocaust studies in Germany are exemplified by the extra-academic research undertaken under the auspices of the Hamburg Institute for Social Research. Unlike their academic colleagues, its members and affiliates have kept alive the political ambitions of the student movement and the polemical tone of earlier debates. The proponents of the so-called Hamburg school set out to document the political economy at the center of the "Final Solution." They contend that an intermediate layer of academically trained professionals designed and implemented the genocidal policies of the Nazi regime in the name of modern Western science, especially economics. In their opinion the Holocaust has to be interpreted within the overall context of state-of-the-art population policies which entailed large scale deportations and relocations as part of far-flung plans to reform the political, economic, and ethnic map of Eastern Europe. The attempted realization of these plans, including the insufficiently prepared relocation of ethnic Germans from the Soviet Union, set off a chain reaction of failed social engineering which led to ethnic cleansing and genocide. Furthermore, they are convinced that the professional 'ethos' and worldview of this planning intelligentsia is alive and well in Western academia, including German historiography.[68] Not surprisingly, their work has met harsh criticism from academic historians, including their generational peers, who pointed out, among more polemical responses, that material unearthed by Götz Aly et al. might attest to *post factum* rationalizations of Nazi policy rather than decision making processes.[69] Nevertheless, the work is an important part of recent interest in the administrative and political personnel which realized the Holocaust. It finally addresses questions which should have been but could not be asked by their predecessors after 1945.

While these recent studies are clearly rooted in the tradition of *Alltagsgeschichte*, they also address research problems and ethical questions which were explicitly and implicitly raised in the writing of their structuralist predecessors. Their students have zoomed in on the functional elites of the Nazi regime and researched how administrators, party officials, and academics constructed the "Final Solution." The best recent works, for instance, Ulrich Herbert's 1996 study of Werner Best, combine an essentially biographical format with a systematic exploration of the structures and worldviews which shaped the generation of young, successful Nazi functionaries.[70] The study illustrates that German historians have finally overcome the sterility of the functionalist-intentionalist debates with their rigid, seemingly irreconcilable theoretical alternatives. Scholars like Herbert contend that the dynamics of violence which led to the Holocaust were motivated by racial anti-Semitism as well as ambitions for economic modernization and colonization steeped in the tradition of modern Western imperialism. The perpetrators' 'irrational' ideological objectives, their seemingly rational, utilitarian interest in social engineering, and their desire to solve pressing organizational and administrative problems caused by mass scale deportations resulted in a gradual process of radicalization, a process which differed significantly in various local settings and among various groups of perpetrators.[71] Moreover, with regard to the bystanders, Herbert has reached the alarming conclusion that acceptance of genocide did not require ideological fanaticism or mass hysteria, as recently alleged by Goldhagen, but that wide-scale, "escalating indifference" to the plight of minorities assured popular consent.[72]

The innovators of German Holocaust studies might differ in tone and emphasis but they agree in their rejection of the singularity metaphor as useless and counter-productive. Again, Ulrich Herbert: "The study of the genocide does not just reveal information about the historically unique situation and the specific German society of the 1930s and 1940s; rather it remains a contemporary, pressing, and depressing concern, not just, but especially here in Germany. These questions will keep us busy for quite some time even beyond all short-term, topical debates and excitement. In that process the insistence on the events' incomprehensibility is as unproductive as any recourse to monocausal and seemingly radical explanations."[73] Not surprisingly, Götz Aly has been even less tempered in his criticism. He rejects the left liberal "feuilleton wisdom" which posits the Holocaust as inexplicable because this approach "opens no avenues for reflection and unnecessarily restricts one's focus" in research as well as teaching.[74] Instead, he argues that the Holocaust is accessible to analysis by conventional historiographical methods partly because the conventional rules of state bureaucratic procedure applied to the "Final Solution."[75] Therefore he concludes: "The deed and the crime is (sic) unique. However, Auschwitz is part of European as well as German history. Only when one has fully understood this context is it possible to talk meaningfully of the 'limits of understanding.' The Holocaust was not a 'reversion to barbarism,' nor a 'break with civilization,' still less an 'Asiatic deed.' But it was also far from being a 'historical black hole,' somehow beyond language, poetry and historical understanding, but rather a possibility inherent in European civilization itself."[76] Finally, the cause of the Holocaust's uniqueness, in Germany as well as in the US, did not profit from the fact that its most recent high-profile proponent, Daniel Goldhagen, presented a methodologically problematic interpretation of perpetrator history. With renewed self-confidence into the methodological integrity of their discipline German historians, in agreement with their colleagues abroad, unanimously rejected Goldhagen's thesis.[77] However, they also abandoned the search for metaphorical language suitable for the representation of Holocaust history.

Conclusion

The rise of metaphor in German historiography, that, for a short period, coexisted with conventional rhetorics of empiricism, was linked to a whole range of factors. The notion of uniqueness was adopted by a generation of German historians who, unlike their predecessors and successors, were either well versed in theoretical language and applied it in their own work or who were used to debate large scale constructs and theoretical models with their colleagues. These theoretical inclinations were themselves linked to the Nazi past because they reflected the ambition of a minority among German historians who wanted to part with traditional academic practices and identities that, they argued, had been discredited during the Third Reich. At the same time, the concern with new historiographical foundations helped them avoid direct confrontation with some of the most troubling concrete aspects of Nazi history. The peculiar mixture of selective avoidance and reformist determination resulted from a specific biographical constellation. The theoretical instruments as well as the concept of uniqueness were used by historians, in Germany as well as abroad, who had themselves experienced the Nazi era. The frustration with conventional methodology and interest in metaphorical language speaks to their desire to come to terms with exceptionally destructive events which had disrupted and devalued their own adolescence *after the fact*.

In addition, the rhetorics of singularity was embraced by academics who, because of their innovative zeal and biographical insecurities, were more tuned into international developments and expectations, both professional and political, than any prior generation of academics in Germany. Therefore, they were also more likely to identify with concepts suggested by historians from abroad. However, despite these theoretical interests and international outlook, it took a historiographical crisis for the uniqueness metaphor to be imported to Germany. The media event *Holocaust* revealed that historians were no longer the guardians of national historical consciousness. Moreover, the discipline was prevented from rising to the challenge by internal division and paralysis. In addition to conventional political disagreements, historians faced unusual methodological and philosophical divisions which they tried to solve, unsuccessfully, through misguided discussions about factual details. The abstract concepts of structure vs. intention and fascism vs. totalitarianism are simply beyond the reach of procedures of historical evidence. The same applies to the concept of uniqueness and the notion of the Holocaust's inexplicability. However, the fact that neither can be proven historically made them even more suitable as temporary lowest common denominators for a divided professoriate.

The fall of metaphor is inherent in the concept itself but it was also actively prepared by its proponents. The notion of uniqueness, especially its inexplicable version, is inherently unstable, which becomes quite obvious when historians announce their belief in the Holocaust's ultimate incomprehensibility but immediately continue espousing its historical meaning in conventional historical prose.[78] In addition, and more important, the language of uniqueness disrupts the principle of contiguity. Historians have no problems emphasizing the exceptional relevance of the case studies which they have singled out for research. But this relevance is based on the belief that their results, however monographic in scope, contain insights into the larger historical context, that the historical world forms a continous whole devoid of radical qualitative shifts which require radically different methods of analysis and representation. Or, to put it differently, historiographical language is located at the metonymic pole of language; too much metaphor does not just change its surface appearance, its 'style,' it also changes the epistemological assumptions which are embedded in the very structure of historiographical discourse.

The limited value of the concept of uniqueness as an historiographical tool became obvious during the Historians' Debate when it quickly turned into a litmus test for the different political alignments without providing any stimulus for research. But the most important reason for the sudden demise of the idea of singularity is again generational. The second generational turn-over in the discipline since the end of the war has reduced the personal stakes involved in the study of the Nazi crimes and it has produced another generation whose members are eager to differentiate themselves from their teachers. In the process, the new historians have shed the cumbersome theoretical instruments and metaphorical language which their predecessors employed to study the "Final Solution." Recent histories of the Holocaust published in Germany illustrate this professionalization and methodological normalization in German historiography in general and Holocaust studies in particular. In the wake of everyday history and microhistory German historians have retained their international perspective but they have methodologically reverted to a methodological stance which preceded not just the debates of the 1970s but even the Nazi period. Fully and seriously engaged in *Vergangenheitsbewältigung*, German historians have again embraced the comforting illusion that their texts are a transparent reflection of the empirical record, that they are simply telling the facts. With hindsight, the historiographically volatile 1970s and the subsequent short reign of metaphor appear just as ripples in a sea of historiographical normality and self-confidence. The notion of the Holocaust's singularity temporarily postponed this inevitable return to business as usual and gave rise to unusual and unusually productive historiographical introspection and in this way attested to the extraordinary challenge which the historicization of events like the Holocaust pose to an academic discipline. [79]

It might take another generation of scholars (although hopefully not another event like the Holocaust) before the unacknowledged implicit premises of the historian's craft are again tested in such stringent fashion. In the meantime, a new consensus seems to have emerged in the discipline, a consensus which is ripe with underlying assumptions about modernity, human nature, and historical continuity and which has eliminated the historical and anthropological distance between us and the Nazi perpetrators that German historians worked so hard to maintain for over 30 years: "Perpetrator research forces one to accept the unwelcome insight that the transformation of human beings into mass murderers requires little time and will power. Neither long biographical adaptation nor time consuming indoctrination appear necessary."[80]

NOTES

1. Wolfgang Sofsky, "An der Grenze des Sozialen: Perspektiven der KZ-Forschung," in Ulrich Herbert/Karin Orth/Christoph Dieckmann, *Die nationalsozialistischen*

Konzentrationslager: Entwicklung und Struktur (Göttingen: Wallstein, 1998), 1141–1169, 1141–2.

2. Ulrich Herbert, "Der Holocaust in the Geschichtsschreibung der Bundesrepublik Deutschland," Ulrich Herbert/Olaf Groehler, *Zweierlei Untergang: Vier Beiträge über den Umgang mit der NS-Vergangenheit in den beiden deutschen Staaten* (Hamburg: Ergebnisse, 1992), 67–86; Ulrich Herbert, "Vernichtungspolitik: Neue Antworten und Fragen zur Geschichte des Holocaust," in Herbert (ed.), *Nationalsozialistische Vernichtungpolitik 1939–1945: Neue Forschungen und Kontroversen* (Frankfurt: Fischer, 1998), 9–66.

3. Peter Novick, *The Holocaust in American Life* (Boston: Houghton Mifflin, 1999); Tim Cole, *Selling the Holocaust: From Auschwitz to Schindler's List* (New York: Routledge, 1999).

4. This applies especially to the work of Steven Katz, *The Holocaust in Historical Context*, vol. 1 (New York: Oxford UP, 1994) who has embarked on a multi-volume study of genocide in world history with the a priori determined objective to prove the historical uniqueness of the Holocaust; see Berel Lang's review "The Second Time? The Fifth? The Question of Holocaust-Uniqueness," Lang, *The Future of the Holocaust*, (Ithaca: Cornell UP, 1999), 77–91.

5. Gavriel Rosenfeld, "The Politics of Uniqueness: Reflections on the Recent Polemical Turn in Holocaust and Genocide Studies," *Holocaust and Genocide Studies* 13/1 (1999), 28–61.

6. Herbert, "Vernichtungspolitik," 21.

7. Jacobson developed this theory of binary opposition in 1956 following Saussure's definition of the syntagmatic and paradigmatic axes in language, see Roman Jacobson, "Two Aspects of Language and Two Types of Aphasic Disturbances," reprinted in Jacobson, *On Language* (Cambridge: Harvard UP, 1990), 115–133; see also Richard Bradford, *Roman Jacobson: Life, language, art* (New York: Routledge, 1994), 9–23; and David Lodge, *The Modes of Modern Writing* (Chicago: University of Chicago Press, 1988), 73–124.

8. Herbert, "Holocaust," 81.

9. For the recent debates about German historians during National Socialism see Winfried Schulze/Otto Gerhard Oexle, eds., *Deutsche Historiker im Nationalsozialismus* (Frankfurt: Fischer, 1999); see also Wulf Kansteiner, "Mandarins in the Public Sphere: *Vergangenheitsbewältigung* and the Paradigm of Social History in the Federal Republic of Germany," *German Politics and Society* 52/17 (1999), 84–120.

10. Martin Broszat, "Holocaust und die Geschichtswissenschaft," Broszat, *Nach Hitler: Der schwierige Umgang mit unserer Geschichte* (München: Oldenbourg, 1986), 271–286, 284.

11. See for example the sources about the history of the "Final Solution" published in the *Vierteljahrshefte für Zeitgeschichte*: "Der Gerstein-Bericht," VfZ 1 (1953), 177–194; "Denkschrift Himmlers über die Behandlung der Fremdvölkischen," VfZ 5 (1957), 194–198; and "Der Generalplan Ost," VfZ 6 (1958), 281–325; and Walter Hofer, *Der Nationalsozialismus: Dokumente 1933–1945* (Frankfurt: Fischer, 1957), 267–312.

12. Regina Holler, *20. Juli 1944: Vemächtnis oder Alibi?* (München: Saur, 1994), 69–87.

13. *Das Tagebuch der Anne Frank* (Frankfurt: Fischer, 1957, originally published in 1949); Eugen Kogon, *Der SS-Staat: Das System der deutschen Konzentrationslager*, 3rd ed. (Frankfurt: Verlag der Frankfurter Hefte, 1949, 1st ed. 1946).

14. See for example Dagmar Barnouw, *Germany 1945: Views of War and Violence* (Bloomington: Indiana UP, 1996).

15. Norbert Frei, "Auschwitz und Holocaust: Begriff und Historiographie," in Hanno Loewy (ed.), *Holocaust: Die Grenzen des Verstehens: Eine Debatte über die Besetzung der Geschichte* (Reinbek: Rowohlt, 1992), 101–109.

16. Jeffrey Herf, *Divided Memory: The Nazi Past in the Two Germany's* (Cambridge: Harvard UP, 1997).

17. Kogon, *SS-Staat*, 392.

18. Alexander Mitscherlich/Fred Mielke (eds.), *Doctors of Infamy: The Story of the Nazi Medical Crimes* (New York: Schuman, 1949), 151.

19. Kogon, *SS-Staat*, viii; see also Mitscherlich/Mielke, *Doctors of Infamy*, 153.

20. Herbert/Orth/Dieckmann, *Die nationalsozialistischen Konzentrationslager*, vol. 2, 19.

21. Kogon, *SS-Staat*, viii.

22. Mitscherlich/Mielke, *Doctors of Infamy*, 152.

23. Kogon, *SS-Staat*, vi and Mitscherlich/Mielke, *Doctors of Infamy*, 151.

24. Werner Bergmann, *Antisemitismus in öffentlichen Konflikten: Kollektives Lernen in der politischen Kultur der Bundesrepublik 1949–1989* (Frankfurt: Campus, 1997), 187 ff.

25. Norbert Frei, "Der Frankfurter Auschwitz-Prozess und die deutsche Zeitge-schichtsforschung," Fritz-Bauer Institut (ed.), *Auschwitz: Geschichte, Rezeption, Wirkung* (Frankfurt: Campus, 1996), 123–136. The expert opinions have been published in Institut für Zeitgeschichte (ed.), *Gutachten des Instituts für Zeitgeschichte*, 2 vols. (München: Institut für Zeitgeschichte, 1958 and 1966); and Hans Buchheim et al., *Anatomie des SS-Staates*, 2 vols. (Olten: Walter, 1965).

26. Herbert, "Holocaust," 75

27. Wolfgang Scheffler, *Judenverfolgung im Dritten Reich 1933–1945* (Berlin: Colloquium, 1960), 5.

28. Martin Broszat (ed.), *Kommandant in Auschwitz: Autobiographische Aufzeichnungen von Rudolf Höss* (Stuttgart: Deutsche Verlagsanstalt, 1958), 14.

29. *Anatomie des SS-Staates*, vol. I, 5,7.

30. Ibid., 8.

31. Uwe Dietrich Adam, Judenpolitik im Dritten Reich (Düsseldorf: Droste, 1972), 360–361; see also H.G. Adler, *Der verwaltete Mensch: Studien zur Deportation der Juden aus Deutschland* (Tübingen: Mohr, 1974) In his voluminous study, already concluded in 1971, the survivor of Theresienstadt reconstructs every detail of the deportation of Germany's Jews in the name of historical objectivity but reserves his empathy for the demise of the liberal constitutional state under the rule of law, xxix-xxx, 1038.

32. Broszat, *Kommandant*, 10,14,18,20,21.

33. Klaus-Dietmar Henke/Claudio Natoli (eds.), *Mit dem Pathos der Nüchternheit: Martin Broszat, das Institut für Zeitgeschichte und die Erforschung des Nationlsozialismus* (Frankfurt: Campus, 1991).

34. Moishe Postone, "After the Holocaust: History and Identity in West Germany," Kathy Harms et al. (eds.), *Coping with the Past: Germany and Austria after 1945* (Madison: University of Wisconsin Press, 1990), 233–251, 236.

35. Heinrich August Winkler, "Die 'neue Linke' und der Faschismus: Zur Kritik neo-marxistischer Theorien über den Nationasozialismus," in Winkler, *Revolution, Staat, Faschismus: Zur Revision des historischen Materialismus* (Göttingen: Vandenhoeck und Ruprecht, 1987), 65–117.

36. For a summary of the debate see Ian Kershaw, *Der NS-Staat: Geschichtsinterpretationen und Kontroversen im Überblick*, 3rd ed. (Reinbek: Rowohlt, 1999), 39–79.

37. Wolfgang Wippermann, "Post-War German Left and Fascism," *Journal of Contemporary History* 4/1 (1976), 192.

38. Georg Iggers, "Introduction," Iggers (ed.), *The Social History of Politics: Critical Perspectives in West German Historical Writing Since 1945* (Leamington Spa: Berg, 1985), 1–48.

39. Kershaw, *NS-Staat*, 112–147.

40. Herbert, "Vernichtungspolitik," 21.

41. Helmut Krausnick/Hans-Heinrich Wilhelm, *Die Truppe des Weltanschauungskrieges: Die Einsatzgruppen des Sicherheitsdienstes und des SD 1938–1942* (Stuttgart: Deutsche Verlagsanstalt, 1981; Eugen Kogon et al. (eds.), *Nationalsozialistische Massentötungen durch Giftgas* (Frankfurt: Fischer, 1983); Militärgeschichtliches Forschungsamt (ed.), *Das Deutsche Reich und der Zweite Weltkrieg*, 6 vols. (Stuttgart: Deutsche Verlagsanstalt, 1979–1988).

42. Otto D. Kulka, "Singularity and Its Relativization: Changing Views in German Historiography on National Socialism and the 'Final Solution,'" *Yad Vashem Studies* 19 (1988), 151–186, 151; Otto D. Kulka, "Major Trends and Tendencies in German Historiography on National Socialism and the "Jewish Question," Yisrael Gutman/Gideon Greif (ed.), *The Historiography of the Holocaust Period* (Jerusalem: Yad Vashem, 1988), 1–51.

43. For such exceptions see for example Falk Pingel, *Häftlinge unter SS-Herrschaft: Widerstand, Sebstbehauptung und Vernichtung im Konzentrationslager* (Hamburg: Hoffmann und Campe, 1978); and Christian Streit, *Keine Kameraden* (Stuttgart: Deutsche Verlagsanstalt, 1978).

44. Hans Mommsen, "Holocaust und die Deutsche Geschichtswissenschaft," Gutman, *Historiography*, 79–97; see also, less equivocally Broszat, "Holocaust," 271.

45. Konrad Kwiet, "Zur historiographischen Behandlung der Judenverfolgung im Dritten Reich," *Militärgeschichtliche Mitteilungen* 27/1 (1980), 149–192, 151.

46. See for instance Elie Wiesel's widely circulated critique of *Holocaust* in which he re-emphasized the singularity and inexplicability of the Holocaust, Wiesel, "Die Trivialisierung des Holocaust: Halb Faktum und halb Fiktion," Peter Märtesheimer/Ivo Frenzel (eds.), *Im Kreuzfeuer: Der Fernsehfilm Holocaust* (Frankfurt: Fischer, 1979).

47. Kershaw, *NS-Staat*, 148–206; and Michael Marrus, *The Holocaust in History* (New York: Meridian, 1987), 31–46.

48. Martin Broszat, "Hitler und die Genesis der 'Endlösung:' Aus Anlass der Thesen von David Irving," Broszat, *Nach Hitler*, 187–229 (originally published in 1977); Hans Mommsen, "Die Realisierung des Utopischen: Die 'Endlösung der Judenfrage' im 'Dritten Reich,'" Mommsen, *Der Nationalsozialismus und die deutsche Gesellschaft* (Reinbek: Rowohlt, 1991), 184–232 (originally published in 1983); see also Adam, *Judenpolitik*.

49. Yehuda Bauer, "Auschwitz," Eberhard Jäckel/Jürgen Rohwer, *Der Mord an den Juden im Zweiten Weltkrieg* (Frankfurt: Fischer, ²1987), 164–173, 172.

50. Jäckel/Rohwer, *Mord*, 242.

51. Rosenfeld, "Politics of Uniqueness," 35.

52. Yehuda Bauer, "A Past That Will Not Go Away," Michael Berenbaum/Abraham Peck (eds.), *The Holocaust and History: The Unknown, the Disputed, and the Reexamined* (Bloomington: Indiana UP, 1998), 12–22, 16; see also Yehuda Bauer, *A History of the Holocaust* (Danbury: Watts, 1982), 332.

53. Saul Friedlander, "The 'Final Solution': On the Unease in Historical Interpretation," Friedlander, *Memory, History, and the Extermination of the Jews of Europe* (Blomington: Indiana UP, 1993), 102–116, 113; see also Saul Friedlander, "Some Aspects of the Historical Significance of the Holocaust," *The Jerusalem Quaterly* 1,1 (1976), 36–59.

54. Steven Aschheim, "On Saul Friedlander," *History and Memory* 9/1+2 (1997), 11–46, 11.

55. Hans Mommsen, "Realisierung des Utopischen," 184; Mommsen, "Der Weg zum Völkermord an den europäischen Juden," Bernd Faulenbach/Helmut Schütte (eds.), *Deutschland, Israel und der Holocaust: Zur Gegenwartsbedeutung der Vergangenheit* (Essen: Klartext, 1998), 19–30, 19; Eberhard Jäckel, "Die Entschlussbildung als historisches Problem," Jäckel/Rohwer, *Mord an den Juden*, 9–17, 9; Jäckel, "The Holocaust: Where we are, where we need to go," Berenbaum/Peck, *The Holocaust and History*, 23–29, 26.

56. Wolfgang Benz, *Der Holocaust* (München: Beck, 1995), 7; see also Wolfgang Benz, *Dimension des Völkermords: Die Zahl der jüdischen Opfer des Nationalsozialismus* (München: Oldenbourg, 1991), 8; and Peter Longerich, *Politik der Vernichtung: Eine Gesamtdarstellung der nationalsozialistischen Judenverfolgung* (München: Piper, 1998), 17.

57. Andreas Hillgruber, "Der geschichtliche Ort der Judenvernichtung," Jäckel/Rohwer, *Mord an den Juden*, 211–224, 223; see also Hillgruber *Zweierlei Untergang* . Martin Broszat embraced the idea of the Holocaust's metahistorical quality in Stuttgart (Jäckel/Rohwer, *Mord an den Juden*, 64) but repeatedly voiced doubts before and afterwards; see for example Broszat, "Genesis," 195; Broszat, "Plädoyer," 159 as well as Christian Meier, "Der Historiker Martin Broszat," Henke/Natoli, *Pathos der Nüchternheit*, 11–38, 27–30.

58. Rudolf Augstein et al., *Historikerstreit: Die Dokumentation der Kontroverse um die Einzigartigkeit der nationalsozialistischen Judenvernichtung* (München, 1987), 165. For an extensive contextualization of the Historians' Debate see Wulf Kansteiner, "Between Politics and Memory: The *Historikerstreit* and West German Historical Culture of the 1980s," Richard Golsan, ed., *Fascism's Return: Scandal, Revision, and Ideology since 1980* (Lincoln, 1998), 86–129; for a recent interpretation of the Historians' Debate from a psychoanalytical perspective see Dominick LaCapra, *Representing the Holocaust: History, Theory, Trauma* (Ithaca, 1994), 43–67; and LaCapra, *History and Memory after Auschwitz* (Ithaca, 1998), 43–72.

59. *Historikerstreit* (see note 54), 73.

60. Ibid., 71.

61. Nicolas Berg, "'Auschwitz' und die Geschichtswissenschaft: Überlegungen zu Kontroversen der letzten Jahre," Berg, Jess Jochimsen, Bernd Stiegler, ed., *Shoah: Formen der Erinnerung* (München: Fink, 1996), 31–52, 37–8.

62. See for example Eberhard Jäckel, "Die elende Praxis der Untersteller: Das Einmalige der nationalsozialistischen Verbrechen lässt sich nicht leugnen," Rudolf Augstein et al., *Historikerstreit: Die Dokumentation der Kontroverse um die Einzigartigkeit der nationalsozialistischen Judevernichtung* (München: Piper, 1987), 115–122; and Hans-Ulrich Wehler, *Entsorgung der deutschen Vergangenheit: Ein polemischer Essay zum 'Historikerstreit'* (München: Beck, 1988), 100.

63. Norbert Frei, "Farewell to the Era of Contemporaries: National Socialism and Its Historical Examination en route into History," *History and Memory* 9/1–2 (1997), 59–79, 69.

64. Not surprisingly this new social history was vigorously criticized by practitioners of the 'old' social history for its methodological naiveté and lack of theoretical foundations; see for example Franz Josef Brüggemeier/Jürgen Kocka (eds.), *Geschichte von unten— Geschichte von innen: Kontroversen um die Alltagsgeschichte* (Hagen: Fernuniversität, 1985).

65. Monika Richarz, *Jüdisches Leben in Deutschland: Zeugnisse zur Sozialgeschichte 1918–1945*, vol. 3 (Stuttgart:, 1982), 7, 40.

66. Dan Diner, "Zwischen Aporie und Apologie: Über Grenzen der Historisierbarkeit des Nationalsozialismus," Diner (ed.), *Ist der Nationalsozialismus Geschichte: Zur Historisierung und Historikerstreit* (Frankfurt: Fischer, 1987), 62–73, 73; see also Diner, "Perspektivenwahl und Geschichtserfahrung: Bedarf es einer besonderen Historik des Nationalsozialismus?," Walter Pehle (ed.), *Der historische Ort des Nationalsozialismus* (Frankfurt: Fischer, 1990), 94–113; and Diner, "Gedächnis und Methode: Über den Holocaust in der Geschichtsschreibung," Fritz-Bauer-Institut, *Auschwitz*, 11–22.

67. Walter Manoschek, *"Serbien ist judenfrei:" Militärische Besatzungspolitik und Judenvernichtung in Serbien 1941/42* (München: Oldenbourg, 1993); Dieter Pohl, *Von der "Judenpolitik" zum Massenmord: Der Distrikt Lublin des Generalgouvernements 1939–1944* (Frankfurt: Lang, 1993); Thomas Sandkühler, *"Endlösung in Galizien: Der Judenmord in Ostpolen und die Rettungsinitiativen von Berthold Beitz 1941–1944* (Bonn: Dietz, 1996); Christian Gerlach, *Krieg, Ernährung, Völkermord: Forschungen zur deutschen Vernichtungpolitik im Zweiten Weltkrieg* (Hamburg: Hamburger Edition, 1998).

68. Most recently, members of the institute mounted a controversial exhibit about the involvement of the Wehrmacht in ethnic cleansing and genocide which has been more successful in undermining the persistent myth of the chivalrous German army than 20 years of scholarship, Hamburger Institut für Sozialforschung (ed.), *Vernichtungskrieg: Verbrechen der Wehrmacht 1941–1944* (Hamburg: Hamburger Edition, 1995).

69. Wolfgang Schneider, *Vernichtungspolitik: Eine Debatte über den Zusammenhang von Sozialpolitik und Genozid im nationalsozialistischen Deutschland* (Hamburg: Junius, 1991); see also Norbert Frei, "Wie modern war der Nationalsozialismus?," *Geschichte und Gesellschaft* 19 (1993), 367–87; Axel Schmidt, "NS-Regime, Modernisierung und Moderne: Anmerkungen zur Hochkonjuktur einer andauernden Diskussion," *Tel Aviver Jahrbuch für deutsche Geschichte* 23 (1994), 3–22; and Michael Burleigh, *Ethics and Extermination: Reflections on Nazi Genocide* (Cambridge: Cambridge UP, 1997), 169–182.

70. Ulrich Herbert, *Best: Biographische Studien über Radikalismus, Weltanschauung und Vernunft 1903–1989* (Bonn: Dietz, 1996).

71. Herbert, "Vernichtungspolitik," 27.

72. Ibid., 65.

73. Ibid., 65.

74. Götz Aly, "Wider das Bewältigungs-Kleinklein," Loewy, *Grenzen des Verstehens*, 42–51, 43; see also Götz Aly et al., "Editorial," *Beiträge zur nationalsozialistischen Gesundheits- und Sozialpolitik* 5 (1987), 7–9, and Aly/Heim, *Vordenker der Vernichtung*, 11.

75. Götz Aly, *'Final Solution:' Nazi Population Policy and the Murder of the European Jews* (New York: Oxford UP, 1999), 245, 253.

76. Götz Aly, "The Planning Intelligentsia and the 'Final Solution,'" Michael Burleigh (ed.), *Confronting the Nazi Past: New Debates on Modern German History* (New York: St. Martin's, 1996), 140–153, 153; see also Aly/Heim, *Vordenker der Vernichtung*, 492.

77. Johannes Heil/Rainer Erb (eds.), *Geschichtswissenschaft und Öffentlichkeit: Der Streit um Daniel J. Goldhagen* (Frankfurt: Fischer, 1998).

78. See for example Ludolf Herbst, *Das nationalsozialistische Deutschland 1933–1945* (Frankfurt: Suhrkamp, 1996), especially 374 and 397.

79. The symbolic, generational change of the guard was theatrically enacted at the Historikertag of 1998 when the new generation did not directly attack their just retired teachers but instead exposed the collaborative behavior of the teachers' teachers during the Third Reich, Kansteiner, "Mandarins in the Public Sphere," 102–109.

80. Sofsky, "KZ-Forschung," 1154.

❧ 13 ❧

Uniqueness as Denial: The Politics of Genocide Scholarship

DAVID E. STANNARD

Forgetting the extermination is part of the extermination itself.
　　　　　　　　　　　　　　　　—*Jean Baudrillard*

I have tried to keep memory alive, I have tried to fight those who would forget. Because if we forget, we are guilty, we are accomplices.
　　　　　　　　　　　　　　　　—*Elie Wiesel*

I

$\mathcal{R}$ecently, the world marked the fiftieth anniversary of the end of World War II. Not a week passed in 1995 without the commemoration of some significant event that happened somewhere on the planet five decades earlier—from the fire-bombings of Dresden and Tokyo to the Yalta Conference and the death of Franklin Roosevelt, from the atomic bombings of Hiroshima and Nagasaki to the opening days of the Nuremberg trials—and much more.

But in the minds of many people the most hideous and stirring images of 1945 are those associated with the opening up of the Nazi confinement and extermination centers. With the evacuation of Auschwitz-Birkenau and the liberations of Mauthausen, Buchenwald, Dachau, and Bergen-Belsen, the world finally got to see up close what many Allied leaders had long denied or appeared indifferent to: the almost unimaginable magnitude and hideousness of the Nazi genocide campaign.[1]

No one will ever know with precision how many people died in the Second World War. The estimates of Chinese deaths, for example, have ranged from 2.5 million to 13.5 million. But, overall, the numbers total in the neighborhood of 50 million people—of whom more than 5 million were Jews. Put another way, by the time the war was over, almost two out of every three Jews in Europe (and one out of three worldwide) had died either in the concentration and death camps, in the ghettoes, or at the hands of mobile killing squads, the *Einsatzgruppen*.[2]

So huge was the carnage that even today it defies comprehension. But it was all too real. And in response to that reality—and to the possibility that something similar could conceivably happen again—many nations both within Europe and beyond have made it illegal to disseminate the hateful idea that the Germans' attempted destruction of European Jewry is an exaggeration or a myth.

Such malignant ideas have, of course, been propagated for many years by extremist groups and individuals. Some have argued that the whole story of the Holocaust is a fabrication. Others admit that it happened but claim that the number killed has been greatly exaggerated. Still more acknowledge that large numbers of deaths occurred but deny that they constitute genocide by claiming that the Jewish deaths, like all others at the time, were merely wartime casualties. Some claim that it was diseases such as typhus, along with the natural deprivations occasioned by war and forced relocation, that killed the Jews—that their deaths were real yet unintentional. Even the genocidal intent of Hitler has never been fully documented, claim others; and without hard proof of his intent the *Führer*, at least, cannot be implicated in whatever extermination effort may have occurred.

Recognizing that these assaults via the pages of history constitute forms of antisemitic cultural violence against Jews in the present, and portend serious danger for the future, the nations of the world have mounted a variety of defensive responses. Some European governments have forcibly prohibited anti-Zionists from speaking in public. A California court has awarded $100,000 to a survivor of Auschwitz for the pain and suffering he endured in an effort to prove untrue the claims of an antisemitic organization that the Nazis did not kill Jews in gas chambers. In Austria the publishers of magazines attempting to minimize Jewish deaths during the Holocaust have been indicted and convicted for their efforts. A professional antisemite who publicly denied the reality of the Holocaust has been sent to prison in Canada. German law states that "denial of the Holocaust" is punishable by up to five years in jail. And the United States has prohibited people who have expressed similar beliefs from entering the country. Other examples abound.[3]

One can imagine, then, the world's reaction if, in 1995, in a sudden eruption of outspoken antisemitism, the most prominent political figures in Germany, including leaders of the German parliament, had publicly ridiculed the Holocaust commemoration ceremonies. Or if they had denied that the Holocaust even happened and threatened to cut off government funds for a film project on World War II unless the word "genocide" was deleted from any references to the Nazis' treatment of the Jews. One can also imagine what the reaction might have been if, throughout that year of somber remembrance, Germany's most important and established newspapers and magazines—across the political spectrum from right to left—had repeatedly mocked the Jews and either denied that the Holocaust ever happened or, conversely, celebrated it as a beneficent event.

Now, clearly, although antisemitism remains far from stamped out in Germany, or anywhere else in the world, such events did not and are not happening in that country. Indeed, they would be illegal there. But they *did* happen in the United States only a few years earlier, when the native peoples of the Americas attempted to commemorate the ghastly destruction that had been visited upon them by European and, later, by white settler military invasions—invasions that brought in their wake wanton slaughter and massive population collapse on a scale and of a duration that dwarf anything that happened in Europe under Nazi rule.

It wasn't *German* politicians who insisted that the word "genocide" not be used in reference to the mass killing of Jews but members of the *U.S. Senate* who threatened to cut funds to the Smithsonian Institution if a film it was partially funding used that word, even in passing, to describe the destruction of the Western Hemisphere's indigenous peoples. And it wasn't German newspapers and magazines that either doubted the reality of the Nazi assault on European Jews or, conversely, admitted and celebrated that genocide. No, it was American publications that routinely denied, or even applauded, the genocide that was carried out against the New World's native inhabitants.

Consider just three examples that represent the "respectable" political spectrum. Scores of other writings—and radio and television presentations—could just as easily be called upon to make the same point.

First, Charles Krauthammer, one of *Time* magazine's regular political columnists, used an entire column to lambaste as "politically correct" opportunists anyone who dared express regret over the killing of millions of innocent people and the destruction of entire ancient cultures in the Americas. What happened in the wake of the European invasion was only what has always characterized human history, Krauthammer claimed, citing the Norman conquest of Britain as an apt (though actually absurd) comparison. "The real question is," he noted, "what eventually grew on this bloodied soil?" For, regardless of the level of destruction and mass murder that was visited upon the indigenous peoples of the Western Hemisphere, it was, in retrospect, entirely justified because in the process it wiped out such alleged barbarisms as the communally based Inca society (which really was only a "beehive," Krauthammer said) and gave the world "a culture of liberty that endowed the individual human being with dignity and sovereignty."[4]

Krauthammer, of course, is a conservative political pundit. But his approach to apologizing for mass murder was not limited to those on the right. Soon after, for example, historian and cold war liberal Arthur Schlesinger Jr. weighed in with much the same argument. Schlesinger, however, was not content to build his case on the purported shortcomings of the *ancient* indigenous societies of the

Americas. No, he gazed into his crystal ball and asserted, in *The Atlantic*, that without the European conquests and slaughter at least some New World societies *today* might be sufficiently unpleasant places to live so as to make eminently acceptable the centuries of genocide that were carried out against the native peoples of the entire Western Hemisphere.[5]

And in the person of Christopher Hitchens, writing in *The Nation*, the political left then sounded its voice. To Hitchens, anyone who refused to join him in celebrating with "great vim and gusto" the annihilation of the native peoples of the Americas was (in his words) self-hating, ridiculous, ignorant, and sinister. People who regard critically the genocide that was carried out in America's past, Hitchens continued, are simply reactionary, since such grossly inhuman atrocities "happen to be the way history is made." And thus "to complain about [them] is as empty as complaint about climatic, geological or tectonic shift." Moreover, he added, such violence is worth glorifying since it more often than not has been for the long-term betterment of humankind—as in the United States today, where the extermination of the Native Americans—the American Indians—has brought about "a nearly boundless epoch of opportunity and innovation."[6]

One possible exception Hitchens allowed to his vulgar social Darwinism, with its quasi-Hitlerian view of the proper role of power in history, was the Euro-American enslavement of tens of millions of Africans.[7] But even then, Hitchens contended, those centuries of massive brutality only "*probably* left Africa worse off than they found it." Clearly, however—as with Krauthammer's and Schlesinger's moral codes—if it could be shown to Hitchens's personal satisfaction that Africa was in fact "better off" following the enslavement and simultaneous mass killing of 40 million to 60 million of its people, he would celebrate the abominations of the slave trade with the same vim and gusto that he did the genocide against the native peoples of the Americas.[8]

These are, of course, precisely the same sort of retrospective justifications for genocide that would have been offered by the descendants of Nazi storm troopers and SS doctors had the Third Reich ultimately had its way: that is, however distasteful the means, the extermination of the Jews was thoroughly warranted given the beneficial ends that were accomplished. In this light it is worth considering again what the reaction would be in Europe and elsewhere if the equivalent of the *actual* views of Krauthammer and Schlesinger and Hitchens were expressed today by the respectable press in Germany—but with Jews, not Native Americans, as the people whose historical near-extermination was being celebrated. And there is no doubt whatsoever that if that were to happen, alarm bells announcing a frightening and unparalleled postwar resurgence of German neo-Nazism would, quite justifiably, be going off immediately throughout the world.

Of course, nothing of the sort happened when those three writers—and the countless others for whom they here stand as establishment representatives—proclaimed their delight in the historical destruction of millions of *non-*

Europeans. And therein lies an apparent paradox: How can we account for this extraordinary difference?

Several answers to this question come immediately to mind, the most obvious of which is the deeply embedded Euro-American ideology of white supremacy. White supremacy of the same everyday sort that some years earlier led prominent British commentators to deride as a topic of inconsequence a detailed published account of genocide against the Brazilian Indians—who have been liquidated into near nonexistence, from a population of at least 2.5 million to barely 100,000 at last count. Such human carnage is unimportant and not worthy of serious attention, one critic put it, because "the tragedy of a civilisation's demise is commensurate with the value of what it achieved" and "the Brazilian Indians created nothing durable in building or in art." Not only unimportant, added another writer, but genocide in this instance was wholly justified, because "the money garnered from the lands, and the unwilling labours, of several million bewildered Indians" had made possible the creation of so much fine European culture—including even an admittedly "modest" Portuguese opera he said he recently had "greatly enjoyed."[9] Presumably, men of such refinement (like their American counterparts) would reject the appropriateness of this same criterion in evaluating the justness of enslaving and killing millions of *white* people—say, those Jews who may not have created much that was durable in the way of building or art but who certainly brought benefit and comfort to the citizens of Nazi Germany with their slave labor and consequent mass deaths in the I. G. Farben chemical plant at Auschwitz or in the coal mines located nearby.

For those who might find such overt racial distinctions distasteful and preferably avoided, however, a more "reasonable" explanation exists for the grossly differential responses that are so commonplace regarding the American and the Nazi holocausts. This explanation simply denies that there is any comparability between the Nazi violence against the Jews and the Euro-American violence against the Western Hemisphere's native peoples. In fact, in most quarters it is held as beyond dispute that the attempted destruction of the Jews in Nazi-controlled Europe was unique, unprecedented, and categorically incommensurable—not only with the torment endured by the indigenous peoples of North and South America, but also with the sufferings of any people at any time in any place during the entire history of humanity.

This rarely examined, taken-for-granted assumption on the part of so many did not appear out of thin air. On the contrary, it is the hegemonic product of many years of strenuous intellectual labor by a handful of Jewish scholars and writers who have dedicated much if not all of their professional lives to the advancement of this exclusivist idea. And it is the work of these people that I shall be addressing in most of the rest of this chapter. For not only is the essence of their argument demonstrably erroneous, the larger thesis that it fraudulently advances is fundamentally racist and violence-provoking. At the same time, moreover, it willingly provides a screen behind which opportunistic governments today attempt to conceal their own past and ongoing genocidal actions.

Before turning to the specific arguments of the Jewish uniqueness proponents, however, something must be said about the ad hominem impugning of motives that almost inevitably is encountered by those who choose to dispute the so-called uniqueness assertion. Indeed, anyone who even raises questions about the alleged uniqueness of the Jewish experience in the Holocaust is, by virtue of that fact alone, immediately in danger of being labeled an antisemite. For example, when President Jimmy Carter once gave a speech commemorating the victims of the Holocaust he mentioned the fact that others besides Jews had died. Because Carter did not limit his commemorative statement to the deaths of Jews, Yehuda Bauer, a professor of Jewish history at Jerusalem's Hebrew University, accused him of attempting to "de-Judaize" the Holocaust, an action, Bauer wrote, that was nothing less than "an unconscious reflection of antisemitic attitudes."[10] To Bauer, the simple acknowledgment of the suffering of others constituted Jew-hating.

But on this matter, Deborah Lipstadt, professor of modern Jewish and Holocaust studies at Emory University and the author of what probably is the most popular book on this topic, holds a place of particular distinction. Lipstadt regards as her enemy anyone who expresses doubt about the utter singularity in all of human history of Jewish suffering at the hands of the Nazis, an enemy situated intellectually and ideologically at one place or another along a posited antisemitic continuum stretching from those she calls Holocaust "deniers" to those she labels Holocaust "relativists." In Professor Lipstadt's considered opinion, a "denier" is someone who flatly rejects the very historical existence of the Holocaust, whereas a "relativist" is someone who recognizes that the mass killing of Jews in Hitler's Germany occurred and was a hideous act of genocide yet who also considers the Holocaust to be, in her words, one among "an array of other conflagrations in which innocents were massacred."[11]

In other words, you are to be considered in the same general category—as an antisemite, as a creator of "immoral equivalencies," as someone trying "to help the Germans embrace their past"—if you are either a neo-Nazi or a comparative historian. For, to Lipstadt, even someone who has no doubt regarding the ghastly horrors of Jewish suffering and death under Hitler—but who has the temerity to dissent from her insistence regarding the unquestionable uniqueness of the Jewish experience—is, in her phrase, merely a *not yet* denier. And "not yet" denial, she writes, is "the equivalent of David Duke without his robes." In short, if you disagree with Deborah Lipstadt that the Jewish suffering in the Holocaust was unique, you are, by definition—and like David Duke—a crypto-Nazi.[12] Needless to say, such intellectual thuggery usually has its intended chilling effect on further discussion.

Mention should also be made of another preliminary difficulty encountered by anyone who takes on the argument regarding the uniqueness of Jews as victims of suffering: locating the actual components of the uniqueness argument itself.

Not only do different advocates of the uniqueness thesis disagree among themselves over the bases for their belief, but the general trend of the argument has shifted over the years and likely will continue transforming itself as new criticisms of specific assertions (such as those contained in this chapter) are raised. This is because, rather than proceeding along a path of open inquiry, virtually all proponents of the uniqueness argument have for years sought out and put forward only those data that appeared to support their own *preexisting* conviction regarding the uniqueness of Jewish suffering—a conviction that in large measure was and is itself an outgrowth not of true scholarly analysis but of straightforward religious dogma. I shall return to this later. But first let us take a look at the arguments themselves; then we can consider the likely motives for advancing them, along with the damage to others that they do.

II

For years it was assumed in many quarters that the sheer size and scope of the mass killing of Jews in Nazi-controlled Europe were unprecedented, and that alone was sufficient to mark Jewish suffering during the Holocaust as unique. As time passed, however, an accumulating body of research began to show that this assumption was false. For example, within the Holocaust itself the Romani people—Gypsies—suffered the same inhuman death camp conditions and probably lost a proportion of their prewar European population equal to that taken from the Jews, a conclusion that now has been accepted by many Jewish students of the Holocaust, including Simon Wiesenthal.[13]

In addition, in just two years between 1915 and 1917, the Armenian population of the Ottoman empire suffered near-obliteration from a Turkish genocide campaign, only two decades after suffering an earlier pogrom in which at least 100,000 Armenians, and probably closer to 200,000, were killed. No one knows for certain how many Armenians died in the second and far larger of these storms of mass killing, but estimates of the pre-genocide population of Armenians have ranged from 1.5 million to 3 million; the actual number of those killed has been put by some writers at under 1 million and by others as high as 2 million, with most serious scholars content to say that at least 1 million and probably closer to 1.5 million people died.[14]

Whether those numbers constitute a proportionate death rate equal to that of Jews in the Holocaust will remain an open question until better statistics become available, but there is little doubt that at least half of the pre-genocide Armenian population was destroyed, and it may have been substantially higher than that. The estimate in one recent analysis—between 50 and 70 percent—is roughly commensurate with the 60 to 65 percent rate of destruction suffered by European Jews during World War II. Moreover, contrary to the assertions of Jewish uniqueness advocates such as Lucy Dawidowicz who claim that "no other people anywhere lost the main body of its population and the fountainhead of its cultural resources," in fact the very hearts of both the Armenian and Gypsy populations were cut out by the genocides waged against them. In the process, the Armenians were also ruthlessly uprooted from 3,000 years of deep cultural relationship with the traditional land of their ancestors. And even today Gypsies remain the targets of ever-mounting racist discrimination wherever they live—including Germany, which recently deported 20,000 Gypsies to Romania, where they predictably have been met with terrorism, violence, and murder.[15]

Yet even if the field of genocide studies must necessarily remain one in which many questions will always go unanswered, there is no question at all regarding at least one matter: that the pre-twentieth-century destruction of native peoples at the hands of European invaders—from Australia to the Americas and elsewhere—frequently resulted in population collapses proportionately much higher than those experienced by any group, including Jews, during the Holocaust. Moreover, not only were *proportionate* losses routinely much higher among indigenous peoples (up to 100 percent in many cases—that is, total extermination—and between 90 and 95 percent generally), but the *gross number* of people destroyed by what I have elsewhere called the "American Holocaust" exceeded by many times over the number of Jews who died under the Nazis and, indeed, was even greater than the number of people of all nations killed worldwide during the entire duration of the Second World War. Even in specific locales—central Mexico and the Andes in particular—the deaths of culturally and ethnically distinct indigenous people in the wake of the European invasions vastly exceeded the mortality figures for Jews during the Holocaust, both in terms of proportional population loss and overall numbers killed.[16]

Most of these facts had become well known by the early 1980s, and thus quantitative criteria quietly began disappearing from the writings of proponents of the Jewish uniqueness argument. To be sure, they did not go away easily. Although acknowledging that, in general, mortality rates or counts could no longer be used as sufficient measures unto themselves to establish uniqueness, some proponents of the uniqueness argument continued to resort to quantification, but only selectively, when it worked to their advantage in establishing differences between the sufferings of Jews and others. Thus, for instance, Lucy Dawidowicz, in *The Holocaust and the Historians,* used the numerical difference between the deaths of Jews in the Holocaust and the deaths of Japanese civilians following the atomic bombings of Hiroshima and Nagasaki as one way of dismissing the possibility that the nuclear destruction of hundreds of thousands of Japanese lives might be termed genocide.[17] When the subjects of comparison are different, however— that is, when discussing other populations that experienced a numerically and proportionately larger loss of life, such as certain huge communities in sixteenth-century Mesoamerica—Jewish uniqueness proponents, of course, now reject any use of quantitative criteria.[18]

Other writers have used the absence of *complete* extermination among a comparison group, such as Armenians, Gypsies, and Native Americans, as a way of denying that genocide was actually perpetrated against the respective non-Jewish group. Michael R. Marrus, for example, distinguishes the suffering of the Armenians from that of the Jews as arising in part from the fact that "however extensive the murder of Armenians . . . killing was far from universal." And, he notes, "the fact is that many thousands of Armenians survived within Turkey during the period of the massacres." Yehuda Bauer concurs, noting that neither the Armenian nor the Gypsy genocides were comparable to the experience of the Jews because "in neither case was the destruction complete." Adds Steven T. Katz: though the mass killing of New England's Pequot Indians was no doubt lamentable (and it is true, he concedes, that their government-sanctioned white killers did act "with unnecessary severity"), at most the destruction of the Pequots can be described as "*cultural* genocide" since, after all, "the number killed probably totaled less than half the entire tribe."[19]

This, to say the least, is a peculiar bit of historical reasoning—since Europe's Jews themselves were far from totally exterminated by the Nazis, with at least 80,000 Jews surviving in Germany alone; since the worldwide population of Jews was "only" reduced by about one-third during the Holocaust; and since the deaths of Jews in Germany, Romania, Hungary, and the USSR, though totaling about 1.3 million people, represented less than 30 percent of those countries' prewar Jewish populations.[20] But it does at least demonstrate the eagerness of some uniqueness advocates to make their case at any cost to logic or probity. In fact, one prominent writer on this topic occasionally defies all connection with reality by proclaiming that "total physical annihilation . . . is what *happened* to the Jews," contending, in a breathtaking somersault of deduction, that the complete extermination of the Jews by the Nazis is a historical *fact*—the survival of one-third of Europe's Jewish population notwithstanding—because those Jews who survived did so despite the "desire" of the Nazis to kill them.[21]

With the exception of this sort of inanity, however, even the most determined uniqueness proponent is today forced to admit, as Steven Katz has acknowledged, that "what might be thought the most acutely self-evident, the most blatantly incontestable grounds for establishing the novelty of Hitler's Judeocide"—that is, the proportions of population destroyed and/or the total numbers killed—do not in fact support the case for Jewish uniqueness.[22]

If the quantitative criterion does not establish the uniqueness of Jewish suffering, particularly when compared with the far more destructive experiences of numerous indigenous peoples, some have then argued that it was the *way* in which the Jews died—that is, the relative speed with which the killing was accomplished—that makes their experience unique. This contention holds that whereas Jews were slaughtered in death camps by the most modern and expeditious methods of mass destruction available at the time, previous and subsequent victims of genocide have been destroyed by far cruder and more prolonged means. The Holocaust, it is said by proponents of this standard, "was unique in quantitive terms" because it destroyed more innocent people "per unit of time" than has any other mass killing event. Even uniqueness advocate Katz now rejects this claim, however, noting the counterexamples of the Soviets under Stalin and other twentieth-century genocides in such places as Bangladesh and Cambodia. More recently, between April and July 1994, as many as 850,000 Tutsi people were slaughtered in Rwanda, primarily with handguns and machetes. This is a rate of about 10,000 per day, a figure equal to the maximum ever achieved during a single 24-hour period at Auschwitz.[23] Surely, though, if speed is to be a criterion, no one has come close to matching the achievements of the United States in killing at least 100,000 people in a matter of hours with the firebombing of Tokyo and the subsequent vaporizing, in virtually a single nuclear instant, of more than 200,000 innocent Japanese civilians in Hiroshima and Nagasaki.

Moreover, beyond the clear factual incorrectness of the assertion that no people have ever been killed in large numbers as efficiently or as quickly as were the Jews under Nazi rule, there is the question of whether the claim itself—correct or not—is especially meaningful or noteworthy. Why, after all, is a genocide campaign that lasts for, say, three years (the approximate duration of the Final Solution) more momentous than one that proceeds at a slower pace but lasts twenty or fifty or a hundred times as long? Might it not just as cogently be argued that the very opposite is the case—that the quantitatively lower level (in the short term) but far more enduring suffering and extinction fear of many generations intrinsically is worse for its victims than the more acute but far briefer agony experienced by only a single historical generation? Who is to say? Who, really, has the *right* to say? Indeed, as Phillip Lopate observes, the very making of the so-called efficiency claim reveals more than anything else its authors' own "narcissistic preoccupations" with Western technology. As he puts it:

> Does it really matter so much if millions are gassed according to Eichmann's timetables, rather than slowly, crudely starved to death as in Stalin's regime, or marched around by ragged teenage Khmer Rouge soldiers and then beheaded or clubbed? Does the family mourning the loved one hacked to pieces by a spontaneous mob of Indonesian vigilantes care that much about abuses of science and technology? Does neatness count, finally, so damn much?[24]

In addition to the claim for distinctiveness based on the *rate* of extermination, uniqueness advocates often point to differences in the *means* of destruction. This is a nuance that appears to take on particular force when Jewish deaths during the Holocaust are contrasted with the historical eradication of the world's indigenous peoples. For native societies fell victim, so the customary argument goes, largely to unintentionally introduced diseases that were simply a by-product of Western imperialism. Steven Katz goes even further than this, contending that not only was the mass destruction of the Western Hemisphere's native peoples by disease "an *unintended* tragedy," it actually, he claims, was "a tragedy that occurred despite the sincere and indisputable desire of the Europeans to keep the Indian population alive." Thus, not only are the Jewish and Native American experiences not comparable, but the alleged good-heartedness of the European conquerors eliminates altogether the charge that the destruction of the aboriginal peoples of the Americas and elsewhere constituted genocide.[25]

Actually, though, the purported means-of-extermination distinction between the deaths of Jews in Nazi-controlled Europe and the deaths of indigenous peoples in their European-invaded homelands is nonsense. Despite frequent undocumented assertions that disease was responsible for the great majority of indigenous deaths in the Americas, there does not exist a single scholarly work that even pretends to demonstrate this claim on the basis of solid evidence. And that is because there *is* no such evidence, anywhere. The supposed truism that more native people died from disease than from direct face-to-face killing or from gross mistreatment or other concomitant derivatives of that brutality such as starvation, exposure, exhaustion, or despair is nothing more than a scholarly article of faith. It seems quite possible that deaths from disease *may* have exceeded those deriving from any other *single* cause, but the plain fact of the matter is that we have no way of ever determining individual degrees of responsibility for the many and various and overlapping factors that were involved in the native peoples' destruction. Because the devastation was so enormous and so complete, few technical demographic details of this sort exist in the historical record. Indeed, if anything is certain regarding this matter it is that most of those tens of millions of deaths— from the islands of the Caribbean to the high country of Mexico, then north and south throughout two huge continents—were in fact caused by intertwined and interacting *combinations* of lethal agents, combinations that took different forms in different locales.

Throughout the Americas, military invasions resulted in the direct massacres of huge numbers of people and the unleashing of bacteria and viruses for which the natives had little or no acquired resistance. In most of what is now the United States—excluding California and the Southwest—the dynamic interaction between military and microbial destruction (in different combinations from time to time and from place to place) was sufficient to lay waste almost an entire continent's indigenous inhabitants. In California and the Southwest, however, as in the Caribbean and Meso- and South America (where at least 90 percent of the Western Hemisphere's population lived) another deadly factor was added. There, survivors of the mass murders and the epidemics commonly were herded together into densely populated *congregaciós* where they either starved in squalor or were worked to death as hired-out slaves in labor camps, in mines, or on plantations—all of which, of course, were hothouses of pestilence and fatal violence. It was under these constantly *interacting* conditions of direct slaughter, disease, and forced labor—combined, as in the Nazi concentration and death camps, with

the consequential reduction of live birth rates to far below replacement levels—
that the indigenous populations of what are now Chile and Peru, for example,
were reduced collectively by 95 percent or more, from somewhere between 9 million and 14 million people to barely 500,000, before the holocaust subsided.[26]

But perhaps the best way to recognize the bankruptcy of this component of the
Jewish uniqueness claim—the outright denial that genocide is an appropriate
term to describe what happened to the indigenous people of the Western
Hemisphere because of the *way* in which the devastation occurred—is simply to
imagine how people like Yehuda Bauer and Steven Katz and Deborah Lipstadt
and other advocates of this position would describe the centuries-long experience
of the Americas' native peoples if that experience instead had been endured by
Jews. Consider, then, the following highly compressed but fully documented historical chronicle, drawn from my book, *American Holocaust*, in which the only departure from reality is the substitution of "Jews" for "native peoples."[27]

At the end of the fifteenth century a huge island in the Caribbean, twice the size of
Switzerland and inhabited by at least a million and perhaps as many as 8 million
Jews, was invaded by Spanish military men in search of gold. The Spaniards also were
carriers of deadly diseases that the Jews had never encountered before, diseases that
killed them en masse. But in their hunt for gold the Spaniards also rounded up and,
under force of arms, enslaved whole communities of Jews, beating and torturing and
working them in mines and on plantations with barely enough food to survive until
they dropped. And all the while that this was happening (and the Jewish population
was plummeting toward zero), the Spaniards' own documents today reveal that their
soldiers took great delight in skewering Jewish babies on yard-long rapiers; of hack-
ing off the breasts of Jewish women just for fun; of burning to death entire towns full
of Jews. And more.

After the total population of Jews on this immense island—plus the hundreds of
thousands of Jews on neighboring islands in the Caribbean—had finally been exterminated in a matter of decades, the horrifying violence then spread to an entire continent. And now still more Jews, numbering by this time in the *tens* of millions, died
from the Spanish onslaught. Scores of Jewish cities were reduced to rubble. Synagogues
beyond counting were crushed. All the religious books that could be found were
burned. Jewish women and children were enslaved and branded on the face with their
owners' initials. Armies of Jews were force-marched to labor in mountain-top silver
mines where they could consider themselves lucky to survive for six months—while
other whole communities of Jews were driven to toil on plantations in tropical forests
where the life expectancy was even shorter. In central Mexico more than 20 million
Jews died before it was over. And there, as elsewhere in Meso- and South America, those
huge numbers of deaths from violence, disease, starvation, and slave labor represented
the destruction of fully 90 to 95 percent of the Jewish population.

Everywhere, entire Jewish towns were obliterated—their residents hacked to death
or burned at the stake—because their leaders did not renounce their religious traditions quickly enough. And all of this was justified by the common and often expressed belief of the murderers—including the wisest and holiest men in the Spanish

realm—that the Jews were semi-human beasts created by God to be the slaves of Christians; that it was the divine right of Christians to hunt Jews down as animals of the forest for no other purpose than to feed their carcasses to dogs.

But the bloodbath didn't stop there—and didn't end with the Spanish. Rather, it was taken up by other Europeans, and with particular delight by the British. Jews were also the original inhabitants of North America in this scenario, and English adventurers and settlers, having decided that Jews were too beast-like to deserve the land that they had cultivated for centuries, launched full-scale extermination campaigns against them—campaigns that, over and over and over again, resulted in the deaths of 19 out of every 20 Jews who happened to live where the English wanted to live. And as the English hunted down and shot and chopped and burned to death every Jew who could not escape into the forest, pious Christian ministers celebrated what they believed to be the imminent extinction of the Jewish people, routinely exclaiming (to quote just one of the most esteemed such leaders) that "it was a fearful sight to see the Jews thus frying in the fire and the streams of blood quenching the same, and horrible was the stink and scent thereof; but the victory seemed a sweet sacrifice, and we gave the praise thereof to God, who had wrought so wonderfully for us."

And, again, it didn't stop there. For years and decades and centuries, Jews were stalked and killed like the animals that the British—and later the Americans—said they were. All the residents of certain Jewish communities, each one numbering in the thousands of people, were herded together and forced to embark on refugee death marches that commonly killed half of their victims—leading at least one hardened veteran and death march overseer to remark that "I fought through the Civil War and have seen men shot to pieces and slaughtered by the thousands, but the Jewish removal was the cruelest work I ever knew." And even after the death marches were over typically another 50 percent and more of such violently dispossessed Jews perished in the concentration camps that were the death marches' established destination points.

During the nineteenth century, meanwhile, the governors of individual states, such as Colorado and California, officially urged the citizenry to exterminate all the Jews they could find, using state funds to finance the actions of mobile killing squads; Jewish children could be—and routinely were—legally taken from their parents and enslaved; and Jews had no legal standing in court to protest against any horrors that were perpetrated against them or against their children. It was during this time as well that a man who was to become President of the United States proudly boasted of personally killing Jews and mutilating their bodies, of supervising the slicing off of Jewish noses and the stripping of flesh from Jewish bodies to be tanned and turned into bridle reins. He also gave specific instructions to kill all the Jewish babies that could be found, pointing out that true extermination could not be accomplished unless all the children as well as the adults were butchered.

Another President of the United States during this era referred to Jews as "beasts of prey," and ordered his military commanders to attack and "lay waste" all the Jewish communities they could find, demanding "that they not be merely overrun but destroyed." Still a third President of the United States instructed his Secretary of War that any Jews who resisted the seizure of their land should be met with the "hatchet" and "exterminated" if necessary. And as time wore on other Presidents over the course of an entire century expressed similar genocidal attitudes, and ordered similar genocidal actions against the Jews.

Even a twentieth-century American President and winner of a Nobel Peace Prize joined the fray, describing one of the many government-launched mass murders of Jewish men and women and children that had occurred during his lifetime (this particular massacre including the clubbing and shooting to death of infants and the proud public display of mutilated Jewish male and female genitals) as a "righteous and beneficial deed," because, after all, as he laughingly put it, "I don't go so far as to think that the *only* good Jews are dead Jews, but I believe nine out of ten are, and I shouldn't like to inquire too closely into the case of the tenth."

When all the dust had settled, throughout the entire North American continent approximately 95 percent of the original Jewish population had been exterminated—from the combined violence, torture, removal, disease, exhaustion, exposure, and other factors that snatched their lives away. The remaining 5 percent were then forcibly driven away to live in abject poverty and squalor on segregated encampments set up by the American government in the most inhospitable environments that could be found.

This description, of course, is far too benign, as it leaves out volumes of ghastly but true accounts. Still, however truncated and thus necessarily understated it is, there can be little doubt that the likes of Yehuda Bauer and Steven Katz and Deborah Lipstadt would describe as "genocide" the account I have just rendered if the tens of millions of victims had indeed been Jews and not the native peoples of the Americas. There also is no doubt that if this were a chronicle of Jewish suffering and a non-Jew referred to it the way Katz has in fact summarized the experience of its *actual* victims—as "an *unintended* tragedy, a tragedy that occurred despite the sincere and indisputable desire of the Europeans to keep the [Jewish] population alive"—he would quite properly be pilloried as a Holocaust denier and a blatant antisemite.

But in fact we needn't have gone to all this trouble. For even if it were accurate to say with assurance that the massive destruction of the native people in the Americas was in large measure the immediate consequence of disease, starvation, and related causes—that is, what the U.S. government now calls the "collateral damage" that follows in the wake of direct violence—*precisely the same thing is true regarding Jewish deaths during the Holocaust.* According to the most authoritative tabulation that exists, the work of Raul Hilberg, Jewish deaths outside of the concentration and death camps during the Holocaust totaled just over 2 million. Of that number, nearly half did not die from direct Nazi violence but rather from what Hilberg describes as "ghettoization and general privation," a category that of course includes very high levels of death from disease. Moreover, within the camps themselves, where more than 3 million Jews died, the mortality rate from disease was even greater. As one recent account, published by the United States Holocaust Memorial Museum and focused on Auschwitz-Birkenau, notes:

Epidemics of lice, typhus, dysentery, and common phlegmon, particularly in Birkenau, resulted in skyrocketing mortality rates in the period from July 1942 [when, under pressure of the Final Solution, the population of the camps had begun to climb sharply] to March 1943; according to available data, they ranged from 19 percent to 25 percent per month. The decline that followed can be attributed to some improvement in the camp conditions in general and in hospitals in particular. In May 1943, the monthly mortality rate dropped to 5.2 percent, and in the main Auschwitz camp it dropped even more.[28]

A death rate of between 19 percent and 25 percent per month, of course, translates into a projected annual mortality rate of between 228 percent and 300 percent. That means the equivalent of the entire camp population was at this time dying from *disease* every four to five months. Moreover, without minimizing the deaths by gassing and other direct means of hundreds of thousands of others, even the subsequent drop to a maximum disease-caused death rate of 5.2 percent per month at Birkenau, once medical conditions improved, still represented a projected mortality rate solely attributable to illness of more than 60 percent per year.

And what was true of Auschwitz was more than equally true in other camps. In Buchenwald, for instance, of the nearly 239,000 persons who were incarcerated there between 1937 and 1945, more than 55,000 (about 23 percent) died in the camp. However, more than 33,000 of those deaths—or approximately 60 percent—were hospital-registered mortalities resulting from disease and related causes.[29] Thus, during the entire time of Buchenwald's existence as a concentration camp, the single greatest cause of death was illness and malnutrition. (These two seemingly separable factors constitute a singular "cause" since, in situations of high disease prevalence and severe nutritional deficiency, it generally is impossible to determine retrospectively which of the two was the principal agent of death.)[30]

Indeed, so extreme were the conditions of illness and deprivation in the camps that more than *half* the nearly 137,000 prisoners brought into *all* the German concentration camps between June and November of 1942 quickly died of disease and/or starvation. Even the SS was alarmed at this degree of mortality, causing the SS Main Economic and Administrative Office to issue a directive to all camp doctors, ordering them to better supervise the care and feeding of prisoners and to "work with all means at their disposal to substantially lower mortality figures," since, "with such a high death toll, the number of prisoners can never be brought to the level that the Reich SS leader has ordered."[31]

A so-called historical revisionist could, of course, use this document (and others like it) to contend, as Katz has done with regard to the destruction of the indigenous peoples of the Americas, that mass death in the Nazi concentration camps was "an unintended tragedy" and a "tragedy that occurred despite the sincere and indisputable desire of the [Nazis] to keep the [concentration camp] population alive." That, of course, would be an assessment equal to Katz's in historical falsity and moral baseness. But all these documents, and many others, do provide powerful support to the assertion of Princeton historian Arno J. Mayer that "from 1942 to 1945, certainly at Auschwitz, but probably overall, more Jews were killed by so-called 'natural' causes than by 'unnatural' ones"—"natural" causes being "sickness, disease, undernourishment, [and] hyperexploitation," as opposed to "unnatural" causes such as "shooting, hanging, phenol injection, or gassing."[32]

There is little doubt that Mayer is correct here regarding Auschwitz, and in his overall claim as well. Even Deborah Lipstadt admits that such "is the case in every war." And on this, at least, she is largely correct. The Japanese ordeal in World War II, during which fully two-thirds of Japan's *military* deaths were the result of illness and starvation, was far from atypical. Indeed, throughout the world today— from Sudan to Angola to Rwanda to Cambodia to Bosnia to Somalia and beyond—literally tens of millions of people who are trapped in the midst of wilfully genocidal warfare are at risk or have died from starvation or disease that is a secondary consequence of the outright killing, a number that often far exceeds the death toll from direct violence itself.[33]

According to the most minimal quantitative translation of Mayer's highly credible claim, then, of the 3.1 million Jewish deaths that took place in the concentration and death camps, at least 1.6 million resulted from "natural" causes, including disease, added to the more than 800,000 Jews outside the camps who died of Hilberg's "ghettoization and general privation." That makes a total of more than 2.4 million of the 5.1 million Jewish deaths during the Holocaust, at a bare minimum, directly attributable to the same so-called natural phenomena—disease, exploitation, malnutrition, and the like—that also were the immediate cause of death for many of the Americas' indigenous people.

Katz and others find that if a significant number of native deaths in the Americas were the result of such causes, then the destruction of the Western Hemisphere's indigenous people was "unintentional" and non-genocidal. The same conclusion should then hold regarding the destruction of Jews during the Holocaust. But does it? Of course not. And why not? The obvious reply is that the so-called natural causes responsible for the deaths of those two and a half million innocent Jews occurred as a corollary to other, more direct, killings during the period that the Jewish people of Europe were either under assault outside the camps or were trapped helplessly within them. But, again, the same thing is true regarding the conditions under which most of the indigenous inhabitants of the Americas contracted the diseases or succumbed to the general privations that led to so many of *their* premature deaths during four long centuries of conquest.

What, then, do Katz and his supporters and like-thinkers propose to *do* about those millions of Jews, fully half the Jewish victims of the Holocaust, who died from disease and destitution? Deny that their deaths were an intrinsic part of the genocide? To do so would be a monumental act of immorality; yet that is precisely the judgment they render when the victims are *not* Jews. As I have written elsewhere, on this point Holocaust scholar Michael R. Marrus has said it as well as anyone:

It is clearly wrong to separate from the essence of the Holocaust those Jews who never survived long enough to reach the camps, or who were shot down by the Einsatzgruppen in the Soviet Union, or who starved in the ghettos of eastern Europe, or who were wasted by disease because of malnutrition and neglect, or who were killed in reprisal in the west, or who died in any of the countless other, terrible ways—no less a part of the Holocaust because their final agonies do not meet some artificial standard of uniqueness.[34]

Of course, Marrus is correct: Jews who died during the Holocaust of disease and malnutrition and neglect or in "countless other, terrible ways" would not have been exposed to those deadly forces if not for the direct violence that was all about them—thus certainly making their deaths part of the genocide that is called the Holocaust. But so too with the native people of the Americas, who died in precisely those same ways, but in vastly higher numbers and proportions, directly as a result of the larger genocidal conditions created by violent European invasions of their communities.

Much has often been made, for example—and rightly so—of the ghastly physical condition of most concentration camp survivors at the moment that they were liberated. In Buchenwald it has been estimated that in the time immediately leading up to liberation most prisoners existed on a greatly restricted diet providing only 600–700 calories per day.[35] That is fewer calories than are provided by a pint of milk and a cup of dry cornmeal and is barely one-quarter the caloric requirement needed simply to maintain the weight of an average adult.

In contrast, much less has ever been made of the fact that during the late eighteenth and early nineteenth centuries (to select just one example among many) the Spanish military in California and the Southwest used the same system of *congregación/reducción* that had been tested with such lethal success in the Andes to imprison tens of thousands of native people in concentration camps euphemistically called missions, forcing inmates to produce the foodstuffs and other goods necessary to sustain the garrisons. In some of these prison workhouses, such as those at San Antonio and San Miguel, the indigenous inmates *routinely*—over the course of half a century—struggled to survive on rations of approximately 640–780 calories per day, roughly the same minuscule caloric intake as that endured by the Buchenwald prisoners on the eve of liberation. Moreover, on average, Indians in all missions in the region lived and worked at slave labor year in and year out, generation after generation, on hardly more than 1,000 calories per day.[36]

Under the prevailing labor requirements these were literally starvation diets, as is apparent in the records of such missions as San Francisco, Santa Clara, and San Jose, where mortality rates regularly exceeded birthrates by ratios of four- and five-to-one. These are life-table statistics that guarantee extremely rapid and wholesale extermination. Nor did the mere fact of being born matter much in these internment camps, since conditions were so abysmal—with individual living space measuring about seven feet by two feet, or about the size of a coffin—

that projected life expectancy at birth could *average* from only eight months to two years—year after year after year.[37]

It should come as no surprise to discover, in light of these circumstances, that by the time the mission camps were shut down starvation, disease, torture, and outright murder had killed a proportion of the native inmate population more than *three times larger* than that ultimately destroyed at Buchenwald a century or so later. Yet, the victims of Buchenwald, quite properly, are memorialized universally as appalling reminders of the Holocaust, while the proportionally far more damaged mission-incarcerated Indians of California rarely are even mentioned in discussions of genocide. Instead, like most native peoples, they are relegated to the status of "unintended" victims of progress—as people, in the words of one writer, who simply "did not wear well."[38]

The identical double-standard regarding deaths from disease and privation is evident in other areas as well. For instance, it sometimes is asserted that the deaths of many native people, particularly in North America, do not "count" as genocide because they occurred in the midst of physical resistance to conquest. Thus, it is said, these must be regarded as wartime deaths rather than genocide. This is an argument similar to one used to downplay the Armenian genocide: The Armenians, it is claimed, "provoked" the Turks to try to exterminate them.[39]

But, of course, if by resisting oppression a group defines itself out of the category of genocide victim, then once again a great many Jewish deaths during the Holocaust cannot qualify as genocide either. Literally tens of thousands of Jews, after all, fought heroically against Nazi repression—from the Warsaw ghetto to the forests of Poland and beyond—most of them dying in the process. According to Yehuda Bauer, Jews mounted armed resistance against the Nazis in more than a hundred ghettoes throughout Poland, and even within death camps there were major uprisings, invariably followed by Nazi massacres of the resistance leaders and others.[40] Are these peoples' brave deaths—like those that were the result of disease and deprivation in the camps or the ghettoes—not to be counted as part of the Holocaust? And if they are to be counted (as surely they must), what kind of perverse logic is it that at the same time *denies* the category of genocide victim to Native American men and women and children who fought valiantly to resist the murderous depredations of invading armies that ultimately overran and obliterated whole Indian nations?

In this regard—that is, the wholesale eradication of many entire Native American communities, peoples, and nations—an important but simple fact must be noted, one that is far too rarely recognized in discussions on this topic. And that is: There were many—indeed, at least 2,000—*distinct* peoples, with deep and complex communal roots, living in the pre-Columbian Americas. Even today, after near total annihilation of the overall indigenous population, the U.S. government officially recognizes more than 500 separate and discrete native nations residing within its political borders. In many cases those peoples differed (and continue to differ) among one another in terms of religion, language, culture, and ethnicity to a much greater extent than do the far fewer separate peoples of Europe, and that includes the differences within Europe between Jews and non-Jews.[41]

Because of the unprecedented immensity of the disaster that befell the people of the Americas as a collectivity, resulting in a population collapse of somewhere between 50 and 100 million—that is, in the annihilation of 90 to 95 percent of the entire hemisphere's indigenous human inhabitants—it has become conventional to speak of genocide in the Americas as a long-term but singular event. On one level, of course, that is apt. But it is much more correct, and much more supportable within the finer points of conventionally accepted genocide terminology, to recognize that even though some (albeit a relative few) ancestrally distinctive groups of people in the Western Hemisphere did not fall victim to genocide, many others most certainly did.

There is a plainly racist "all-of-them-look-alike" bias in the Euro-American tendency to lump the native peoples of North and South America into one or a handful of large and nondistinctive categories of "Indians" (as often is done as well with Africans and Asians), while insisting on fine points of differentiation among European religious, cultural, ethnic, and national groups. One consequence of this lack of discrimination is the failure to recognize that numerous entirely distinct and separate native peoples (some of them now long since completely exterminated) met, or meet, all the strictest criteria for categorization as genocide victims.

In fact, if this all-too-common failure to discriminate ethnically, culturally, and religiously among indigenous peoples was applied to the study of internal violence in Europe during the 1940s, it might be difficult to sustain the argument—solely in quantitative terms—that the killing of Jews that did occur during the Nazis' reign was of sufficient *proportional* magnitude to be historically significant. This is because the comparable group in Europe to "Indians," or to "Africans" or "Asians" on other continents, is "Caucasians"—that is, all 400 million or so "Native Europeans" at the time of the Nazi rise to power. Among this number, Jews, at less than 3 percent of the overall population, would constitute only a small and *invisible because undifferentiated* collectivity whose loss of life under the Third Reich reduced the population of Europe by hardly more than 1 percent between 1939 and 1945. Again, focusing only on quantitative concerns, such a death rate, during a comparable six-year period, is barely one-half of that caused by heart disease in the United States today. Although this admittedly represents an unpleasant number of deaths, as a percentage of the overall population—again, in this unfair and undiscriminating context—it is hardly worthy by itself of being called historically important, let alone "unique." Yet that is precisely the same misleadingly aggregative numerical context that, in calculating death rates, is *routinely* imposed on *non*-European victims of genocide.

Indeed, had the collective and undifferentiated indigenous populations of the Americas been reduced in number by only the same 1 percent that Europe's over-all population was reduced by the deaths of Jews in the Holocaust, few people would even think of describing what happened in the Americas as genocide. Conversely, for the European experience to equal that of North and South America in proportional terms, between 360 million and 380 million people—that is, 90 to 95 percent of Europe's pre-Nazi population—would have to have been annihilated by Nazi violence and related causes, a figure that is nearly *ten times* the number of Europeans, including Russians, who actually did die in the war from all causes. If this all begins to seem like a recondite numbers game, it is—but one that conventionally is played only in reverse, and more guilefully, to advance the Jewish uniqueness agenda and to diminish the significance of every other people's historical suffering.

It is of particular irony, moreover, that some of the points used to establish the alleged uniqueness of the Jewish genocide experience, especially those pertaining to the dehumanizing language used by the Nazis to describe their victims, are in fact *derivative* of expressed Euro-American attitudes toward Native Americans—who, characteristically, never have claimed uniqueness for their own sufferings. Yehuda Bauer, for example, makes much of the fact that in their antisemitic descriptions of Jews the Nazis often used the imagery of "a virus, parasite, or a pest of some sort . . . that had to be destroyed, as vermin would be." And indeed, SS Chief Heinrich Himmler was not alone among Nazis who thought that anti-semitism "is exactly the same as delousing."[42] But decades before Hitler or Himmler were even born it had become a cliché in the United States to refer to Indians as vermin, particularly as lice, often as prelude to launching a new wave of annihilative violence against them. The function of this parasitic terminology can best be seen by examining the full phrase within which it most commonly was used: "Nits make lice," the killers would say, as justification for killing all the children, as well as the adults, in an Indian group slated for extermination. For to fail to destroy the nits—the eggs of the lice—was to invite reinfestation.[43]

Similarly, in a discussion of the uniqueness of the Holocaust in contrast to earlier genocides, Zygmunt Bauman sees one aspect of the singularity of "modern" genocide in what he describes as the Nazis' image of the world as a garden in which the Jews were weeds. "And weeds," he writes, "are to be exterminated." It's really quite an unemotional business, he notes, a coldly calculating implementation of the perverse demands of instrumental reason—for weeds are pests, and "modern genocide, like modern culture in general, is a gardener's job."[44] "Modern" though such consciousness may or may not be, however, there is nothing unique about Jews or any other victims of the Holocaust being viewed in this way. For it was G. Stanley Hall, often regarded as the founder of American psychology, who at the turn of the twentieth century described Native Americans and the other indigenous peoples who made up "nearly one-third of the human race, occupying two-fifths of the land surface of the globe" as "weeds in the human garden" that are in the process of being "extirpated . . . both by conscious and organic processes," adding that "in many minds this is inevitable and not without justification" since "the world will soon be overcrowded, and we must begin to take selective agencies into our own hands."[45]

Bauer certainly is correct when he observes that the repeated Nazi descriptions of Jews as germs and as other lower forms of life served the function of dehumanization, of establishing that the Jew was "not really a human being at all." And once such imagery is internalized by an oppressor it greatly facilitates the psychological distancing, as Christopher Browning puts it, "in which 'the enemy' is easily objectified and removed from the community of human obligation," thus making mass killing and extermination "acceptable" behavior.[46] But Bauer is equally *incorrect* in thinking that the Jewish experience in this regard is unique or even especially distinctive.

For the native peoples of the Americas such dehumanization began more than 400 years before the rise of Hitler, with published descriptions of the inhabitants of the Caribbean and Central America (while they were being enslaved and annihilated) as "beasts in human form," as "*homunculi* in whom you will scarcely find even vestiges of humanity," as "a third species of animal between man and monkey," and much more. In addition, these and other comparable terms, describing Indian peoples as subhuman creatures deserving of liquidation, became commonplace among the Euro-American conquerors throughout the Western Hemisphere for the next few centuries—as they fed native babies to their dogs for food, as they hung native carcasses on their porches like sides of beef, as they sliced off native women's breasts and native men's scrotums for use as exotic change purses, as they decorated their hats with excised female genitals, as they skinned Indian bodies from the hips down to make boot tops and leggings from human flesh. And as, in general, they deliberately erased entire peoples from the face of the earth.[47]

Finally there is the matter of what has become not only a central claim of the Jewish uniqueness argument but actually the very core of that position, now that other, earlier assertions have withered under scrutiny: The Jewish experience is unique among other genocides throughout history, it is now said, because of the Nazis' unrestrained *intent* to destroy all Jewish people, not only those residing in Europe, but throughout the entire world. And though Jewish uniqueness proponents have begun to back away from most other traditional uniqueness criteria in the face of telling criticism, here they seem determined to make their stand.

Both Yehuda Bauer and Steven Katz, probably the leading and certainly the most prolific advocates of the uniqueness of the Jewish Holocaust, have now admitted that on every other significant point previously asserted as grounds for proclaiming the uniqueness of Jews as victims one or more other groups have at least an equal claim to recognition. But no other group, they assert, can claim that their tormentors were seized with what Bauer calls the Nazis' "pseudo-religious, pseudo-messianic" obsession with not allowing a single Jew on the face of the earth to escape. "To date," says Bauer, "this has happened once, to the Jews under Nazism." What was and remains unprecedented about the Jewish experience, Katz adds in concurrence, was "the Nazi racial imperative that *all* Jews must die, and that they must die here and now."[48]

Confronted with this claim, one might easily cite numerous sources attesting to the fact that throughout the course of the Holocaust Gypsies were slated to receive, and did receive, precisely the same murderous treatment as Jews.[49] But the historical record also reveals many pre-twentieth-century examples of unambiguous official calls by European or white American political leaders for the total annihilation of any number of individual Native American peoples. Such examples might begin (although in fact there were precedents) with the plan of William Berkeley, Virginia's colonial governor during the mid-seventeenth century, as conveyed to his military commander, "to Destroy *all* these Northern Indians," a scheme, incidentally, that was carried out successfully and with dispatch: By the time the century came to a close, 95 percent of the native population of Virginia that had been on hand to welcome the first English settlements had been killed off.[50]

We might then leap forward in time nearly two centuries, to witness the direct call from the first governor of the state of California to his legislature, that a war be waged upon the numerous individual native peoples of that region "until the Indian race becomes extinct." By this time, three-fourths of the original native population of California had already been killed off by the Spanish. Now, within the course of just eight bloody years following the gubernatorial death warrant, the state spent more than $1.5 million (subsequently reimbursed by the U.S. Congress) in determinedly destroying fully 60 percent of the remaining Indians. This is approximately the same rate of extermination, during roughly the same number of years, as that suffered by all of Europe's Jews in the Holocaust. And then 50 percent of that remnant group of Indians was *further* annihilated in the next few decades, leading to an overall rate of destruction, under combined Spanish and American rule, of more than 95 percent—far higher even than the hideous death rate, from all causes, endured by the inmates of Auschwitz during the time of that extermination camp's operation.[51]

Moreover, during the period between the Virginia and California exterminations there were numerous other genocidal proclamations and statements of intent—often as a part of the express plans of government officials, including state governors and U.S. presidents—to totally exterminate this or that group of native people, any one of which was as well recognized an independent cultural or religious or ethnic entity in its time and place as were the Jews of twentieth-century Europe. And lest anyone during those years have moral qualms about such savage behavior (as later did even many of Hitler's *Einsatzkommandos*), the popular President Andrew Jackson had words of reassurance. He, himself, had on more than one occasion supervised the mutilation of the corpses of Indians his troops had killed, so as to take home body parts as prizes—and he, himself, had urged the murder of Indian babies (referring to them as "wolves") in order to be certain that *no* one would survive his men's murderous depredations. Killing off entire peoples, after all, as he later advised the U.S. Congress, was only like causing "the extinction of one generation to make room for another."[52]

In addition to such overwhelming evidence, from one side of North America to the other, regarding the clear *non*-uniqueness of the alleged Nazi intent to kill all the Jews, there is the obvious (but rarely asked) built-in question of whether a *failed* intent to kill all the members of a given group—as in the case of the Nazis and the Jews—is truly a distinction more notable than the *successful* extermination of an entire people (for example, the Tasmanians of Oceania or the Beothuk people of Newfoundland, among many others), regardless of whether there is left behind any record of an ideology of extermination on the part of the perpetrators.[53] Thus, if one were to follow Bauer and Katz to their extreme but inevitable conclusions, a nation today that publicly announced its intent to kill all the members of an ethnically defined group of people—and then launched a failed campaign that succeeded in killing only, say, 10 percent of the targeted victims— *would* be guilty of genocide because of its stated and recorded intent. On the other hand, a different nation that actually killed 90 or even 100 percent of a defined population, however large, but left no evidence of clear intent, would *not* be found to have committed genocide. This is sophistry.

But finally, there is the most elementary question that must be asked of those who claim that the keystone of the argument in favor of Jewish uniqueness resides in the Nazi determination to kill all Jews everywhere: Is the very assertion regarding Nazi intent *itself* true? The answer is no.

Apart from the clear comparability—and more—of numerous other peoples who have been slated for (and sometimes suffered) complete extermination, the fundamental problem with the intent argument is its amateurish and simplistic understanding of historical process. Within the conventional range of explanations for the Holocaust, from the so-called intentionalist perspective (which views the unfolding of events in Nazi Germany as directed and controlled by a powerful, single-minded, and consistent core of ideologues) to the so-called functionalist interpretation (in which decisions of the Reich are seen as largely improvisational and even chaotic, in response to changing circumstances), the claim that Jews and only Jews have ever been singled out for total extermination emanates from the extreme intentionalist position.[54] This is the way of thinking that also undergirds most conspiracy theories on a variety of topics. Unable or unwilling to accept the fact that human history proceeds by compromise and accommodation among competing, complex, and ever-unfolding forces—in the case of the Holocaust, as Arno J. Mayer puts it, the "constant interplay of ideology and contingency in which both played their respective but also partially indeterminate roles"—intentionalists and conspiracy theorists seek out and interpret to suit their own unsubtle predispositions any pieces of data that can be made to smack of willful stratagem or intrigue.[55]

This is not, by any means, to say that historians should ignore such information, only to insist that materials of this sort—particularly as regards the Holocaust—are usually scattered and piecemeal, requiring a good deal of attention to nuance and context. For the fact of the matter is, as Holocaust scholar Christopher Browning notes:

> There are no written records of what took place among Hitler, Himmler, and Heydrich concerning the Final Solution, and none of them survived to testify after the war. Therefore, the decision-making process at the center must be reconstructed by the historian, who extrapolates from events, documents, and testimony originating outside the inner circle. Like the man in Plato's cave, he sees only the reflection and shadows, but not reality.[56]

Thus, even the widely accepted belief in a Nazi plan to kill all the Jews of Europe (putting aside for the moment the alleged plot aimed at *worldwide* destruction) is based largely on a combination of hearsay recollection and the interpretation of nonexplicit language in such writings as the infamous Wannsee Protocol. This document consists of the minutes of a meeting held on January 20, 1942, attended by a number of high- and mid-level Nazi officials and convened by Reinhard Heydrich, chief of Security Police and the Security Service. At this meeting, which commonly is regarded as the "smoking gun" for those seeking solid evidence for the Nazi plan to kill all the Jews in Europe, Heydrich is recorded as discussing a proposed "final solution" that involved the forced evacuation "to the East" of all the Jews of Europe, including those in countries that were not yet under German military control, such as England and Spain and Switzerland. "Able-bodied Jews will be taken in large labor columns to these districts for work on roads, separated according to sexes, in the course of which action a great part will undoubtedly be eliminated by natural causes," read the minutes of that meeting—followed by this crucial sentence: "The possible final remnant will, as it must undoubtedly consist of the toughest, have to be treated accordingly, as it is the product of natural selection, and would, if liberated, act as a bud cell of a Jewish reconstruction (see historical experience)."[57]

Never, in this, the key document establishing the plan for a Final Solution, is the outright killing of Jews discussed. To reach the conclusion that this is what in fact was being described requires both an interpretation of the phrase "treated accordingly" and additional supporting documentation. Careful historians, recognizing this problem, have begun by analyzing the phrase in its larger context. Raul Hilberg, for instance, points out that although "Heydrich did not elaborate on the phrase 'treated accordingly' . . . we know from the language of the Einsatzgruppen reports that he meant killing." Others have connected the Wannsee Protocol to other documentary evidence, including Adolf Eichmann's postwar trial interrogation in which he recalls, as the recorder at the Wannsee meeting, that discussions at the conference actually took place "in very plain terms—not in the language that I had to use in the minutes, but in absolutely blunt terms . . . [and] the discussion covered killing, elimination, and annihilation."[58]

Based on this and other, more voluminous, evidence, there seems little doubt that by late 1941 or early 1942 a plan was being put into place that, if carried out, would eventuate in the extermination of most Jews residing "in the German sphere of influence in Europe" (to quote an earlier letter, which had been drafted by Eichmann and signed by Hermann Göring, authorizing the development of plans for a Final Solution), or in "the Lebensraum of the German people" or "Reich territory," to cite the Wannsee Protocol itself. Further, it is true that the inclusion in the Protocol of a statistical table listing estimated numbers of Jews residing in European countries that were at the time outside of German control clearly suggests that *if* those countries were to fall under German domination Heydrich wished to include those Jews as well in the Final Solution. However, it is an enormous and unjustified leap to take the *potential* inclusion of other *European* Jews in Heydrich's report to the furthest extreme possible and claim, as Yehuda Bauer has, that *therefore* the Nazis regarded "the so-called 'Jewish Problem' [as] not a German, or ultimately even European issue, but a *global, universal, even cosmic problem* of the greatest magnitude"—and that therein, with the Nazis' alleged "pseudo-religious" and "pseudo-messianic" plan to kill every Jew on the face of the earth, lies the central proof of Jewish suffering as historically unique.[59]

In the first place, there is no documentary evidence to suggest that any plan to kill even most of the Jews in Nazi-controlled Europe existed prior to the year 1941. As Christopher Browning, among many others, has demonstrated in detail, "The practice of Nazi Jewish policy until 1941 does not support the thesis of a long-held, fixed intention to murder the European Jews."[60] That is, unlike religious and messianic convictions that focus on "universal" and "cosmic" problems, the Final Solution—though certainly rooted in the deep history of German antisemitism and in Hitler's particularly pathological hatred of Jews—was not a long-premeditated and ideologically irresistible Nazi plan or doctrine, as the extreme intentionalist interpretation (and its "uniqueness" offshoot) would have it. Rather, the decision to exterminate the Jews of Europe emerged in the *midst* of the war because of specific mundane and intra-European historical circumstances. And it ended (following the appalling destruction of millions of innocent people) because of changes in those same thoroughly profane and materialist conditions.

This is demonstrable by a large and disparate body of evidence, but one particularly compelling series of incidents irrefutably makes the point. It has long been known that representatives from the highest levels of Nazi leadership, including Adolf Eichmann and *Reichsführer* Heinrich Himmler himself, offered in

1944—that is, two years following the initial implementation of the Final Solution and a year before the war ended—to *release* from Nazi captivity 1 million Jews. (One report says "all the European Jews.") In return, the Nazis wanted 10,000 trucks from the western Allies, to be used only in the Soviet Union, and an unspecified amount of money. (Himmler, at one point, was even supposed to have said that he "wanted to bury the hatchet between us and the Jews.") This was but one of several attempts made by Nazi authorities in 1944 to receive ransom in exchange for the freedom of incarcerated Jews and to begin the process of negotiating a separate peace with the western Allies. Some Jews in fact were freed by the Nazis in this way, though not in numbers close to those that Himmler was proposing. Indeed, as numerous Jewish scholars, including Yehuda Bauer, have long contended, the Nazis were willing to release Jews; the *Allies* were the ones who refused to negotiate. In Bauer's words: "It was the West that failed."[61]

In November 1944, without any major ransom agreements worked out and six months prior to the end of war in Europe, the *Reichsführer* called a halt to the Jewish exterminations and directed that the killing machinery at Auschwitz be dismantled, since "for practical purposes the Jewish question had been solved"— although at least one-third of Europe's Jews, and two-thirds of the world's Jewish population, remained alive.[62] This series of events, to say the least, hardly seems appropriate or consistent behavior for a group that allegedly is obsessed with a messianic, global, even cosmic racial imperative commanding (to quote Katz again) "that *all* Jews must die, and that they must die here and now." And this claimed imperative, it is important to remember, is the final criterion said to establish the uniqueness of the Jewish experience, now that all previous criteria have been found wanting.

That this is a serious problem for proponents of the Jewish uniqueness thesis has not gone unnoticed. Thus, in a recent book entitled *Jews for Sale?*, Bauer tackles head-on the dilemma posed by the Nazi leadership's willingness to trade Jewish lives for money and materiel. His answer:

> Is it not possible to argue that there was no inherent contradiction between the Nazi design to murder all the Jews everywhere and their willingness to compromise temporarily, to permit the flight of some Jews from their domain in return for real advantages to the Reich? If the Nazis expected to be in control, directly or indirectly, of the whole world, might they not have seen the flight of *some* Jews as purely temporary, because they would catch up with those escapees sooner or later?[63]

Following more than 200 pages of further discussion, Bauer not surprisingly answers his own rhetorical questions in the affirmative. While acknowledging the ransom efforts of the Nazis, he contends that this does not constitute contradictory behavior for a group bent on the utter destruction of world Jewry because "the Nazis expected to win the war, and if they did, they would finally 'solve' the

'Jewish question' by total annihilation; any Jews who might escape momentarily would in the end be caught and killed."[64]

Now, it must be said that this is a very imaginative attempt on Bauer's part to wriggle free from an otherwise unsolvable factual and logical dilemma. But it doesn't work. Indeed, it is founded on fantasy. This is so, first, because there is still no evidence whatsoever of any Nazi effort or "plan" (as distinct from bombastic public oratory) to kill every Jew on earth; and second, because the serious Nazi offers regarding the ransoming of Jews were first extended in the late spring and summer of 1944, by which time it was clear to any and all that Germany was in the throes of inevitable and increasingly imminent defeat. Thus, contrary to Bauer's claim, the Nazis at this time did *not* "expect to be in control, directly or indirectly of the whole world," and they had no hope (or apparent desire) of ever "catching up" with those Jews whose liberation they were proposing.

To quote an earlier publication of Bauer's (evidently written before the contradiction had occurred to him): "Were they [the Nazis] willing to release Jews against such materials and in the process of talks regarding peace feelers? Yes, most probably. *They knew that the war was lost* and the hoped-for talks, as well as possible materials, were more important to them than the Jews, whether alive or dead." In fact, no other conclusion is possible. Even as early as the previous winter, with the devastating collapse of Germany's Sixth Army at Stalingrad, discussion of capitulation was being heard in Berlin. To note just one example of how German attitudes toward the war were changing: Whereas in 1941 the Nazis had issued sixty-five *Sondermeldungen,* or special propaganda announcements, to tell the nation how well the war was going, in all of 1943 there were only three *Sondermeldungen*—and one of them was a desperate effort to turn the most massive military defeat of the war into an exhortation on behalf of collapsing national pride. By late summer of 1944, as Himmler and others acting on his behalf were offering to free all the remaining Jews in exchange for money and supplies, a plot among German military leaders to kill Hitler had been attempted, German troops were suffering enormous losses in the field, their front lines collapsing everywhere, and Paris was in the process of being liberated. No Nazi leader, even probably Hitler, who by this time was almost totally withdrawn and speaking at all only rarely, thought that victory for the Germans was still possible.[65]

In short, the supposed Nazi pseudo-religious mania for pursuing and murdering every Jew on earth, thus distinguishing Jews as the victims to end all victims who had ever lived, melted rapidly away (to the largely imaginary extent that it ever truly existed) once defeat was apparent and the possibility occurred to Nazi leaders that living Jews might be more valuable to them than dead ones. Moreover, from the earliest years of Nazi rule until the collapse of the Reich and the liberation of the camps, the German government had always had a policy of excluding from imprisonment and destruction various categories of Jews, including different subdivisions of *Mischlinge,* or part-Jews. Even the Wannsee Protocol devoted as much space to discussing categories of Jews and part-Jews who would be included in or excluded from extermination (based on such matters as age, record of military service, degree of "mixed blood," and ethnicity of marriage partner) as it did to the Final Solution itself. And from the start those categories of exclusion from persecution, especially as they pertained to the matter of ancestry, were far more liberal for Jews than they were for Gypsies.[66]

Thus, the final justification for the contention that Jewish suffering during the Holocaust, stupendously evil and hideous as it was, was unique in human history—that it was a *novum*, something utterly new and unprecedented in all the world's experience—turns out, like its predecessor arguments, to be more rhetorically apparent than real.[67]

❀ ❀ ❀

In fact, the entire process of seeking grounds for Jewish victim uniqueness is one of smoke and mirrors. Uniqueness advocates *begin* by defining genocide (or the Holocaust or the Shoah) in terms of what they already believe to be experiences undergone only by Jews. After much laborious research it is then "discovered"—*mirabile dictu*—that the Jewish experience was unique. If, however, critics point out after a time that those experiences were not in fact unique, *other* allegedly unique experiences are invented and proclaimed. If not *numbers* killed, then how about *percentage* of population destroyed? If not *efficiency* or *method* of killing employed, how about perpetrator *intentionality*? Ultimately, as we have seen, such insistent efforts extend to the point of frivolousness, as one after another supposedly significant criterion is found to have been either nonexistent or shared by others.

Of course, those other groups could, if they so chose, do precisely the same thing. It might well and logically be asserted by American Indians, for instance, that for the word "genocide" to be properly applicable in describing mass destruction in which there were at least *some* survivors, a minimum of, say, 90 percent of the victim group would have to be wiped out. Is this an arbitrary criterion? Perhaps, although it could certainly be argued that short of total extermination (the only "pure" definition of genocide) 90 percent is a reasonable and round figure that identifies real genocide and prohibits the indiscriminate use of the word in comparatively "insignificant" cases of mass killing—say, the roughly 65 percent mortality rate suffered by European Jews during the Holocaust.

Were it pointed out that this figure is self-serving, since by its standard only American Indians and some other indigenous peoples would be characterized as victims of genocide, it would be easy to demonstrate that the 90 percent criterion is no more self-serving—and no more arbitrary—than those criteria put forward over the years (and time after time found wanting) by advocates of Jewish uniqueness. But in fact both cases are examples of cultural egotism driving scholarship before it. As Stephen Jay Gould has described its equivalent in the work of would-be scholars on another topic: "They began with conclusions, peered through their facts, and came back in a circle to the same conclusions," a matter of "advocacy masquerading as objectivity."[68] The fact that Gould was writing of nineteenth-century scientists bent on proving the superiority of their race over others just makes the citation more apt, as we shall see momentarily.

And, finally, as for restricting use of the word "holocaust" to references having to do with the experience of Jews under the Nazis, that copyright was filed at least three centuries too late. Although "The Holocaust," in what has become conventional usage, clearly applies exclusively to the genocide that was perpetrated by the Nazis against their various victims, "holocaust" in more general parlance, as a term to describe mass destruction or slaughter, belongs to anyone who cares to use it. It is a very old word, after all, and as the *Oxford English Dictionary* points out, apart from previous uses that may have been applied to violent assaults on specific peoples, it was used in this way by Milton in the seventeenth century as well as by Ireland's Bishop George Berkeley in 1732—to describe the Druids' brutal treatment of free-thinkers.

III

And yet, the Jewish experience in the Holocaust *was* unique. In certain ways. Just as the Armenian genocide was. Just as the genocide against the Gypsies was. Just as the many genocides against the native peoples of the New World were. And just as, more recently, the genocides in Cambodia, East Timor, Bosnia, Rwanda, and elsewhere have been—despite the fact that Steven Katz, ever obsessed with his Jewish uniqueness *idée fixe*, crassly has dismissed the killing in Bosnia as a mere "population transfer supported by violence" and has described the massive slaughter of up to a million people in Rwanda as "not genocidal" but simply a struggle for "tribal domination."[69]

Some of these horrendous purges killed more people than others. Some killed higher percentages of people than others. Some were carried out with highly advanced death technology harnessed to coldly bureaucratic planning. Others resulted from crude weapons of war, purposeful mass starvation, enslavement, and forced labor. Some were proudly announced by their perpetrators. The intentions of other mass killers were never publicly made known or have been lost to history. There are, of course, numerous other ways in which individual genocides differed, and on this or that specific point many of them no doubt have been "unique." For no two events, even though they commonly may be acknowledged to fall within a single large classification, are ever precisely alike.

The same thing is true with other major historical phenomena that, however different in particular respects, are conceded by historians to fall within certain general categories of definition. Take political revolution, for instance. Consider, for purposes of discussion, the revolutions in colonial America, France, Russia, and China. In an extraordinary variety of ways—including motivation, duration, and outcome—these revolutions greatly differed from one another. That is, there were certain circumstances and occurrences that were unique to each of them. Yet all of them are agreed to have *been* revolutions. That is why, as serious scholars sift through the data and analyze this or that or another characteristic that marks as particular the American or the French or the Russian or the Chinese revolutions, none among them has ever attempted to proclaim any one of these to be the "unique" revolution—the revolution so different from all others, not only in degree but in fundamental essence, that a special capitalized word must be used to identify it. This has not been done, because to do so would be to depart from the world of scholarship and enter the world of propaganda and group hagiography—which in fact quite clearly is what Holocaust uniqueness proponents are up to: elevating the Jewish experience to a singular and exclusive hierarchical category, thereby reducing all other genocides to a thoroughly lesser and wholly separate substratum of classification.

Uniqueness advocates do not, of course, represent, by any means, the whole of Jewish scholarship on the Holocaust or on genocide. Indeed, if anything, they are something of a cult within that scholarly community—though a cult quite skilled at calling attention to itself and one with powerful friends in high places. In contrast, for example, Princeton historian Arno J. Mayer, a self-described "unbelieving yet unflinching Jew whose maternal grandfather died in the Theresienstadt concentration camp," writes critically of "the dogmatists who seek to reify and sacralize the Holocaust" and of "the exaggerated self-centeredness" of the uniqueness proponents, "which entails the egregious forgetting of the larger whole and of all other victims."[70] Similarly, Israel W. Charny, executive director of the Institute on the Holocaust and Genocide in Jerusalem, rebukes what he calls the "leaders and 'high priests' of different cultures who insist on the uniqueness, exclusivity, primacy, superiority, or greater significance of the specific genocide of their people," adding elsewhere:

> I object very strongly to the efforts to name the genocide of any one people as the single, ultimate event, or as the most important event against which all other tragedies of genocidal mass death are to be tested and found wanting. . . . For me, the passion to exclude this or that mass killing from the universe of genocide, as well as the intense competition to establish the exclusive "superiority" or unique form of any one genocide, ends up creating a fetishistic atmosphere in which the masses of bodies that are not to be qualified for the definition of genocide are dumped into a conceptual black hole, where they are forgotten.

Indeed, it is partly in response to these lamentable tendencies of the uniqueness "high priests" that Charny recently has constructed a sophisticated, and inclusive rather than exclusive, generic typology of genocides.[71]

The thoughtful efforts of such scholars are a welcome and important contribution to understanding in this highly charged and contested field of study. But neither the basic and obvious recognition of certain aspects of uniqueness in all genocidal events, nor Charny's carefully worked out scholarly model, is of interest to Jewish uniqueness advocates. On the contrary, so intense in some quarters is the insistence on the a priori and unchallengeable status of Jews as the most damaged people in the history of the world—what Phillip Lopate calls "extermination pride" affording Jews "a sort of privileged nation status in the moral honor roll"—that any effort to place the admittedly horrifying Jewish experience at the hands of the Nazis within the context of comparative genocide analysis is described by some as "stealing the Holocaust."[72]

According to uniqueness advocate Edward Alexander, for instance, the experience of the Holocaust provided "a Jewish claim to a specific suffering that was of the 'highest,' the most distinguished grade available." Even to mention the genocidal agonies suffered by others, either during the Holocaust or at other times and places, is, Alexander says, "to plunder the moral capital which the Jewish people, through its unparalleled suffering in World War II, had unwittingly accumulated."[73] One of the most ghastly amassments of genocidal suffering ever experienced is thereby made the literal equivalent for its victims of a great bounty of jealously guarded "capital" or wealth. It is unlikely that there exists any more forthright expression than this of what Irving Louis Horowitz calls Holocaust "moral bookkeeping," nor any clearer indication of how obstinate, even in the face of overwhelming evidence to the contrary, true believers in the Jewish uniqueness orthodoxy are certain to remain.[74]

But why? To be sure, as psychologist Charny points out, on one level subjective expressions of belief in the uniqueness of one's own particular suffering, or that of one's compatriots, are a natural and quite common accompaniment to an "outpouring of grief, disbelief, horror and rage at the tragedy and infamy done to one's people."[75] But we are not addressing that phenomenon here. Rather, we are concerned with a small industry of Holocaust hagiographers arguing for the uniqueness of the Jewish experience with all the energy and ingenuity of theological zealots. For that is what they are: zealots who believe literally that they and their religious fellows are, in the words of Deuteronomy 7:6, "a special people . . . above all people that are on the face of the earth," interpreting in the only way thus possible their own community's recent encounter with mass death.

Jews, of course, are not the only people who consider themselves Chosen. The Afrikaners also view themselves as a people of the Covenant, as do the Ulster-Scots of Northern Ireland, and as did America's New England Puritan settlers, among others.[76] In each of these cases the corporate self-identity of Chosenness may, on a day-to-day level, be no more harmful to others than the commonplace ethnocentrism displayed by most of the world's religions or cultures. But with its special emphasis on the maintenance of blood purity (e.g., Deuteronomy 7:3; Joshua 23:12–13), and on the either tacit or expressed pollution fear of corrupting that purity with the defiling blood of others, the ideology of the Covenant intrinsically is but a step away from full-blown racism and, if the means are available, often violent oppression of the purportedly threatening non-Chosen.

Thus, the Afrikaners' self-identification with the ancient Hebrews, and with their own Great Trek regarded by them as a second Exodus—combined with their explication of the biblical story of Ham as meaning that black Africans were divinely ordained to be their servants—formed the theologically legitimizing core of the reprehensible doctrine of apartheid. Thus, the covenantal belief of the Ulster-Scots in their self-defined status as one of God's predestined "elect" peoples has served to justify their occupation of the "promised land" of Northern Ireland, along with their historical persecution of that land's native Irish people. And thus, on one occasion (among many) that the Puritan settlers of New England laid waste an entire neighboring Indian nation with barely a pretext of provocation—shooting and stabbing and burning to death every man, woman, and child that they could find—they wrote in justification that "sometimes the Scripture declareth women and children must perish with their parents," and noted that as Chosen People (alluding to Deuteronomy 20:16) the Lord had given them the Indians' "Land for an Inheritance." Citing the rest of the scriptural passage—"thou shalt save alive nothing that breatheth"—was unnecessary as it would have been redundant.[77]

Justifications for Israel's territorial expansionism and suppression of the Palestinian people, when it has been admitted that the Palestinians *are* a people, of course have long followed this same path of Chosen People self-righteousness. Moreover, it is a self-righteousness that commonly is yoked to the Holocaust's role as part of the founding myth of the Israeli state. That is why an Israeli government official confidently can expect a favorable hearing when he defends his nation's policy of expansionism by saying that to move back from the pre-1967 frontier would be equivalent to returning to the "borders of Auschwitz." And it is why an Israeli military leader can anticipate widespread support for assertions that it is "the holy martyrs of the Holocaust" from whom Israel's army "draws its power and strength" and that the Holocaust is nothing less than "the root and legitimation of our enterprise." As Zygmunt Bauman has observed, Israel uses the Holocaust "as the certificate of its political legitimacy, a safe-conduct pass for its past and future policies, and above all as the advance payment for the injustices it might itself commit."[78]

If, then, the claimed historical uniqueness of Jewish suffering during the Holocaust serves an important function in a theocratic state that perceives itself as under siege—the function served by all "life-sustaining lies," in Karl Jaspers's phrase—it is a falsehood for which others have had to pay a very high price.[79] For implicit in—indeed, *essential* to—the notion of the uniqueness and incomparability of the Jews' genocidal suffering is the concomitant trivialization or even outright denial of the genocidal suffering of *others*, since those others (Armenians, Gypsies, Native Americans, Cambodians, Rwandans, and more) by plain and unavoidable definition are *un*-Chosen beings whose deaths, in the larger scale of things, simply don't matter as much. And this is racist, just as the diminution or denial of Jewish suffering during the Holocaust is antisemitic.

This, of course, is a grave and solemn matter despite the fact that on occasion the transparent superficiality of uniqueness supporters in dealing with non-Jewish peoples is almost comical. Yehuda Bauer, for example, is fond of pretending to be a scholar who has studied the claim that genocide was carried out against the native peoples of the Americas, specifically, he says, "the Pierce Nez" Indians—when in fact there are not now and never have been any such people. Presumably he means the Nez Percé people of the American Northwest, whose noses, incidentally, were not pierced and whose Westernized name apparently is a corruption of the French *nez près*.[80] In any case, the Nez Percé people never have been known by anyone, save Professor Bauer, as "Pierce Nez," and to refer to them as such demonstrates the same level of serious scholarly concern for and knowledge of the topic at hand as would someone, say, claiming to be writing Jewish history who couldn't spell the word "Jew." Clearly, one should avoid declaiming in feigned seriousness on the historical experiences of people whose very name one does not know. For to treat the Nez Percé and others in this way is only to confirm Jean Baudrillard's insight that "the deepest racist avatar is to think that an error about earlier societies is politically or theoretically less serious than a misinterpretation of our own world. Just as a people that oppresses another cannot be free, so a culture that is mistaken about another must also be mistaken about itself."[81]

Deborah Lipstadt provides another variant on this sort of thing when she decries a statement by a Holocaust denier who makes claims for moral comparability between the United States internment of Japanese-American citizens during the Second World War and the Nazi "internment" of Jews. She is quite correct in rejecting this comparison, of course (Manzanar and Tule Lake were outrages, to be sure, but they were not Treblinka or Sobibór), but in doing so she contends that, however improper it was to intern the Japanese, the attempted comparison breaks down because "the Jews had not bombed Nazi cities or attacked German forces in 1939."[82] No, but neither did those Americans of Japanese ancestry who were interned by the U.S. government bomb American cities or attack American forces. Indeed, by equating Japanese-American citizens with the armed forces of the nation of Japan, Lipstadt betrays in herself the very same racist sentiment that led the United States to intern Americans of Japanese ancestry in the first place.

And then there is the case of Rabbi Seymour Siegel, former professor of ethics at the Jewish Theological Seminary and executive director of the U.S. Holocaust Memorial Council. When asked if room might be made on the council for a representative of the Romani, or Gypsy, people who had suffered so horrendously under the Nazis—side by side, in the same death camps and gas chambers and ovens as the Jews—Siegel described such a proposal as "cockamamie" and expressed doubt that the Gypsies even existed as a people.[83]

If such examples of intellectual or moral malfeasance, demonstrating at best wilful ignorance and racist disdain for the non-Jewish group whose sufferings allegedly are being compared with the Jewish experience, are legion among upholders of the Jewish uniqueness persuasion—and they are—further evidence of callous scorn for and *organized* denial of the sufferings of others are even more insidious. For example, for many years now the Turkish government has employed an extraordinary range of strong-arm tactics to prevent international recognition of the Armenian genocide. It is understandable, if still detestable, that perpetrator governments would deny their own complicity in mass murder. It is quite another thing, however, for a group that itself has been terribly victimized by an extermination campaign to collaborate with a historically murderous state in denying that state's documented participation in genocide.

Yet that is precisely what happened only a few years ago when Turkish and Israeli government officials together pressured the White House, which was then involved in planning for the United States Holocaust Memorial Museum, to reject any mention of the Armenian genocide in the museum's exhibits. It is what happened on another occasion when the head of the Jewish community in Turkey, Jewish lobbyists in the United States, and Israeli officials of the Foreign Office conspired with the Turkish government to prevent the United States from holding an official Armenian day of remembrance. And it is what continues to happen today, when, among many other examples, a documentary film on the Armenian genocide remains banned on Israeli television, and when an effort by people in Israel's Education Ministry to produce high school curricula on the Armenian and Gypsy genocides recently was quashed by an oversight committee of government-paid historians.[84]

All this, of course, did not happen without some quid pro quo. So the Turkish government has repaid these generous efforts on its behalf by publicly stating not only that (as their Jewish friends obligingly have confirmed for them) there never was an Armenian genocide but that the Nazi assault on the Jews was indeed historically unique. This is the process, aided in the current instance by the complicity of Holocaust uniqueness proponents and the Israeli government, that Roger W. Smith has called "denying genocide by acknowledging the Holocaust."[85]

For a government with the blood of genocide on its hands—such as Turkey or the United States—to deny the presence of that blood is disgraceful enough. But in certain ways it is worse, because it is so gratuitous, for former *victims* of genocide to befriend such nations and promote their lies purely in the interest of preserving one's own fabricated self-image as history's Victim of victims. For whether it is Israeli government officials conspiring with the Turkish government to conceal the Armenian genocide or Jewish-American Holocaust scholars ridiculing the idea that Native Americans were or are victims of genocide, the damage and the dangers are the same.

The damage done by such actions is what international peace scholar Johan Galtung has called "cultural violence": the systematic degradation and denial of a group's sense of dignity or self-worth and the concealment (by "normalization" of their reduced status) of past and ongoing direct and structural violence that they have suffered. Building on a previously elaborated typology of "direct violence" (straightforward maiming and killing) and "structural violence" (the institutionalization of gross inequality), Galtung demonstrates some of the ways in which cultural violence resides and operates in the intellectual and symbolic infrastructures of certain societies. (For instance, in their manufactured and self-serving but subsequently taken-for-granted history and ideology that use the socially constructed notion of a group's allegedly inborn degeneracy to legitimize continuing direct and structural violence against it.) As Galtung puts it: "Cultural violence makes direct and structural violence look, even feel, right—or at least not wrong."[86]

Jews, of course, have long suffered from all three types of violence, and few better examples exist of attempted cultural violence than the ongoing actions today of neo-Nazi Holocaust deniers. "The general public tends to accord victims of genocide a certain moral authority," observes Deborah Lipstadt, adding, in a good capsule description of one of the things that cultural violence does: "If you devictimize a people you strip them of their moral authority"—and you thereby make more acceptable whatever the amount of their past or present suffering that you cannot simply conceal.[87] Lipstadt understands this quite well, of course, precisely because she sees discussion of genocide as a competitive endeavor and devotes much of her work to devictimizing and thus stripping of their possible moral authority any and all victim groups other than Jews.

In addition to the damage that is inherent in the cultural violence of genocide denial, there is the matter of the future dangers that it promotes. As Roger Smith, Eric Markusen, and Robert Jay Lifton recently have written regarding the continuing denial of the Armenian holocaust:

> Where scholars deny genocide, in the face of decisive evidence that it has occurred, they contribute to a false consciousness that can have the most dire reverberations. Their message, in effect, is: murderers did not really murder; victims were not really killed; mass murder requires no confrontation, no reflection, but should be ignored, glossed over. In this way scholars lend their considerable authority to the acceptance of this ultimate human crime. More than that, they encourage—indeed invite—a repetition of that crime from virtually any source in the immediate or distant future. By closing their minds to truth, that is, such scholars contribute to the deadly psychohistorical dynamic in which unopposed genocide begets new genocides.[88]

This, of course, is one of the great and justified fears that Jews long have harbored regarding the threat of Holocaust denial—that it invites repetition of anti-Jewish mass violence and killing. But when advocates of the allegedly unique suffering of Jews during the Holocaust *themselves* participate in denial of *other* historical genocides—*and such denial is inextricably interwoven with the very claim of uniqueness*—they thereby actively participate in making it much easier for those other genocides to be repeated. And, in the case of genocides against the native peoples of the Americas, not to be repeated but to continue. As, indeed, they are at this very moment. For never, really, have they stopped.

Elie Wiesel is one of the few proponents of the Jewish uniqueness idea who has ever examined with care and seriousness any documents on genocide in the Americas. Those materials, which he studied in the 1970s, related to the Paraguayan government's then ongoing effort to exterminate the Aché Indians. Wiesel was stunned, horrified, and overwhelmed; he said: "Until now, I always forbade myself to compare the Holocaust of European Judaism to events which are foreign to it." Yet, he now conceded, "there are here indications, facts which cannot be denied: it is indeed a matter of a Final Solution. It simply aims at exterminating this tribe. Morally and physically. So that nothing will remain, not even a cry or a tear. Efficient technique, tested elsewhere."[89]

But why hadn't this acclaimed student of genocide spoken out on these ghastly events earlier? "I didn't know," was all he could say. "But is that only an excuse? I can't think of any other." Of course he was not alone in his ignorance, as he was more than ready to point out. After listing some of the horrors he now knew that the Aché people were experiencing—"men hunted, humiliated, murdered for the sake of pleasure . . . young girls raped and sold . . . children killed in front of their parents reduced to silence by pain . . . ghettos, collective murders, manhunts, tortures, and agonies"—he concluded:

> Our society prefers not to know anything of all that. Silence everywhere. Hardly a few words in the press. Nothing is discussed in the U.N., nor among the politicized intellectuals or the moralists. The great consciences kept quiet. Of course, we had an excuse! We didn't know. But now, after having read these testimonies, we know. Henceforth we shall be responsible. And accomplices.[90]

That was written twenty years ago in a book that has long been out of print. How many Americans today have heard of the Aché Indians? Or of the scores of other separate and independent indigenous peoples of Central and South America who have been totally exterminated, under equally ghastly conditions, during our lifetimes? Or of those who are being destroyed in the same way even now? Who knows of the many more still—tens of millions of people from Alaska in the far north to Tierra del Fuego in the far south, and on the 16 million square miles of land between—who were liquidated by outside invaders and settlers during past centuries? There is nothing left of most of them. Not a trace. Others cling on to existence, their numbers tiny fractions of what they were before the waves of violence swept over them.

The willful maintenance of public ignorance regarding the genocidal and racist horrors against indigenous peoples that have been and are being perpetrated by many nations of the Western Hemisphere, including the United States—which contributes to the construction of a museum to commemorate genocide only if the killing occurred half a world away—is consciously aided and abetted and legitimized by the actions of the Jewish uniqueness advocates we have been discussing. Their manufactured claims of uniqueness for their own people are, after all, synonymous with dismissal and denial of the experience of others—others much weaker, more oppressed, and in far more immediate danger than they. Further—and this would be ironic were it not so tragic—in their denial of genocide victim status to other groups, Jewish uniqueness advocates almost invariably mimic *exactly* the same pattern of assertions laid out by the antisemitic historical revisionists who deny Jewish suffering in the Holocaust: The number of people killed is said to be exaggerated, the deaths that did occur are labeled as provoked or wartime casualties, most of the victims are claimed to have succumbed to natural causes such as disease, there is alleged to be no evidence of official intent to commit genocide, and so on. In this way, narcissistic, false claims of uniqueness are joined with brutal, racist denials of the sufferings of others, becoming two sides of the same debased coin.

But as uniqueness proponents never tire of reminding anyone who will listen, denial encourages more violence against those who truly are its victims. Jews suffered horrendously during the reign of the Third Reich—to say nothing of the millennium of oppression and exile and pogrom that led inexorably toward the Holocaust—and so all people of conscience must be on guard against Holocaust deniers who, in many cases, would like nothing better than to see mass violence against Jews start again.

By that same token, however, as we consider the terrible history and the ongoing campaigns of genocide against the indigenous inhabitants of the Western Hemisphere and other peoples elsewhere, there no longer is any excuse for maintaining the self-serving masquerade of Jewish genocide uniqueness—the endlessly refined and revised deception that serves equally to deny the sufferings of others, and thus, in murderous complicity with both past and present genocidal regimes, to place those terribly damaged others even closer to harm's way. It is a moral issue. And a serious one. As Elie Wiesel has said: "Now we know. Henceforth we shall be responsible. And accomplices."

NOTES

This essay is a revised and expanded version of a lecture given on May 2, 1995, at the University of Colorado, Boulder. I am grateful to the consortium of organizations and academic departments at the university that invited me to speak—particularly the Center for Studies of Ethnicity and Race in America—and for the spirited and enlightening post-lecture discussion that ensued.

1. See, among other discussions of the Allies' wartime denial and indifference, David S. Wyman, *The Abandonment of the Jews: America and the Holocaust, 1941–1945* (New York: Pantheon Books, 1984); and Christopher Simpson, *The Splendid Blond Beast: Money, Law, and Genocide in the Twentieth Century* (Monroe, Maine: Common Courage Press, 1995).

2. The overall death toll of the war, including the range of figures for China, is summarized in Peter Calvocoressi, Guy Wint, and John Pritchard, *Total War: Causes and Courses of the Second World War*, rev. 2d ed. (New York: Pantheon, 1989), pp. 576–578. The most exhaustive quantitative study of Jewish deaths during the Holocaust, putting the total figure at 5.1 million, is Raul Hilberg, *The Destruction of the European Jews*, rev. and definitive ed. (New York: Holmes and Meier, 1985), three volumes; for the cited total and percentages of Jewish deaths, see especially volume 3, pp. 1047–1048 and 1201–1220. Hilberg's figures have, of course, been criticized (ineffectively) by neo-Nazis and so-called historical revisionists as being far too high. Conversely, others have claimed that they are too low, some even arguing that in Auschwitz alone as many as 4 million people—including 2 million Jews—perished. Hilberg's estimate of 1.1 million as the number of Jewish deaths at Auschwitz has received confirmation in subsequent research, however, lending further credence to his widely accepted overall figure as well. For recent and authoritative discussion of the death toll at Auschwitz, see Franciszek Piper, "The Number of Victims," in *Anatomy of the Auschwitz Death Camp*, ed. Yisreal Gutman and Michael Berenbaum (Bloomington: Indiana University Press in association with the United States Holocaust Memorial Museum, 1994), pp. 61–76.

3. For discussion of some of the more prominent of these cases, see Deborah Lipstadt, *Denying the Holocaust: The Growing Assault on Truth and Memory* (New York: Free Press, 1993), pp. 11–12, 14, 141, 157–170, 219–222. See also Erich Kulka, "Denial of the Holocaust," in *Genocide: A Critical Bibliographic Review*, vol. 2, ed. Israel Charny (London: Mansell, 1991), pp. 38–62. It should be noted that following the case of Ernst Zundel, who was twice sentenced to prison terms in Canada for disseminating hate literature denying the existence of the Holocaust, the Canadian Supreme Court found the statute in question to be unconstitutional. One of the more infamous cases of a Holocaust denier being hailed before the bar of justice involves the French academic Robert Faurisson, discussed most fully in Pierre Vidal-Naquet, *Assassins of Memory: Essays on the Denial of the Holocaust* (New York: Columbia University Press, 1992). Such prosecutions continue today. Thus, during the summer of 1995, a young man named Bela Ewald Althans was sentenced by a Berlin court to three and one-half years in prison for telling tourists at Auschwitz that the Holocaust "is a giant farce." Centre for Comparative Genocide Studies (Macquarie University, Australia), *Newsletter* 2(1) (1995):14. The term "cultural violence" in this paragraph is borrowed from Johan Galtung, whose work on the topic is discussed later in this chapter.

4. *Time*, 27 May 1991, p. 74.

5. *The Atlantic*, September 1992, pp. 16–30.

6. *The Nation*, 19 October 1992, p. 422. That people on the left can be as racist as their partners on the right, especially regarding indigenous peoples, is a matter too often overlooked. For another example, see the exchanges in Ward Churchill, ed., *Marxism and Native Americans* (Boston: South End Press, 1983).

7. Here I do not use the term "quasi-Hitlerian" lightly. For example, compare Hitchens's expressed sentiments in his essay in praise of power and historical inevitability with those of Hitler in a speech he delivered in Munich in April of 1923: "The whole work of Nature is a mighty struggle between strength and weakness—an eternal victory of the strong over the weak. There would be nothing but decay in the whole of Nature if this were not so. States which offend against this elementary law fall into decay. . . . History proves: He who

has not the strength—him the 'right in itself' profits not a whit." Quoted in Alan Bullock, *Hitler: A Study in Tyranny*, rev. ed. (New York: Harper and Row, 1962), pp. 398–399.

8. Emphasis added in Hitchens quote. Traditional estimates suggest that about 10 million captured Africans survived the ordeal of forced migration to become plantation laborers in North or South America or the Caribbean. Recent research puts the figure at closer to 12 million or 15 million. However, for every African who survived to become a working slave, between three and four died during the enslavement process. With a total of 10–15 million Africans surviving to become slaves, this makes for an overall death rate directly attributable to enslavement of anywhere from 40 million to 60 million—and this was *prior* to the surviving Africans' beginning to labor under further horrendous and life-diminishing conditions as New World bondsmen and bondswomen. For a brief bibliographical discussion of this matter, see David E. Stannard, *American Holocaust: Columbus and the Conquest of the New World* (New York: Oxford University Press, 1992), pp. 317–318.

9. Quoted and discussed in Desmond C. Derbyshire and Geoffrey K. Pullum, eds., *Handbook of Amazonian Languages*, vol. 1 (Berlin: Mouton de Gruyter, 1986), pp. 4–8. I am grateful to Professor Pullum for calling these writings to my attention.

10. Yehuda Bauer, "Whose Holocaust?" *Midstream* 26(9) (November 1980):42, 45.

11. Lipstadt, *Denying the Holocaust*, pp. 20, 74.

12. Ibid., pp. 212–215. Although Lipstadt's technique of preemptively villifying anyone who might disagree with her is especially egregious, she is far from alone in employing it. And for such ire to be raised the issue at hand does not have to be limited to the uniqueness question. For many years now, for instance, even the most eminent Jewish scholars who have failed to follow the established historical line regarding the causes and conduct of the Nazi campaign against the Jews have thereby courted withering ad hominem criticism from within certain segments of the Jewish intellectual community. Prominent examples, among many, include the attacks on Hannah Arendt for writing *Eichmann in Jerusalem* more than thirty years ago, critical responses to which included the *New York Times Book Review* calling it a defense of the Nazis and an attack on their Jewish victims and the *Intermountain Jewish News* headlining its report on the book while it was being serialized in the *New Yorker*: "Self-Hating Jewess Writes Pro-Eichmann Series." At about that same time, Raul Hilberg was "showered with criticism" (to use Michael R. Marrus's words) for making some remarks about limited Jewish resistance to the Nazis at the end of his monumental study, *The Destruction of the European Jews*. More recently some Jewish students organized a boycott of classes conducted by distinguished Princeton scholar Arno J. Mayer, because in his book *Why Did the Heavens Not Darken?* he wrote critically both of "'revisionists' who categorically deny the Judeocide" *and* of "dogmatists who seek to reify and sacralize the Holocaust." For a contemporary discussion of the response to Arendt's book, see Dwight Macdonald, "Hannah Arendt and the Jewish Establishment," *Partisan Review* (spring 1964), reprinted in Macdonald's *Discriminations: Essays and Afterthoughts, 1938–1974* (New York: Grossman, 1974), pp. 308–317. The harsh treatment accorded Hilberg is discussed in Michael R. Marrus, "Jewish Resistance to the Holocaust," *Journal of Contemporary History* 30 (1995):83–110. On the Princeton students and Professor Mayer, see his "Memory and History: On the Poverty of Remembering and Forgetting the Judeocide," *Radical History Review* 56 (1993):5–20. Mayer is also included in a rogues' gallery of "Hitler apologists" compiled by the Anti-Defamation League because he does not

toe the line on the uniqueness question. See *Hitler's Apologists: The Anti-Semitic Propaganda of Holocaust "Revisionism"* (New York: Anti-Defamation League, 1993), pp. 3–4, 48–49.

13. Ian Hancock, "'Uniqueness' of the Victims: Gypsies, Jews, and the Holocaust," *Without Prejudice* 1 (1988):55; and the same author's "Uniqueness, Gypsies, and Jews," in *Remembering for the Future: Working Papers and Addenda,* ed. Yehuda Bauer et al. (Oxford: Pergamon Press, 1989), vol. 2, pp. 2017–2025. For an excellent bibliography of writings on the Gypsies as Holocaust victims, see Michael Burleigh and Wolfgang Wippermann, *The Racial State: Germany, 1933–1945* (Cambridge: Cambridge University Press, 1991), pp. 364–367.

14. A good recent summary discussion of the Armenian genocide, including biblio-graphical suggestions, is Richard G. Hovannisian, "Etiology and Sequelae of the Armenian Genocide," in *Genocide: Conceptual and Historical Dimensions,* ed. George J. Andreopoulos (Philadelphia: University of Pennsylvania Press, 1994), pp. 111–140. For discussion of a va-riety of issues on this matter, see also Richard G. Hovannisian, ed., *The Armenian Genocide in Perspective* (New Brunswick, N.J.: Transaction Books, 1986); and Florence Mazian, *Why Genocide? The Armenian and Jewish Experiences in Perspective* (Ames: Iowa State University Press, 1990). On the legitimacy of these numbers it is worth noting that decades ago even Bernard Lewis, regarded by many as an apologist for the Turks, put the Armenian death toll at 1.5 million and described it as a "terrible holocaust." Bernard Lewis, *The Emergence of Modern Turkey* (Oxford: Oxford University Press, 1961), p. 356.

15. Gerard J. Libaridian, "The Ultimate Repression: The Genocide of the Armenians, 1915–1917," in *Genocide and the Modern Age: Etiology and Case Studies of Mass Death,* ed. Isidor Wallimann and Michael N. Dobkowski (Westport, Conn.: Greenwood Press, 1987), pp. 203–235. The Dawidowicz reference is from Lucy S. Dawidowicz, *The Holocaust and the Historians* (Cambridge: Harvard University Press, 1981), p. 13.

16. Stannard, *American Holocaust,* part 2.

17. Dawidowicz, *The Holocaust and the Historians,* pp. 15, 17. Considering that there has been some controversy on the number of Japanese deaths in Hiroshima and Nagasaki fol-lowing the bombings, note that the most thorough review of the topic remains that by the Committee for the Compilation of Materials on Damage Caused by the Atomic Bombs in Hiroshima and Nagasaki, *Hiroshima and Nagasaki: The Physical, Medical, and Social Effects of the Atomic Bombings,* trans. Eisei Ishikawa and David L. Swain (New York: Basic Books, 1981), pp. 363–369.

18. See note 22.

19. Michael R. Marrus, *The Holocaust in History* (Hanover, N.H.: Brandeis University Press and University Press of New England, 1987), pp. 21–22 (emphasis in original); Bauer, "Whose Holocaust?" p. 45; and Steven T. Katz, "The Pequot War Reconsidered," *New England Quarterly* 64 (1991):206–224 (emphasis in original). (In this essay Katz also rec-ommends that "we hold our charges of racism in reserve" if we are adequately to under-stand the white colonists' slaughter of the Indians—a suggestion as obtuse as saying that we should hold our charges of antisemitism in reserve if we wish to understand the Nazi destruction of the Jews. I previously commented on this article in *American Holocaust,* p. 318, note 11.)

20. Hilberg, *Destruction of the European Jews,* vol. 3, pp. 1047–1048 and 1220.

21. Yehuda Bauer, "Holocaust and Genocide: Some Comparisons," in *Lessons and Legacies: The Meaning of the Holocaust in a Changing World,* ed. Peter Hayes (Evanston, Ill.: Northwestern University Press, 1991), p. 40 (emphasis added).

22. Steven T. Katz, *The Holocaust in Historical Context, Volume I: The Holocaust and Mass Death Before the Modern Age* (New York: Oxford University Press, 1994), pp. 97–98. As of this writing only the first volume of Katz's proposed multivolume study has been published. Both Marrus and Bauer are among those who also now explicitly make this concession. See Marrus, *The Holocaust in History*, pp. 23–24; and Yehuda Bauer, "Is the Holocaust Explicable?" in Bauer et al., *Remembering for the Future*, pp. 1969–1970.

23. George M. Kren and Leon Rappoport, *The Holocaust and the Crisis of Human Behavior* (New York: Holmes and Meier, 1980), p. 2. Katz, *Holocaust in Historical Context*, p. 98, note 128. Gérard Prunier, *The Rwanda Crisis: History of a Genocide* (New York: Columbia University Press, 1995), pp. 264–265. For the maximum rate of killing ever achieved at Auschwitz, see the statement by the camp's commandant, Rudolf Hoess, quoted in Burleigh and Grimes, *The Racial State*, p. 106.

24. Phillip Lopate, "Resistance to the Holocaust," in *Testimony: Contemporary Writers Make the Holocaust Personal*, ed. David Rosenberg (New York: Times Books, 1989), p. 292.

25. Katz, *Holocaust in Historical Context*, p. 20 (emphasis in original).

26. For convenient overviews, see Noble David Cook, *Demographic Collapse: Indian Peru, 1520–1620* (Cambridge: Cambridge University Press, 1981); and John Hemming, *The Conquest of the Incas* (New York: Harcourt Brace Jovanovich, 1970). On sexual inactivity and infertility in the Nazi camps, see Terrence Des Pres, *The Survivor: An Anatomy of Life in the Death Camps* (New York: Oxford University Press, 1976), pp. 189–191.

27. All of the accounts and information that follow are documented in detail—along with much else for which there is no room here—in my *American Holocaust*, especially part 2.

28. Yisrael Gutman, "Auschwitz—An Overview," in Gutman and Berenbaum, *Anatomy of the Auschwitz Death Camp*, p. 27.

29. David A. Hackett, ed., *The Buchenwald Report* (Boulder: Westview Press, 1995), pp. 109–115.

30. For examples of efforts to deal with this problem in historical analysis, see Andrew B. Appleby, "Disease or Famine? Mortality in Cumberland and Westmorland, 1580–1640," *Economic History Review*, 2d ser., 26 (1973):403–431; and John D. Post, "The Mortality Crises of the Early 1770s and European Demographic Trends," *Journal of Interdisciplinary History* 21 (1990):29–62.

31. Hilberg, *Destruction of the European Jews*, vol. 3, p. 1220, table B-3; Hackett, *Buchenwald Report*, pp. 226–227.

32. Arno J. Mayer, *Why Did the Heavens Not Darken? The "Final Solution" in History*, with a new foreword by the author (New York: Pantheon, 1990), pp. 365, 462.

33. Lipstadt, *Denying the Holocaust*, p. 215; John W. Dower, *War Without Mercy: Race and Power in the Pacific War* (New York: Pantheon, 1986), p. 298. For a concise summary of the situation in the world today, see Laurie Garrett, *The Coming Plague: Newly Emerging Diseases in a World Out of Balance* (New York: Farrar, Straus, and Giroux, 1994), pp. 607–608.

34. Marrus, *The Holocaust in History*, p. 20. See also Des Pres, *The Survivor*, p. 114, where he wonders at the notion of a hierarchy of death, depending on whether one was confined to a death camp or a concentration camp: "What, really, is the difference," Des Pres asks, "if Buchenwald was not classified as an extermination camp and had no gas

chamber, but had special rooms for mass shooting and a level of privation so severe that prisoners died in hundreds every day?"

35. Hackett, *Buchenwald Report*, p. 7.

36. On the calories provided in the diets supplied to California's mission-concentration camp Indians, see Sherburne F. Cook, *The Conflict Between the California Indian and White Civilization* (Berkeley: University of California Press, 1976), p. 37, table 2, and pp. 42–43, where a downward adjustment of at least 10 percent of the table 2 figures is discussed.

37. For the ghastly statistics of life and death in the northern California missions, see Robert H. Jackson, "The Dynamic of Indian Demographic Collapse in the San Francisco Bay Missions, Alta, California, 1776–1840," *American Indian Quarterly* 16 (1992):141–156. For a still more recent analysis of a wide variety of lethal life conditions in the California missions that provides strong support for Cook's pioneering statistical computations, see Robert H. Jackson, *Indian Population Decline: The Missions of Northwestern New Spain, 1687–1840* (Albuquerque: University of New Mexico Press, 1995). For discussion of inmate living space in the missions, see Cook, *Conflict Between the California Indian and White Civilization*, pp. 89–90. Modern osteological analysis of native skeletal remains from California mission burials has confirmed the devastating impact of malnutrition in these death camps—in marked contrast to the skeletal remains at preinvasion burial sites. See, for example, Phillip L. Walker et al., "The Effects of European Contact on the Health of Alta California Indians, in *Columbian Consequences, Volume 1: Archeological and Historical Perspectives on the Spanish Borderlands West*, ed. David Hurst Thomas (Washington, D.C.: Smithsonian Institution Press, 1989), p. 351.

38. Despite constant infusions of new inmates to replace those who were perishing in the mission compounds, by the time the missions closed they had killed off at least 72 percent of their native prisoners—including up to one-third of the imprisoned children each year—compared with the previously cited 23 percent at Buchenwald. See Cook, *Conflict Between the California Indian and White Civilization*, p. 346. While the idea is commonplace that the destruction of the native peoples of the Americas was, as Katz has put it, "an *unintended* tragedy" (see note 25), the specific reference to them as people who "did not wear well" comes from Alfred W. Crosby, "Infectious Disease and the Demography of the Atlantic Peoples," *Journal of World History* 2 (1991): 124.

39. For a brief discussion, see Robert Melson, "Revolution and Genocide: On the Causes of the Armenian Genocide and the Holocaust," in *The Armenian Genocide: History, Politics, Ethics*, ed. Richard G. Hovannisian (New York: St. Martin's Press, 1992), esp. pp. 86–87.

40. See the recent discussion in Marrus, "Jewish Resistance to the Holocaust."

41. Putting aside religion and ethnicity—which in themselves were greatly varied—in linguistic terms alone the native peoples of the Western Hemisphere were astonishingly diverse, speaking at least 1,500 to 2,000 different and mutually unintelligible languages. These have been traced to a cluster of more than 150 highly distinct language families, each one as different from the others as Indo-European is from Sino-Tibetan. In contrast, there are hardly more than forty comparably distinct language families that are ancestral to the entirety of Europe and the Middle East. For discussion, see, among many sources, L. Campbell and M. Mithun, eds., *The Languages of Native America: Historical and Comparative Assessment* (Austin: University of Texas Press, 1979), and an early but still valuable overview, Harold E. Driver, *Indians of North America*, 2d rev. ed. (Chicago: University of Chicago Press, 1969), ch. 3. For more recent discussion of certain specific points of controversy, cf.

Joseph H. Greenberg, *Language in the Americas* (Stanford: Stanford University Press, 1988), and James Matisoff, "On Megalocomparison," *Language* 66 (1990):106–120.

42. Yehuda Bauer, *The Holocaust in Historical Perspective* (Seattle: University of Washington Press, 1978), pp. 8–9, 32–33; and Bauer, "Whose Holocaust?" pp. 44–45. Himmler is quoted in Robert Jay Lifton, *The Nazi Doctors: Medical Killing and the Psychology of Genocide* (New York: Basic Books, 1986), p. 477.

43. See, for example, David Svaldi, *Sand Creek and the Rhetoric of Extermination: A Case Study in Indian-White Relations* (New York: University Press of America, 1989), p. 291; and Lynwood Carranco and Estle Beard, *Genocide and Vendetta: The Round Valley Wars of Northern California* (Norman: University of Oklahoma Press, 1981), ch. 4.

44. Zygmunt Bauman, *Modernity and the Holocaust* (Cambridge: Polity Press, 1989), pp. 91–92, 98.

45. G. Stanley Hall, *Adolescence: Its Psychology*, vol. 2 (New York: D. Appleton, 1904), pp. 648, 651.

46. Bauer, *Holocaust in Historical Perspective*, p. 8; Christopher R. Browning, *Ordinary Men: Reserve Police Battalion 101 and the Final Solution in Poland* (New York: HarperCollins, 1992), p. 162.

47. Stannard, *American Holocaust*, pp. 83, 88, 120, 133, 204, 210–212, 240–246.

48. Bauer, "Is the Holocaust Explicable?" p. 1970; Bauer, *Holocaust in Historical Perspective*, p. 38; Katz, *Holocaust in Historical Context*, vol. 1, p. 580.

49. For example, Benno Müller-Hill, *Murderous Science: Elimination by Scientific Selection of Jews, Gypsies, and Others, 1933–1945* (Oxford: Oxford University Press, 1988); Burleigh and Wippermann, *The Racial State*, pp. 113–135; and Hancock, "'Uniqueness' of the Victims," pp. 53–54. See also Brenda Davis Lutz and James M. Lutz, "Gypsies as Victims of the Holocaust," *Holocaust and Genocide Studies* 9 (1995):346–359, who contend that the proportion of Gypsies killed during the Holocaust was lower than the Jewish figure, but who demonstrate that the Nazi *intent* was identical for Gypsies and Jews.

50. Edmund S, Morgan, *American Slavery—American Freedom: The Ordeal of Colonial Virginia* (New York: W. W. Norton, 1975), p. 233 (emphasis added); Stannard, *American Holocaust*, p. 107.

51. Albert L. Hurtado, *Indian Survival on the California Frontier* (New Haven: Yale University Press, 1988), p. 135; Edward D. Castillo, "The Impact of Euro-American Exploration and Settlement," in *Handbook of North American Indians*, vol. 8, ed. William C. Sturtevant (Washington: Smithsonian Institution Press, 1978), p. 108; Stannard, *American Holocaust*, pp. 107, 142–145, 240–246. In Auschwitz 1.1 million of the 1.3 million prisoners died—a rate of 84.6 percent (Piper, "The Number of Victims," p. 71); the 95 percent rate of destruction for California Indians is the most conservative of the current scholarly estimates—that of Douglas H. Ubelaker, "North American Indian Population Size: Changing Perspectives," in *Disease and Demography in the Americas*, ed. John W. Verano and Douglas H. Ubelaker (Washington: Smithsonian Institution Press, 1992), p. 174, table 5. It is based on a pre-European contact population estimate that most scholars would increase by at least 50 percent—for example, Russell Thornton, *American Indian Holocaust and Survival: A Population History Since 1492* (Norman: University of Oklahoma Press, 1987), p. 109, table 5-4—and likely much more. Similarly, whereas Ubelaker's total population decline estimates for the native peoples of North America (excluding Mexico) result in a continent-wide collapse of 73 percent—compared with about 65 percent among

European Jews during the Holocaust—the estimates of other scholars, based on projections of much higher pre-Columbian population figures, result in an overall reduction of 95 percent of the indigenous population in the aftermath of the European invasion. Ubelaker's 73 percent figure is based on a pre-Columbian population estimate of less than 2 million people for the area of what is now the United States, a figure that most contemporary scholars would at least double and more likely multiply by a factor of at least five. For a range of such figures, from roughly 4 million to 12 million or more, compare William M. Denevan, *The Native Population of the Americas in 1492*, 2d ed. (Madison: University of Wisconsin Press, 1992), p. xxviii, table 1, and Ann F. Ramenofsky, *Vectors of Death: The Archaeology of European Contact* (Albuquerque: University of New Mexico Press, 1987), p. 162.

52. On the psychological resistance of *Einsatzkommandos* to their massive killing assignments, see Lifton, *The Nazi Doctors*, pp. 159–162. Jackson is quoted in Ronald T. Takaki, *Iron Cages: Race and Culture in 19th-Century America* (New York: Alfred A. Knopf, 1979), pp. 96, 102–103.

53. Lyndall Ryan, *The Aboriginal Tasmanians* (St. Lucia: University of Queensland Press, 1981); L.F.S. Upton, "The Extermination of the Beothuks of Newfoundland," *Canadian Historical Review* 58 (1977):133–153.

54. Originally developed by Tim Mason in his essay, "Intention and Explanation: A Current Controversy About the Interpretation of National Socialism," in *Der Führerstaat: Mythos und Realität*, ed. Gerhard Hirschfeld and Lothar Kettenacker (Stuttgart, 1981), pp. 21–40, these terms are discussed insightfully in Christopher R. Browning, *Fateful Months: Essays on the Emergence of the Final Solution* (New York: Holmes and Meier, 1985), pp. 8–38.

55. Mayer, *Why Did the Heavens Not Darken?* p. 459.

56. Browning, *Fateful Months*, pp. 13–14.

57. John Mendelsohn and Donald S. Detwiler, eds., *The Holocaust: Selected Documents in Eighteen Volumes* (New York: Garland, 1982), pp. 22–25. This is a reproduction and translation of the only known extant copy of the Wannsee Protocol.

58. Hilberg, *Destruction of the European Jews*, vol. 2, p. 405; Gerald Fleming, *Hitler and the Final Solution* (Berkeley: University of California Press, 1982), pp. 91–92.

59. Hilberg, *Destruction of the European Jews*, vol. 2, p. 401; Mendelsohn and Detwiler, *The Holocaust*, p. 20; Bauer, "Is the Holocaust Explicable?" p. 1970. Much is sometimes made of the fact that the Wannsee Protocol refers to "the Reich Fuehrer-SS and the Chief of the German Police"—namely, Heinrich Himmler—being "entrusted with the official handling of the final solution of the Jewish problem centrally *without regard to geographic borders*" as if this suggests a worldwide plan (emphasis added). See, for instance, Leni Yahil, *The Holocaust: The Fate of European Jewry, 1932–1945* (New York: Oxford University Press, 1990), p. 313. Clearly, however, this phrase must be read in context—and that context is unambiguously provided by the immediately preceding two sentences that twice refer to "the final solution of the Jewish problem *in Europe*" (emphasis added). The geographic borders in question, then, plainly were European borders.

60. On the absence of evidence (or even grounds for logical deduction) concerning a pre-1941 plan for the Final Solution, see the thoughtful and evenhanded discussion in Browning, *Fateful Months*, pp. 8–38.

61. For general discussion of this topic, see Arthur D. Morse, *While Six Million Died: Chronicle of American Apathy* (New York: Random House, 1967), pp. 353–361; Wyman,

Abandonment of the Jews, pp. 243–249; and Bauer, *The Holocaust in Historical Perspective*, pp. 94–155. For recent interpretations, see also Paul L. Rose, "Joel Brand's 'Interim Agreement' and the Course of Nazi-Jewish Negotiations, 1944–1945," *Historical Journal* 34 (1991):909–929; and Richard Breitman and Shlomo Aronson, "The End of the 'Final Solution'? Nazi Plans to Ransom Jews in 1944," *Central European History* 25 (1993): 177–203. The reprehensibly cynical "bury the hatchet" quotation attributed to Himmler appears in Monty Noam Penkower, *The Jews Were Expendable: Free World Diplomacy and the Holocaust* (Urbana: University of Illinois Press, 1983), p. 281. The quotation from Bauer is on p. 155 of *The Holocaust in Historical Perspective*.

62. Hilberg, *Destruction of the European Jews*, vol. 3, pp. 980–981.

63. Yehuda Bauer, *Jews for Sale? Nazi-Jewish Negotiations, 1933–1945* (New Haven: Yale University Press, 1994), p. 2.

64. Ibid., p. 252.

65. Bauer, *The Holocaust in Historical Perspective*, p. 154 (emphasis added). For a convenient summary of Germany's military situation at this time, see Calvocoressi, Wint, and Pritchard, *Total War*, esp. pp. 512–54.

66. On the grotesque Nazi efforts to create a "third race" between Aryans and Jews, see Hilberg, *Destruction of the European Jews*, vol. 1, pp. 65–80. The substantive portions of the Wannsee Protocol, in translation, cover thirteen pages, of which more than six are concerned with the proposed treatment of various categories of "mixed blood" persons, and of elderly Jews and Jews with distinguished war records, who might be exempt from evacuation—and thus from extermination. On the more stringent categorization of Gypsies than Jews—from 50 to 100 percent stricter in terms of "desirable blood quantum" sufficient to exclude one from persecution—see Donald Kenrick and Grattan Puxon, *The Destiny of Europe's Gypsies* (New York: Basic Books, 1972), pp. 67, 85; and Angus Fraser, *The Gypsies* (Oxford: Blackwell, 1992), p. 260.

67. The term *novum* in this context is derived from Katz's claim at the beginning of the recently published first volume of his Holocaust study that the *Endlösung*—the Final Solution—was a *novum*—a "singularity as a historical phenomenon." Katz, *Holocaust in Historical Context*, vol. 1, p. 3.

68. Stephen Jay Gould, *The Mismeasure of Man* (New York: W. W. Norton, 1981), p. 85.

69. Liz McMillen, "The Uniqueness of the Holocaust," *Chronicle of Higher Education* 40(42) (June 22, 1994):A13.

70. Mayer, "Memory and History," pp. 6 and 17.

71. Israel W. Charny, "Introduction" to Charny, *Genocide*, p. xxiv; and Israel W. Charny, "Toward a Generic Definition of Genocide," in Andreopoulos, *Genocide*, pp. 72, 91–92.

72. Lopate, "Resistance to the Holocaust," pp. 299, 300.

73. Edward Alexander, *The Holocaust and the War of Ideas* (New Brunswick, N.J.: Transaction Publishers, 1994), p. 195; Edward Alexander, "Stealing the Holocaust," *Midstream* 26(9) (November 1980):47.

74. Irving Louis Horowitz, "Genocide and the Reconstruction of Social Theory: Observations on the Exclusivity of Collective Death," in Wallimann and Dobkowski, *Genocide and the Modern Age*, p. 62.

75. Charny, "Toward a Generic Definition of Genocide," p. 72.

76. Donald Harman Akenson, *God's Peoples: Covenant and Land in South Africa, Israel, and Ulster* (Ithaca, N.Y.: Cornell University Press, 1992).

77. On the Afrikaners and the Ulster-Scots, see ibid., esp. pp. 72–77, 94–95, and 119–122; on the Ulster-Scots also see Steve Bruce, *God Save Ulster: The Religion and Politics of Paisleyism* (Oxford: Clarendon Press, 1986). The quotation from a Puritan writer is from John Mason, *A Brief History of the Pequot War* (Boston: Kneeland and Green, 1736 [reprint]), p. 21, discussed in Stannard, *American Holocaust*, pp. 111–115.

78. Israeli officials quoted in Mayer, "Memory and History," p. 13; Bauman, *Modernity and the Holocaust*, p. ix.

79. Jaspers is quoted by Gordon Craig in his review of the Hannah Arendt–Karl Jaspers correspondence, *New York Review of Books*, May 13, 1993, p. 12.

80. Bauer, "Is the Holocaust Explicable?" p. 1969; Robert H. Ruby and John A. Brown, *Indians of the Pacific Northwest: A History* (Norman: University of Oklahoma Press, 1981), p. 16.

81. Jean Baudrillard, *The Mirror of Production* (St. Louis: Telos Press, 1975), p. 107.

82. Lipstadt, *Denying the Holocaust*, pp. 213–214.

83. Edward T. Linenthal, *Preserving Memory: The Struggle to Create America's Holocaust Museum* (New York: Viking Press, 1995), pp. 242–243.

84. Judith Miller, *One, by One, by One: Facing the Holocaust* (New York: Simon and Schuster, 1990), p. 259; Linenthal, *Preserving Memory*, pp. 238–239; and Yossi Klein Halevi, "The Forgotten Genocide," *Jerusalem Report* 6(2) (June 1995):20–21. For good discussion of the relentless Turkish campaign to conceal the Armenian holocaust, see Roger W. Smith, "Denial of the Armenian Genocide," in Charny, *Genocide*, vol. 2, pp. 63–85. See also the incredible tale of political manipulation and scholarly dishonesty on this subject in Roger W. Smith, Eric Markusen, and Robert Jay Lifton, "Professional Ethics and the Denial of Armenian Genocide," *Holocaust and Genocide Studies* 9 (1995):1–22.

85. Smith, "Denial of the Armenian Genocide," p. 71.

86. Johan Galtung, "Cultural Violence," *Journal of Peace Research* 27 (1990):291–305.

87. Lipstadt, *Denying the Holocaust*, pp. 7–8.

88. Smith, Markusen, and Lifton, "Professional Ethics and the Denial of Armenian Genocide," p. 16.

89. Elie Wiesel, "Now We Know," in *Genocide in Paraguay*, ed. Richard Arens (Philadelphia: Temple University Press, 1976), pp. 165–166.

90. Ibid., pp. 166–167.

About the Book and Contributors

*E*valuating the Jewish Holocaust is by no means a simple matter, and one of the most controversial questions for academics is whether there have been any historical parallels for it. Have Armenians, Gypsies, American Indians, or others undergone a comparable genocide? In this fiercely controversial volume, distinguished scholars offer new discussions of this question. Presenting a wide range of strongly held views, they provide no easy consensus.

Some critics contend that if the Holocaust is seen as fundamentally different in kind from other genocides or mass deaths, the suffering of other persecuted groups will be diminished. Others argue that denying the uniqueness of the Holocaust will trivialize it. Alan S. Rosenbaum's introductions provide a much-needed context for readers to come to terms with this multi-dimensional dispute, to help them understand why it has recently intensified, and to enable them to appreciate what universal lessons might be gleaned from studying the Holocaust.

This volume makes an important contribution to our comprehension of one of the defining events of modern history. It should be essential reading for scholars, students, and general readers interested in the Holocaust and its relationship to other instances of politically inspired mass murder.

Israel W. Charny is professor of psychology and family therapy at the Hebrew University of Jerusalem, Israel, and is executive director of the Institute on the Holocaust and Genocide (Jerusalem). He is the author of *How Can We Commit the Unthinkable? Genocide, The Human Cancer* (1982), and the editor of *Toward the Understanding and Prevention of Genocide* (1980) and three volumes in the series, *Genocide: A Critical Bibliographic Review* (1988, 1991, 1994). His writings have appeared as chapters in other edited works and in professional journals.

Vahakn N. Dadrian is former professor of sociology at the State University of New York at Geneseo (1970–1991) and is currently director of a major genocide studies project supported by the H. F. Guggenheim Foundation. He is the author of two monographs on Armenian genocide in the issues of *International Journal of Middle Eastern Studies* (1986, 1991). His monograph entitled "Genocide as a Problem of National and International Law: The World War I Armenian Case and Its Contemporary Legal Ramifications" first appeared in the *Yale Journal of International Law* (1989) and has now been published as a book in Turkish and French. His articles have appeared in many professional publications. He recently published a comprehensive study on the Armenian genocide entitled *History of the Armenian Genocide: Ethnic Conflict from the Balkans to Anatolia to the Caucasus* (1995, with French translation to come).

Seymour Drescher is professor of history at the University of Pittsburgh, Pennsylvania. His books include: *The Meaning of Freedom: Economics, Politics and Culture After Slavery* (with Frank McGlynn, 1992); *Capitalism and Anti-Slavery: British Mobilization in Comparative Perspective* (1986); *Econocide: British Slavery in the Era of Abolition* (1977); and many other writings in professional journals.

Richard J. Goldstone is a Justice of the Constitutional Court of South Africa. From 15 August 1994 to September 1996 he served as Chief Prosecutor of the United Nations International Criminal Tribunals for the former Yugoslavia and Rwanda. Among his many distinguished accomplishments are the 1998 Chairpersonship of a high level group of international experts which met in Spain and drafted a Declaration of Human Duties and Responsibilities for the Director General of UNESCO (the Valencia Declaration); the Head of the Board of the Human Rights Institute of South Africa; the Chancellor of the University of the Witwatersrand, Johannesburg; and a member of the International Panel established in August 1997 by the Government of Argentina to monitor the Argentinean Inquiry to elucidate Nazi activities in the Argentine Republic since 1938. Of the many awards he has received are the International Human Rights Award of the American Bar Association (1994); Honorary Doctorates of Law from the University of Cape Town, Hebrew University (Jerusalem), Maryland University College, the University of Glasgow, and others; also, he is an Honorary Fellow of St. Johns College (Cambridge); a Fellow of the Centre for International Affairs of Harvard University; and a Foreign Member of the American Academy of Arts & Sciences.

Barbara B. Green is professor of political science (and former associate provost and vice president) at Cleveland State University, Ohio. She is the author of *The Dynamics of Russian Politics: A Short History* (1994). Her other writings have appeared in many professional journals. In a recent issue of *Wellesley* magazine (Winter 1994), First Lady Hillary Rodham Clinton cited Green as among the best and most brilliant teachers she ever had.

Ian Hancock is professor of linguistics and English at the University of Texas at Austin. He is United Nations representative for the International Romani Union. He is the author of *The Pariah Syndrome: An Account of Gypsy Slavery and Persecution* (1988), and many articles in professional journals.

Wulf Kansteiner is a professor of modern German history and holocaust studies. He has taught at the University of Tennessee, Kent State University, SUNY Binghamton, and currently Ohio State University. Among his publications are articles in professional journals and books, including *German Politics and Society* (1999); *Journal of Contemporary History* (1996); *History and Theory* (1993, 1994); and in R. J. Golsan (ed), *Fascism's Return* (1998); and in K. Jenkins (ed), *The Postmodern History Reader* (1997).

Steven T. Katz is professor of Jewish history and thought at Cornell University in Ithaca, New York, and editor of *Modern Judaism*. His latest books include: *The Holocaust in Historical Context*, vol. 1 (1994); *Mysticism and Philosophical Analysis* (1978); *Mysticism and Religious Traditions* (1983); and *Mysticism and Language* (1992). His writings have also appeared as chapters in other edited works and in professional journals.

Robert F. Melson is professor of political science at Purdue University and co-director of the Jewish Studies Program. His books include: *Nigeria: Modernization and the Politics of Communalism* (1971); and *Revolution and Genocide* (1992), and his writings have appeared in numerous professional journals.

Alan S. Rosenbaum is professor of philosophy at Cleveland State University, Ohio. He is the author and/or editor of four books: *The Philosophy of Human Rights: International Perspectives* (ed.) (1980); *Coercion and Autonomy: Foundations, Issues and Practices* (1986);

Constitutionalism: The Philosophical Dimension (ed.) (1988); and *Prosecuting Nazi War Criminals* (1993). His articles have appeared in numerous professional journals.

John K. Roth is the Russell K. Pitzer Professor of Philosophy at Claremont McKenna College, where he has taught since 1966. In addition to service on the U.S. Holocaust Memorial Council and on the editorial board for *Holocaust and Genocide Studies*, he has published more than 25 books and hundreds of articles and reviews, including *A Consuming Fire: Encounters with Elie Wiesel and the Holocaust, Approaches to Auschwitz* (with Richard L. Rubenstein), *Holocaust: Religious and Philosophical Implications* (with Michael Berenbaum), *Ethics After the Holocaust,* and major contributions to *The Holocaust Chronicle.* In 1988, Roth was named U.S. National Professor of the Year by the Council for Advancement and Support of Education (CASE) and the Carnegie Foundation for the Advancement of Teaching.

Richard L. Rubenstein is currently president of the University of Bridgeport. He is the former Robert O. Lawton Distinguished Professor of Religion at Florida State University. His books include: *After Auschwitz* (1966); *The Cunning of History* (1975); *Approaches to Auschwitz* (with John K. Roth) (1987); and many other books and articles.

Shimon Samuels earned his doctorate from a joint program of the University of Pennsylvania and the Paris Sorbonne. He is currently director for International Liaison of the Simon Wiesenthal Centre, Paris, France. His work includes the containment of resurgent antisemitism in the former Soviet Union; restitution claims of Holocaust victims against banks and insurance companies; and Vatican diplomacy. Moreover, he has published as a journalist more than 200 articles on combating racism, antisemitism, and prejudice.

David E. Stannard is professor of American studies at the University of Hawaii. His books include: *Death in America* (1975); *The Puritan Way of Death* (1977); *Shrinking History* (1980); *Before the Horror: The Population of Hawai'i on the Eve of Western Contact* (1989); and *American Holocaust: The Conquest of the New World* (1992). He has published in numerous professional journals.

Kinue Tokudome is a Japanese writer/journalist. She is the author of a collection of interviews on the Holocaust and its historical significance entitled *Courage to Remember* (St. Paul, Minn.: Paragon House, 1999); she is the translator of Raul Hilberg's memoir *The Politics of Memory* in Japanese (1998); and is currently at work on a project on Japanese war crimes as an Abe fellow of the Japan Foundation Center for Global Partnership.

Index